W9-BQV-150

AIRCRAFT
OF WORLD WAR II

AIRCRAFT
OF WORLD WAR II

BILL GUNSTON

CHANCELLOR
PRESS

First published in 1980 by Octopus Books

This edition published in 1997 by Chancellor Press, an imprint of Reed International Books Limited, Michelin House, 81 Fulham Road, London SW3 6RB

© Copyright Fabbri Editori S.p.A., Milan 1973 in the illustrations
© Copyright Reed International Books Limited 1980 the text and this edition

ISBN 1 85152 865 2

Printed in Malaysia

Page 4 He 111H-22, III/KG 3, Gilze-Rijen, Netherlands. Note Fi 103 flying bomb underneath.

Page 5 P-40E, USAAF 343rd FG, Adak, Aleutians, 1943.

Page 6 B-17G Flying Fortress, 447th BG, 8th Air Force, Rattlesden, Great Britain, 1944–5.

Page 7 Lancaster B.I, 15 Squadron, Mildenhall, Great Britain.

Page 208 Belgian Hurricane I of 2nd Squadron, 1st Fighter Group, 2nd Air Regiment, at Schaffen. Armed with four 0.5in FN-Browning guns in wings.

Contents

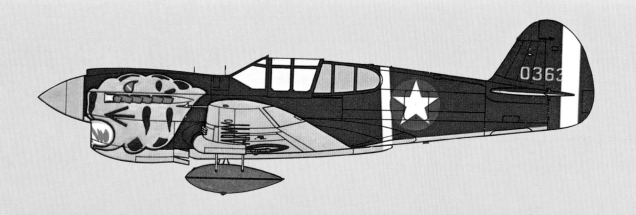

Introduction

Aircraft of World War 2 means the aircraft that fought in that great conflict. Most of the important types were designed long before that war began, and represented technology of an earlier generation. For example, the leading warplanes of the Luftwaffe, such as the Bf 109, He 111, Do 17 and Ju 87, had all flown by 1935; the Ju 52/3m, by far the most important transport for Hitler's armies, flew in 1932. Even the very newest machines that took part in the war were started as programmes in the late 1930s; for example the design of the B-29 and Me 262 was under way in 1938. Only one or two very exceptional aircraft, such as the P-51 Mustang, represented the technology of the 1940s.

Aircraft design has always been in a state of flux, reflecting galloping new technology and the introduction of an endless succession of new techniques. But the 1930s was especially important as the era in which aircraft design reached its first state of maturity. Around 1930 the Americans and Germans introduced to the production line a technique that had been known since before 1914: all-metal stressed-skin construction. By using a covering of strong but light aluminium alloy the skin of the aircraft could be made to bear the major part of the loads, and do so more efficiently than the traditional type of structure in which fabric was stretched over a framework of either wire-braced wood or welded steel tubing. In turn the new structure facilitated the design of aerodynamically 'cleaner' aircraft with monoplane wings devoid of bracing struts or wires.

This tremendous improvement came at the same time as retractable landing gear, advanced engine installations offering more power and reduced drag, enclosed cockpits and flight decks, variable-pitch propellers, all-weather de-icing systems, power-driven gun turrets, flaps on the wings to improve take-off and landing despite dramatic increases in wing-loading (weight supported by a given area of wing), and much-needed radio aids to assist navigation and bad-weather landing. On top of all this, so-called 'back-room boffins' made such progress in the development of the totally new subject of radar, and the contrary technique of ECM (electronic countermeasures), that the electronic equipment often rivalled in importance the aircraft that carried it. In other words, in some important missions a poor aircraft with the right electronics was more valuable than a brilliant one with out-of-date systems.

Major participating nations in World War 2 tended to stamp their own imprint on their aircraft. Though this book rightly concentrates on the most important aircraft, there were actually hundreds of types involved, used in numbers transcending anything seen in the sky before or since.

Britain clung to outmoded methods of construction, so that the RAF entered the war with even its trim Spitfire fitted with an old-fashioned two-blade propeller carved from wood, and with fabric covering on the Hurricane and many other types. The absence of a modern gun was rectified by importing the American Browning (which itself dated from 1916) and later the Hispano cannon. A fixation on the gun turret caused aberrations in fighter design and also left heavy bombers well-protected against attack from the front, top or rear but defenceless underneath, where the German night-fighters enjoyed a perfect no-deflection shot with the bomber silhouetted against the palest part of the sky.

Germany entered the war with a

range of aircraft which were advanced in design and generally very formidable; but Nazi long-term planning was abysmal, so that the same types had to soldier on to the bitter end, by which time they were obsolescent. Only in the bold early planning for jet aircraft, at a time when all Britain had was a single engine described by Whittle as 'a running heap of scrap', did Germany throw a scare into the Allies in 1944; but the Me 262 could not stave off defeat.

In the United States an admitted lag in military technology in 1940 was made up with immense energy, and combined with production on a giant scale to yield the greatest air armadas ever seen. Though all major US engine companies were by 1938 working on extremely advanced liquid-cooled engines, the American war effort in the air rested on the air-cooled radials of Pratt & Whitney, with Wright not too far behind; these two companies provided 85 per cent of US horsepower and roughly 52 per cent of the total power of the Allies. To an even greater extent the Italians and Japanese relied on the air-cooled radials, but their much more limited capacity for development and production soon began to tell.

Both Italy and Japan began the war convinced that the key factors for a fighter were manoeuvrability and pilot view. Speed, climb, toughness and firepower took second place, and the Italians even clung to the biplane. In one classic design, the so-called Zero, the Japanese achieved such dominance as almost to be equated with invincibility, but in fact this nimble fighter was like the German types in having to continue in production because nothing arrived to replace it. In general, in 1936–8 Japanese design was outstandingly advanced (at a time when the Western nations fondly believed the opposite, because of non-existent intelligence) but as World War 2 progressed it was overtaken until in the final year of the war surviving combat aircraft were largely consumed in fruitless and unrepeatable suicide missions.

The Soviet Union was another country where non-existent Western intelligence created a warped and outdated picture. Nothing was known of the amazing profusion of interesting military aircraft and air weapons of the period 1928–41 other than two 1933-vintage fighters and a bomber that served in Spain. Russian fighters of

World War 2 were initially made of wood, for strategic reasons, but gradually incorporated more and more light alloy. They were made powerful yet small, with very limited firepower, while some of the opposing German fighters carried a veritable arsenal of hard-hitting cannon. Russian designers never changed their view that their small and nimble fighters were a better answer – at least for their purpose – than such massive machines as the American P-47, P-38, F4U and F6F. On the other hand the Americans never doubted that, with their R-2800 engine putting out powers up to 3,400hp with emergency water injection in combat, their big fighters combined long range and firepower to defeat the enemy.

America, more than most combatants, built many unconventional fighter prototypes during World War 2. Yet none was as good as the conventional designs (except for the P-38 Lightning, flown before the war). The same was true in other countries, and two aircraft, the Ju 88 and Mosquito, proved to have such a combination of qualities that they were able to serve in almost every role to which aircraft were put in World War 2.

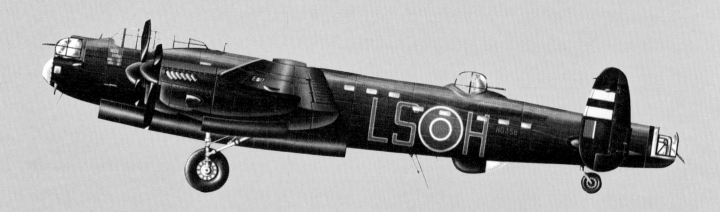

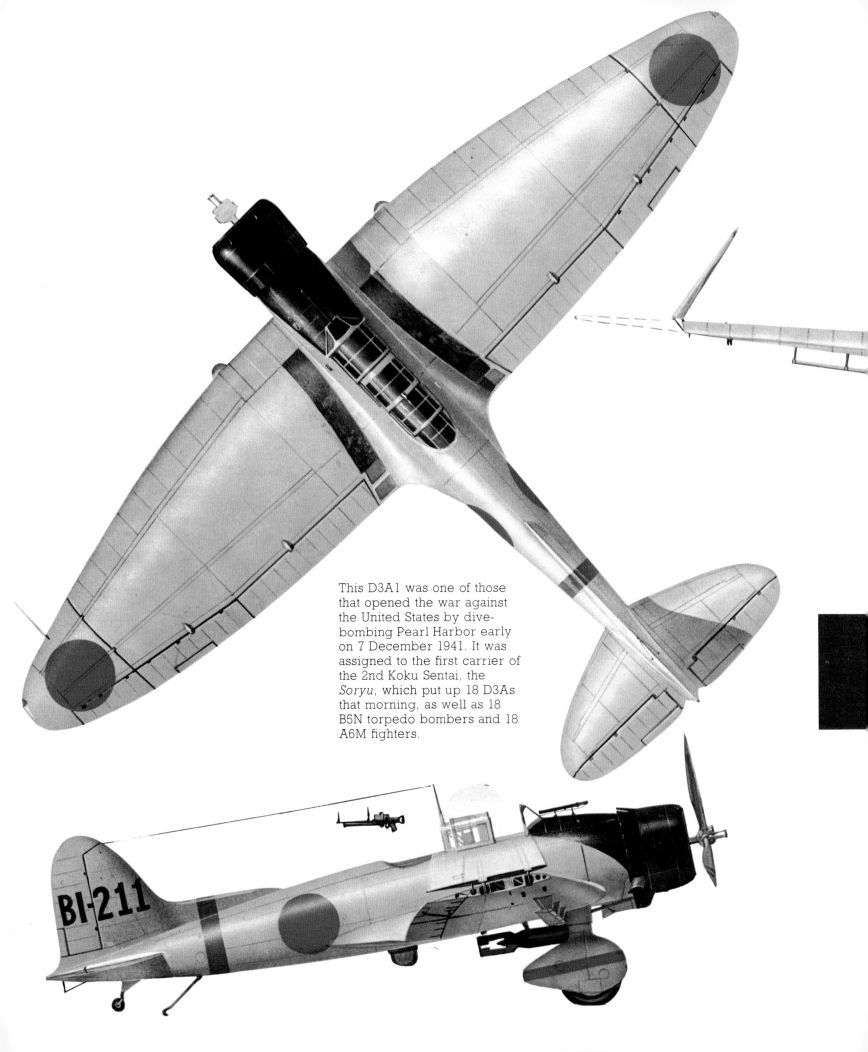

This D3A1 was one of those that opened the war against the United States by dive-bombing Pearl Harbor early on 7 December 1941. It was assigned to the first carrier of the 2nd Koku Sentai, the *Soryu*, which put up 18 D3As that morning, as well as 18 B5N torpedo bombers and 18 A6M fighters.

BI-211

Aichi D3A1 Val

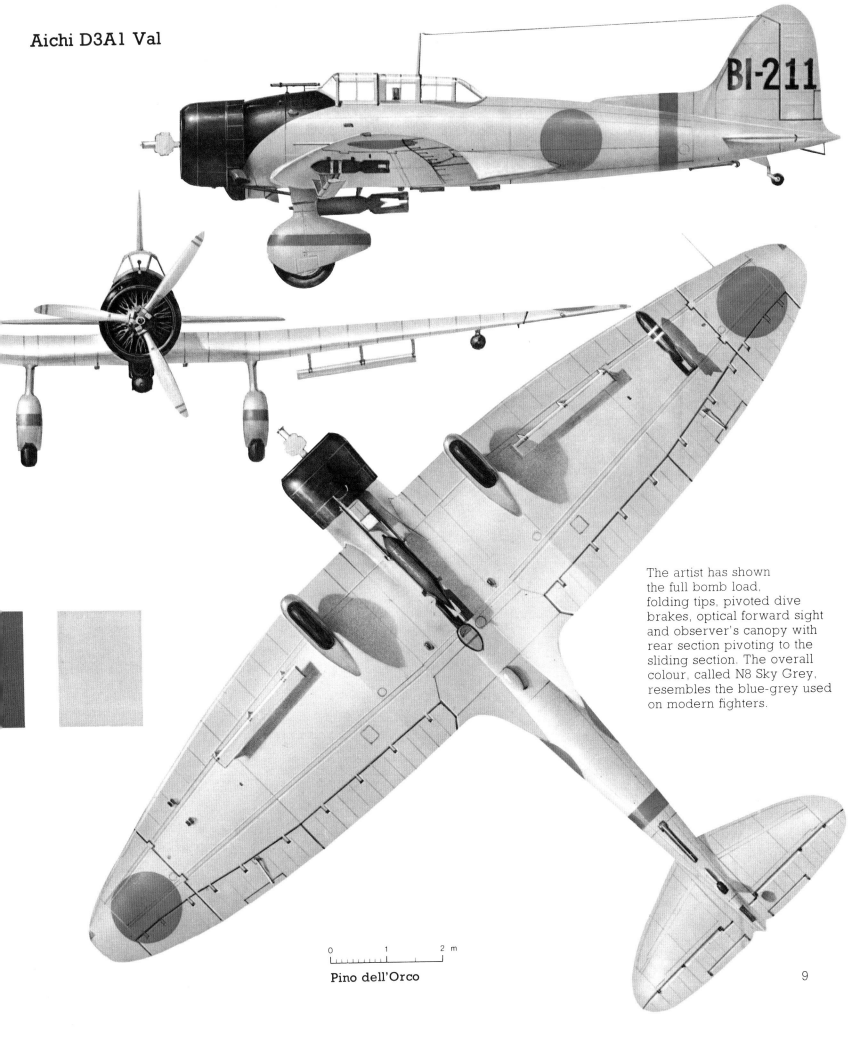

BI-211

The artist has shown the full bomb load, folding tips, pivoted dive brakes, optical forward sight and observer's canopy with rear section pivoting to the sliding section. The overall colour, called N8 Sky Grey, resembles the blue-grey used on modern fighters.

0   1   2 m

Pino dell'Orco

9

Aichi D3A Val

1 This D3A1 is shown as it appeared on the morning of 7 December 1941 over Pearl Harbor. It flew with the 2nd Koku Sentai from the carrier *Hiryu*.

2 This D3A1 was flown by the commander of the 1st Koku Sentai, operating from the *Akagi*. Note the depressed dive brakes and bomb swung down prior to release.

3 The second Aichi AM-17 prototype, which flew about six months after the low-powered first aircraft (probably in June 1938).

4 One of the first D3A1 production aircraft, used from land bases in China and Indo-China from the beginning of 1940.

5 This D3A1 survived until 1944, operating with the 5th Koku Sentai from *Shokaku* and then from a land base in the Philippines.

6 Numerically much more important than the earlier model, the D3A2 was better-looking and cleaner aerodynamically. This one served with the 55th Kokutai, from an island base.

7 This is how most surviving D3A2s looked by 1945, especially when stripped down for a suicide mission. This example was seen at Misawa, near Aomori.

8 The Yokosuka D3Y1 Myojo (Venus) was intended as a simple wooden version of the D3A but ended up as a new type. Only two prototypes and three production examples of this design were completed by VJ-Day.

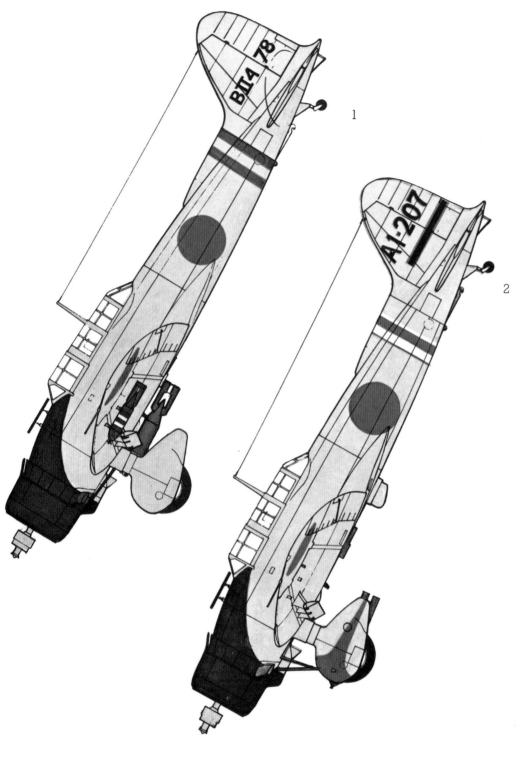

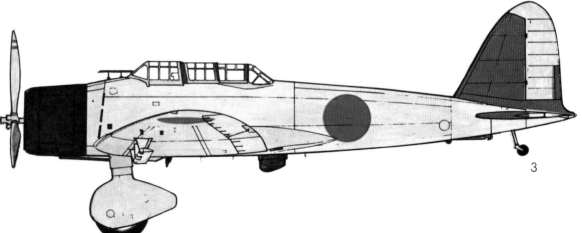

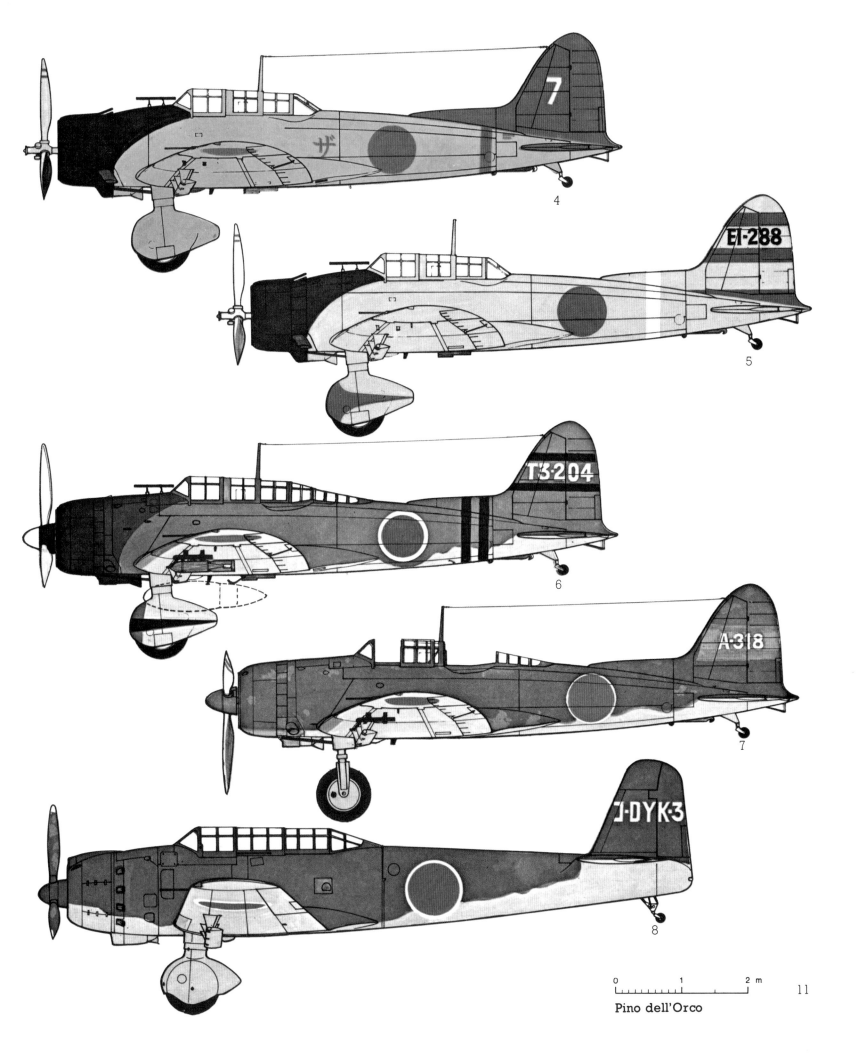

7

EI-288

T3-204

A-318

J-DYK-3

4

5

6

7

8

0   1   2 m

Pino dell'Orco

11

Aichi D3A Val

Neither especially large nor powerful, and in many respects obsolescent, the Imperial Navy's D3A dive bomber came as a most unpleasant shock to the Allies. On 7 December 1941 it was the first type of Japanese aircraft to go into action against American targets, and it caused devastation at Pearl Harbor on that day. For almost a year it carried all before it, protected by the supposedly invincible A6M 'Zero' fighters. During this period it wiped out most of the Allied surface vessels in the south-west Pacific and Indian Ocean areas, achieving far more than even the Japanese commanders dared to hope. Then, quite suddenly, it was confronted by properly defended warships and formidable Allied fighters, while replacement crews steadily deteriorated in quality and degree of training. The day of this once-feared aircraft was virtually over by mid-1943.

Prior to 1941 Allied intelligence on Japanese warplanes was almost non-existent. One of the few types known to exist – because of the fuss one caused in 1937 when it sank the US Navy gunboat *Panay* – was the Aichi D1A, a fabric-covered biplane derived from the German He 50. It was fondly thought that all Japanese combat aircraft were still of this general vintage in 1941, but in fact moves to replace the D1A had started in May 1936 with the drafting of an 11-Shi (meaning an experimental specification in the 11th year of Emperor Hirohito's reign) for a new carrier-based dive bomber of stressed-skin monoplane design.

The ultimate winner of an industry competition was again Aichi Tokei Denki, whose design team leader, Tokuhishiro Goake, was one of a number of Japanese fully experienced in the new form of all-metal construction. According to legend he adopted an elliptical wing plan because he was impressed by another earlier Heinkel type, the He 70. Like the Spitfire, the Aichi monoplane gained little from its curving wing shape which mainly had the effect of making it more difficult to construct. Goake decided against both internal bomb stowage and retractable landing gear, but did adopt a modern full-length engine cowling with cooling gills, a Hamilton type three-blade variable-pitch propeller and hydraulically powered flaps and dive brakes, the latter being carried on three blade-pylons well below the underside of the wing and rotating 90˚ to limit speed in the dive. Only the tips of the wings folded to reduce stowage space when embarked.

The prototype flew in January 1938 and, after numerous improvements, the aircraft beat a rival from Nakajima and Aichi received a production contract in December 1939. The Navy designation was Type 99 Carrier Bomber Model 11, and the Allies bestowed the terse code-name Val, once the D3A had been positively identified. Code names were essential in order to report accurately aircraft whose true designation was seldom known and in any case difficult to remember. In general the policy was to assign a short and distinctive boy's name to fighters and reconnaissance seaplanes, names of trees to trainers, birds to gliders and girl's names to all other types.

D3A carrier trials took place in autumn 1940, and an increasing number of the D3A1 version flew operational missions in China and Indo-China from this time on, without the fact being appreciated in Washington. At Pearl Harbor 126 dive-bombers took part, and the number grew to over 250 by mid-1942. In April 1942 a small force placed from 82 to 87 per cent of their bombs on target in sinking the British carrier *Hermes* and heavy cruisers *Dorsetshire* and *Cornwall*.

Altogether Aichi made 470 D3A1s, followed by 815 of the more powerful and better streamlined D3A2, which replaced the earlier version on the company's assembly line in August 1942. A further 201 D3A2s were also constructed by the Japanese Showa company.

From mid-1942 losses were heavy, and by mid-1944 none were left in first-line service except for the growing number of kamikaze suicide conversions.

COUNTRY OF ORIGIN Japan.

CREW 2.

TOTAL PRODUCED 1,495.

DIMENSIONS Wingspan 14·365m (47ft 2in); length 10·195m (33ft 5½in); wing area 34·9m² (375·66ft²).

WEIGHTS Empty **D3A1**: 2408kg (5,309lb), **D3A2**: 2570kg (5,666lb); maximum loaded **1**: 3650kg (8,047lb) **2**: 3800kg (8,378lb).

ENGINE **D3A1**: 1,070hp Mitsubishi Kinsei 44 14-cylinder two-row radial; **D3A2**: 1,300hp Kinsei 54.

MAXIMUM SPEED **1**: 389km/h (242mph) at 3000m (9,845ft); **2**: 430km/h (267mph) at 6200m (20,340ft).

SERVICE CEILING **1**: 9300m (30,500ft); **2**: 10500m (34,450ft)

RANGE **1**: 1473km (915 miles); **2**: 1352km (840 miles).

MILITARY LOAD Two fixed forward-firing 7·7mm Type 97 machine guns and one 7·7mm Type 92 aimed by observer; one 250kg (551lb) bomb on hinged crutches under fuselage and one 60kg (132lb) bomb on rack under each outer wing.

Avro Lancaster

In the final years before World War 2 the three new heavy bombers planned for RAF Bomber Command were the Short Stirling, Handley Page Halifax and Avro Manchester. It was confidently predicted that the Stirling would win the war, the Halifax would be a close second and the twin-engined Avro come a poor third. In fact, while the Halifax was immensely useful and served in great numbers (6,176) in many versions for numerous roles, the Stirling was a great disappointment and the Manchester was in most ways the best of the lot. It was by far the easiest to build and maintain, and it could carry the giant light-case 'blockbuster' bombs that had not been thought of when the bombers were first designed.

The one thing the Manchester lacked was a good engine. Eventually the Air Ministry fell for Rolls-Royce's proposal to replace the troublesome Vultures with four reliable Merlins, though this meant longer-span outer wings. Existence of a standard powerplant, already flying in the Beaufighter II, made the scheme possible, and the prototype 'Manchester III', soon renamed Lancaster, flew on 9 January 1941. Its performance and fighter-like handling were a complete surprise. From the start the four-Merlin conversion was a tremendous success.

Large-scale production was organized with all speed, bringing in Avro, Armstrong Whitworth, Austin Motors, Metrovick and Vickers-Armstrongs. Manchesters on the line were completed as 'Lancs', easily distinguished by their rows of small rectangular windows in the fuselage. One batch of 300 was built with Hercules engines, bulged bomb bays and a ventral turret. Deliveries to 44 (Rhodesia) Sqn at Waddington began in September 1941, and on 17 April 1942 this unit with some from 97 Sqn made a rather foolhardy daylight low-level raid on a factory at Augsburg. Altogether 156,000 sorties were flown by Lancasters, nearly all against German targets, dropping 618,273 tonnes (608,612 UK tons) of bombs of all sizes up to the 10-tonne Grand Slam and including the spinning drum weapons that burst the Ruhr dams on 17 March 1943.

Nearly all Lancasters looked alike, the 3,425 Mk I aircraft being followed by 3,039 Mk III with Packard Merlins, usually with broad paddle-blade propellers and with a growing array of radar and ECM equipment. Most Bomber Command aircraft carried the bulky and heavy H_2S mapping radar whose scanner caused a prominent bulge under the rear fuselage, and whose emissions were like a lighthouse to the patrolling Luftwaffe night-fighters. A small number carried Gee-H precision navigation (see main five-view drawing), and 100 Group used many special Lancasters for Elint (electronic reconnaissance), spoofing and general countermeasures.

Total production amounted to 7,377, of which 430 were made in Canada by an organization called Victory Aircraft which after the war became Avro Canada. Non-bomber versions included the Coastal Command ASR.III with air-dropped lifeboat installation engineered by Cunliffe-Owen Aircraft, and the GR.III maritime reconnaissance version. Late in the war there were several special versions including the B.VI with high-altitude Merlin 87 engines and a fuselage packed with ECM gear, the B.IV which became the Lincoln, the long-range B.I(FE) model for Tiger Force in the Far East with large dorsal overload fuel tank, and two machines with a tail sighting position for twin-20mm cannon barbettes above and below the rear fuselage. (Curiously, except for the small number of Mk II aircraft, no Lancaster had any defence or even crew-vision on its vital underside, which was where German night fighters were most likely to attack.)

Post-war additional new versions appeared including the unarmed Lancastrian high-speed transport which, as well as serving in the RAF in three versions (64 aircraft), also became an important interim civil transport along with large numbers of Lancasters. A true transport based on the Lancaster was the high-wing York.

COUNTRY OF ORIGIN Great Britain.

CREW Normally 7.

TOTAL PRODUCED 7,377.

DIMENSIONS Wingspan 31·1m (102ft 0in); length 21·1m (69ft 4in); wing area 119·49m² (1,297ft²).

WEIGHTS Empty **Mk I**: 16705kg (36,900lb); maximum gross 30845kg (68,000lb); max overload with Grand Slam bomb, 31750kg (70,000lb).

ENGINES **I**: Four 1,460hp Rolls-Royce Merlin 20 or 22 or 1,640hp Merlin 24 vee-12 liquid-cooled; **II**: four 1,650hp Bristol Hercules VI 14-cylinder sleeve-valve radials; **III**: four 1,390hp Packard V-1650 (Merlin 28, 38 or 224).

MAXIMUM SPEED (all bombers, typical) 462km/h (287mph) at 3500m (11,500ft).

SERVICE CEILING (typical) 7467m (24,500ft).

RANGE Maximum with full bomb-load 2675km (1,660 miles); with 3175kg (7,000lb) bomb-load 4075km (2,530 miles).

MILITARY LOAD Normal bomb load 6350kg (14,000lb), with many options and in special versions unusual loads; defensive armament, tail turret with four 7·7mm (0·303in) Browning machine guns (late models in some cases two 12·7mm/0·5in); mid-upper turret if fitted two 7·7mm (0·303in) (**Mk VII**, two 12·7mm/0·5in); nose turret if fitted, two 7·7mm (0·303in); Mk II also ventral barbette, two 7·7mm (0·303in).

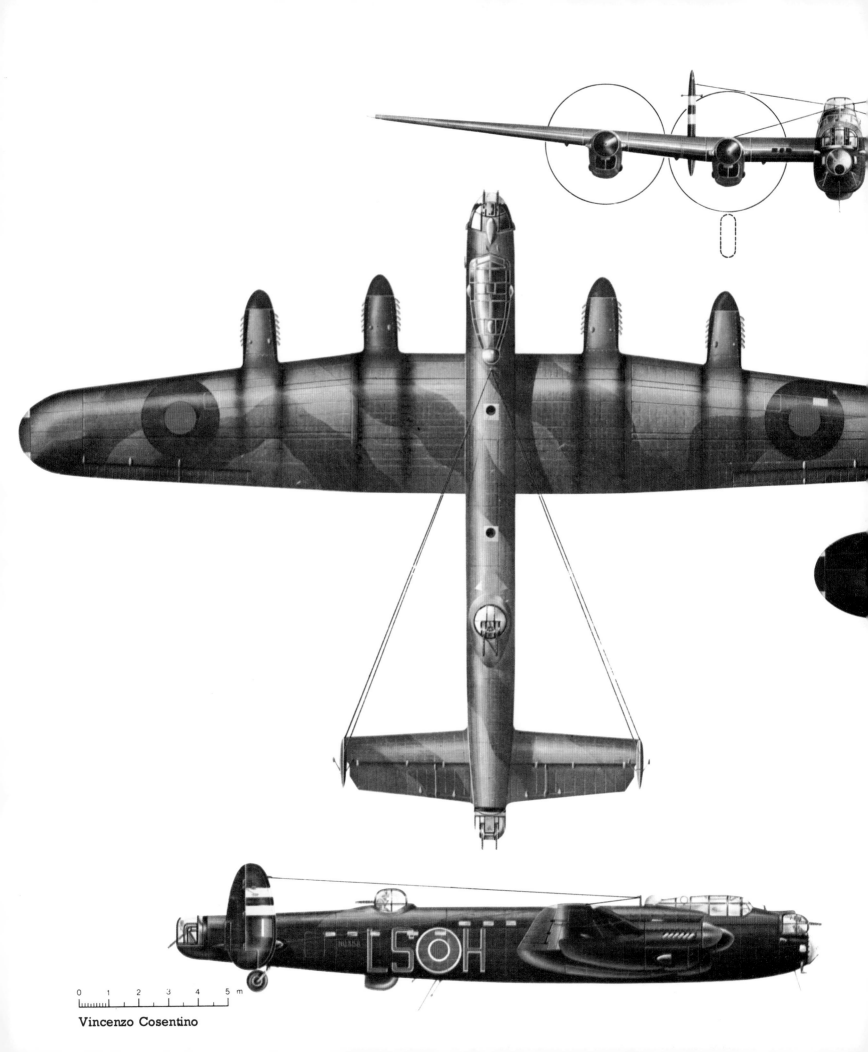

0 1 2 3 4 5 m

Vincenzo Cosentino

Avro Lancaster B.I

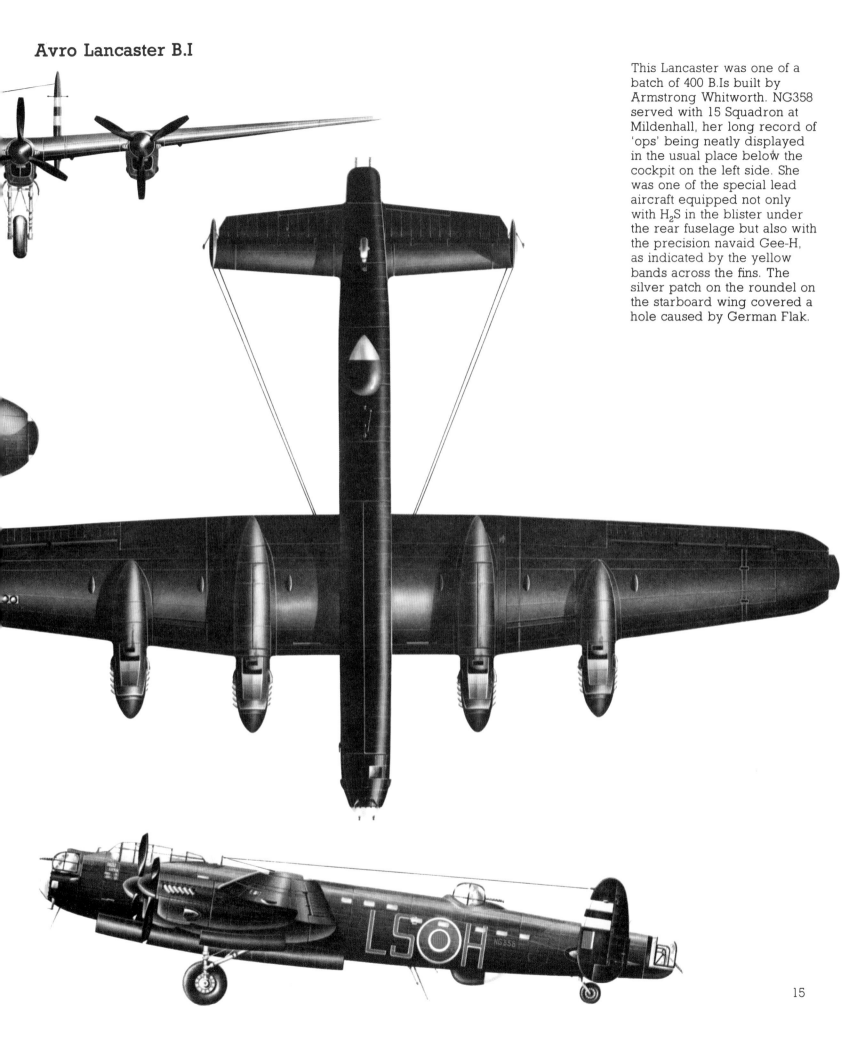

This Lancaster was one of a batch of 400 B.Is built by Armstrong Whitworth. NG358 served with 15 Squadron at Mildenhall, her long record of 'ops' being neatly displayed in the usual place below the cockpit on the left side. She was one of the special lead aircraft equipped not only with H_2S in the blister under the rear fuselage but also with the precision navaid Gee-H, as indicated by the yellow bands across the fins. The silver patch on the roundel on the starboard wing covered a hole caused by German Flak.

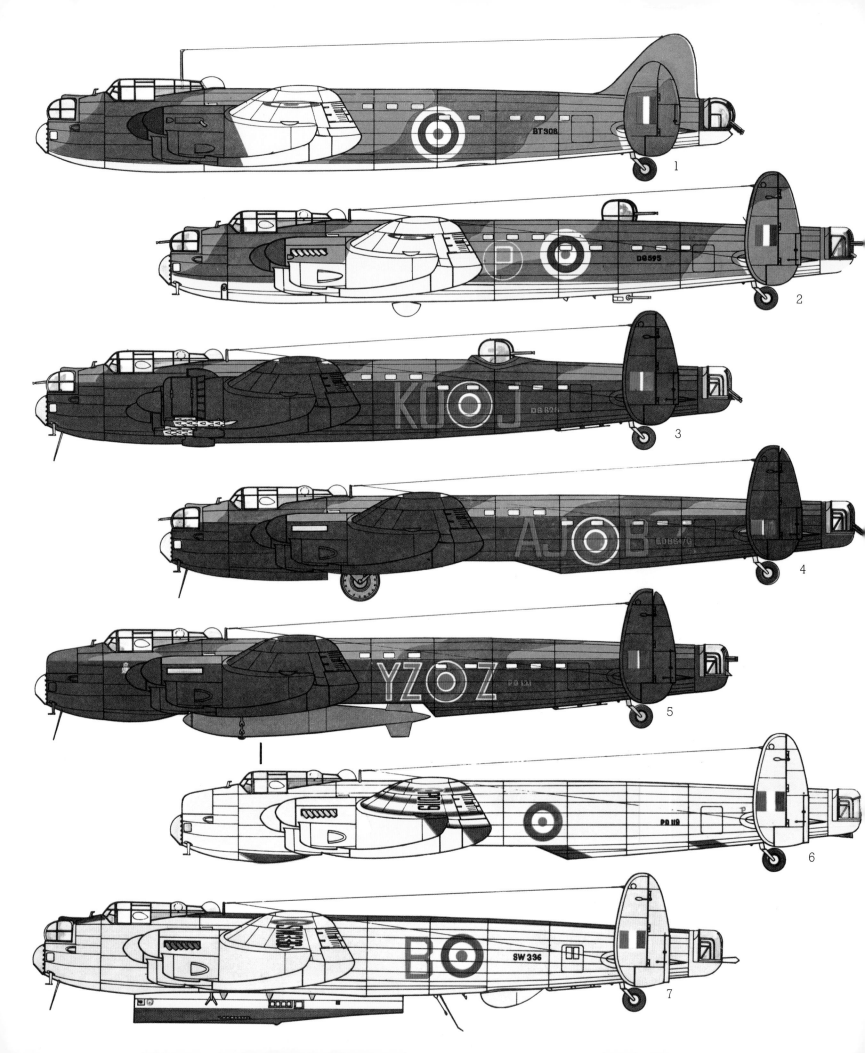

1

2

3

4

5

6

7

Avro Lancaster

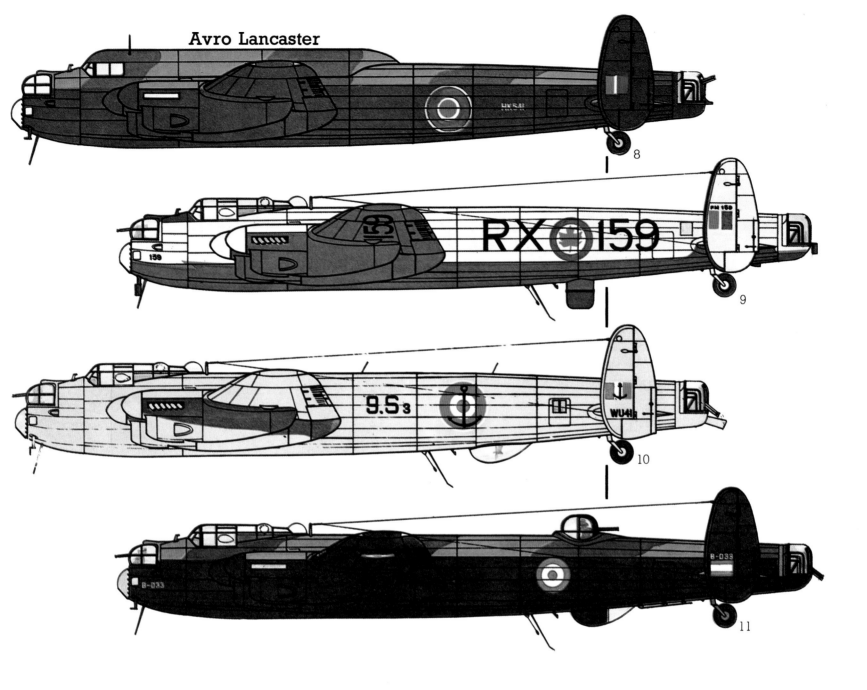

1 First designated Avro Manchester III, this aircraft was a Manchester fitted with extended outer wings and four Merlins. It flew on 9 January 1941, and later did air testing of a Metropolitan-Vickers F2 turbojet fitted in the tail.

2 The second prototype flew on 13 May 1941 and introduced the new tail, mid-upper turret and ventral barbette.

3 The Lancaster II had Hercules sleeve-valve engines with long flame-damped exhausts, a bulged bomb bay and ventral barbette.

4 ED864/G was one of the 23 Mk Is rebuilt for 617 Sqn's dam-busting mission.

5 PD121 was a Mk I (Special), in this case burdened by the 10-tonne (9·8-UK ton) Grand Slam bomb.

6 PD119 was a Mk I (Special) used in 1948 for research at the Royal Aircraft Establishment.

7 SW336 was built at Yeadon, near Leeds, as a B.III but then converted to ASR.III with lifeboat, used by 36 Sqn at Luqa.

8 HK541 was a B.I(FE) with saddle tank for Far East missions.

9 Built by Victory Aircraft as a B.X (FM159) this MR.10 served post-war with 407 Sqn RCAF at Comox, BC.

10 The penultimate B.I appeared post-war with the French Aéronavale 9S based at Noumea in New Caledonia.

11 Built at Chester as PA377, this B.I went to Argentina in 1948.

Vicenzo Cosentino

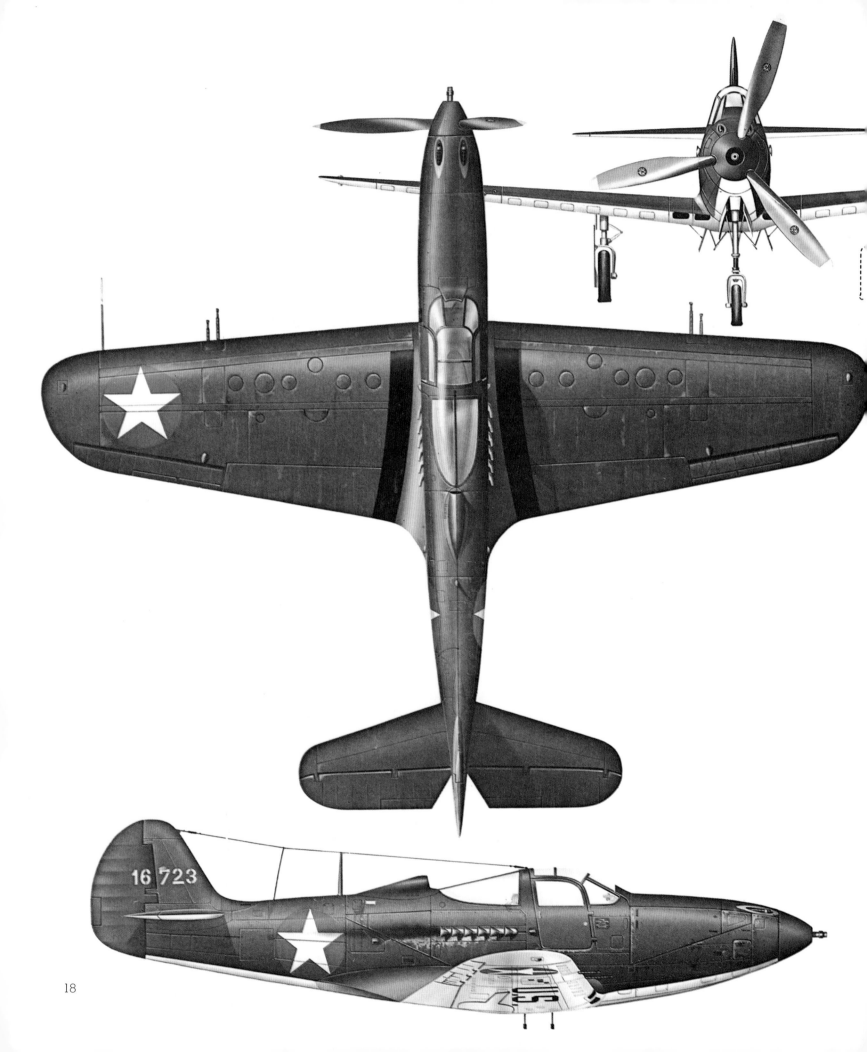

Bell P-39D Airacobra

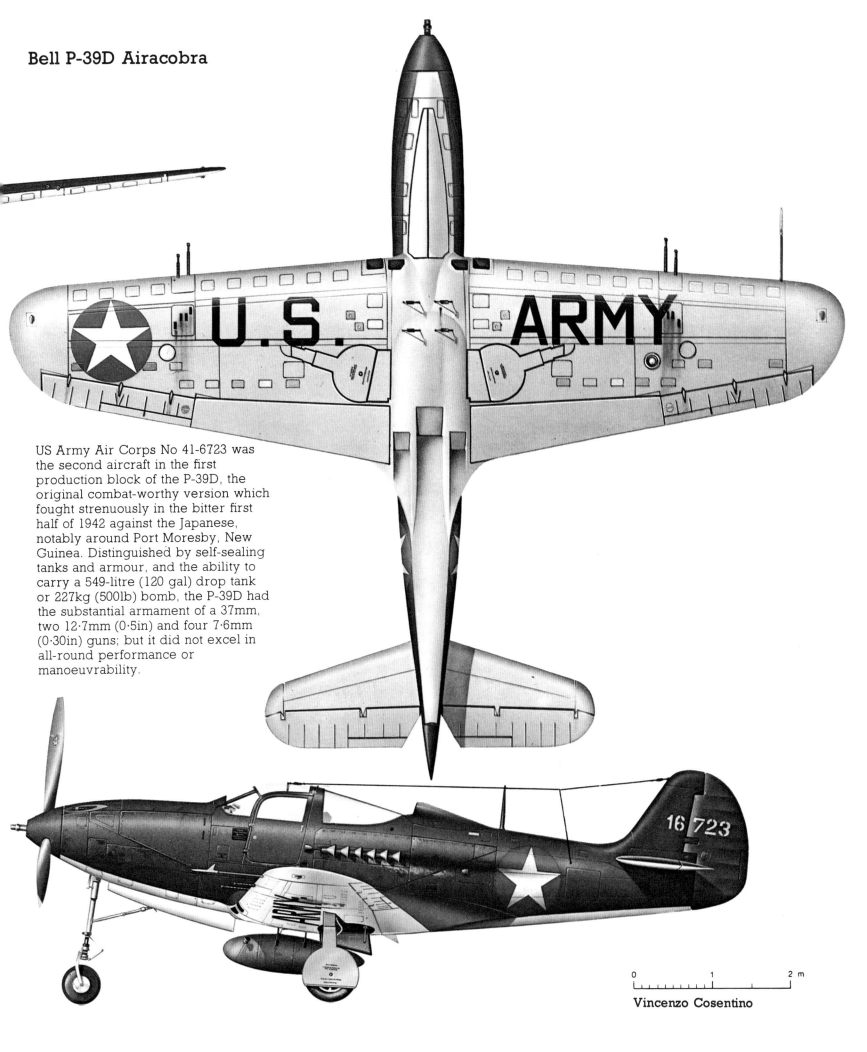

US Army Air Corps No 41-6723 was the second aircraft in the first production block of the P-39D, the original combat-worthy version which fought strenuously in the bitter first half of 1942 against the Japanese, notably around Port Moresby, New Guinea. Distinguished by self-sealing tanks and armour, and the ability to carry a 549-litre (120 gal) drop tank or 227kg (500lb) bomb, the P-39D had the substantial armament of a 37mm, two 12·7mm (0·5in) and four 7·6mm (0·30in) guns; but it did not excel in all-round performance or manoeuvrability.

Vincenzo Cosentino

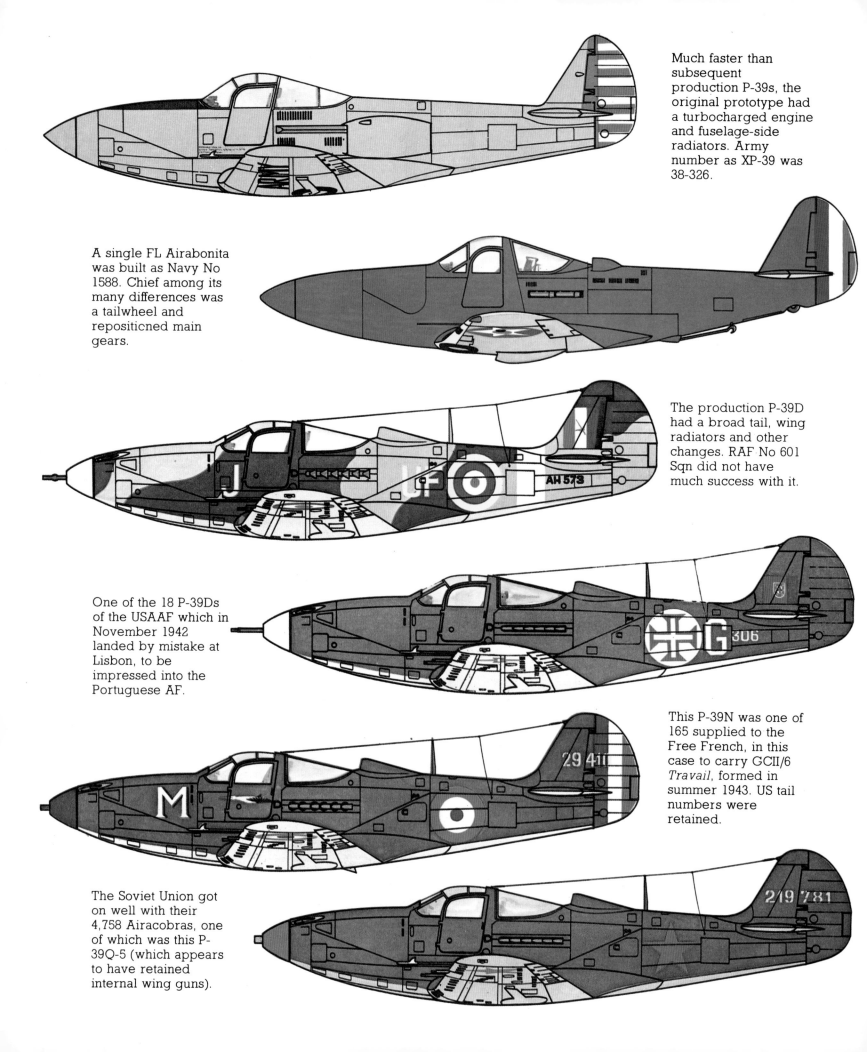

Much faster than subsequent production P-39s, the original prototype had a turbocharged engine and fuselage-side radiators. Army number as XP-39 was 38-326.

A single FL Airabonita was built as Navy No 1588. Chief among its many differences was a tailwheel and repositioned main gears.

The production P-39D had a broad tail, wing radiators and other changes. RAF No 601 Sqn did not have much success with it.

One of the 18 P-39Ds of the USAAF which in November 1942 landed by mistake at Lisbon, to be impressed into the Portuguese AF.

This P-39N was one of 165 supplied to the Free French, in this case to carry GCII/6 *Travail*, formed in summer 1943. US tail numbers were retained.

The Soviet Union got on well with their 4,758 Airacobras, one of which was this P-39Q-5 (which appears to have retained internal wing guns).

Bell P-39 Airacobra

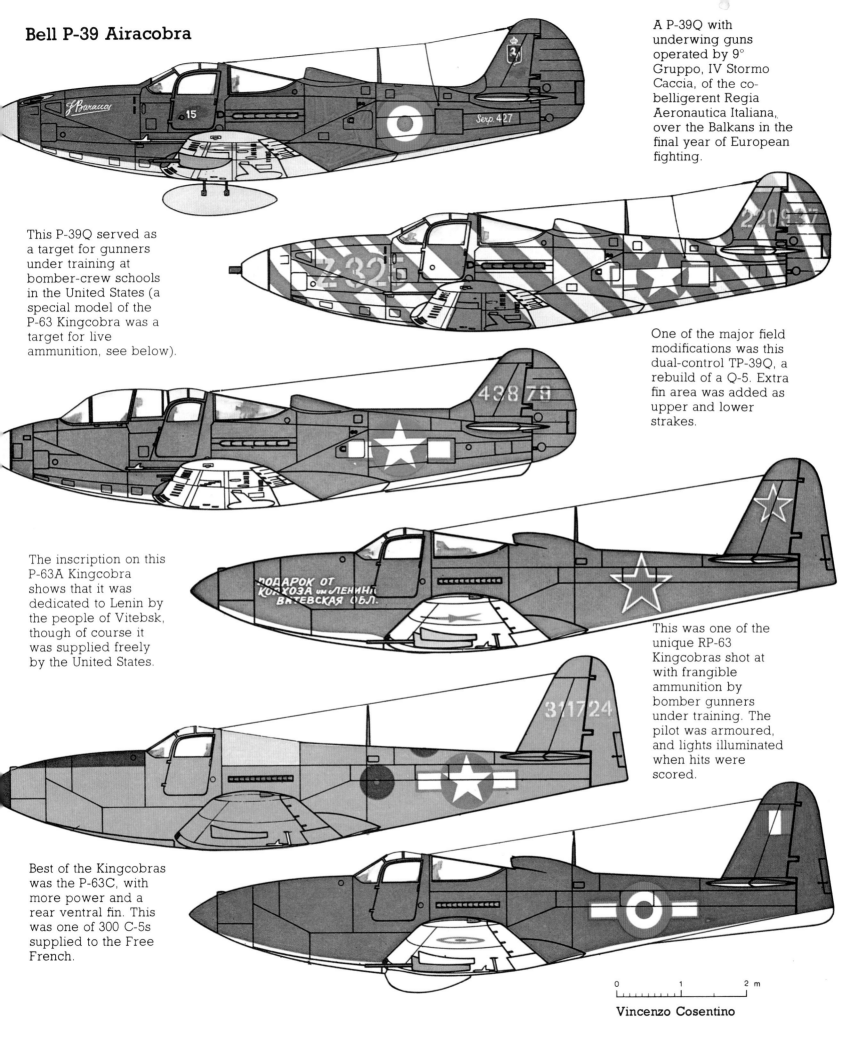

A P-39Q with underwing guns operated by 9° Gruppo, IV Stormo Caccia, of the co-belligerent Regia Aeronautica Italiana, over the Balkans in the final year of European fighting.

This P-39Q served as a target for gunners under training at bomber-crew schools in the United States (a special model of the P-63 Kingcobra was a target for live ammunition, see below).

One of the major field modifications was this dual-control TP-39Q, a rebuild of a Q-5. Extra fin area was added as upper and lower strakes.

The inscription on this P-63A Kingcobra shows that it was dedicated to Lenin by the people of Vitebsk, though of course it was supplied freely by the United States.

This was one of the unique RP-63 Kingcobras shot at with frangible ammunition by bomber gunners under training. The pilot was armoured, and lights illuminated when hits were scored.

Best of the Kingcobras was the P-63C, with more power and a rear ventral fin. This was one of 300 C-5s supplied to the Free French.

0   1   2 m

Vincenzo Cosentino

Bell P-39 Airacobra

Bell Aircraft was started by Larry Bell in 1935 as a result of Consolidated deciding to move from Buffalo to San Diego. The new company took over most of the Buffalo factory, and designers R.J. Woods and O.L. Woodson began to design new fighters of radical design. The only one to be built in large numbers was the model P-400 Airacobra, called P-39 by the US Army Air Corps, the first example of which made its maiden flight on 6 April 1939. Like many American pursuit (fighter) designs of this period it was unconventional in major respects. The result was not all that had been hoped; yet in a time of crisis when fighters were in short supply, this tough machine gave good service on every Allied front.

Like a dozen fighters before it, the Airacobra put the engine behind the cockpit in order to get it on the centre of gravity and thus achieve maximum manoeuvrability. This meant driving the propeller reduction gearbox via a long tubular shaft passing between the pilot's legs, but this proved to be one of the few parts of the P-39 that gave hardly any trouble. A secondary advantage of the rear engine location was that it facilitated installing heavy gun armament in the nose, and a third was that it protected the pilot from behind. In theory it could have crushed the pilot in a severe forced landing, but this seldom happened.

Another feature of the Bell that at the time was radical was the nosewheel (so-called tricycle) landing gear. This also proved relatively trouble-free, though its novelty caused great problems in air forces unfamiliar with it, though with proper training the problems vanished. A minor novelty was the use of a car-type hinged door on each side of the roomy and well-equipped cockpit, the roof of which was fixed.

Despite its unconventionality the prototype demonstrated an excellent all-round performance, the speed with a turbo-supercharged engine being 628km/h (390mph) at medium altitudes, then probably faster than any other fighter in the world. Unfortunately, as often happens, it was all downhill from

then on, as the turbo was removed from the engine, the cooling system was moved from fuselage to wing, and more than a ton of weight was added in armour, self-sealing tanks, bullet-proof transparencies and armament.

The US Army ordered 80 P-45 Airacobras in August 1939, soon changing the designation to P-39C, and large batches were ordered by the frantic French. In 1940 the French orders were taken over by Britain, and by September 1941 No 601 Sqn RAF had equipped with what at the time was called the Caribou I (later the US name was adopted). A combination of poor serviceability and deep distrust of this unfamiliar fighter resulted in a pathetic experience, culminating in rejection by the RAF after one combat mission.

The USAAF, however, found fewer snags and received 429 of the P-39D version (in most respects similar to that supplied to the RAF), despite lack of a nosewheel training aircraft. Production built up fast, with 229 P-39Fs (Aeroproducts instead of Curtiss Electric propeller), 210 P-39Ks with revised engine, 250 Ls, 240 Ms, 500 N-0s, 900 N-1s, 695 N-5s and finally no fewer than 4,905 of the P-39Q with revised wing guns and in later batches a four-blade propeller.

Production was curtailed in early 1944 and stopped in July, partly to release the newly built Marietta, Georgia, factory for production of the B-29. About 5,000 Airacobras were flown via Iran to the Soviet Union where they proved satisfactory in close-air support operating from rough dirt and board airstrips. Other important users were the Free French and co-belligerent Italian air forces.

Having got into high-rate production, Bell were permitted to build 3,303 of the P-63 Kingcobra which, though based on the P-39, had a new airframe. Of these, 2,421 went to the Soviet Union and about 350 to the Free French. Standard armament of the P-63A and C (the latter having a more powerful V-1710 engine) was one 37mm and four 12·7mm (0·5in), two of the latter being in underwing fairings similar to those of the P-39Q.

COUNTRY OF ORIGIN USA.

CREW 1

TOTAL PRODUCED 9,588.

DIMENSIONS Wingspan 10·363m (34ft 0in); length 9·195m (30ft 2in); wing area 19·79m² (213ft²).

WEIGHTS Empty, **L**: 2540kg (5,600lb), **Q**: 2707kg (5,968lb); maximum gross **L**: 3530kg (7,780lb), **Q**: 3656kg (8,052lb).

ENGINE Allison V-1710 vee-12 liquid-cooled. **C,D,F** 1,150hp V-1710-35; **K,L**: 1,325hp V-1710-63; **M,N,Q**: 1,200hp V-1710-83 or -85.

MAXIMUM SPEED (typical) 612km/h (380mph) at 3355m (11,000ft).

SERVICE CEILING (typical) 10670m (35,000ft).

RANGE (typical with bomb) 1207km (750 miles), (with drop tank) 2360km (1,466 miles).

MILITARY LOAD Normal armament one 37mm Oldsmobile T-1 cannon with 15 rounds (**C**) or (other models except RAF) 30 rounds (RAF aircraft, 20mm with 60 rounds) and two 12·7mm (0·5in) Brownings (200 rounds) in nose; four 7·7mm (0·303in) Brownings in wings (1,000 rounds) in P-39**D** to **N**, two 12·7mm (0·5in) (200 rounds) in **Q**; **D** onwards, provision for 227kg (500lb) bomb under fuselage.

Boeing B-17 Flying Fortress

Difficult as it may be to believe, the most famous American bomber of all time was conceived as a defensive aircraft. As no hostile nation appeared to be within bombing range the only threat to the United States was thought to be a hostile fleet, and in May 1934 the Army Air Corps issued a specification for a multi-engined anti-ship bomber. The term 'multi-engined' had universally been taken to mean a twin, but Boeing's entry, the Model 299, had four of the most powerful engines available, in order that the speed and height over the target should be greater.

First flown on 28 July 1935, the impressive 299 soon crashed, through no fault of the aircraft. The concept of a large formation of high-flying strategic bombers, bristling with guns and defending each other by massed firepower, took firm root in Washington. It was a concept soon to be sternly tested, and after titanic and bloody struggles was eventually to prove triumphant: but this was to no small degree due to the long-range escort-fighters.

A vital part of the concept was the General Electric turbosupercharger, and these were fitted to the production B-17B, officially named Fortress, first delivered in June 1939 after prolonged service trials with test and evaluation models. From the start the B-17 had a conservative wing-loading which made it sedate and generally popular, though cruising speed was low (especially in a sky filled with flak or fighters) and once the two pilots had left their seats the aircraft tended to indulge in violent gyrations making escape difficult.

With the B-17C of 1940 came armour, self-sealing tanks, a ventral bathtub for underside protection and flush side guns. This was the fastest production model, and 20 were supplied to the RAF, which managed to eliminate the first eight in a matter of weeks. The USAAF, building up strength with the better-protected B-17D, spent 1941 learning how to operate long high-flying missions and had a handful of these valuable machines on hand in the Philippines in December 1941. Meanwhile Boeing had largely redesigned the B-17 with a larger fin and tailplane and wholly new turreted armament, the resulting B-17E flying on 5 September 1941. Production built up at a group of vast factories run by Boeing, Douglas and Vega (Lockheed), and on 17 August 1942 the E began three years of relentless missions against German targets with the 8th Air Force.

In April 1942 the E gave way to the F, with frameless Plexiglas nose, paddle-blade propellers and more than 400 minor improvements. Boeing built 2,300, Douglas 600 and Vega 500, and in July 1943 all three switched to the final model, the G, with chin turret to discourage head-on attacks, and many other changes. By this time the heavy and costly olive-drab paint had been eliminated, because the growing massed formations, trailing contrails, could be seen from great distances. When production stopped in April 1945 Boeing had built 4,035 of the G model, Douglas 2,395 and Vega 2,250, the grand total being 12,731.

USAAF B-17s dropped 581,851 tonnes (640,036 US tons) of bombs on Europe, and shot down an unknown but enormous number of hostile fighters. Weapons dropped · included the rocket-propelled bomb for U-boat pens, 1814kg (4,000lb) bombs hung under the wings and the GB-1 radio-controlled glide bomb. Some 'Forts' were converted into YB-40 escort fighters, others into BQ-7 radio-controlled missiles, and many served as tankers, strategic reconnaissance aircraft, transports, air/sea rescue lifeboat carriers and Navy and RAF ocean-patrol aircraft. RAF 100 Group used many Fortress IIIs (B-17Gs) as ECM (electronic countermeasures) platforms, and in 1945 the Navy PB-1W was the first aircraft ever to operate with airborne early-warning radar in a large bulge under the nose. A proportion of regular USAAF bombers had carried H_2X blind-bombing radar in place of the spherical ball turret, and one of the most curious war stories concerns the use of a considerable number of B-17s - at least 14 - by the Luftwaffe, for all kinds of clandestine purposes.

COUNTRY OF ORIGIN USA.

CREW 6 to 10, most **F** and **G** models in bomber role having 8.

TOTAL PRODUCED 12,731.

DIMENSIONS Wingspan 31·6m (103ft 9in); length, **C**: 20·7m (67ft 11in), **E**: 22·5m (73ft 10in), **F,G**: 22·8m (74ft 9in); wing area 131·92m² (1,420ft²).

WEIGHTS Empty **C**: 13880kg (30,600lb), **E**: 14628kg (32,250lb), (**G**, typical) 17240kg (38,000lb); maximum loaded **C**: 22520kg (49,650lb), **E**: 24040kg (53,000lb), **G**: normal 29756kg (65,600lb), (**G**, overload) 32660kg (72,000lb).

ENGINES Four 1,200hp Wright Cyclone R-1820-65 or (**F** and **G**) R-1820-97.

MAXIMUM SPEED **C**: 520km/h (323mph), **E**: 499km/h (310mph), **G**: 462km/h (287mph) all at 9144m (30,000ft).

SERVICE CEILING **C**: 11278m (37,000ft), **G**: 10850m (35,600ft).

RANGE (Max bomb-load, typical) 1760km (1,100 miles), over 4830km (3,000 miles) in ferry condition.

MILITARY LOAD Normal internal bomb load 2722kg (6,000lb), but maximum overload up to 5800kg (12,800lb); defensive armament of **C**, one 7·62 or 7·7mm (0·30 or 0·303in) gun in nose, one 12·7mm (0·5in) in each waist window and twin 12·7mm (0·5in) in dorsal and ventral positions, all manually aimed; **G**: 12 or 13 guns of 12·7mm (0·5in) in twin-gun chin, dorsal, ball and tail turrets, two waist windows, two lateral nose sockets and (optional) roof of radio compartment.

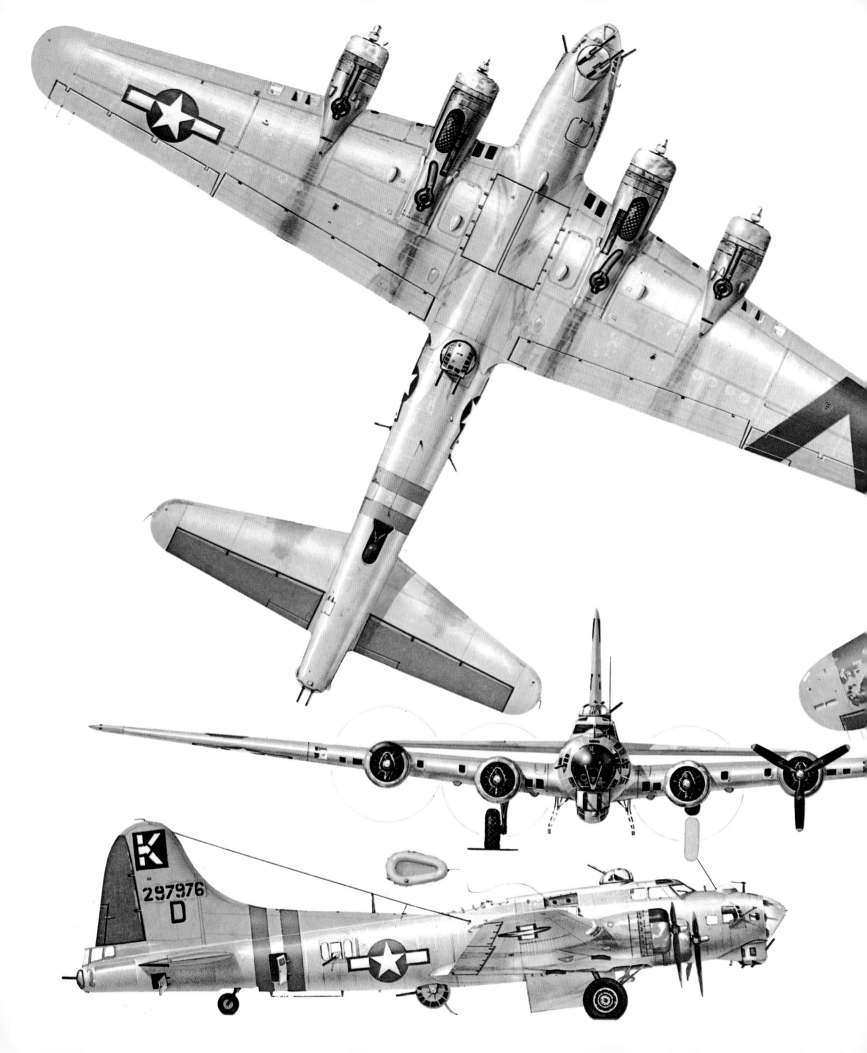

Boeing B-17G Flying Fortress

A BIT Ó LACE

This late-model B-17G was one of the famous Fortresses with a long record of missions with the 8th Air Force; it was also notable in that its nose art was signed by Milton Caniff (see inset). Users were the 711th Bomb Squadron of the 447th Bomb Group, based at Rattlesden. Aircraft 42-97976 was delivered after March 1944, at first to the same group's 709th BS, and is shown in end-of-war markings with yellow wing tips and tail. Squadron codes were not worn by the 447th. Note dinghy in the lower side elevation.

0 1 2 3 4 5 m

Pino dell'Orco

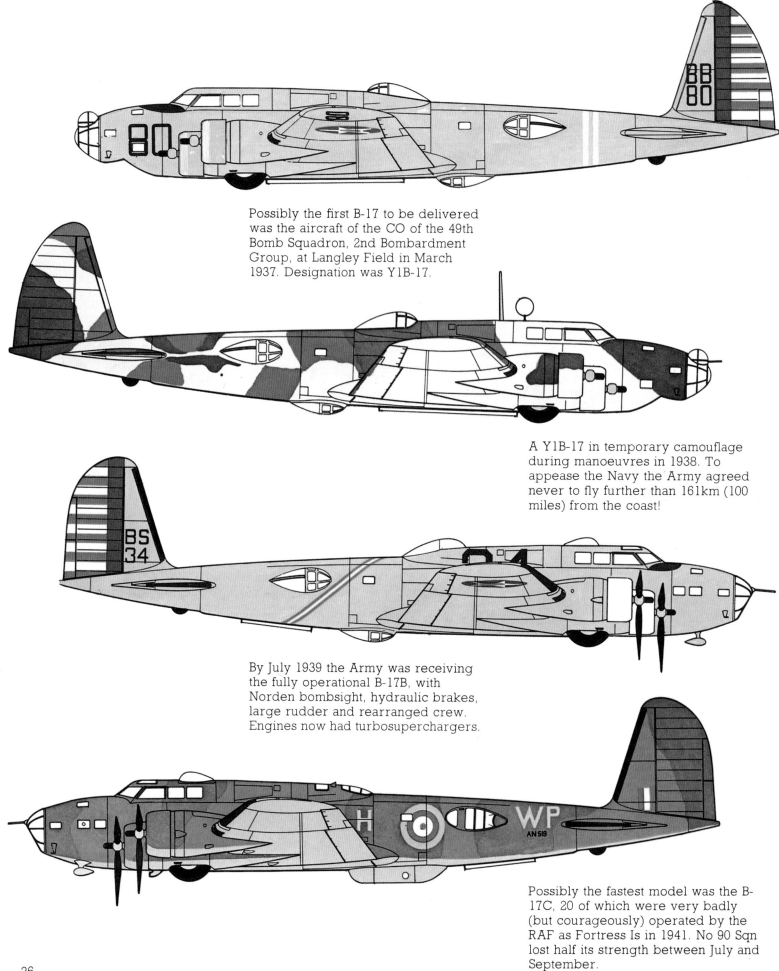

Possibly the first B-17 to be delivered was the aircraft of the CO of the 49th Bomb Squadron, 2nd Bombardment Group, at Langley Field in March 1937. Designation was Y1B-17.

A Y1B-17 in temporary camouflage during manoeuvres in 1938. To appease the Navy the Army agreed never to fly further than 161km (100 miles) from the coast!

By July 1939 the Army was receiving the fully operational B-17B, with Norden bombsight, hydraulic brakes, large rudder and rearranged crew. Engines now had turbosuperchargers.

Possibly the fastest model was the B-17C, 20 of which were very badly (but courageously) operated by the RAF as Fortress Is in 1941. No 90 Sqn lost half its strength between July and September.

Boeing B-17 Flying Fortress

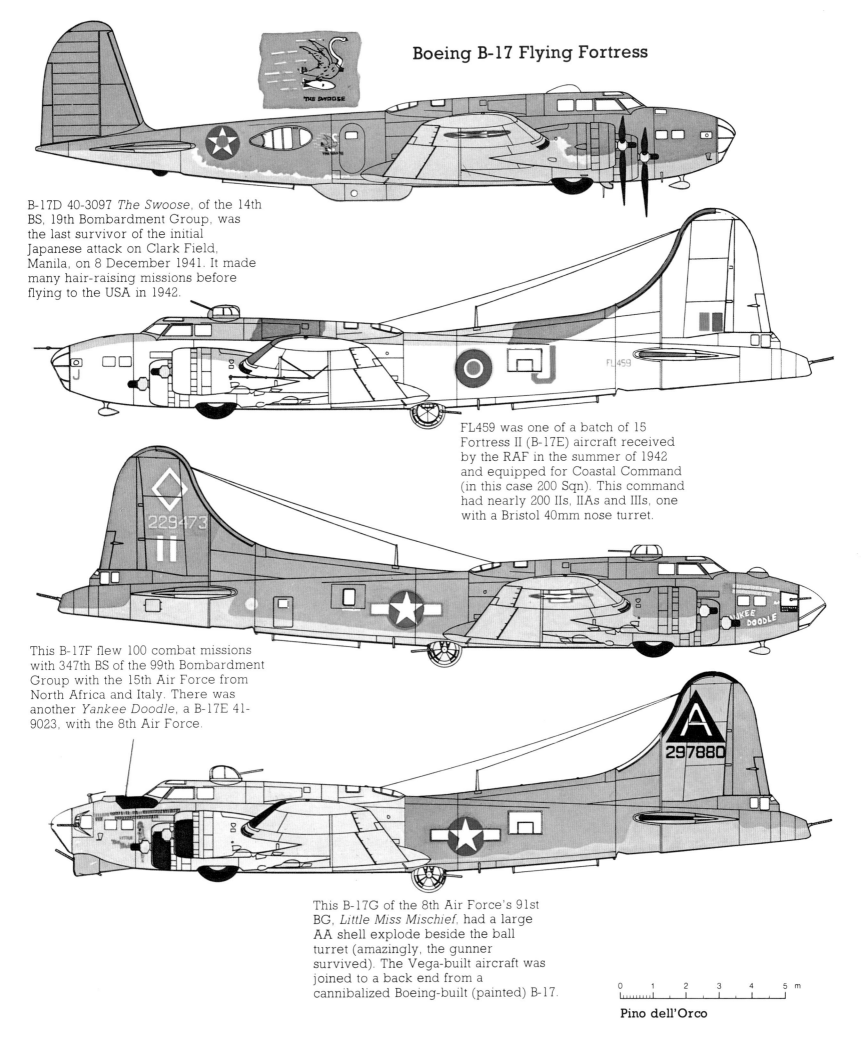

B-17D 40-3097 *The Swoose*, of the 14th BS, 19th Bombardment Group, was the last survivor of the initial Japanese attack on Clark Field, Manila, on 8 December 1941. It made many hair-raising missions before flying to the USA in 1942.

FL459 was one of a batch of 15 Fortress II (B-17E) aircraft received by the RAF in the summer of 1942 and equipped for Coastal Command (in this case 200 Sqn). This command had nearly 200 IIs, IIAs and IIIs, one with a Bristol 40mm nose turret.

This B-17F flew 100 combat missions with 347th BS of the 99th Bombardment Group with the 15th Air Force from North Africa and Italy. There was another *Yankee Doodle*, a B-17E 41-9023, with the 8th Air Force.

This B-17G of the 8th Air Force's 91st BG, *Little Miss Mischief*, had a large AA shell explode beside the ball turret (amazingly, the gunner survived). The Vega-built aircraft was joined to a back end from a cannibalized Boeing-built (painted) B-17.

0 1 2 3 4 5 m

Pino dell'Orco

Boeing B-29-97-BW Superfortress

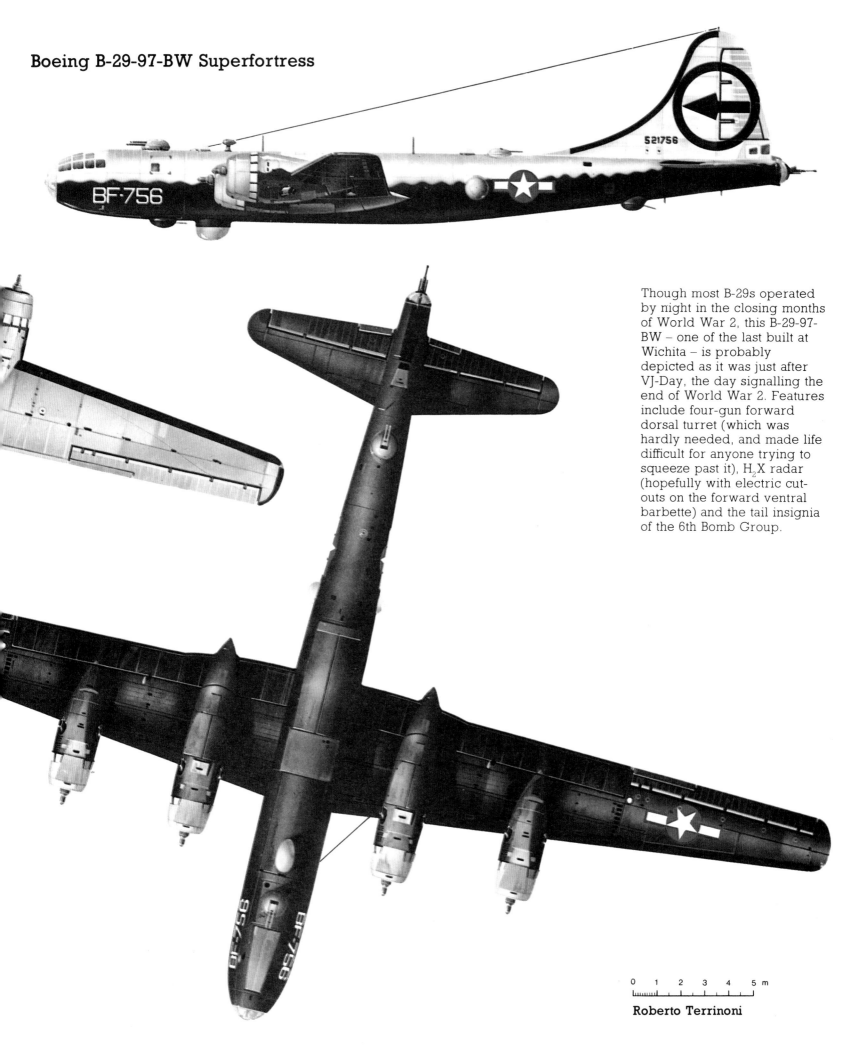

Though most B-29s operated by night in the closing months of World War 2, this B-29-97-BW – one of the last built at Wichita – is probably depicted as it was just after VJ-Day, the day signalling the end of World War 2. Features include four-gun forward dorsal turret (which was hardly needed, and made life difficult for anyone trying to squeeze past it), H_2X radar (hopefully with electric cut-outs on the forward ventral barbette) and the tail insignia of the 6th Bomb Group.

0 1 2 3 4 5 m

Roberto Terrinoni

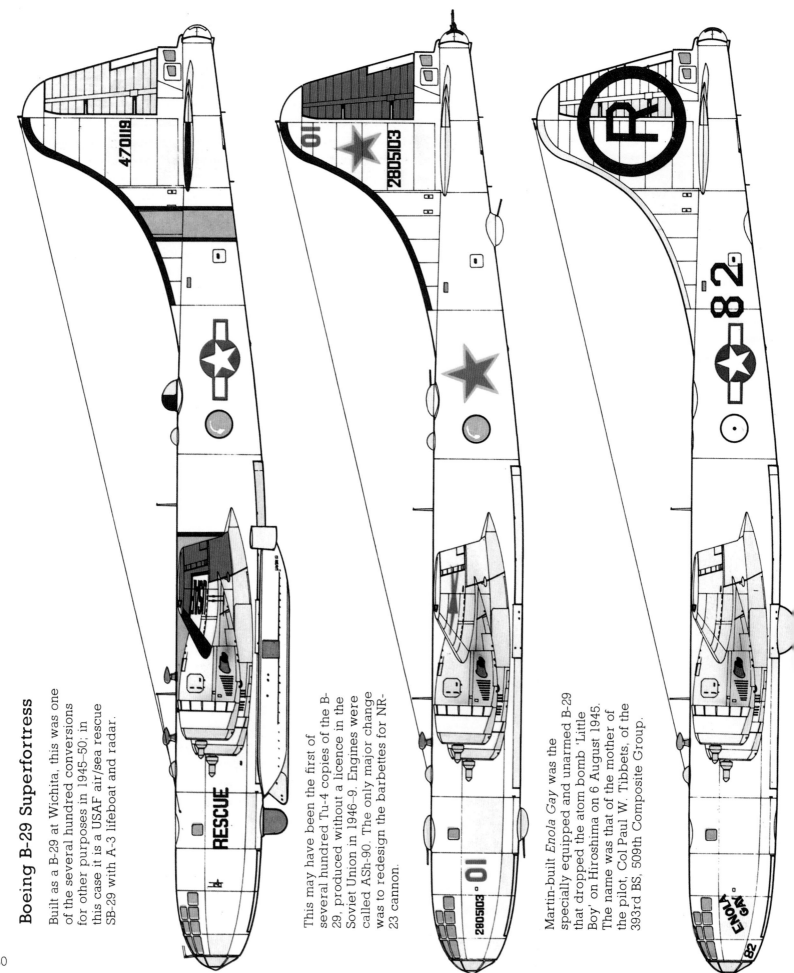

Boeing B-29 Superfortress

Built as a B-29 at Wichita, this was one of the several hundred conversions for other purposes in 1945–50; in this case it is a USAF air/sea rescue SB-29 with A-3 lifeboat and radar.

This may have been the first of several hundred Tu-4 copies of the B-29, produced without a licence in the Soviet Union in 1946–9. Engines were called ASh-90. The only major change was to redesign the barbettes for NR-23 cannon.

Martin-built *Enola Gay* was the specially equipped and unarmed B-29 that dropped the atom bomb 'Little Boy' on Hiroshima on 6 August 1945. The name was that of the mother of the pilot, Col Paul W. Tibbets, of the 393rd BS, 509th Composite Group.

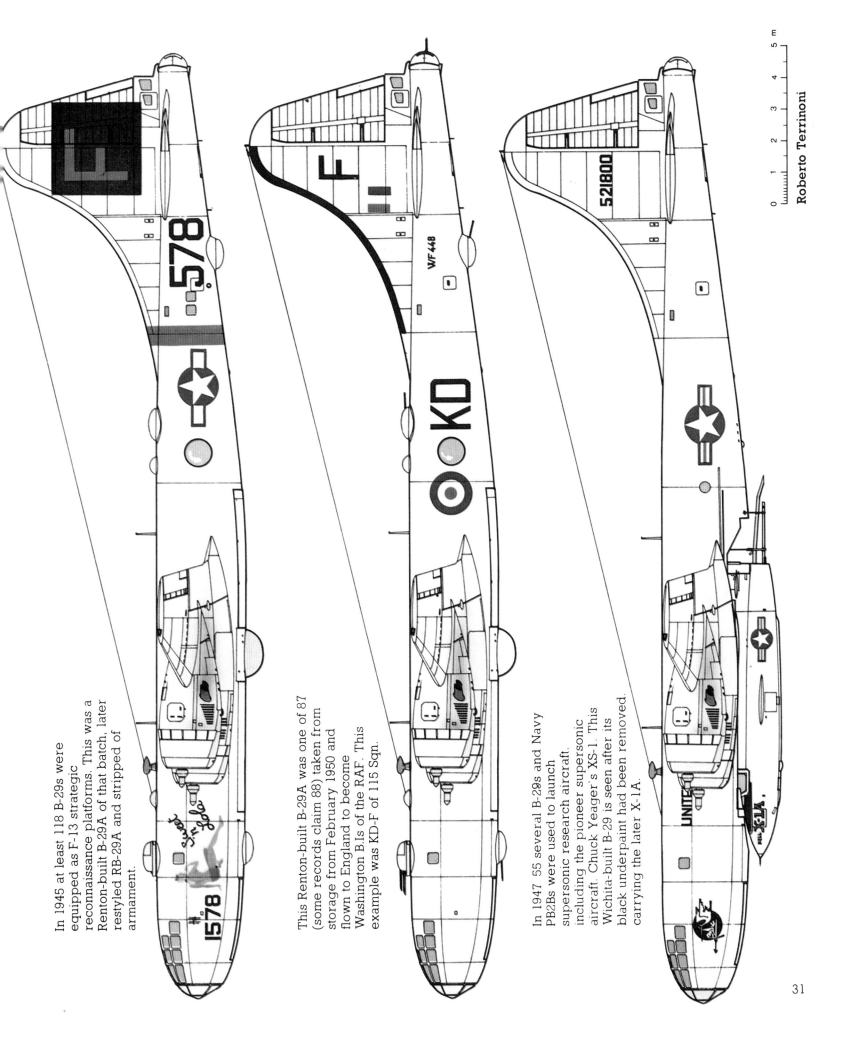

In 1945 at least 118 B-29s were equipped as F-13 strategic reconnaissance platforms. This was a Renton-built B-29A of that batch, later restyled RB-29A and stripped of armament.

This Renton-built B-29A was one of 87 (some records claim 88) taken from storage from February 1950 and flown to England to become Washington B.Is of the RAF. This example was KD-F of 115 Sqn.

In 1947 55 several B-29s and Navy PB2Bs were used to launch supersonic research aircraft. including the pioneer supersonic aircraft. Chuck Yeager's XS-1. This Wichita-built B-29 is seen after its black underpaint had been removed. carrying the later X-1A.

Roberto Terrinoni

Boeing B-29 Superfortress

No aircraft in history made a greater contribution to aviation technology than the B-29 Superfortress, which thrust boldly forward in structure, materials, systems, propulsion, armament and even flight environment. Thanks to an early start, at a time when the USAAC was finding it difficult even to get Congress to pay for the first B-17s for inventory service, the whole mighty programme led to production aircraft in time to play a major role in the final year of World War 2. Indeed, in partnership with the atomic bomb, the B-29 ended the war and made the feared bloody invasion of Japan unnecessary.

It was in March 1938 that Chief of Staff Oscar Westover requested from industry proposals for a completely new strategic bomber with a pressurized cabin so that it could fly higher than the B-17, and much faster. Boeing took the job on, and in January 1939 a frighteningly costly nationwide production programme was planned for what was clearly going to be the most advanced aircraft ever contemplated, at a time when there was no money and not a single piece of a prototype. This bold decision was instrumental, $6\frac{1}{2}$ years later, in shortening the war.

After immense engineering effort the Boeing Model 345 finally crystallized as a design in the summer of 1940, and the first prototype flew in olive-drab paint, without armament, on 21 September 1942. Orders mounted rapidly, and as well as the unused Sea Ranger plant at Renton, a few miles from the Boeing parent factory, a completely new production line was set up at Wichita, backed by another run by Martin at Omaha and yet another operated by Bell at Marietta, Georgia. Fisher Body division of General Motors began making the engine nacelles, each bigger and much more complex than many fuselages and fitted with two GE turbosuperchargers. From stem to stern the B-29 was impressive, with a pressurized crew compartment in the nose, a tunnel to a second pressure cabin in the rear fuselage, an all-glazed nose with instrument panels on each side for the two pilots, five powered turrets driven by gunners who could transfer control from one man to another, and vast front and rear bomb bays from which weapons were sequenced alternately to keep centre of gravity.

Wing loading easily exceeded that of any previous aircraft in service, as did take-off and landing speeds. Throughout 1944 USAAF crews found the great new bomber almost too much of a challenge, and there was prolonged difficulty over engine cooling, cruise technique (which began at an abysmal level and, for the crews who survived, gradually worked up until miles-per-gallon had been doubled) and knitting the crew together as a tight and proficient team. Finally, the day before D-Day (i.e., on 5 June 1944), a small B-29 formation bombed the marshalling yard at Bangkok. Increasingly strong B-29 forces in China, each supplied with all the necessities except food by perilous airlift 'over the Hump' from Burma, began missions against Japan itself. In November the new 20th Air Force began attacks from the Marianas, and as deliveries of B-29s grew to a flood so did the scale of attacks.

Crews steadily matured, mastered the challenging Superfortress, and by 1945 were going out in their hundreds with bellies filled with firebombs that razed city after city to the ground. The Tokyo mission of 9 March 1945 wiped out more than 40km² ($15\frac{1}{2}$ square miles) of the city, killed 84,000 and injured over 100,000 – never equalled in any other aerial attack. Finally on 6 August 1945 the special unarmed and modified aircraft of Col Paul Tibbetts dropped the nuclear weapon Little Boy on Hiroshima. Three days later another B-29 dropped a different type of atom bomb, named Fat Man, on Nagasaki. This brought World War 2 to a close.

But the B-29 still had a giant task to perform in Korea, where its weapons often included the monster Tarzan radio-controlled bomb. The USAF brought 88 out of storage and lent them to the RAF, which named them the Washington. And in the Soviet Union the Tupolev bureau copied the B-29 and put it into production as the Tu-4.

COUNTRY OF ORIGIN USA.

CREW As bomber, usually 11–13.

TOTAL PRODUCED 3,970.

DIMENSIONS Wingspan 43·05m (141ft 3in); length 30·175m (99ft 0in); wing area 161·28m² (1,739ft²).

WEIGHTS Empty 32368kg (71,360lb) varying with equipment and armament to 33795kg (74,500lb); maximum loaded either 61240kg (135,000lb) or 64000kg (141,000lb).

ENGINES Four 2,200hp Wright Duplex Cyclone R-3350-23 18-cylinder radials.

MAXIMUM SPEED With full armament 575km/h (357mph) at 9144m (30,000ft).

SERVICE CEILING 9708m (31,850ft).

RANGE With 4540kg (10,000lb) bomb load, 5230km (3,250 miles).

MILITARY LOAD Normal bomb load of up to 9072kg (20,000lb); normal armament, two or four 12·7mm (0·5in) Browning guns in forward dorsal turret, two 12·7mm (0·5in) in each of rear dorsal and two ventral turrets, and two 12·7mm (0·5in) and one 20mm in tail turret. B-29C had defensive armament removed, except for tail guns, for increased speed and over-target height, and most special-purpose versions were unarmed.

Bristol Blenheim

Britain, the country that in 1918–21 set new standards in stressed-skin construction in which a metal skin bears most of the loads, was curiously reluctant to adopt such aircraft for its airlines or air force. The Blenheim, the first modern bomber to reach the RAF, was never planned for by the RAF but arose because a newspaper tycoon had in March 1934 asked the Bristol Aeroplane Co to build him a comfortable executive transport faster than anything available elsewhere. Bristol were afraid a streamlined monoplane might offend their chief customer, the RAF, by highlighting the outmoded appearance of contemporary British warplanes. After much dragging of feet, so that the Bristol 142 missed the great air race to Melbourne in October 1934, the aircraft flew on 12 April 1935. When two Hamilton variable-pitch propellers had been bought from the United States, replacing the wooden units originally fitted, the 142 was timed at 494km/h (307mph), more than 129km/h (80mph) faster than any fighter in the RAF.

Accordingly, on 9 July 1935 the Air Ministry held a conference, drafted bomber specification B.28/35 and later placed an order for 150 of the bomber designed to meet it. Named Blenheim, the Bristol 142M differed from the 142 in having the wing raised to the mid-position to leave room under it for a bomb bay. A retractable turret was added in the rear fuselage and there were many other changes. Blenheims reached the RAF in March 1937, flying rings round other service machines but also suffering many crashes caused by lack of familiarity with modern aircraft. By late 1939 no fewer than 1,134 Mk I Blenheims had been delivered, including 200 by Avro and 250 in the new Shadow Factory scheme organized by car manufacturers led by the Rootes group. About 200 were rebuilt as fighters, with four fixed belly machine-guns; and from the summer of 1939 some of these Mk IF Blenheims were the first in the world to go into service as night fighters with rudimentary airborne radar.

Via a coastal reconnaissance proto-type called Bolingbroke, a name later adopted for numerous Blenheim versions made in Canada, Bristol produced the Mk IV with a longer nose occupied by the navigator/bomb-aimer. It also carried more fuel, but thanks to more powerful engines was even faster than the Mk I. The Mk IV was probably the busiest aircraft in the RAF in the first six months of World War 2, and 3,297 were built. Some were IVF fighters, and the IVL had extra fuel and aft-facing chin turret. Early in the war Blenheims attacked the German fleet, served in France and flew many kinds of combat mission, and throughout 1941 even made dangerous low-level daylight raids against targets as far as Bremen and Cologne. By late 1941 Blenheims were being replaced in Britain and served increasingly in overseas theatres such as Greece, North Africa, Iraq, the Soviet Union, India, Burma and Singapore.

The final model was the Mk V, with a better dorsal turret, more armour, new nose, more power and numerous other changes. Rootes made 940 in 1942–3, but by this time the Blenheim was obsolescent and losses were heavy. On one occasion in December 1942 ten Mk Vs went out over Tunisia, met 60 Bf 109s and were almost annihilated, a single wreck of a survivor returning to base. Part of the trouble was that the gross weight had risen by 50 per cent compared with the Mk I, but the chief problem was that an aircraft which had been the last word in modernity in 1935 was totally inadequate in 1942.

Altogether 6,260 Blenheims (including Canadian Bolingbrokes) were made in 1936–44. Large numbers were exported in the final months of peace, and 40 were made under licence in Yugoslavia and 60 in Finland. In Canada Bolingbrokes often operated on skis, and one was a twin-float seaplane. There were large numbers of special versions, including a clipped-wing prototype for high-speed photographic sorties at low level and a heavily armoured two-seat ground-attack version called the Bisley. Single specimens of this famous machine exist in Britain, Canada and Finland.

COUNTRY OF ORIGIN Great Britain.

CREW 3.

TOTAL PRODUCED 6,260.

DIMENSIONS Wingspan 17·17m (56ft 4in); length, **I**: 12·1m (39ft 9in), **IV**: 12·9m (42ft 7in), **V**: 13·4m (44ft 0in); wing area 43·57m² (469ft²).

WEIGHTS Empty, **I**: 3674kg (8,100lb), **IV**: 4441kg (9,790lb); maximum loaded, **I**: 5670kg (12,500lb), **IV**: 6532kg (14,400lb), **V**: 7711kg (17,000lb).

ENGINES Two Bristol Mercury nine-cylinder radials. **Mk I**: 840hp Mercury VIII, **IV**: 920hp Mercury XV, **V**: 950 hp Mercury 30; Bolingbrokes included versions with Cyclone and Twin Wasp Junior engines.

MAXIMUM SPEED **I**: 455km/h (283mph), **IV** early: 472km/h (293mph), **IVL**: 429km/h (266mph), **V**: 418km/h (260mph).

SERVICE CEILING **I, IV**: 9000m (29,500ft).

RANGE **I**: 1810km (1,125 miles), **IV**: 2350km (1,460 miles), **V**: 2575km (1,600 miles), in each case with bombs, max fuel.

MILITARY LOAD **I**: 454kg (1,000lb) bomb load, fixed 7·7mm (0·303in) Browning machine gun in nose, 7·7mm (0·303in) Vickers K or Lewis in turret; **IV**: same bomb load plus optional 145kg (320lb) external; 7·7mm (0·303in) in nose, two 7·7mm (0·303in) Browning in dorsal turret and two more in chin turret; **V**: usually as IV.

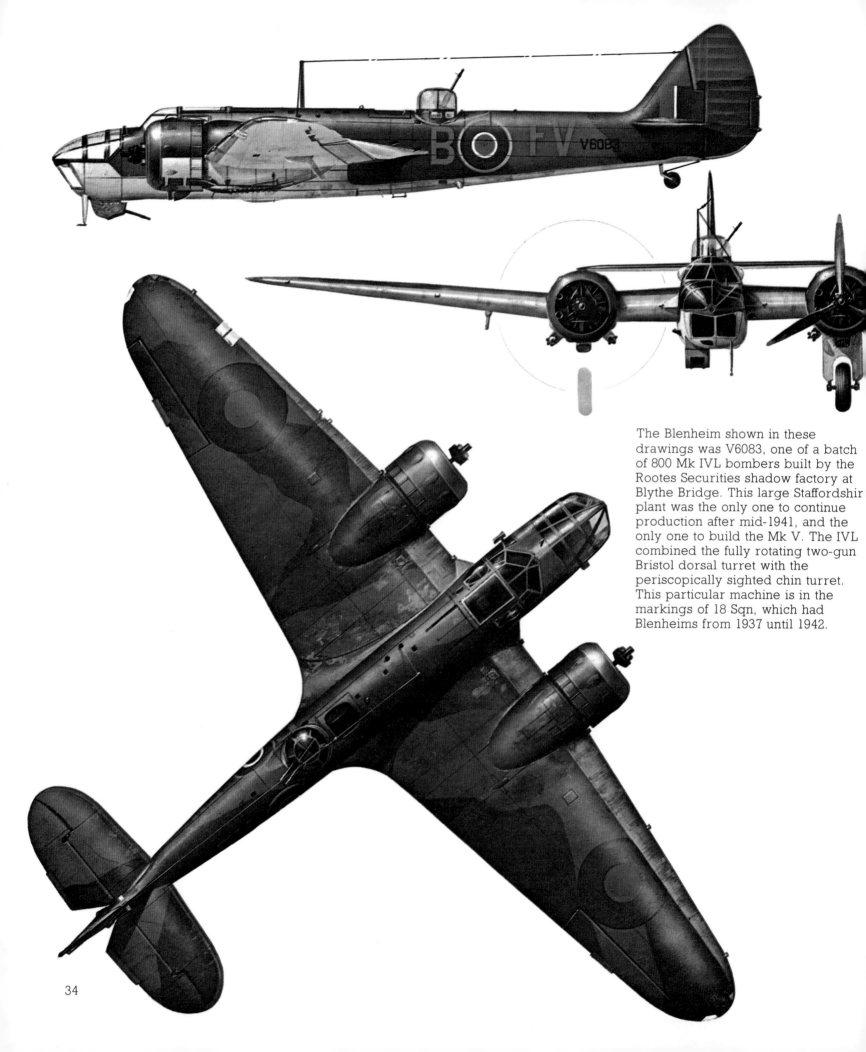

The Blenheim shown in these drawings was V6083, one of a batch of 800 Mk IVL bombers built by the Rootes Securities shadow factory at Blythe Bridge. This large Staffordshir plant was the only one to continue production after mid-1941, and the only one to build the Mk V. The IVL combined the fully rotating two-gun Bristol dorsal turret with the periscopically sighted chin turret. This particular machine is in the markings of 18 Sqn, which had Blenheims from 1937 until 1942.

Bristol Blenheim Mk IVL

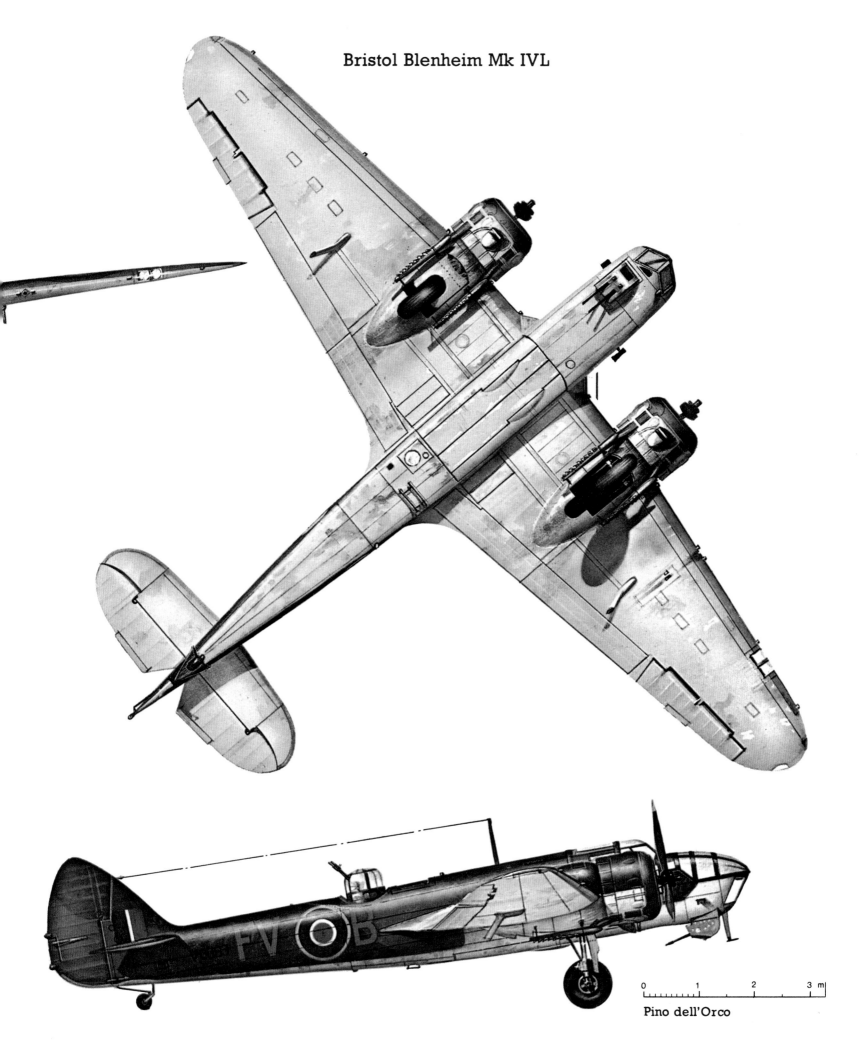

FV D

0   1   2   3 m

Pino dell'Orco

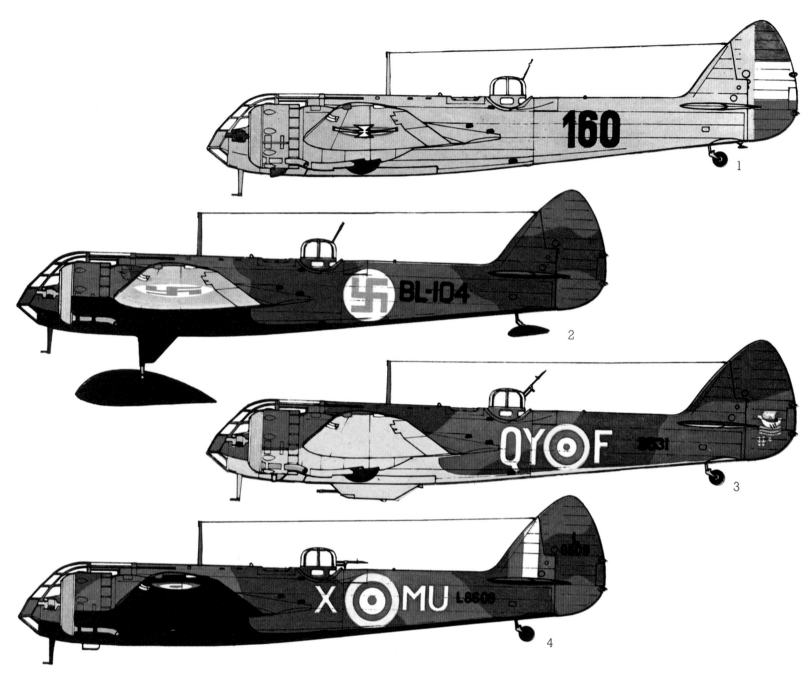

1 The first Blenheim I flown out (as G-AFCE) to Yugoslavia in November 1937. Subsequently Ikarus AD built the type under licence at Zemun.

2 The first of 18 Mk I aircraft for Finland, modified to carry Swedish bombs and fitted with skis. Subsequently Blenheims were made under licence at Tampere.

3 Blenheim IF fighter of 235 Sqn, with the final Mk IV turret with two belt-fed Brownings, and four more in a belly installation.

4 This Mk I served with 60 Sqn at Lahore, India, in 1940, subsequently being based at Mingaladon in the defence of Burma in early 1942.

Bristol Blenheim

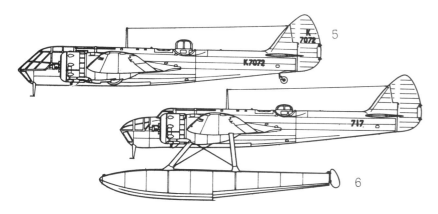

5 Early Blenheim I rebuilt as prototype Bolingbroke in October 1937: subsequently converted as first Blenheim IV.

6 Canadian Fairchild Bolingbroke III with Edo floats. 1939: subsequently reconverted to landplane.

7 One of 12 Blenheim IV bombers supplied to the Royal Hellenic air force in 1939 40. shown with 32 Sqn.

8 Blenheim IV of Free French unit in Cyrenaica in 1942 with first (single-gun) chin turret.

9 Mk IVF of 15 Sqn South African Air Force, Tunisia. 1942.

10 First pre-production Mk V, from Blythe Bridge.

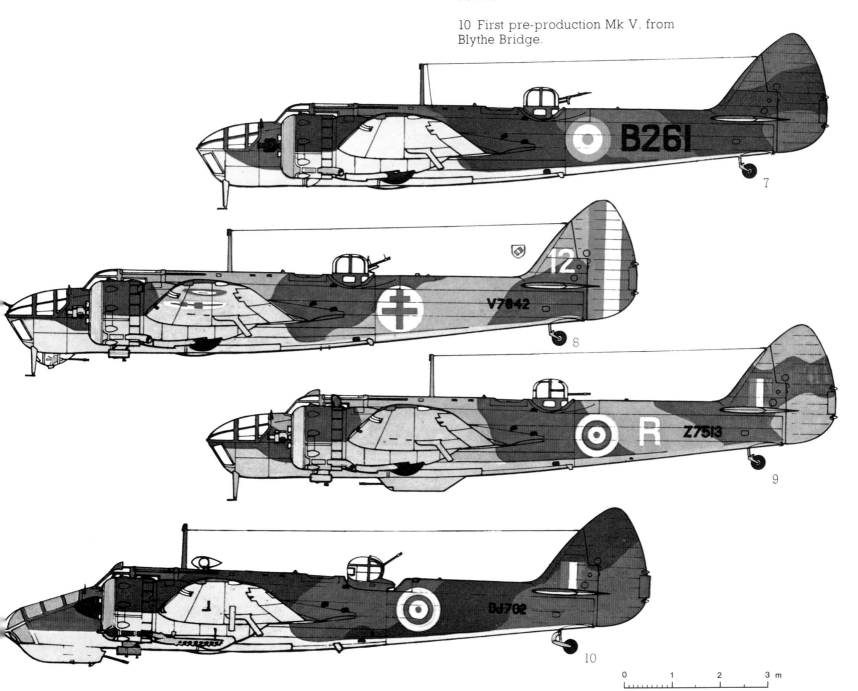

Pino dell'Orco

One of the most important of all Corsair versions was the F4U-1D, of which 1,675 were delivered by Chance Vought and 2,303 by Goodyear (as FG-1Ds). This 1D served aboard one of the last big *Essex* carriers to become operational during World War 2, USS *Franklin* (CV-13) Nearly all the American Corsairs that fought in that

Chance Vought F4U-1D Corsair

conflict belonged to the Marine Corps, with a few notable exceptions. While the Marines shot down 2,140 enemy aircraft with their Corsairs, the Navy score was 136 from land bases and 384 from carriers, 127 being gained by VF-17 in 75 days. This 1D has the standard Midnight Blue finish of 1945.

0   1   2 m

Massimo Jacoponi

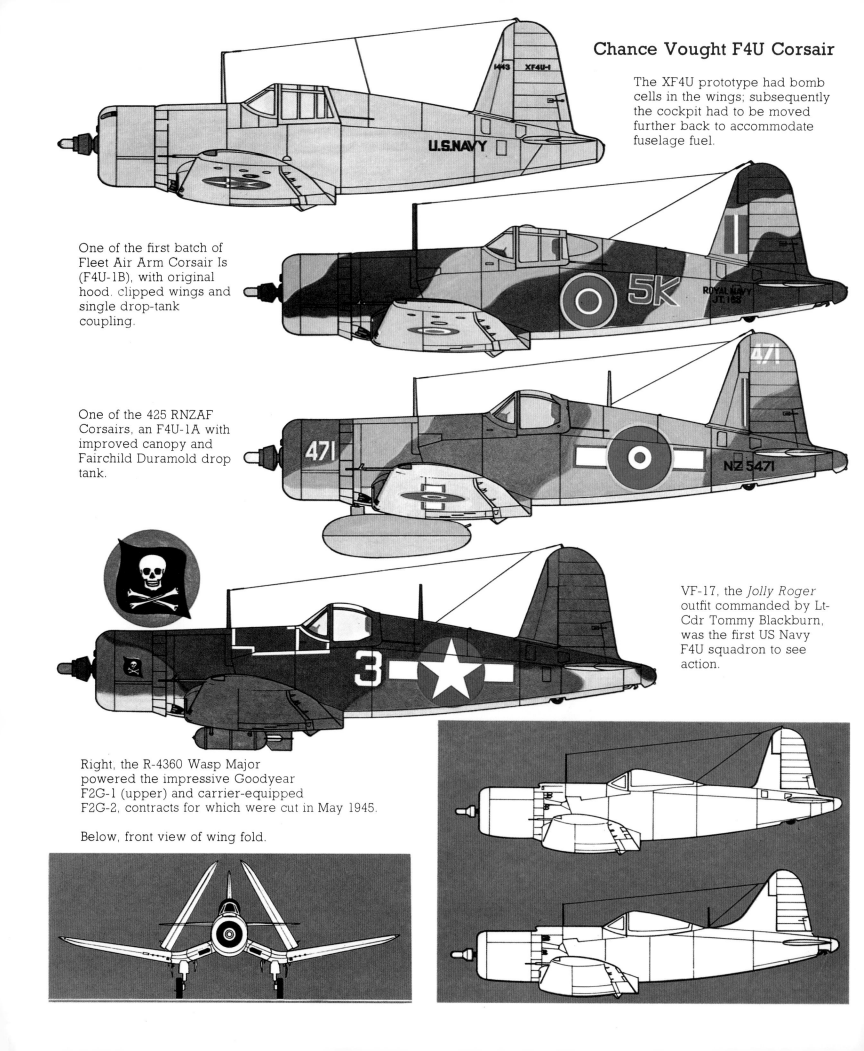

Chance Vought F4U Corsair

The XF4U prototype had bomb cells in the wings; subsequently the cockpit had to be moved further back to accommodate fuselage fuel.

One of the first batch of Fleet Air Arm Corsair Is (F4U-1B), with original hood. clipped wings and single drop-tank coupling.

One of the 425 RNZAF Corsairs, an F4U-1A with improved canopy and Fairchild Duramold drop tank.

VF-17, the *Jolly Roger* outfit commanded by Lt-Cdr Tommy Blackburn, was the first US Navy F4U squadron to see action.

Right, the R-4360 Wasp Major powered the impressive Goodyear F2G-1 (upper) and carrier-equipped F2G-2, contracts for which were cut in May 1945.

Below, front view of wing fold.

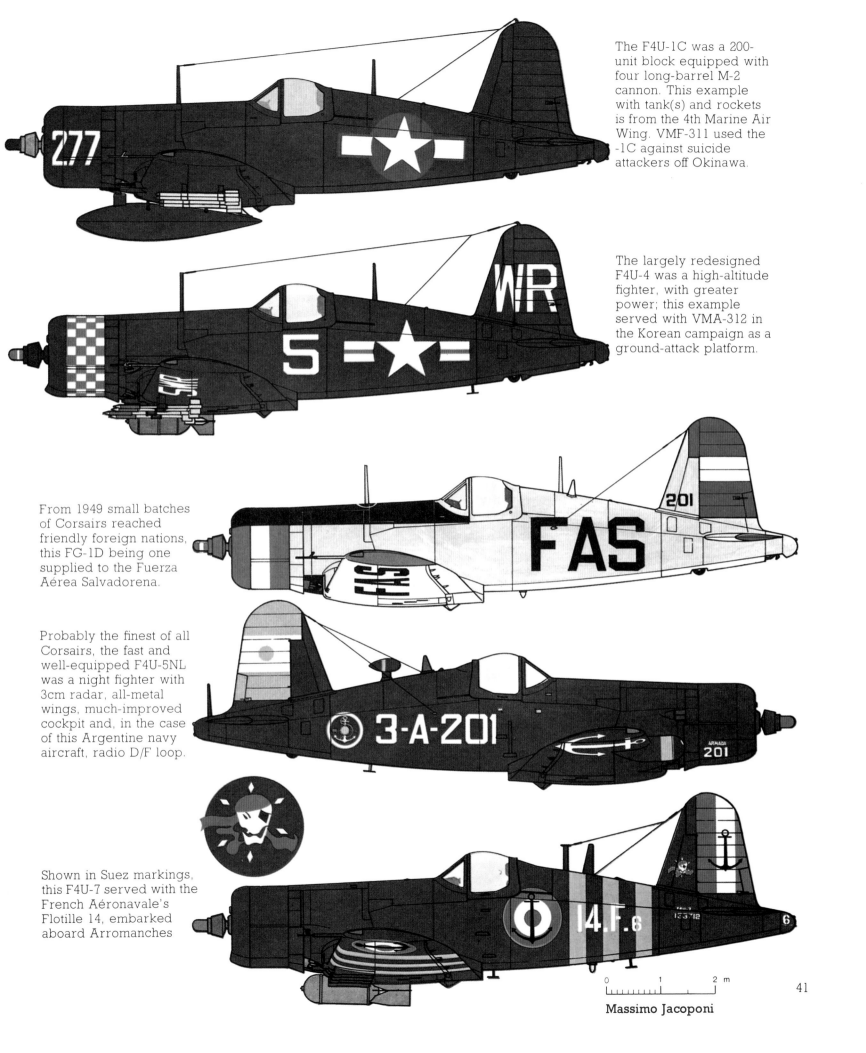

The F4U-1C was a 200-unit block equipped with four long-barrel M-2 cannon. This example with tank(s) and rockets is from the 4th Marine Air Wing. VMF-311 used the -1C against suicide attackers off Okinawa.

The largely redesigned F4U-4 was a high-altitude fighter, with greater power; this example served with VMA-312 in the Korean campaign as a ground-attack platform.

From 1949 small batches of Corsairs reached friendly foreign nations, this FG-1D being one supplied to the Fuerza Aérea Salvadorena.

Probably the finest of all Corsairs, the fast and well-equipped F4U-5NL was a night fighter with 3cm radar, all-metal wings, much-improved cockpit and, in the case of this Argentine navy aircraft, radio D/F loop.

Shown in Suez markings, this F4U-7 served with the French Aéronavale's Flotille 14, embarked aboard Arromanches

0   1   2 m

41

Massimo Jacoponi

Chance Vought F4U Corsair

Though not one of the most famous wartime fighters, the bent-wing Corsair was truly exceptional. When the prototype was built it had the biggest and most powerful engine, largest propeller and probably largest wing on any fighter in history. In 1940 it was rebuilt after being almost destroyed in a wheels-down forced landing on the wet grass of a golf-course, and in a matter of days became the first fighter in history, and first American aircraft of any sort, to exceed 644km/h (400mph). At this time most of the new crop of US fighters were being designed around new liquid-cooled engines; the impressive performance of the Corsair resulted in cancellation of most of these engines, and Pratt & Whitney concentrated on the air-cooled radial.

First flown on 29 May 1940, the V-166 prototype, called XF4U by the Navy, was one of the first products of the merged United Aircraft Vought and Sikorsky divisions at Stratford, Connecticut. (This merger was unpopular, and was dissolved on the last day of 1942, so it is preferable to call the Corsair a Chance Vought rather than a Vought-Sikorsky aircraft.) The prototype reflected Navy requirements of the day in having internal cells in the wing for small bombs; fixed gun armament comprised two 7·7mm (0·303in) Brownings above the engine and two of 12·7mm (0·5in) calibre in the wings. The wings were of unusual inverted-gull form partly to achieve the ideal 90° junction with the fuselage (which would otherwise have needed a mid-wing like the Wildcat) and partly to match the 4·06m (13ft 4in) propeller with the length of landing gear that could retract backwards, the wheels rotating 87° on the legs to lie neatly inside the wing. Carburettor-air and oil coolers were placed in the inner leading edge, leaving the tightest and neatest radial cowling then achieved.

During 1941 the Corsair was redesigned to incorporate lessons from combat in Europe. This delayed the emergence of production aircraft, but despite a very large increase in weight – resulting from extra fuel, armament and armour – the all-round performance was enhanced. Most obvious of the changes was a 0·8m (32in) rearward shift of the cockpit, in order to increase the fuel capacity, and this slightly worsened the pilot's forward view at low speeds or on the ground.

In late 1941 production started, and the importance of the powerful new fighter is underlined by the fact that two additional companies were brought in to make it; eventually Goodyear delivered 3,941 and the inefficient Brewster company 735. The first unit to form was Marine squadron VMF-124 in September 1942, but the first to use the Corsair from carriers were squadrons of the British Fleet Air Arm whose aircraft had clipped wings in order to fit inside the cramped hangars with wings folded. Subsequent to a shaky start on 14 February 1943 the Corsair enjoyed a career of total ascendancy over the Japanese in the Pacific. Notable units included VMF-214 'The Black Sheep' and the first carrier-based Navy squadron VF-17 'Skull and Crossbones'. Nine squadrons of the RNZAF (Royal New Zealand Air Force) also used the Corsair in this theatre, with 370 aircraft, the British FAA total being 2,012.

Altogether the number of F4U-1 variants built was 9,444, including the -1C and -1D with changed armament or engine model. The F4U-2 had night-fighter radar, the 32 in service being modified -1s. Next major version was the F4U-4, with more powerful engine. This series, the standard production model at the end of the war, included -4P photo-reconnaissance models with fuselage cameras. Production continued after VJ-day and in 1946 the uprated -32W engine became available for the F4U-5 series. Together with the low-altitude AU-1 attack version and a batch of F4U-7s for the French used in Indo-China these completed production in December 1952, the longest run of any American piston-engined fighter. In the Korean war more than 1,800 Corsairs saw action in all kinds of ground attack and air combat missions, partnering the new jets in offering short field-length and long flight endurance.

COUNTRY OF ORIGIN USA.

CREW 1.

TOTAL PRODUCED 12,571.

DIMENSIONS Wingspan 12·497m (41ft 0in); length -1: 10·16m (33ft 4in), -4: 10·26m (33ft 8in); wing area 29·172m² (314ft²).

WEIGHTS Empty, -1: 4074kg (8,982lb); -4: 4175kg (9,205lb); maximum loaded, -1: 6350kg (14,000lb), -4: 6654kg (14,670lb).

ENGINE Pratt & Whitney R-2800 Double Wasp 18-cylinder radial. -1: 2,000hp R-2800-8; -4: 2,100hp -18W; -5: 2,300hp -32W.

MAXIMUM SPEED -1: 671km/h (417mph) at 6066m (19,900ft); -4: 718km/h (446mph) at 7986m (26,200ft).

SERVICE CEILING -1: 11247m (36,900ft); -4: 12650m (41,500ft).

RANGE (-1, -4, no bombs) 1633km (1,015 miles).

MILITARY LOAD Most versions, six 12·7mm (0.5in) Browning MG 53-2 in outer wings each with 375 rounds (outer guns) or 400 rounds (remainder); F4U-1C and -4B, four 20mm M-2; most versions from -1C onwards, fittings for fuselage drop tank plus two 454kg (1,000lb) bombs or eight 127mm (5in) rockets under wings.

Consolidated B-24 Liberator

Though it did not noticeably improve on the all-round performance of the B-17, which was conceived five years earlier, the B-24 Liberator was made in even greater quantity, and used by more Allied air forces on every front of World War 2. The original Model 32 prototype flew on 29 December 1939, just 11 months after Mac Laddon and his team began the design, and over the next 18 months matured with the addition of turbocharged engines, armour, self-sealing tanks and defensive armament.

Fundamental features included the long and aerodynamically efficient Davis wing, with Fowler flaps and fuel cells between the spars, the tall main landing gears with single wheels and legs retracting outwards to lie inside the wing, and the stumpy fuselage with a vast central bomb bay fitted with doors like roll-top desks, the front and rear fuselage being joined across the bay by a catwalk.

The first operational models were the British LB-30A, used as a transport on the North Atlantic return ferry service, and the RAF Liberator I used both as a bomber in North Africa and as a long-range Coastal Command patroller with ASV (air-to-surface vessel) radar and in many aircraft a battery of four 20mm Hispano cannon in the belly. One machine even had stub wings on each side of the nose carrying rocket projectiles. The RAF Liberator II introduced powered turrets in the tail and mid-upper positions. Later in 1941 the USAAF began to receive the first mass-produced version, the B-24D, with strange flattened oval engine cowlings resulting from the relocation of the oil coolers on each side, the turbo being underneath. With paddle-blade propellers this was a good performer at high altitude, though of course it was unpressurized and the waist gunners were almost in the open.

To build the B-24 an industrial team greater than anything previously seen took over vast windowless plants built in a matter of months: Consolidated at San Diego, and in a new mile-long plant at Forth Worth; Douglas at Tulsa, and the Ford works at Willow Run, near Detroit, where B-24s were made at approximately the rate of one every two hours. The B-24D was designated Liberator III in British service, and in many aircraft the rear fuselage contained either a ball turret or one of two types of mapping/bombing radar. This version was also the first to have a C-87 transport counterpart, as well as the first F-7 strategic reconnaissance machines, each carrying 11 cameras. Special versions included the XB-41 escort fighter, the whole military load comprising guns and ammunition.

The E differed little from the D, but the B-24G introduced a nose turret, and this led to the very similar H, J and M. The most numerous model was the J, 6,678 of these being delivered, not including the Navy PB4Y-1 ocean-patrol version. The L had a lightweight twin-gun tail position instead of a powered turret, many being modified as gunner trainers for B-29 crews. The XB-24K showed better performance with a single fin, and this went into production on the B-24N, and an even taller fin was fitted to the Navy RY-3 transport and to Prime Minister Churchill's famed Liberator C.IX *Commando*. The same lofty fin was fitted to the totally redesigned US Navy PB4Y-2 Privateer, a much longer and heavier machine which saw most of its extensive service after the war. In the Privateer the engine cowlings became oval in the vertical plane, and operational equipment and armament were completely changed for ocean reconnaissance at low altitudes. The Privateer production total was 739, the majority delivered just after the war; these are not included in the total of B-24 production.

In late 1942 yet another factory had come on stream with B-24 deliveries: North American Aviation at Dallas. By 1944 a total of over 180,000 people were engaged in Liberator production, the output being better than one per hour for long periods. These aircraft handled almost every kind of wartime mission, and large numbers of B-24 Liberators continued in many air forces into the 1950s.

COUNTRY OF ORIGIN USA.

CREW 5–11 according to role, most bombers having 10.

TOTAL PRODUCED 19,203, not including 1,800 complete airframes as spares and 739 PB4Y-2 Privateer.

DIMENSIONS Wingspan 33·5m (110ft 0in); length, **B-24J**: 20·47m (67ft 2in); wing area 97·36m² (1,048ft²).

WEIGHTS Empty, **D**: 14789kg (32,600lb), **J**: 16783kg (37,000lb); maximum loaded, **D**: 27216kg (60,000lb), **J**: 29484kg (65,000lb).

ENGINES Four Pratt & Whitney R-1830 Twin Wasp 14-cylinder radials, usually 1,200hp R-1830-65.

MAXIMUM SPEED **D**: 488km/h (303mph), **J**: 467km/h (290mph).

SERVICE CEILING All, about 8500m (28,000ft).

RANGE Varied greatly according to weapon load, but typically 4000km (2,500 miles) with bomb load of 2268kg (5,000lb).

MILITARY LOAD More than 20 types of defensive armament, usual for E/G/H/J being ten 12·7mm (0·5in) Browning machine guns in twin-gun nose, tail, dorsal and ventral turrets and two manual waist positions; normal bomb load 3630kg (8,000lb).

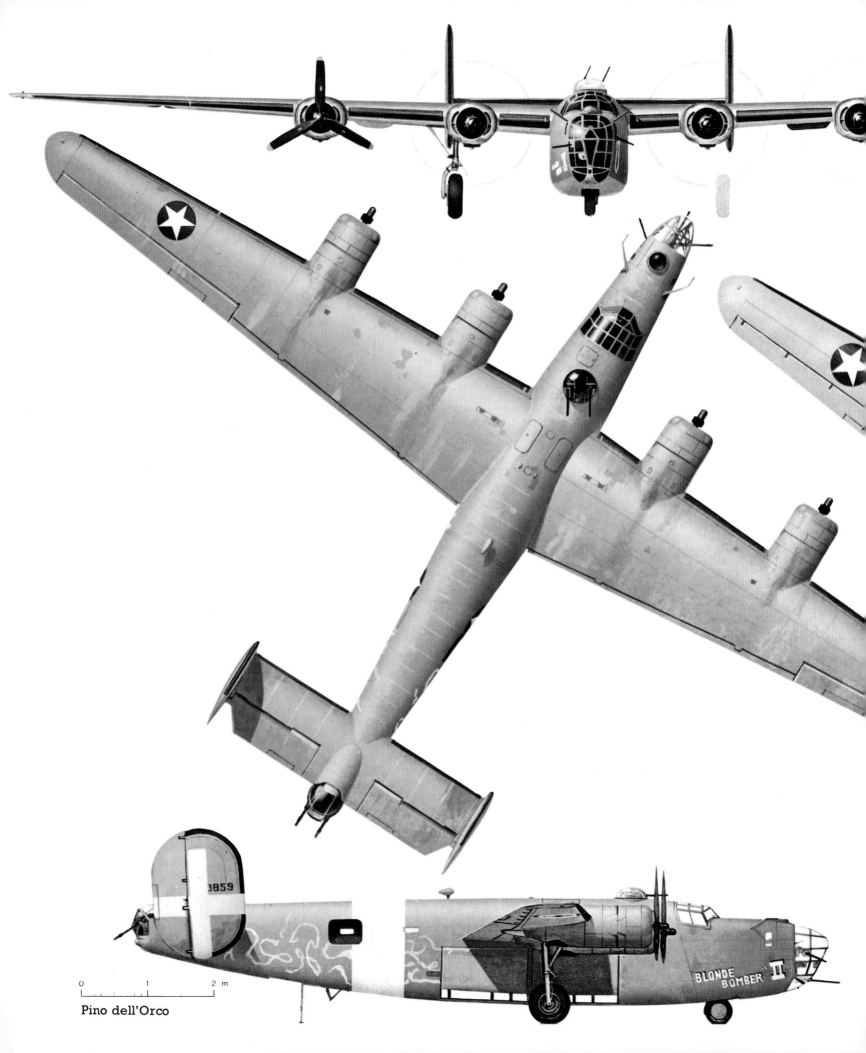

BLONDE BOMBER II

3859

0 1 2 m

Pino dell'Orco

Consolidated B-24D Liberator

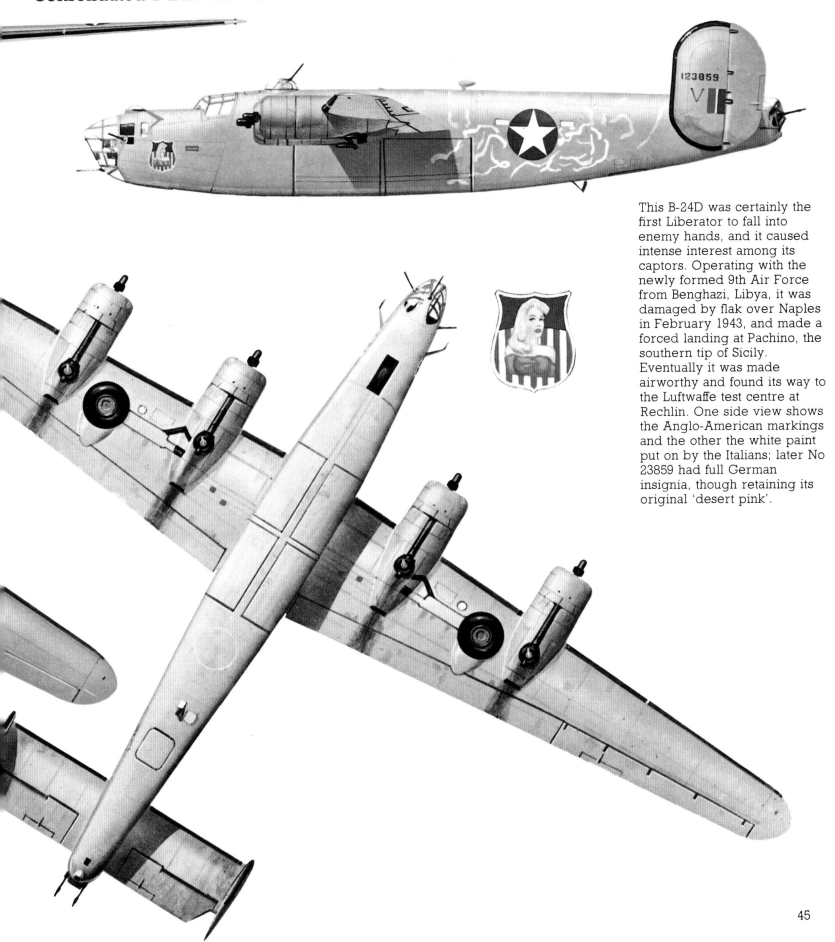

This B-24D was certainly the first Liberator to fall into enemy hands, and it caused intense interest among its captors. Operating with the newly formed 9th Air Force from Benghazi, Libya, it was damaged by flak over Naples in February 1943, and made a forced landing at Pachino, the southern tip of Sicily. Eventually it was made airworthy and found its way to the Luftwaffe test centre at Rechlin. One side view shows the Anglo-American markings and the other the white paint put on by the Italians; later No 23859 had full German insignia, though retaining its original 'desert pink'.

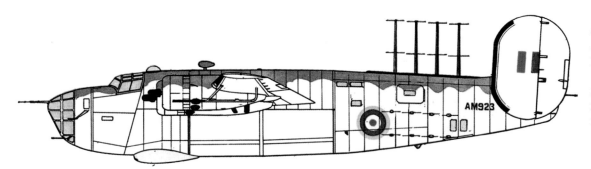

One of the many interesting early versions was the Mk I Liberator of RAF Coastal Command; this one with 120 Sqn has ASV Mk II radar and four 20mm Hispanos in a belly installation.

The USAF had no version resembling the RAF Liberator II, with circular cowlings, two power turrets (both four-gun Boulton Paul) and lengthened nose. This one served 159 Sqn in Libya.

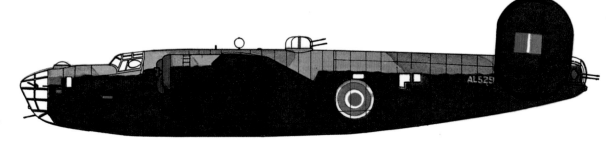

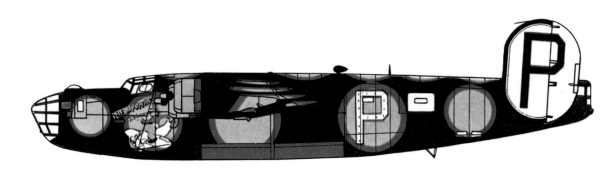

Pete the Pom Inspector was one of the brilliantly painted lead-ships, usually war-weary ex-bombers, on which the mighty wings and divisions of the 8th Air Force formed up before going to Germany. This one, a B-24D, belonged to the 467th BG.

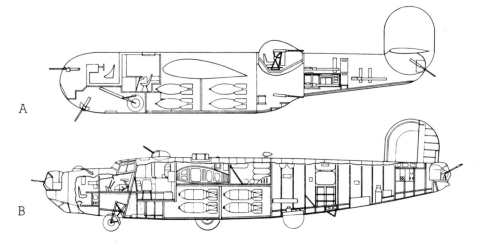

Comparative longitudinal sections of (A) the original proposal by Mac Laddon's team for the Model 32 in March 1939, and (B) a late production B-24J. In some respects the original layout was preferable.

Consolidated B-24 Liberator

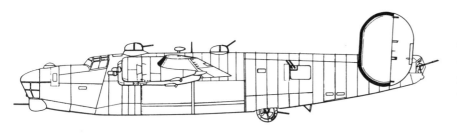

The XB-41 was a converted B-24D with fourteen 12·7mm (0·5in) guns, intended as an escort fighter. Only one aircraft (41-11822) was flown.

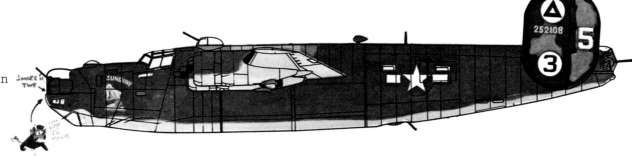

A standard B-24H, with Emerson electric nose turret, which made a landing at Varese, still in enemy hands, in March 1944 (according to the Italians the crew was flying to Switzerland where they intended to desert).

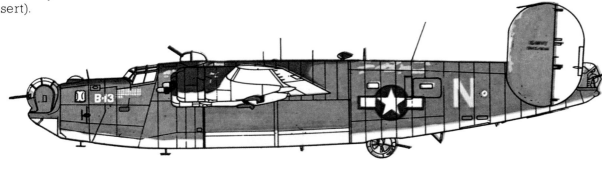

The US Navy operated 977 Liberators, nearly all basically similar to the B-24J but with the comfortable Erco nose turret: designation was PB4Y-1.

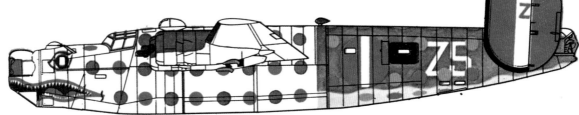

Another of the lurid lead-ships, this was the B-24H used by the 458th Bombardment Group based at Horsham St Faith, Norwich. Lead-ships left the assembled formation after it had formed up.

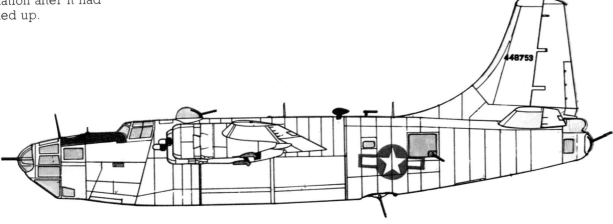

Prototype of the ultimate model, the single-fin B-24N: this was appreciably faster and had completely different turrets, but only seven were built before B-24 production was cancelled on 31 May 1945

0 1 2 3 4 m

Pino dell'Orco – Claudio Tatangelo

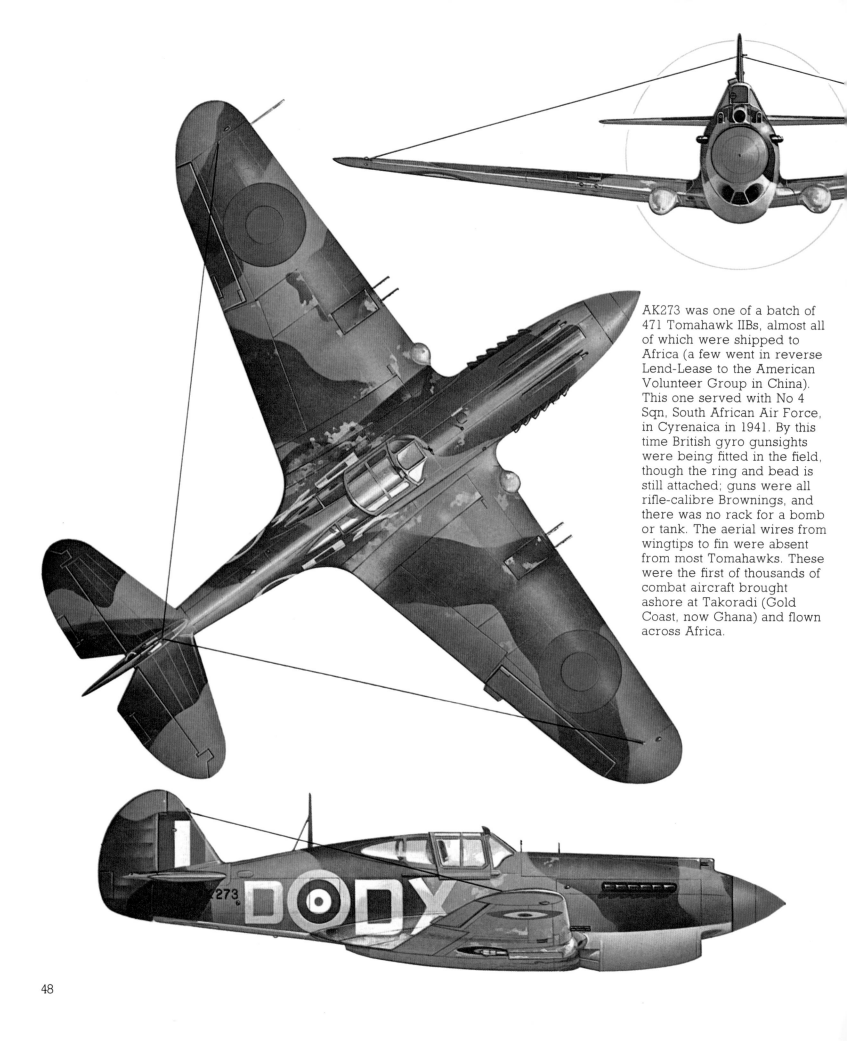

AK273 was one of a batch of 471 Tomahawk IIBs, almost all of which were shipped to Africa (a few went in reverse Lend-Lease to the American Volunteer Group in China). This one served with No 4 Sqn, South African Air Force, in Cyrenaica in 1941. By this time British gyro gunsights were being fitted in the field, though the ring and bead is still attached; guns were all rifle-calibre Brownings, and there was no rack for a bomb or tank. The aerial wires from wingtips to fin were absent from most Tomahawks. These were the first of thousands of combat aircraft brought ashore at Takoradi (Gold Coast, now Ghana) and flown across Africa.

Curtiss Tomahawk IIB

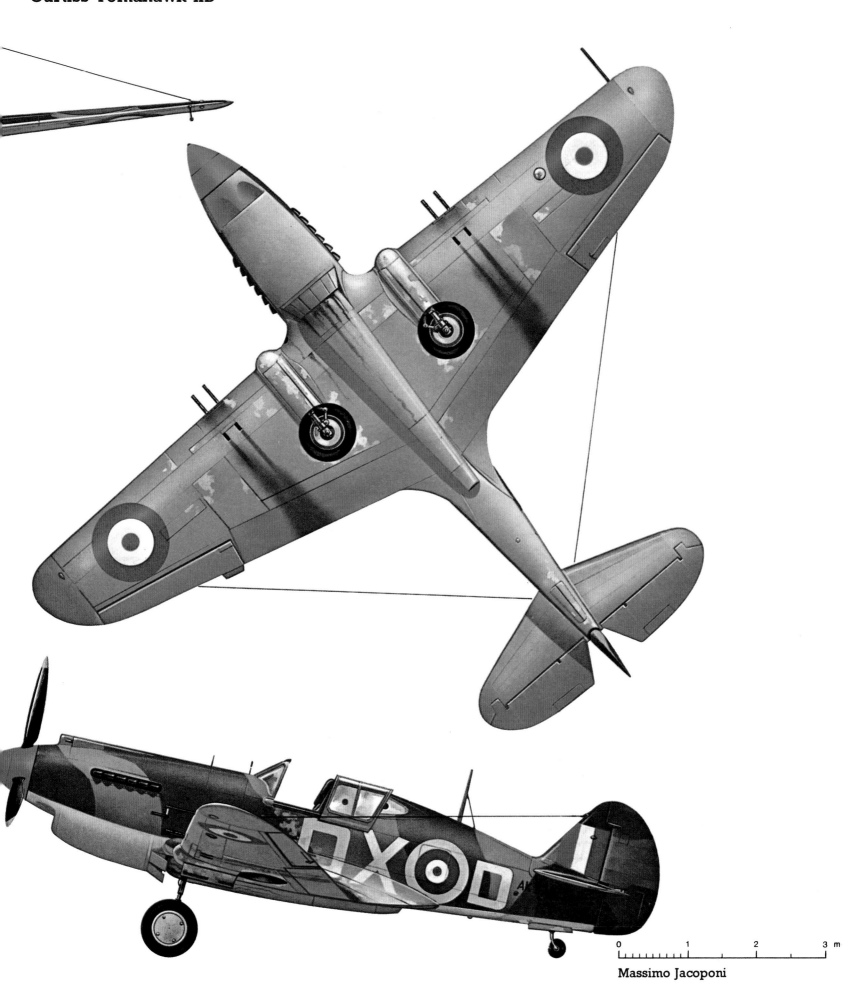

Massimo Jacoponi

0   1   2   3 m

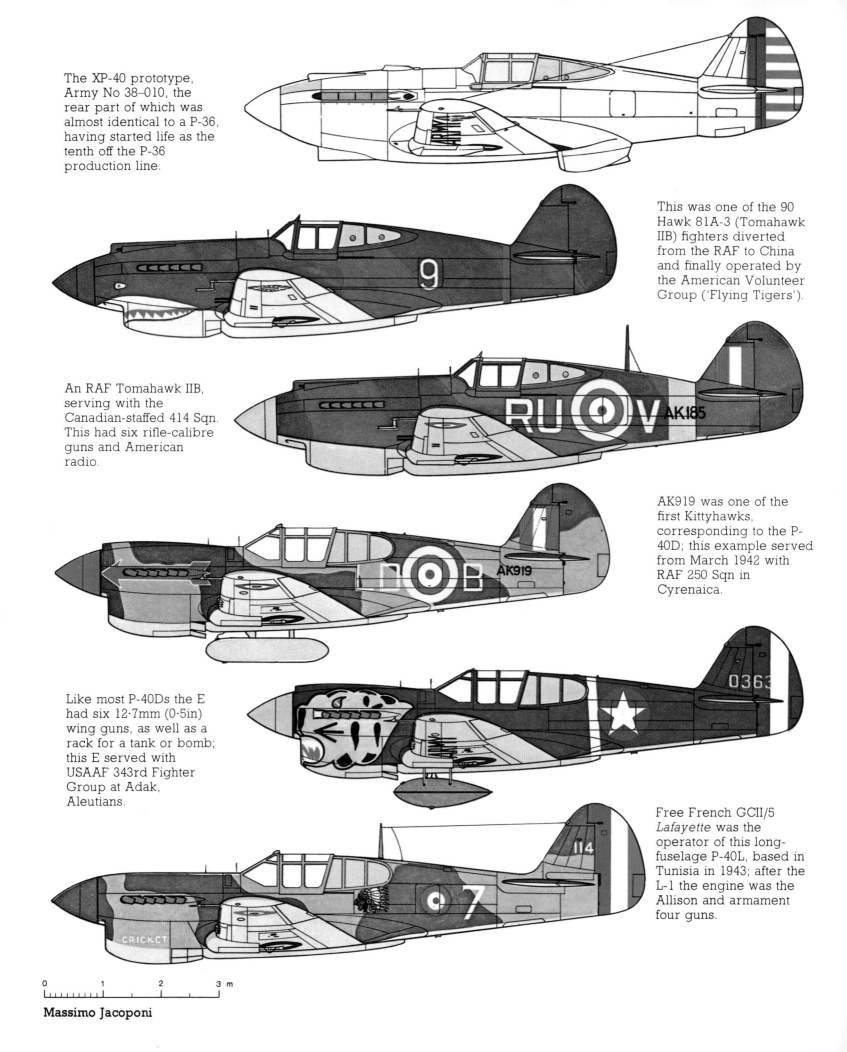

The XP-40 prototype, Army No 38–010, the rear part of which was almost identical to a P-36, having started life as the tenth off the P-36 production line.

This was one of the 90 Hawk 81A-3 (Tomahawk IIB) fighters diverted from the RAF to China and finally operated by the American Volunteer Group ('Flying Tigers').

An RAF Tomahawk IIB, serving with the Canadian-staffed 414 Sqn. This had six rifle-calibre guns and American radio.

AK919 was one of the first Kittyhawks, corresponding to the P-40D; this example served from March 1942 with RAF 250 Sqn in Cyrenaica.

Like most P-40Ds the E had six 12·7mm (0·5in) wing guns, as well as a rack for a tank or bomb; this E served with USAAF 343rd Fighter Group at Adak, Aleutians.

Free French GCII/5 *Lafayette* was the operator of this long-fuselage P-40L, based in Tunisia in 1943; after the L-1 the engine was the Allison and armament four guns.

0   1   2   3 m

Massimo Jacoponi

Curtiss P-40

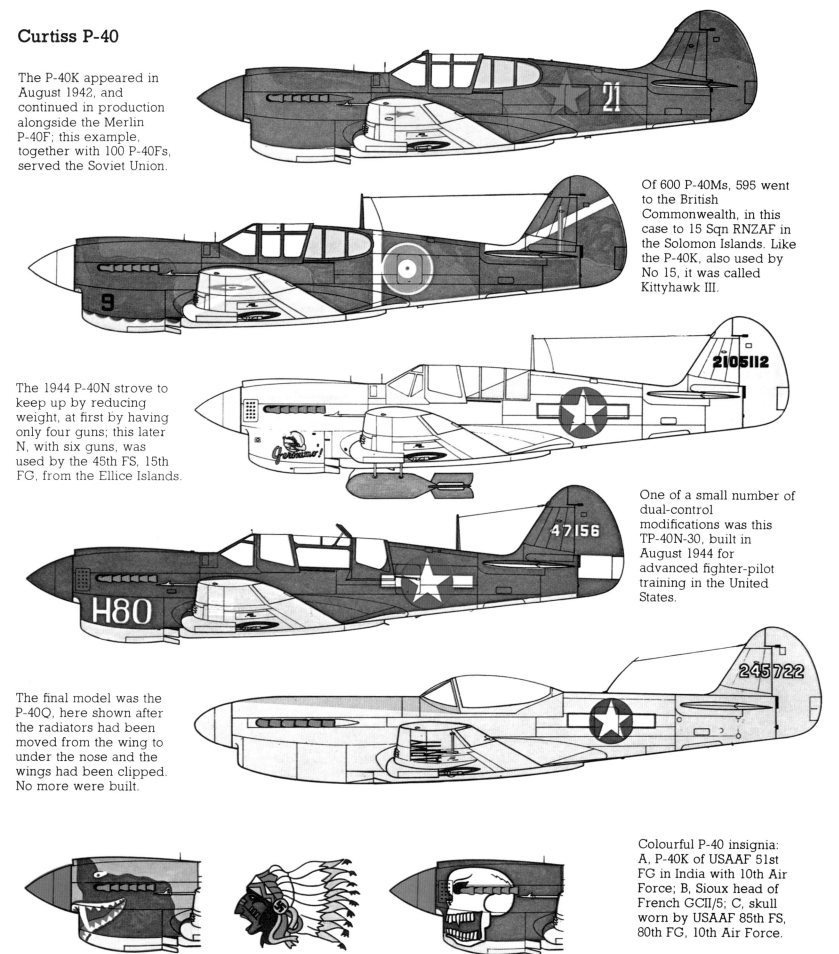

The P-40K appeared in August 1942, and continued in production alongside the Merlin P-40F; this example, together with 100 P-40Fs, served the Soviet Union.

Of 600 P-40Ms, 595 went to the British Commonwealth, in this case to 15 Sqn RNZAF in the Solomon Islands. Like the P-40K, also used by No 15, it was called Kittyhawk III.

The 1944 P-40N strove to keep up by reducing weight, at first by having only four guns; this later N, with six guns, was used by the 45th FS, 15th FG, from the Ellice Islands.

One of a small number of dual-control modifications was this TP-40N-30, built in August 1944 for advanced fighter-pilot training in the United States.

The final model was the P-40Q, here shown after the radiators had been moved from the wing to under the nose and the wings had been clipped. No more were built.

Colourful P-40 insignia: A, P-40K of USAAF 51st FG in India with 10th Air Force; B, Sioux head of French GCII/5; C, skull worn by USAAF 85th FS, 80th FG, 10th Air Force.

A

B

C

Curtiss P-40

During the 1930s the leading American builders of pursuit (fighter) aircraft were Boeing and Curtiss. From 1935 Boeing concentrated on other types, but by this year Curtiss had completed the design of its first stressed-skin monoplane fighter, with wheels retracting backwards into the wings and with every other modern refinement. This led to a prolonged succession of improved versions which, though never in the top league, were tough and serviceable, and were important in World War 2 in putting extra Allied aircraft into the sky – especially in the ground-attack role – on every front. Yet, from its position of ascendancy in 1939, Curtiss went steadily downhill, failed to produce a next-generation fighter, and stopped making aircraft altogether in 1948.

The first Model 75 prototype flew in May 1935 and, after many changes, matured in March 1937 as the US Army Air Corps P-36, a standard production machine made in large numbers for export as the Hawk 75A and one of the most important of the Armée de l'Air fighters in the spring of 1940 when these tough but rather slow machines were credited with 311 victories over the Luftwaffe. Subsequent deliveries with both Cyclone and Twin Wasp engines to the RAF were named Mohawks, and they served with especial distinction in the Middle East and Burma.

In 1937 a prototype XP-37 flew with the Allison liquid-cooled engine, and in the summer of that year an order was placed for a better conversion designated XP-40. By May 1940 production P-40s were emerging, and though the Hawk 81 version did not reach France before the collapse the same machines were snapped up by the RAF as the Tomahawk, and by late 1941 more than 1,200 of several versions had reached the RAF and Commonwealth air forces, mainly in North Africa. The P-40B and C was the best USAAF fighter available in the first weeks after Pearl Harbor, scoring the first US kills.

In May 1941 Curtiss flew the first Hawk 87 with an improved engine and better equipment, called Kittyhawk I by the RAF. The USAAF also placed orders for the P-40D, and production switched to the more heavily armed P-40E, Packard Merlin-powered F, Allison-engined K (late models of which introduced a lengthened fuselage) and mass-produced later models with numerous improvements, all with the Allison engine. As well as a succession of quite different fighter prototypes, Curtiss never ceased building improved P-40 versions, all of them eventually named Warhawk by the USAAF. Unfortunately all suffered from a fundamentally early conception, so that compared with other World War 2 fighters they were lacking in performance and often in manoeuvrability and other factors. The one thing all enjoyed was the ability to get back to base after suffering severe battle damage, and this played a part in the controversial decision to keep P-40 versions in production until December 1944, when the whole series was obsolescent.

By 1942 the Tomahawk family had been largely relegated to training, army co-operation (they helped form RAF Army Co-operation Command) and low-level reconnaissance in areas that were less heavily defended. The Kittyhawk/Warhawk, however, remained in front-line service on every front except Great Britain itself, a large number going to the Soviet Union which received many Merlin P-40Fs and some 2,000 of the later N model. Throughout the war the P-40 in most major versions was one of the most important fighters of the Flying Tigers (American Volunteer Group) in China and of the Chinese air force itself, and several versions were standard types with Canada, Australia, New Zealand, South Africa and the Free French. Commonwealth name for the N and other late models was Kittyhawk IV. Late in the war one of the Curtiss attempts to improve the P-40 was the Q, with shorter span, much longer body and many other changes. This succeeded in reaching 679km/h (422mph), still slower than contemporary Spitfires or Mustangs, but 160km/h (100mph) faster than most earlier P-40 models.

COUNTRY OF ORIGIN USA.

CREW 1.

TOTAL PRODUCED Radial engined about 1,400; liquid-cooled (excluding prototypes) 13,738.

DIMENSIONS Wingspan 11·38m (37ft 4in); length (radial) typically 8·73m (28ft 7¾in), **C**: 9·68m (31ft 9in), (most later) 10·24m (33ft 4in); wing area 21·925m² (236ft²).

WEIGHTS Empty **Hawk 75A-4**: 2060kg (4,541lb), **N**: 2812kg (6,200lb); maximum loaded **75A-4**: 3022kg (6,662lb), **N**: 5008kg (11,400lb).

ENGINE **P-36, Hawk 75**: either Wright R-1820 Cyclone, usually of 1,200hp, or Pratt & Whitney R-1830 Twin Wasp of 1,050–1,200hp; **B,C**: 1,150hp Allison V-1710-33 vee-12; **F**: 1,300hp Packard V-1650-1; **K**: 1,325hp V-1710-73; **N**: 1,200hp V-1710-81.

MAXIMUM SPEED **Hawk 75**: typically 520km/h (323mph), **B to N**, typical: 563km/h (350 mph).

SERVICE CEILING Typical of all versions 10050m (33,000ft).

RANGE Typical of all versions without drop tank 1130km (700 miles).

MILITARY LOAD **P-36**: one 12·7mm (0·5in) and one or three 7·62mm (0·30in) fixed Browning machine guns; **Hawk 75A**: six 7·5mm or (RAF) 7·7mm (0·303in); **most Tomahawks**: six 7·7mm (0·303in); (most later versions) six 12·7mm (0·5in) plus fuselage rack for bomb or tank of 272kg (600lb) and wing racks for two 227kg (500lb).

De Havilland D.H.98 Mosquito

Like most of the world's greatest combat aircraft the Mosquito owed nothing to any official specification but was the result of dogged persistence by far-sighted engineers. In this case the de Havilland Aircraft Company even had to overcome two years of official disinterest, and flat disbelief in the whole idea. Fortunately the company prevailed, and once the first aircraft was in the air it dominated every field it entered until by the end of the war – which it did much to hasten – it was by far the most versatile Allied aircraft.

The original idea in 1937 was a fast bomber version of the Albatross transport, but by October 1938 this had changed to a twin-Merlin machine with such speed it could dispense with defensive armament and fly with just pilot and navigator. Like the Albatross, however, it was to be made of wood, pressed and bonded into smooth curving shapes and using low-density but rigid panels with inner and outer ply layers linked by spruce stringers or solid but light balsa-wood. The trouble was that nobody believed in an unarmed bomber, far less a wooden one.

By sheer relentless effort Sir Geoffrey de Havilland and C.C. Walker managed to get specification B.1/40 written in January 1940, and, after the D.H.98 Mosquito had twice been cancelled in the panics of that summer, the yellow prototype flew at Hatfield on 25 November 1940. According to Walker, 'When they saw it fly, even the RAF understood what the Mosquito was all about.'

In September 1941 a Mosquito PR.I unarmed reconnaissance aircraft took photographs down the French Atlantic coast, and simply outdistanced Bf 109s sent to intercept it. Two months later 105 Sqn began to receive the B.IV with 907kg (2,000lb) bomb load and this went into action next May, later making a long succession of daring pinpoint raids on Gestapo offices, headquarters, Nazi rallies and even Amiens prison where many Resistance fighters escaped from execution through the shattered walls. BOAC used Mosquitoes to carry VIPs and urgent cargo to Sweden and other places under the noses of Fw 190s, and the bomber family grew with the B.IX and its two-stage engines, paddle propellers and ever new electronic devices for the Master Bombers leading the way for the four-engined heavies. The B.XVI introduced a pressure cabin, even more new devices and a bulged bomb-bay for a 'cookie' as big as those carried by Lancasters.

Back on 15 May 1941 the first Mosquito F.II fighter had taken the air, with thick flat windscreen, pilot stick instead of spectacles, side door and four cannon under the floor, as well as four machine guns in the nose. AI Mk IV radar was fitted, and at once here was the world's best night fighter, replaced from 1942 by a succession of later marks with centimetric radar in various kinds of bluff nose radome that took the place of the machine guns. The most numerous model of all was the FB.VI fighter/bomber, with no radar but cannon, machine guns, bombs and equipment to hit anything at any time. Later, rockets were hung under the outer wings, and the Mk XVIII even had a 6-pounder 57mm Molins ship-busting gun mounted internally on the lower centreline.

Photo-reconnaissance Mosquitoes leaped ahead with pressurized high-flying models, some of which were popular in the USAAF as the F-8, and culminated in the PR.34, with an unprecedented combination of speed and range, from which stemmed the B.35 and NF.36, respectively a high-altitude bomber and night fighter. These, along with several other versions, were mainly post-war developments. Total production of all versions amounted to 7,781, of which well over 1,000 were made at Toronto and 212 in Sydney, Canadian and most Australian examples having Packard V-1650 Merlin engines.

So many were the exploits of the 'Mozzie' that only a few can be noted; not least was the ability of this extremely fast and manoeuvrable aircraft to range with impunity through the sky over Germany, to a degree that made it appear almost supernaturally invincible to its opponents.

COUNTRY OF ORIGIN Great Britain.

CREW 2.

TOTAL PRODUCED 7,781.

DIMENSIONS Wingspan, most: 16·51m (54ft 2in), **NF.XV**: 17·98m (59ft 0in); length, most: 12·34m (40ft 6in), **NF.II**: 12·6m (41ft 4in), NF with radomes, within 50mm (2in) of Mk II, **Sea Mosquito 33**: 12·88m (42ft 3in); wing area 42·18m^2 (454ft^2).

WEIGHTS Empty, **F.II**: 6058kg (13,356lb), **B.XVI**: 6759kg (14,901lb); maximum loaded, **F.II**: 8459kg (18,649lb), **B.IV**: 9886kg (21,749lb), heaviest **B.XVI**: 11756kg (25,917lb).

ENGINES Two Rolls-Royce or Packard Merlin vee-12 liquid-cooled; **II,III,IV, early VI**: 1,230hp Mk 21, **late VI and 33**: 1,640hp Mk 25, **IX,XVI**: 1,680hp Mk 72 or 1,710hp Mk 77, **34–36**: 1,690hp Mk 113/114.

MAXIMUM SPEED **Mk II**: 595km/h (370mph), **III,IV,VI**: 612km/h (380mph), **IX,XVI,30**: 660km/h (410mph), **34,35**: 684km/h (425mph).

SERVICE CEILING From 9144m (30,000ft) for Mk 33 to 10973m (36,000ft) for Mk VI and 13000m (42,650ft) for 34, and slightly higher for long-span XV.

RANGE Typically 2990km (1,860 miles) with full internal fuel and small drop tanks, Mk 34 with large tanks reaching 5633km (3,500 miles).

MILITARY LOAD **PR versions**: cameras and electronics only; **bombers**: Mk IV internal bomb load 907kg (2,000lb), Mk IX could have modification for 1814kg (4,000lb) bomb in bulged bay, standard on later bombers; **night fighters**: four 20mm Hispano cannon (Mk II: also four 7·7mm (0·303in) machine guns), except NF.XV four 7·7mm (0.303in) only in belly blister; **fighter/bombers**: four 20mm and four 7·7mm (0·303in) and 227kg (500lb) bombs internal plus 454kg (1,000lb) or eight 27kg (60lb) rockets under wings, except Mk XVIII exchanged cannon for single gun of 57mm with 25 rounds.

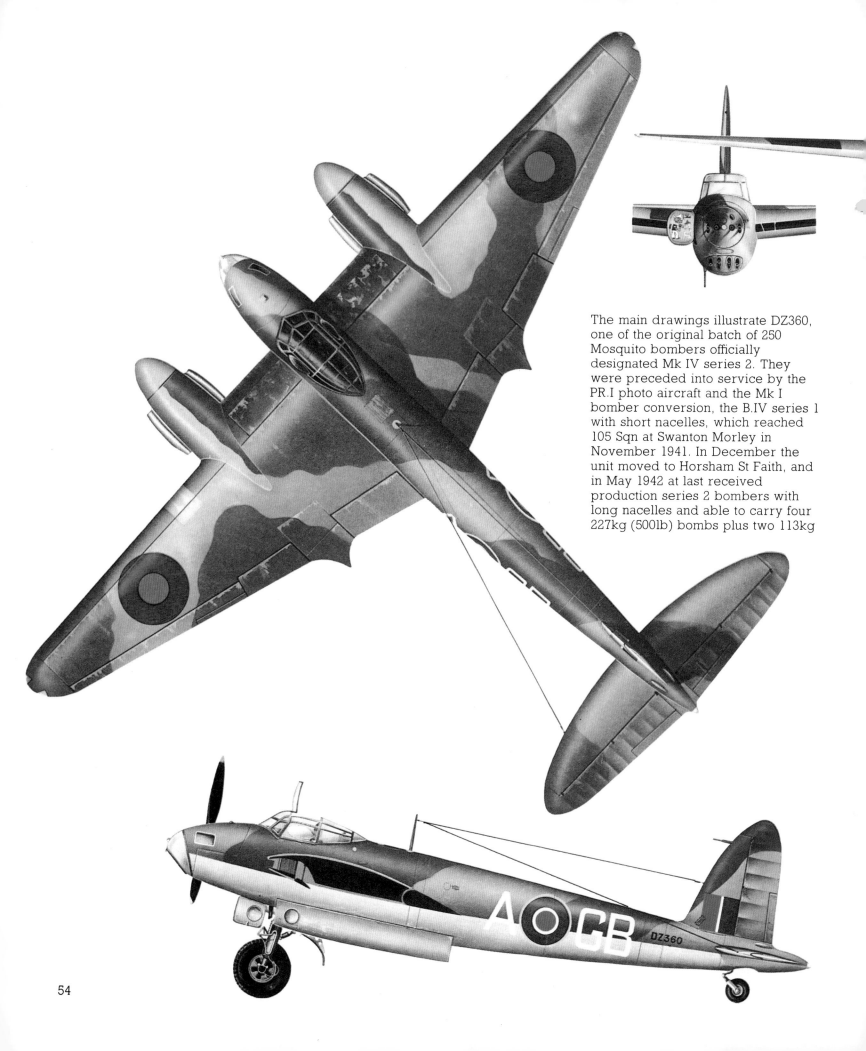

The main drawings illustrate DZ360, one of the original batch of 250 Mosquito bombers officially designated Mk IV series 2. They were preceded into service by the PR.I photo aircraft and the Mk I bomber conversion, the B.IV series 1 with short nacelles, which reached 105 Sqn at Swanton Morley in November 1941. In December the unit moved to Horsham St Faith, and in May 1942 at last received production series 2 bombers with long nacelles and able to carry four 227kg (500lb) bombs plus two 113kg

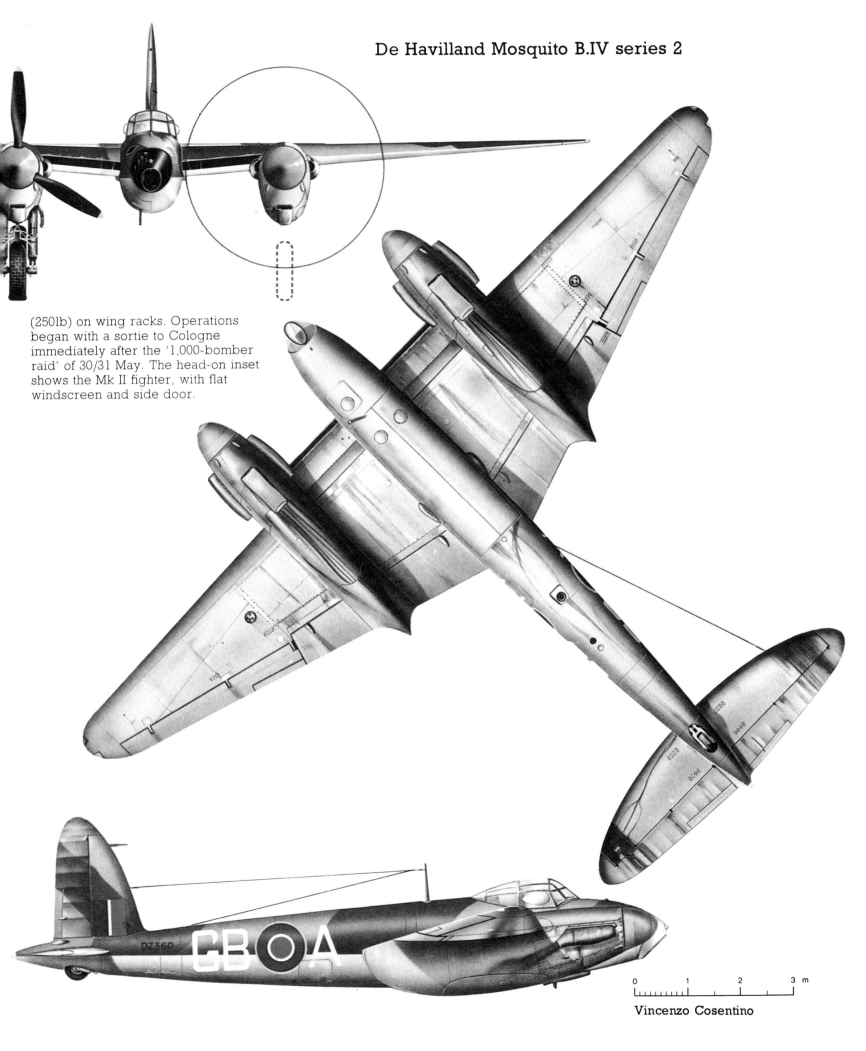

De Havilland Mosquito B.IV series 2

(250lb) on wing racks. Operations
began with a sortie to Cologne
immediately after the '1,000-bomber
raid' of 30/31 May. The head-on inset
shows the Mk II fighter, with flat
windscreen and side door.

Vincenzo Cosentino

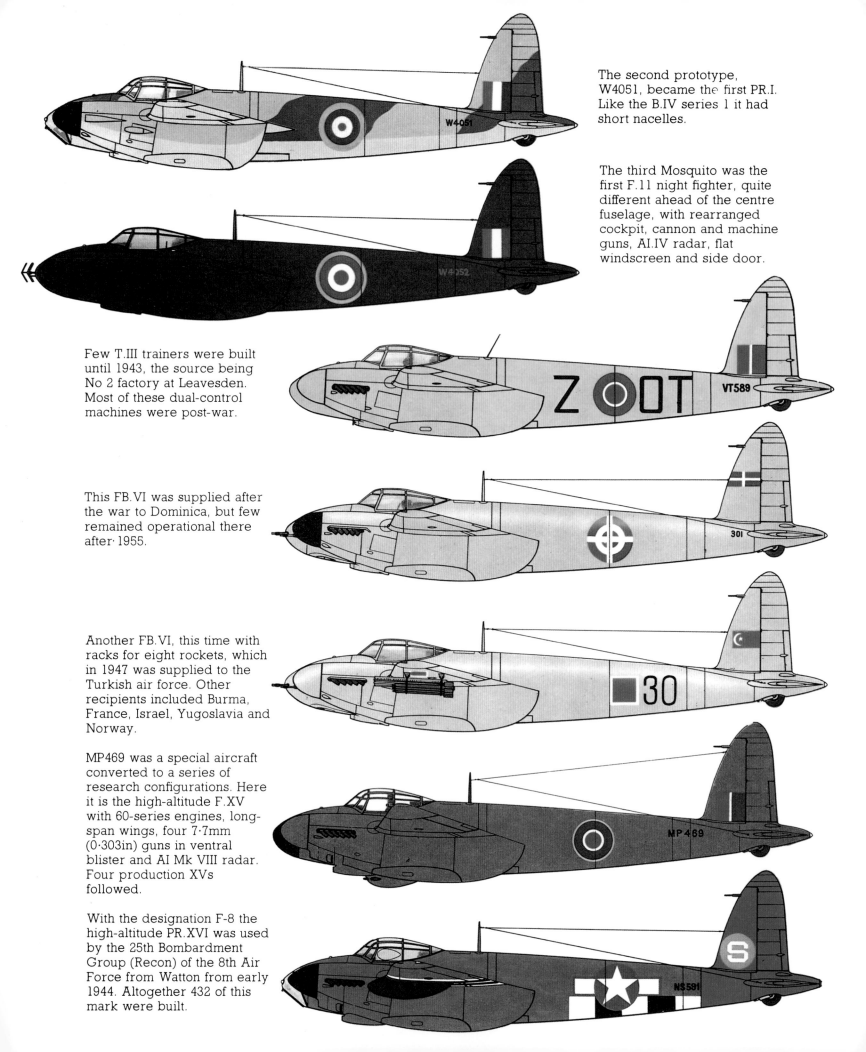

The second prototype, W4051, became the first PR.I. Like the B.IV series 1 it had short nacelles.

The third Mosquito was the first F.11 night fighter, quite different ahead of the centre fuselage, with rearranged cockpit, cannon and machine guns, AI.IV radar, flat windscreen and side door.

Few T.III trainers were built until 1943, the source being No 2 factory at Leavesden. Most of these dual-control machines were post-war.

This FB.VI was supplied after the war to Dominica, but few remained operational there after·1955.

Another FB.VI, this time with racks for eight rockets, which in 1947 was supplied to the Turkish air force. Other recipients included Burma, France, Israel, Yugoslavia and Norway.

MP469 was a special aircraft converted to a series of research configurations. Here it is the high-altitude F.XV with 60-series engines, long-span wings, four 7·7mm (0·303in) guns in ventral blister and AI Mk VIII radar. Four production XVs followed.

With the designation F-8 the high-altitude PR.XVI was used by the 25th Bombardment Group (Recon) of the 8th Air Force from Watton from early 1944. Altogether 432 of this mark were built.

De Havilland D.H.98 Mosquito

Dubbed Tsetse Fly, the FB.XVIII had a 6-pounder 57mm Molins gun for attacking shipping. This example served 248 Sqn, the original exponent of this mark in October 1943.

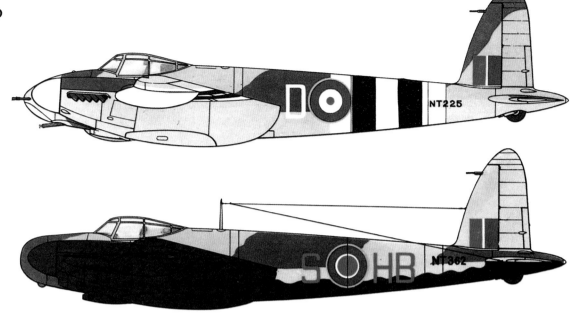

The best wartime night fighter was the NF.30, with two-stage engines (originally the Mk 76) with flame-dampers, and advanced AI Mk X radar. This one was assigned to 239 Sqn.

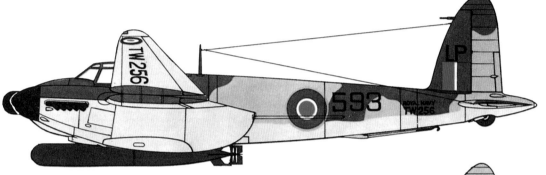

Too late for war operations, the Sea Mosquito TR.33 was a much modified FB.VI with (eventually) Merlin 25s, folding wings, oleo landing gear, arrester hook and ASH radar. The 50 of this mark were followed by six TR.37s with large ASV radar.

Ultimate Mosquito bomber, the B.35 combined the B.XVI's bulged bomb bay and pressure cabin with the Mk 113/114 engines. This one went to 139 Sqn.

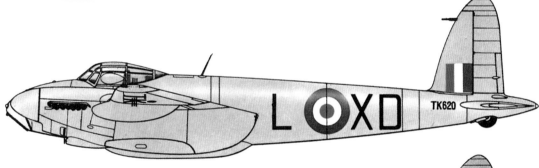

A Yugoslavian NF.36, the ultimate night fighter (with the NF.38, with British radar) which was basically a Mk 30 with Merlin 113 engines. Belgium and Sweden also operated late-model night fighters.

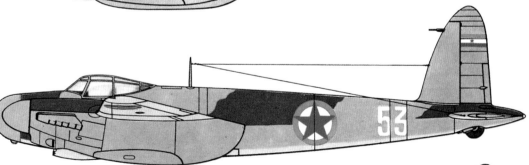

Developed in 1944–5 by General Aircraft, the ungainly TT.39 was a dedicated target tug produced by rebuilding Percival-built B.XVI or PR.34 aircraft to Navy specification.

Vincenzo Cosentino

Dornier Do 217E-5

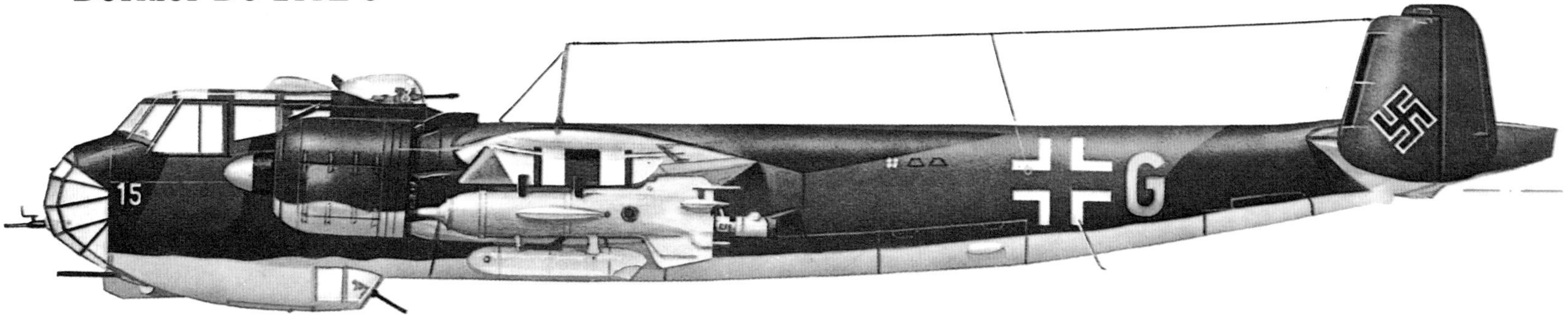

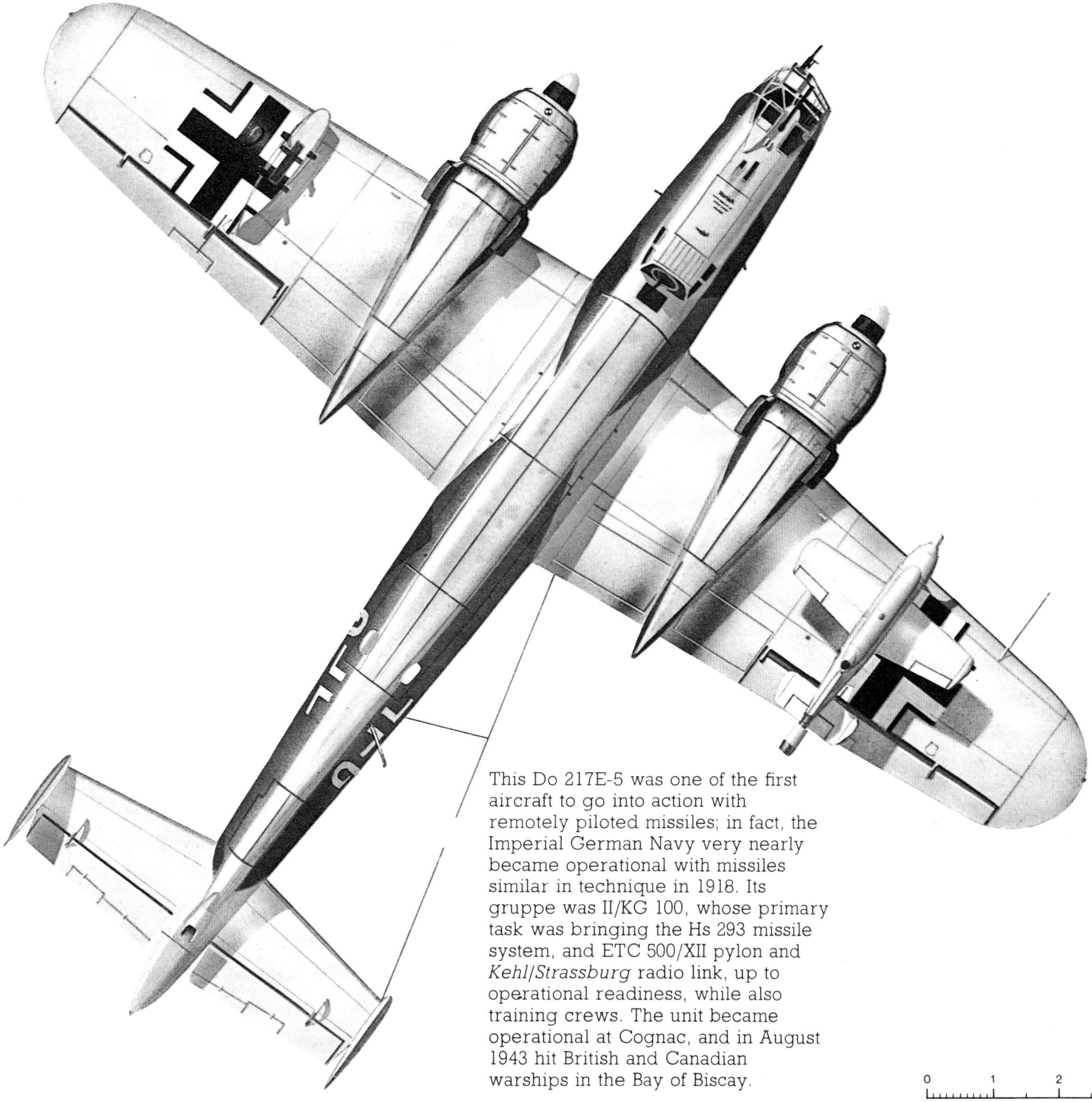

This Do 217E-5 was one of the first aircraft to go into action with remotely piloted missiles; in fact, the Imperial German Navy very nearly became operational with missiles similar in technique in 1918. Its gruppe was II/KG 100, whose primary task was bringing the Hs 293 missile system, and ETC 500/XII pylon and *Kehl/Strassburg* radio link, up to operational readiness, while also training crews. The unit became operational at Cognac, and in August 1943 hit British and Canadian warships in the Bay of Biscay.

0   1   2   3   4 m

Pino dell'Orco

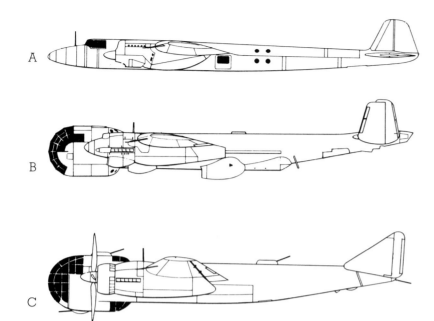

A

B

C

Three totally different prototypes covering a span of only ten years but with gross weight and power multiplied by four. A, the original 'Flying Pencil', the Do 17 VI civil transport, really a mailplane but with cramped accommodation for six passengers. B, the Do 217P VI of June 1942 with pressure cabin and third *HZ-Anlage* engine in the rear fuselage to supercharge the main DB603s. C, the Do 317B which in 1944 remained unfinished, with 2,870hp DB 610 double engines.

0 1 2 3 4 5 m

Pino dell'Orco

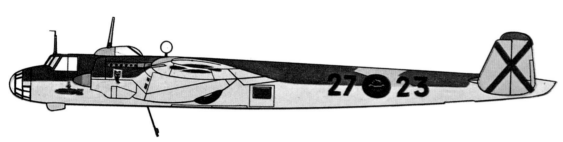

First version of the Do 17 to see action was the Do 17F-1 reconnaissance aircraft with the Legion Kondor's 1.A/88 in Spain in March 1937. Later in the year this Do 17E-1 bomber was one of a batch which joined 1. and 2.K/88, performing with impressive reliability and few casualties.

The Yugoslavs were so impressed by the high-power Do 17M at the Zurich display in July 1937 that they took out a licence for the Do 17K, powered by 980hp Gnome-Rhone 14N radials, and also bought 20 from Dornier. This Ka-2 was a photo model, while the bomber was the Kb-1.

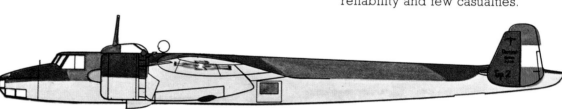

Exceptionally, this Do 17Z-1 is depicted while operational with a Bf 110 *Zerstörer* unit, the famous ZG 26 *Horst Wessel*, in Libya in 1941–2. No Do 17 unit as such took any part in the African campaign; after the capture of Crete all surviving units went to the Eastern front.

Apart from a Croatian staffel the only operator of the Do 17 in combat after the end of 1941 was the Finnish air force, one of whose Z-2s is seen here. Goering gave the Finns 15 war-weary bombers which began operating on the Eastern front in April 1942. The unit was PLeLv46.

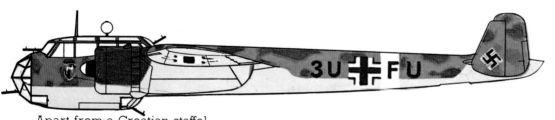

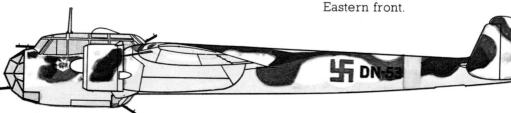

Dornier Do 17, 215 and 217

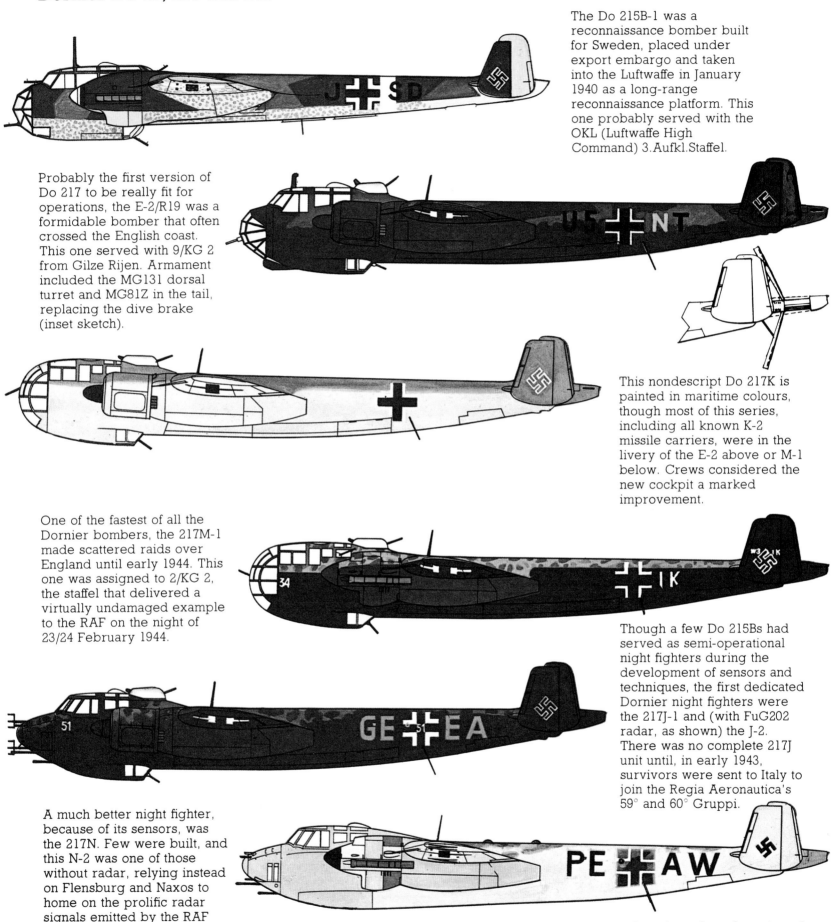

The Do 215B-1 was a reconnaissance bomber built for Sweden, placed under export embargo and taken into the Luftwaffe in January 1940 as a long-range reconnaissance platform. This one probably served with the OKL (Luftwaffe High Command) 3.Aufkl.Staffel.

Probably the first version of Do 217 to be really fit for operations, the E-2/R19 was a formidable bomber that often crossed the English coast. This one served with 9/KG 2 from Gilze Rijen. Armament included the MG131 dorsal turret and MG81Z in the tail, replacing the dive brake (inset sketch).

This nondescript Do 217K is painted in maritime colours, though most of this series, including all known K-2 missile carriers, were in the livery of the E-2 above or M-1 below. Crews considered the new cockpit a marked improvement.

One of the fastest of all the Dornier bombers, the 217M-1 made scattered raids over England until early 1944. This one was assigned to 2/KG 2, the staffel that delivered a virtually undamaged example to the RAF on the night of 23/24 February 1944.

Though a few Do 215Bs had served as semi-operational night fighters during the development of sensors and techniques, the first dedicated Dornier night fighters were the 217J-1 and (with FuG202 radar, as shown) the J-2. There was no complete 217J unit until, in early 1943, survivors were sent to Italy to join the Regia Aeronautica's 59° and 60° Gruppi.

A much better night fighter, because of its sensors, was the 217N. Few were built, and this N-2 was one of those without radar, relying instead on Flensburg and Naxos to home on the prolific radar signals emitted by the RAF bombers.

0 1 2 3 4 5 m

Pino dell'Orco

Dornier Do 17, 215 and 217

It is strange that, while some early Luftwaffe aircraft were planned as warplanes in the guise of civil machines, the Dornier company built the Do 17 as a most unsuitable passenger transport, had it rejected by Lufthansa, and saw it rescued from storage by one man who thought it would make a good bomber. The man was Robert Untucht, who as well as being on the RLM (Air Ministry) staff was the airline's chief test pilot. He happened to see the slim machine at the Löwenthal factory, liked the look of it and tested it. The inevitable result was that the Do 17 became a bomber, which in a prototype version in 1937 walked away from all the non-German fighters in a big flying meeting at Zurich. Early Do 17E bombers and F reconnaissance machines did well in the Spanish Civil War, becoming famous as 'the Flying Pencil' on account of their slim fuselage.

By World War 2 the Do 17Z was a major type, losing the slim outline but giving much better accommodation to an enlarged crew, and carrying twice the bomb-load despite having much better defensive armament. In the ensuing combats with Allied fighters the Dornier proved vulnerable, but it could be flung about the sky with no limitations and could dive with remarkable speed. It was extremely popular with its crews, and continued to bomb targets in the Balkans, and, from 1941, the Soviet Union. A handful of models designated Do 215 with a different engine were used by the Luftwaffe and Hungary, and a radar-equipped 215 scored the first radar night-fighter kill of the Luftwaffe in 1941.

This was the end of the rather limited 17/215 family, but back in 1938 Dornier had flown a slightly larger bomber designated Do 217, which promised to carry a far heavier bomb-load. After many problems a good 217 with an outstanding new radial engine entered service at the end of 1940, and within a year many fresh variants were being designed. Over England the 217 proved as vulnerable as the 17Z, though scattered examples made haphazard raids until spring 1944. Over the Eastern Front the 217E bombers were tough and effective, while the 217J and N were radar-equipped night fighters, though not very good ones.

In 1943 the crack KG 100 wing went into action with the 217E-5 carrying two Hs 293 radio-controlled missiles, followed by the long-span bulged-nose 217K-2 carrying a pair of the giant FX missiles. These precision-guided weapons scored many hits on Allied warships, one notable event being a mission against the Italian fleet on 9 September 1943 as it sailed to try to join the Allies: the biggest battleship, *Roma*, was promptly sunk, and her sister *Italia* just managed to limp into Malta.

There followed several further versions, notably the fast 217M bomber with liquid-cooled engines, which was the last of the Dornier bombers to remain in production in the summer of 1944. One that ventured over England early in 1944 made a beautiful wheels-up landing near Cambridge (it was flying with the RAF within weeks) 80km (50 miles) from where its crew had taken to their parachutes. However, Dornier failed to produce the elusive new bomber that the Luftwaffe was forever seeking during the war years, spending large amounts of money and engineering effort on an extraordinary machine designated Do 217P with pressure cabin and three engines, the third being in the rear fuselage driving high-capacity blowers to supercharge the engines on the wings. At the same time Dornier worked on its candidate for the new-generation 'Bomber B' requirement, the Do 317. Though this looked very like a 217, apart from having triangular fins, it was actually much heavier and more powerful, and was planned to carry a bomb load of 5600kg (12,346lb) as well as a further pair of 1800kg (3,968lb) bombs on underwing racks, a load much heavier than the big four-engined Allied bombers could manage. Typically, the whole programme failed to lead to a production article, and in late 1944 the Nos 2 to 5 prototypes of this potentially impressive aircraft were completed as carriers of the Hs 293 missile and thrust into service to try to stem Allied attacks.

COUNTRY OF ORIGIN Germany.
CREW **Early Do 17**: 3, **Do 17Z** and subsequent plus virtually all **217**: 4.
TOTAL PRODUCED **17/215**: 1,700; **217**: 1,905.
DIMENSIONS Wingspan, **17**: 18·0m (59ft 0½in), **most 217**: 19·0m (62ft 4in), **17K-2**: 24·8m (81ft 4½in); length, typical **early 17**: 16·1m (52ft 9¾in), **17Z**: 15·79m (51ft 9½in), **217E**: (except early version with long dive brake): 17·3m (56ft 9¼in), **217K,M**: 16·98m (55ft 9in), **217J,N**: 17·9m (58ft 9in); wing area, **17/215**: 55m² (592ft²), **most 217**: 57m² (613·4ft²), **217K-2**: 67m² (721·2ft²).
WEIGHTS Empty, **17E**: 4500kg (9,921lb), **17Z**: 5209kg (11,484lb), **217E**: 8850kg (19,512lb), **M-1**: 10950kg (24,140lb); max loaded, **17E**: 7050kg (15,542lb), **17Z**: 8587kg (18,931lb), **217E-2**: 16465kg (36,299lb), **217M-1**: 16700kg (36,817lb).
ENGINES **17E,F**: two 750hp BMW VI vee-12; **17Z**: 1,000hp BMW-Bramo 323P nine-cyl radial; **215**: 1,100hp DB 600Aa inverted-vee-12; **217E**: 1,580hp BMW 801A 18-cyl radial; **217K**: 1,700hp BMW 801D; **217M,N**: 1,750hp DB 603A inverted-vee-12.
MAXIMUM SPEED **17E**: 355km/h (220mph), **17Z**: 425km/h (263mph), **217E**: 515km/h (320mph), **K-2**: 533km/h (331mph) no missiles, **217J,N**: 498km/h (309mph), **217M**: 557km/h (346mph).
SERVICE CEILING **17E**: 5100m (16,730ft), **17Z**: 7000m (22,960ft), **217E,M,J,N**: 7500m (24,600ft), **K-2** no missiles: 9000m (29,520ft), **P**: 16154m (53,000ft).
RANGE **17E**: 1000km (621 miles), **17Z**: 1160km (721 miles), **217E,M,J,N,K-2** (weapon load): 2100km (1,305 miles).
MILITARY LOAD **17E**: bomb load of 750kg (1,653lb) and two 7·92mm MG15 (upper and lower rear hatches); **17Z**: bomb load of 1000kg (2,205lb) and six MG15, two in nose, two above and below at rear and one from each side; **217E**: bomb load of 4000kg (8,818lb), one 20mm MG151, one 13mm MG131 in dorsal, one MG131 in lower rear, three MG15 or 81 from nose and side, plus (some) two MG81 in tail; **217K,M**: As E but no tail guns and MG15 replaced by MG81; **217J,N**: usually four MG151 and four MG17 firing ahead and (late N-2/R22) four MG151 firing obliquely upwards.

Douglas A-20 Havoc and Boston

The Douglas family of shoulder-wing attack bombers and night interceptors were in many ways outstanding aircraft, typical of designs conceived much later. Planned by Ed Heinemann in 1937 to meet a US Army Air Corps specification, the original concept first flew as the Douglas 7B on 26 October 1938. This prototype was soon lost in a crash, but Heinemann and Jack Northrop (who at that time worked for Douglas) saw several ways in which the 7B could be improved, and with Army agreement recast it as the DB-7 with narrow but deep fuselage, nosewheel landing gear, deep low-slung nacelles and many other changes. The first order, for 100, was placed by the French Armée de l'Air in February 1939. The first of the new aircraft flew on 17 August of that year.

Development was swift, and service delivery to France via Casablanca began on 2 January 1940. Despite the DB-7's advanced design and contrast with previous French equipment it got into action fast, and over 100 reached North Africa, some 80 seeing action with GB I/19, II/19, I/32, II/32 and I/61 before the collapse. By this time Britain had increased the order to 270, and took all Douglas could supply. A giant depot had already been set up at Burtonwood for modifying American aircraft, and through here passed hundreds of DB-7s in 1940–41. Many emerged as Boston attack bombers, but most of the early batches were rebuilt as Havoc night fighters. Some had radar, a few experimented with the Long Aerial Mine in which explosive charges were towed on steel cables, while many had a glass nose housing an extremely powerful searchlight called a Turbinlite.

By late 1940 the US Army A-20 was flying with the much more powerful R-2600 engine with turbosuperchargers, but the turbo installation had to be abandoned. This caused severe loss of performance at high altitude, making the A-20 less useful for fighting or reconnaissance, but orders grew swiftly for R-2600 models called Boston III by Britain and A-20C by the US Army, these and all subsequent models

having a broader vertical tail. Boeing had been brought in to build 240 DB-7s for France and eventually made the A-20C and Boston IIIA. The RAF Havoc II had a 12-gun nose, while others had upward-firing guns or both guns and bombs. From late 1941 additional batches of DB-7s went to the Soviet Union. Small numbers served with the US Navy as the DB-1 and -2.

By 1943 production was centred on a new series of which the basic model was the A-20G. This incorporated numerous small and large modifications, and soon was fitted with a power-driven dorsal turret. The USAAF had previously used small numbers of early models as night fighters designated P-70, with British AI Mk IV radar, and the A-20G was the basis for improved night fighters with different armament, some of which trained P-61 crews. The USAAF standardized on the name Havoc, and supplemented the G with the A-20J, called Boston IV by the RAF, with a navigator/bombardier in a glazed nose. The A-20H was similar to the G but had slightly more powerful engines, and this also had a glazed-nose equivalent in the K. Usually these three-crew aircraft were used as lead-ships by large formations of G and H Havocs, the latter keeping close behind the leader and bombing when they saw the lead-ship do so. The F-3 was an early photo-reconnaissance version, but lack of turbocharged engines restricted this series, and most Havocs and Bostons operated at low or medium level, in almost all theatres of war, making level bombing runs and, in some areas, using their heavy front armament to good effect in low-level attacks on surface targets. Nearly half of all DB-7 type aircraft were freely supplied to the Soviet Union, where their strength and high performance were much appreciated. Many machines of this basic type had a rudimentary flight-control system in the rear cockpit behind the wing, occupied by the radio operator/gunner, who could thus (it was thought) land the aircraft if the pilot were to be incapacitated. This was seldom fitted after installing a turret.

COUNTRY OF ORIGIN USA.

CREW Glazed nose versions: 3; others: 2.

TOTAL PRODUCED 7,385.

DIMENSIONS Wingspan 18·695m (61ft 4in); length, always within 0·25m (10in) of **A-20G**: 14·73m (48ft 4in); wing area, 43·2m² (465ft²).

WEIGHTS Empty, **DB-7**: 5171kg (11,400lb), **A-20G/Boston IV**: typically 7700kg (16,975lb); maximum loaded, **DB-7**: 7725kg (17,030lb); **A-20G/Boston IV**: 12340kg (27,200lb).

ENGINES **Prior to Boston III**: two Pratt & Whitney R-1830 Twin Wasp 14-cylinder radials each rated at 1,050hp or 1,200hp; **from Boston III/A-20C**: two Wright R-2600 Cyclone 14-cylinder two-row radials each rated at 1,600hp or (A-20H, K) 1,700hp.

MAXIMUM SPEED **DB-7**: 505km/h (314mph), **Havoc I** (RAF): 475km/h (295mph), **Boston III/A-20C/A-20G**: 549km/h (342mph), **A-20H,K**: 565km/h (351mph).

SERVICE CEILING All versions, about 7700m (25,250ft).

RANGE With full bomb load and normal fuel, **DB-7**: 1050km (650 miles), **A-20C/Boston III**: 1207km (750 miles), **A-20G/H/J/K**: 1610km (1,000 miles).

MILITARY LOAD Extremely varied; early versions prior to G had internal bomb load of 907kg (2,000lb), and defensive armament of four 7·7mm (0·303in) or two 12·7mm (0·5in) guns fixed firing ahead and two 7·7mm (0·303in) or one 12·7mm (0·5in) dorsal and one or two 7·62mm (0·30in) or 7·7mm (0.303in) ventral; **Havoc** night fighters, see text; **P-70**: four 20mm M-2 cannon in belly tray; **later P-70A and B**: six 12·7mm (0·5in) firing ahead; **A-20G,H**: bomb load of 1814kg (4,000lb) and nine 12·7mm (0·5in) guns, six in nose, two in turret and one at lower rear; **A-20J,K**: as G but only two forward-firing 12·7mm (0·5in) guns.

Douglas Boston IV

This Boston IV, handed over after being built as an A-20J, served with No 342 Sqn RAF, composed of Free French personnel, initially part of 170 Wing in North Africa. In 1944 it became part of 137 Wing in Bomber Command's 2 Group, moving to the Continent in August as part of the 2nd Tactical Air Force with these French markings. The unit had a dual French identity as GB1 Lorraine bomber group, whose badge was worn on the fin together with the Free French cross of Lorraine on the nose.

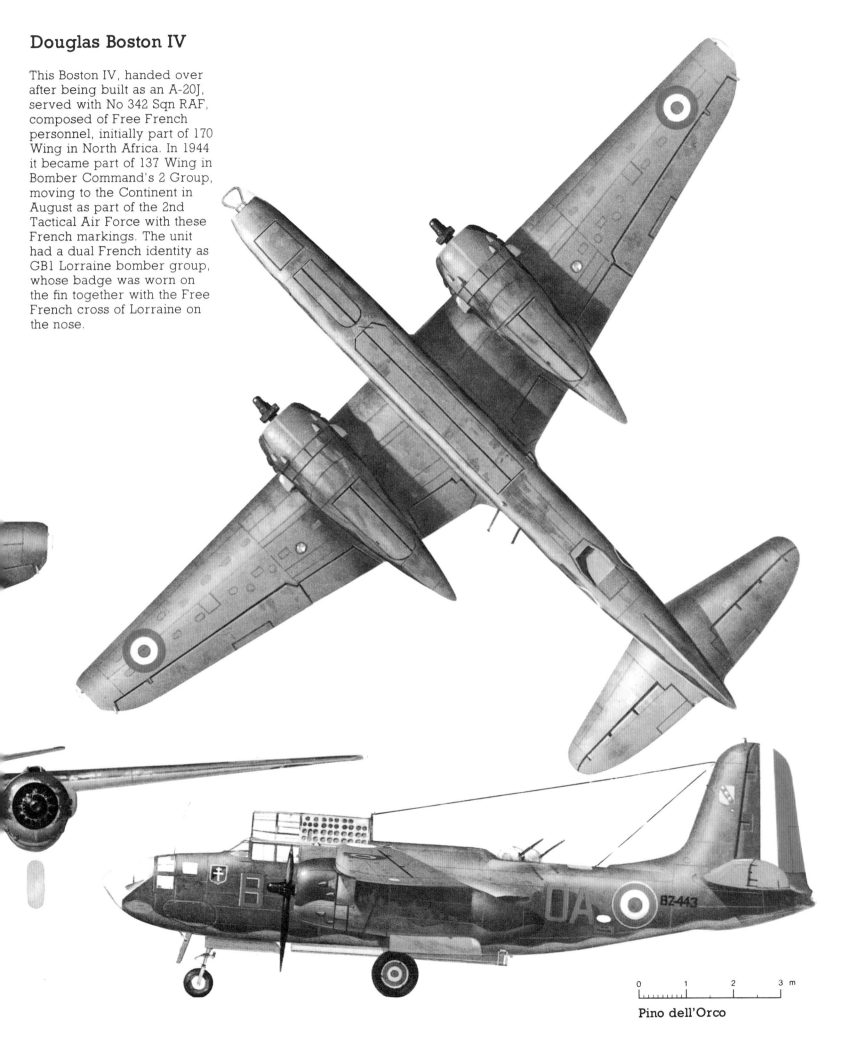

OA · BZ-443

0   1   2   3 m

Pino dell'Orco

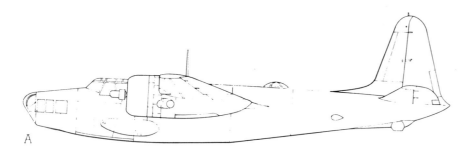

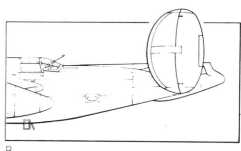

A The original project by Heinemann and Northrop was the Model 7B, with Twin Wasp engines, retractable turret and four 7·62mm (0·30in) package guns firing ahead. It was redesigned to meet demands of the French.

B The twin-fin tail originally intended for the more powerful French DB-7A with Cyclone R-2600 engines. Three were flown before it was decided to use a broader single fin.

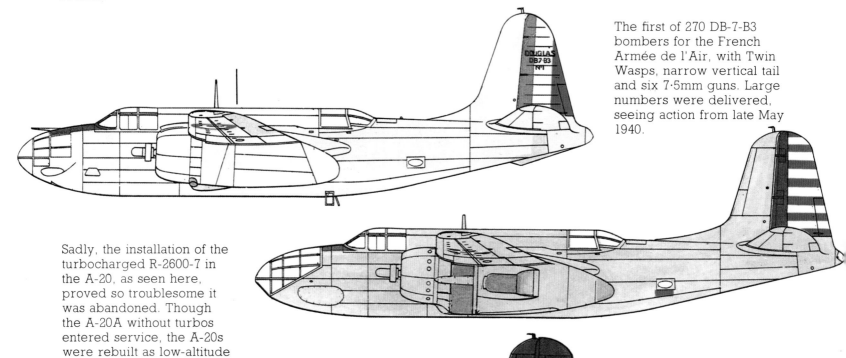

The first of 270 DB-7-B3 bombers for the French Armée de l'Air, with Twin Wasps, narrow vertical tail and six 7·5mm guns. Large numbers were delivered, seeing action from late May 1940.

Sadly, the installation of the turbocharged R-2600-7 in the A-20, as seen here, proved so troublesome it was abandoned. Though the A-20A without turbos entered service, the A-20s were rebuilt as low-altitude P-70 night fighters.

A standard Boston III, AL296, serving with 107 Sqn RAF at Great Massingham in early 1942. The RAF used 781, including 240 Boeing-built Mk IIIAs.

Olive and 'desert pink' were often used in camouflage schemes applied locally in North Africa from November 1942. This was a typical result, seen on an A-20C Havoc of the 47th BG (Light), 12th Air Force, at Medioura, Morocco, in December 1942.

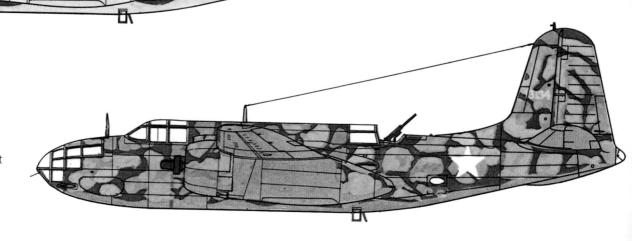

Douglas A-20 Havoc and Boston

USAAF 39-771 was one of the P-70 Havoc night fighters produced by rebuilding unsuccessful turbocharged A-20 bombers. They were first-class except above 9400m (20,000ft), with British AI.IV radar and four 20mm M-2 cannon. This one was with the 481st NF training group.

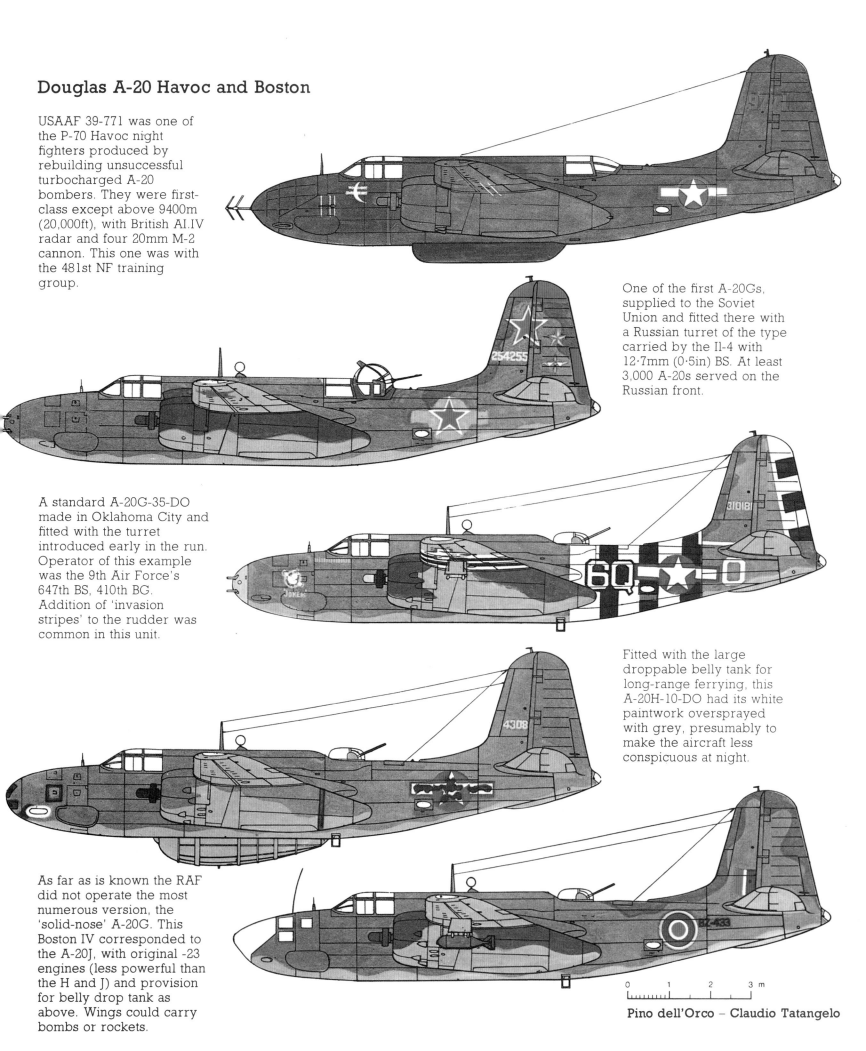

One of the first A-20Gs, supplied to the Soviet Union and fitted there with a Russian turret of the type carried by the Il-4 with 12·7mm (0·5in) BS. At least 3,000 A-20s served on the Russian front.

A standard A-20G-35-DO made in Oklahoma City and fitted with the turret introduced early in the run. Operator of this example was the 9th Air Force's 647th BS, 410th BG. Addition of 'invasion stripes' to the rudder was common in this unit.

Fitted with the large droppable belly tank for long-range ferrying, this A-20H-10-DO had its white paintwork oversprayed with grey, presumably to make the aircraft less conspicuous at night.

As far as is known the RAF did not operate the most numerous version, the 'solid-nose' A-20G. This Boston IV corresponded to the A-20J, with original -23 engines (less powerful than the H and J) and provision for belly drop tank as above. Wings could carry bombs or rockets.

Pino dell'Orco – Claudio Tatangelo

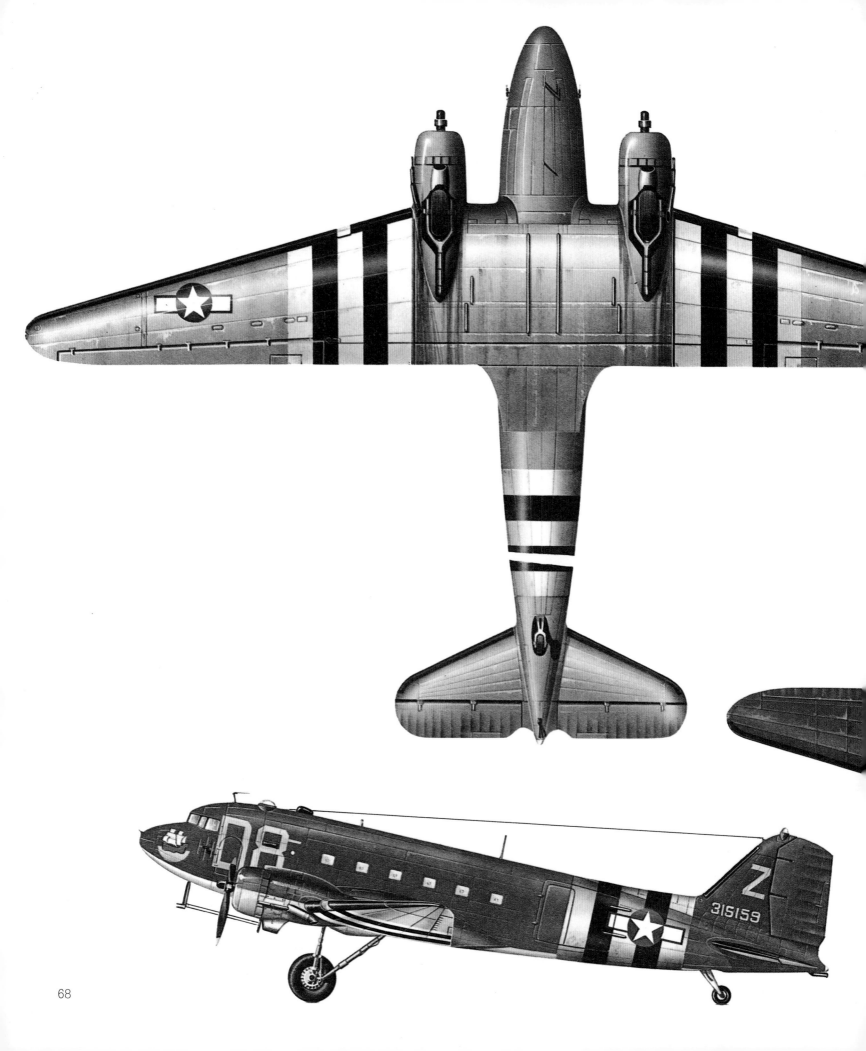

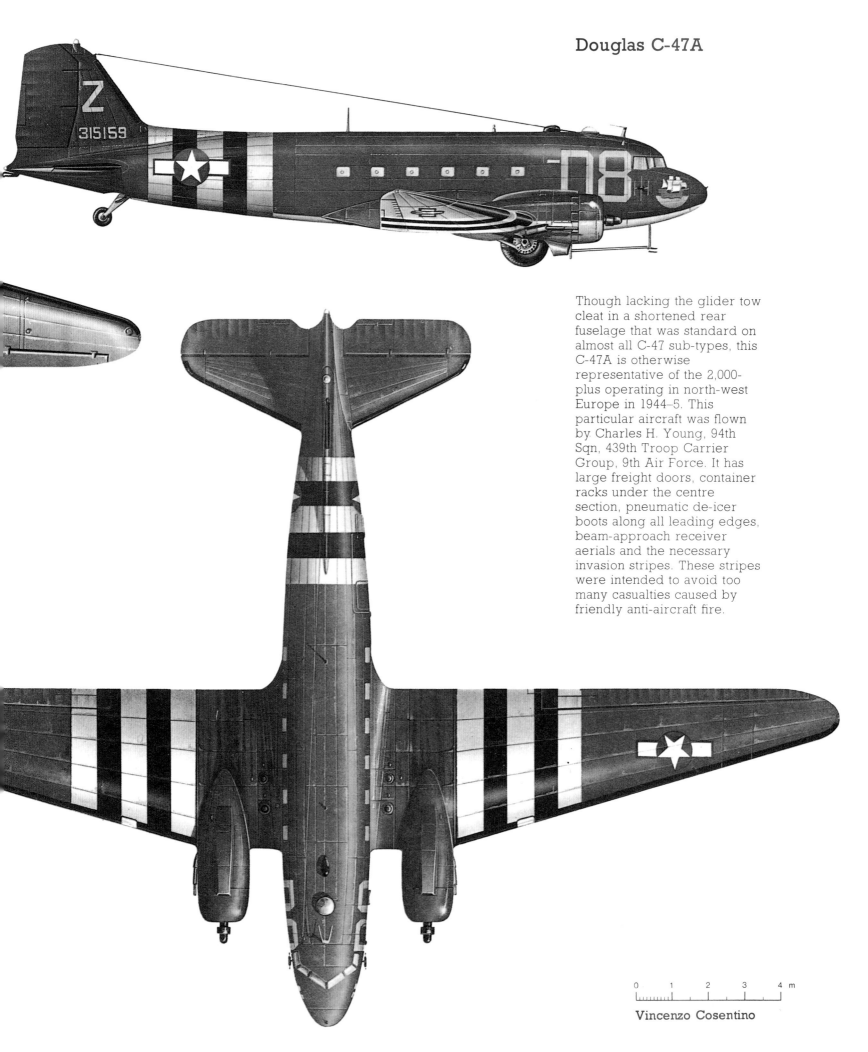

Douglas C-47A

Z
315159

D8

Though lacking the glider tow cleat in a shortened rear fuselage that was standard on almost all C-47 sub-types, this C-47A is otherwise representative of the 2,000-plus operating in north-west Europe in 1944–5. This particular aircraft was flown by Charles H. Young, 94th Sqn, 439th Troop Carrier Group, 9th Air Force. It has large freight doors, container racks under the centre section, pneumatic de-icer boots along all leading edges, beam-approach receiver aerials and the necessary invasion stripes. These stripes were intended to avoid too many casualties caused by friendly anti-aircraft fire.

0 1 2 3 4 m

Vincenzo Cosentino

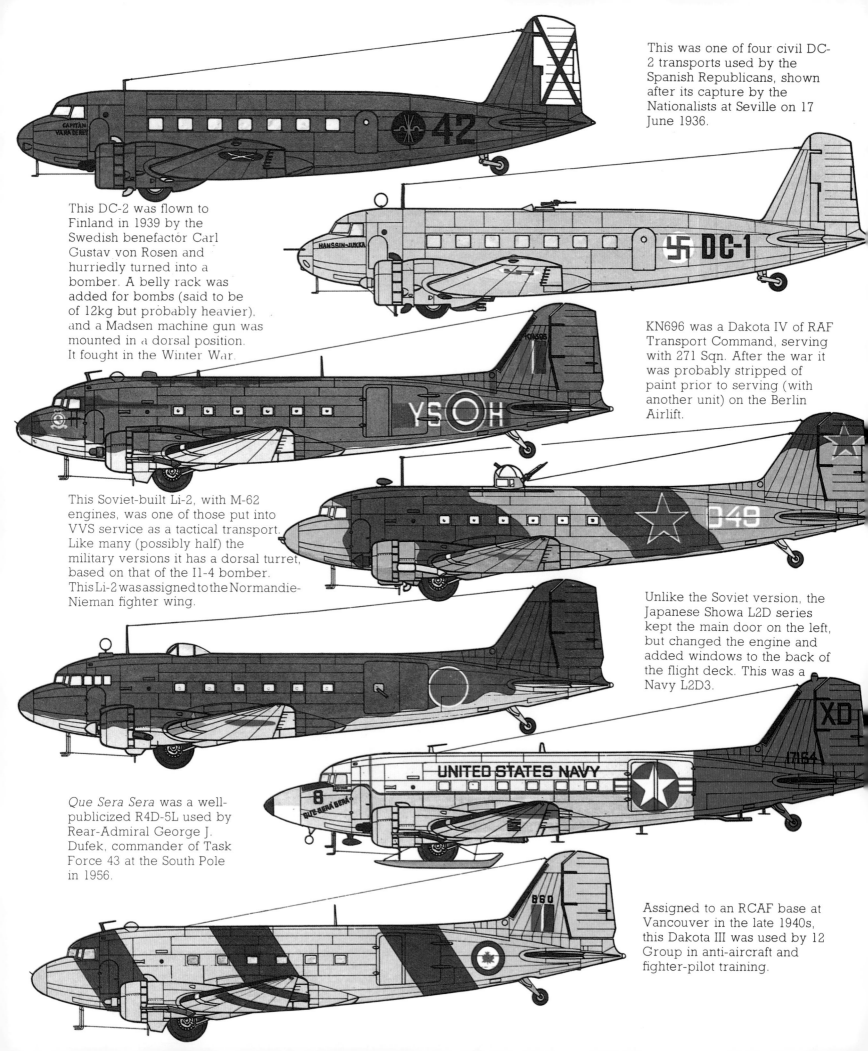

This was one of four civil DC-2 transports used by the Spanish Republicans, shown after its capture by the Nationalists at Seville on 17 June 1936.

This DC-2 was flown to Finland in 1939 by the Swedish benefactor Carl Gustav von Rosen and hurriedly turned into a bomber. A belly rack was added for bombs (said to be of 12kg but probably heavier), and a Madsen machine gun was mounted in a dorsal position. It fought in the Winter War.

KN696 was a Dakota IV of RAF Transport Command, serving with 271 Sqn. After the war it was probably stripped of paint prior to serving (with another unit) on the Berlin Airlift.

This Soviet-built Li-2, with M-62 engines, was one of those put into VVS service as a tactical transport. Like many (possibly half) the military versions it has a dorsal turret, based on that of the Il-4 bomber. This Li-2 was assigned to the Normandie-Nieman fighter wing.

Unlike the Soviet version, the Japanese Showa L2D series kept the main door on the left, but changed the engine and added windows to the back of the flight deck. This was a Navy L2D3.

Que Sera Sera was a well-publicized R4D-5L used by Rear-Admiral George J. Dufek, commander of Task Force 43 at the South Pole in 1956.

Assigned to an RCAF base at Vancouver in the late 1940s, this Dakota III was used by 12 Group in anti-aircraft and fighter-pilot training.

Douglas C-47 and Dakota

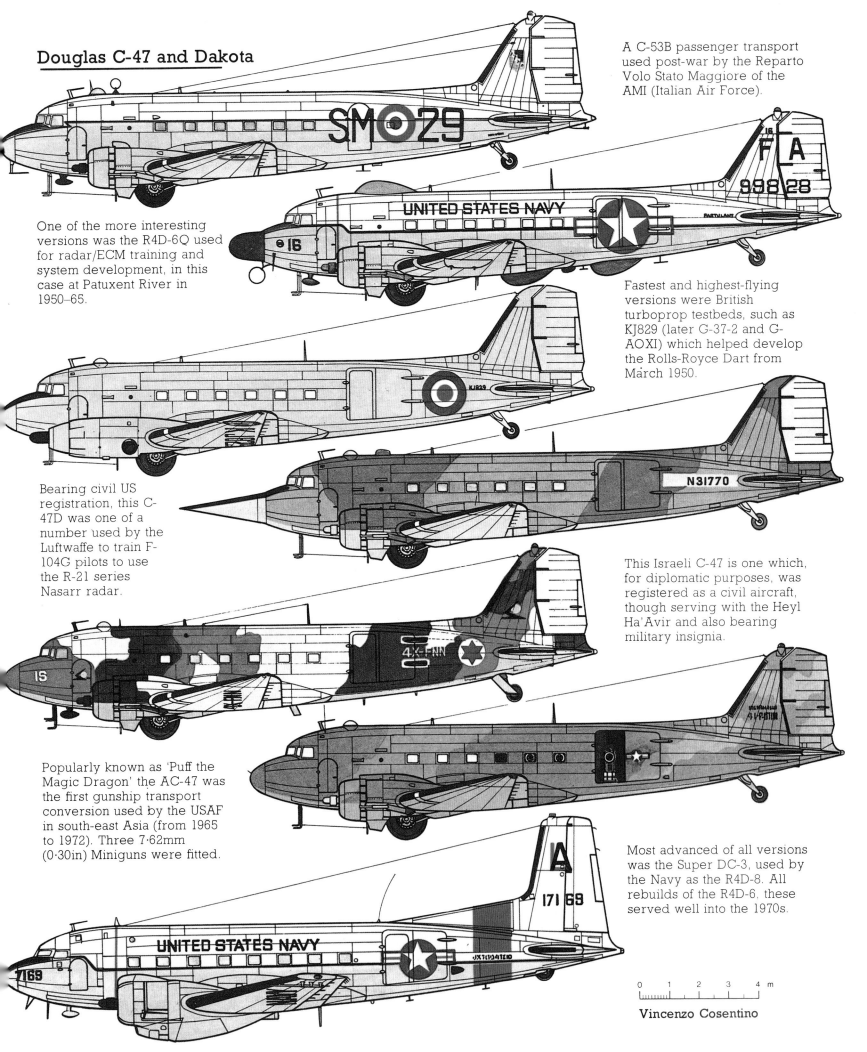

A C-53B passenger transport used post-war by the Reparto Volo Stato Maggiore of the AMI (Italian Air Force).

One of the more interesting versions was the R4D-6Q used for radar/ECM training and system development, in this case at Patuxent River in 1950–65.

Fastest and highest-flying versions were British turboprop testbeds, such as KJ829 (later G-37-2 and G-AOXI) which helped develop the Rolls-Royce Dart from March 1950.

Bearing civil US registration, this C-47D was one of a number used by the Luftwaffe to train F-104G pilots to use the R-21 series Nasarr radar.

This Israeli C-47 is one which, for diplomatic purposes, was registered as a civil aircraft, though serving with the Heyl Ha'Avir and also bearing military insignia.

Popularly known as 'Puff the Magic Dragon' the AC-47 was the first gunship transport conversion used by the USAF in south-east Asia (from 1965 to 1972). Three 7·62mm (0·30in) Miniguns were fitted.

Most advanced of all versions was the Super DC-3, used by the Navy as the R4D-8. All rebuilds of the R4D-6, these served well into the 1970s.

Vincenzo Cosentino

Douglas C-47 and Dakota

Probably the most famous transport aeroplane in history, and certainly the one made in the largest numbers (unless one includes all the Soviet-designed An-2 biplanes as transports), the DC-3 emerged almost by chance as the result of American Airlines wanting a DST (Douglas Sleeper Transport) bigger than the existing DC-2. Douglas took it upon themselves to offer a 'day-plane' version for seated passengers called DC-3. It swiftly became almost the world standard civil airliner, but from 1941 production of military versions far outstripped anything seen previously.

Like most of the world's most widely used aircraft the military versions came in a profusion of guises. After Pearl Harbor the USAAF took over numerous civil DC-3s and gave them designations ranging from C-48 to C-84. The basic military model was the C-47 Skytrain, with large side doors, strong freight door, glider tow attachment and folding wooden seats along the sides of the cabin. The C-53 Skytrooper was a troop transport, with small door, wood floor and fixed metal seats. US Navy versions were designated R4D, while to the British Commonwealth all variants were Dakotas, identified by mark numbers. To the Soviet Union, where large numbers were made under licence in about 1938–44 under the direction of the Lisunov bureau, it was the Li-2. In Japan, where 571 were constructed by Showa and Nakajima, it was the L2D, which in turn was code-named 'Tabby' by the Allies.

Underlying the exceptional longevity of the DC-3 in all versions is the fatigue-resistant structure, entirely of stressed skin and with a multi-spar wing offering a number of alternative load paths in the way now done with modern jets. When the DC-3 was designed in 1934–5 all the advances in flaps, landing gear, propellers, radial cowlings, de-icer boots on the leading edges and, by no means least, warm and soundproofed interiors were all developed and available off the shelf. Despite the much greater weight, compared with the equally pioneering DC-

2, the more powerful engines allowed safe flying on one engine, something hardly ever enjoyed by transport aircraft previously.

During World War 2 thousands of C-47 and C-53 versions were the standard workhorses of the Allies from the North African landing in November 1942 onward. The chief gliders towed were the Horsa and the CG-4A Hadrian, the Hamilcar being much too large for such a tug. The TC-47 series were dual trainers, the C-47C was a prototype twin-float amphibian (which flew very well but was not procured in quantity) and the XCG-17 was a remarkably efficient glider.

At the end of World War 2 Douglas developed a largely redesigned Super DC-3, with greatly modified airframe, different engines and improved equipment. This did not sell to the airlines but the US Navy bought kits for the conversion of 98 R4Ds to this standard, calling them R4D-8s. While regular transports, most of them based on wartime C-47s, formed the backbone of the transport strength of nearly all the world's postwar air forces, the US Air Force, Navy, Marines and Coast Guard operated many special-purpose versions. Some of these were concerned with electronic research or reconnaissance, others with radar training (usually sprouting a profusion of bumps and other kinds of aerial), while ski-equipped versions were winterized for use in Polar exploration.

One of the more unexpected developments was the AC-47, popularly known as 'Puff the Magic Dragon', the pioneer example of a so-called gunship transport conversion equipped with night sensors, sighting systems and a battery of automatic weapons (in this case usually three 7·62mm (0·30in) GE Miniguns on pintle mounts along the left side of the fuselage) to deliver suppressive fire against ground targets in Vietnam. By 1980 American usage of C-47 variants was restricted to a handful of special test aircraft, but ordinary transport versions were still in service with at least 75 of the world's air forces or para-military organizations.

COUNTRY OF ORIGIN USA.

CREW Usually 3.

TOTAL PRODUCED 10,691 by Douglas, plus 571 in Japan and at least 2,000 in Soviet Union.

DIMENSIONS Wingspan 28·96m (95ft 0in), except **R4D-8**: 27·43m (90ft 0in); length, **DC-3**, **C-53**: 19·65m (64ft 6in), **C-47** with tow attachment: 19·64m (64ft 5½in), **R4D-8**: 20·65m (67ft 9in); wing area 91·7m² (987ft²), **R4D-8**: 90·02m² (969ft²).

WEIGHTS Empty (typical of all C-47) 7700kg (16,970lb), **R4D-8**: 8862kg (19,537lb); maximum loaded, **C-47** normal: 11432kg (25,200lb), alternate and **C-53**: 11794kg (26,000lb), emergency overload: 14969kg (33,000lb).

ENGINES Standard for **C-47, -53**: two Pratt & Whitney R-1830-92 Twin Wasp 14-cylinder radials each rated at 1,200hp; some **DC-3** conversions: Wright R-1820 Cyclone; **Li-2**: 1,000hp M-62R based on Cyclone; **L2D**: Ki-43 or -51 Kinsei of 1,050 or 1,300hp; **R4D-8**: 1,475hp Wright R-1820-80.

MAXIMUM SPEED Typical of all, 370km/h (230mph), **R4D-8**: 435km/h (270mph).

SERVICE CEILING Typical of all, 7000m (23,000ft).

RANGE Typical of all, 3420km (2,125 miles), **R4D-8**: 4023km (2,500 miles).

MILITARY LOAD Typical cargo load, 3900kg (8,600lb) or 27, 28 or 32 troops.

Focke-Wulf Fw 190 and Ta 152

So good was the Bf 109 considered in 1937 that many experts thought there was no need to consider a successor. A successor was, however, ordered. Dubbed Würger (Shrike), a name which did not stick, it was designed at Focke-Wulf at Bremen under Kurt Tank, the project team being headed by R. Blaser. They did a fantastic job. The little Fw 190 which flew on 1 June 1939 was at that time the most advanced fighter in the world. Apparently unknown to Allied intelligence, despite the highly public nature of the Fw factory, it burst on the scene in northern France in the summer of 1941. At first RAF intelligence officers concluded the radial-engined fighters must be captured Hawk 75s, but it was soon realized they were in a rather different class entirely. When a flyable example happened to fall into RAF hands in June 1942 the Fw 190 was held in even greater respect.

Originally designed for the BMW 139 radial engine, the Fw 190A production version actually had a heavier but generally more powerful unit in an extremely advanced low-drag installation. The neat airframe was designed for rapid manufacture in dispersed facilities, a factor that was important when, by 1943, 190 production was taking place at 24 separate locations. The need for simple maintenance was also designed for from the start, as was a wide landing gear, neat frameless canopy and virtually all-electric systems. Luck entered into the programme to some degree with the swift attainment of wholly exceptional handling, without the shortcomings of the later 109s. Combined with excellent combat protection, heavy armament and the ability to carry offensive loads far greater than the limits for any other wartime single-engined fighter – indeed, heavier than many large bombers – the chief wonder is that the Bf 109 was not only kept in production but actually outstripped the rate of manufacture of the 190 to the end of the war.

The early 190A series were among the first aircraft to carry the outstanding new Mauser MG151 cannon, as well as the old MG FF and machine guns. The cockpit was especially modern and impressive, and the fan-cooled engine was controlled by an automatic system which in emergency could allow an override boost to be selected for even greater temporary performance. Later versions of the 190 usually had special power-boost systems such as MW50 using methanol-water or GM-1 using nitrous oxide. As early as March 1942 tests were exploring the 190's suitability as a fighter/bomber, and the result was not only a range of special-purpose variants, such as the 190F family of close-support machines (which replaced almost all the Ju 87s) and 190G long-range attack aircraft, but also a great variety of field conversion kits with which a 190 could speedily be transformed into almost any special version. Among the duties which these amazing aircraft undertook were dive bombing, tank-busting, torpedo attacks, bombing with the heaviest bombs, reconnaissance, rocket firing, missile guidance, anti-bomber attacks with special weapons, night fighting, long-range anti-ship attacks and dual training. The 190 was also an important guidance aircraft for the Mistel pilotless Ju 88 missiles, on which the fighter rode pick-a-back.

During 1943 the 190 became by far the most important tactical attack aircraft of the Luftwaffe, replacing many earlier types on the Eastern and Italian fronts and not only delivering a greater weight of firepower against surface targets but also proving a difficult aircraft to intercept. Many of the field kits added to the already heavy armament, as indicated by the data.

Fundamental lack of high-altitude performance led to prolonged attempts to fit turbochargers or a different engine, and in August 1944 the long-nosed 190D-9 entered service with a liquid-cooled engine. Right at the end of the war this was joined by a superficially similar high-altitude fighter with a pressure cabin which, such was chief engineer Tank's prestige, was designated Ta 152H. Few reached the Luftwaffe before VE-Day.

COUNTRY OF ORIGIN Germany.

CREW 1.

TOTAL PRODUCED At least 20,051, plus about 200 Ta 152s and 64 Fw 190A-5s and A-8s made in 1945–6 by SNCASO in France as the NC.900.

DIMENSIONS Wingspan 10·5m (34ft 5½in), except **Ta 152C**: 11·0m (36ft 1in) and **Ta 152H**: 14·45m (47ft 4½in); length, **A,F,G-series**: 8·8m (28ft 10½in) to 8·96m (29ft 4¼in), **D-9**: 10·2m (33ft 5¼in), **Ta 152**: 10·8m (35ft 5½in); wing area, **A,F,G,D**: 18·3m² (196·98ft²), **152H**: 23·3m² (250·8ft²).

WEIGHTS Empty, **A-3**: 2899kg (6,391lb), **A-8**: 3471kg (7,652lb), **D-9**: 3490kg (7,694lb), **Ta 152H-1**: 3920kg (8,642lb); maximum loaded, **A-3**: 3970kg (8,752lb), **A-8**: 4900kg (10,802lb), **D-9**: 4840kg (10,670lb), **Ta 152H-1**: 5217kg (11,502lb).

ENGINE **A,F,G**: 1,700hp BMW 801D 18-cylinder two-row radial, **D-9**: Junkers Jumo 213A inverted-vee-12 rated at 2,240hp with special boost, **Ta 152H**: Jumo 213E rated at 1,776hp.

MAXIMUM SPEED **A,F,G**: 650–675km/h (404–419mph), **D-9**: 685km/h (426mph), **152H**: 760km/h (472mph).

SERVICE CEILING Typical **A**: 11400m (37,400ft), **D-9**: 12000m (39,400ft), **152H**: 14800m (48,560ft).

RANGE **A,F,G**: Typically 800km (497 miles) on internal fuel, **D-9**: 837km (520 miles), **152H**: 1215km (755 miles) at max-continuous cruise.

MILITARY LOAD Basic **A-3**: two 7·92mm MG17 machine guns above fuselage, two 20mm MG151 in wing roots and two 20mm MG FF outboard; **A-8**: same but fuselage guns 13mm MG131 and addition of racks for 250kg (551lb) bomb and four 50kg (110lb) bombs; **late A, F and G**: various including 30mm MK103 guns, several rockets and projectors, torpedoes, BT700 and Bv 246 missiles and bombs up to 1800kg (3,968lb); **D-9**: two MG131, two MG151 and 500kg (1,102lb) bomb; **H-1**: one MK108 of 30mm and two MG151; **Ta 152C**: three 30mm MK108 and 500kg (1,102lb) bomb. Special variants carried as many as six MG151.

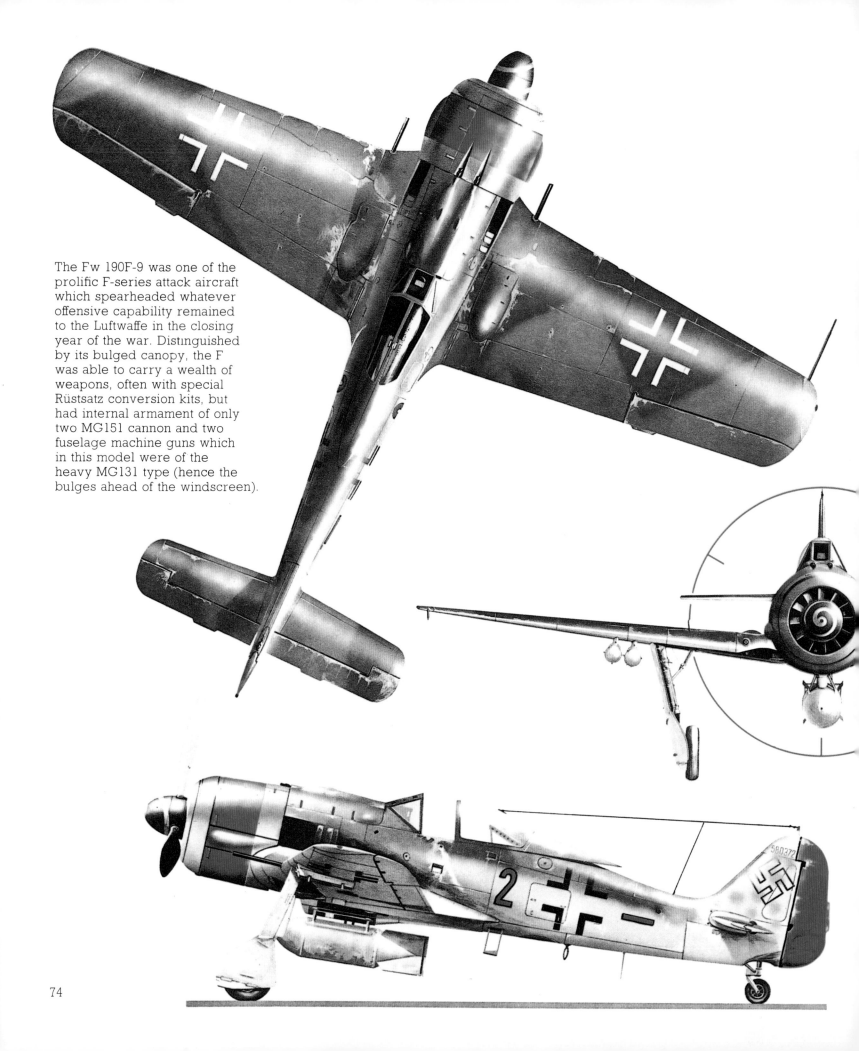

The Fw 190F-9 was one of the prolific F-series attack aircraft which spearheaded whatever offensive capability remained to the Luftwaffe in the closing year of the war. Distinguished by its bulged canopy, the F was able to carry a wealth of weapons, often with special Rüstsatz conversion kits, but had internal armament of only two MG151 cannon and two fuselage machine guns which in this model were of the heavy MG131 type (hence the bulges ahead of the windscreen).

Focke-Wulf Fw 190F-9

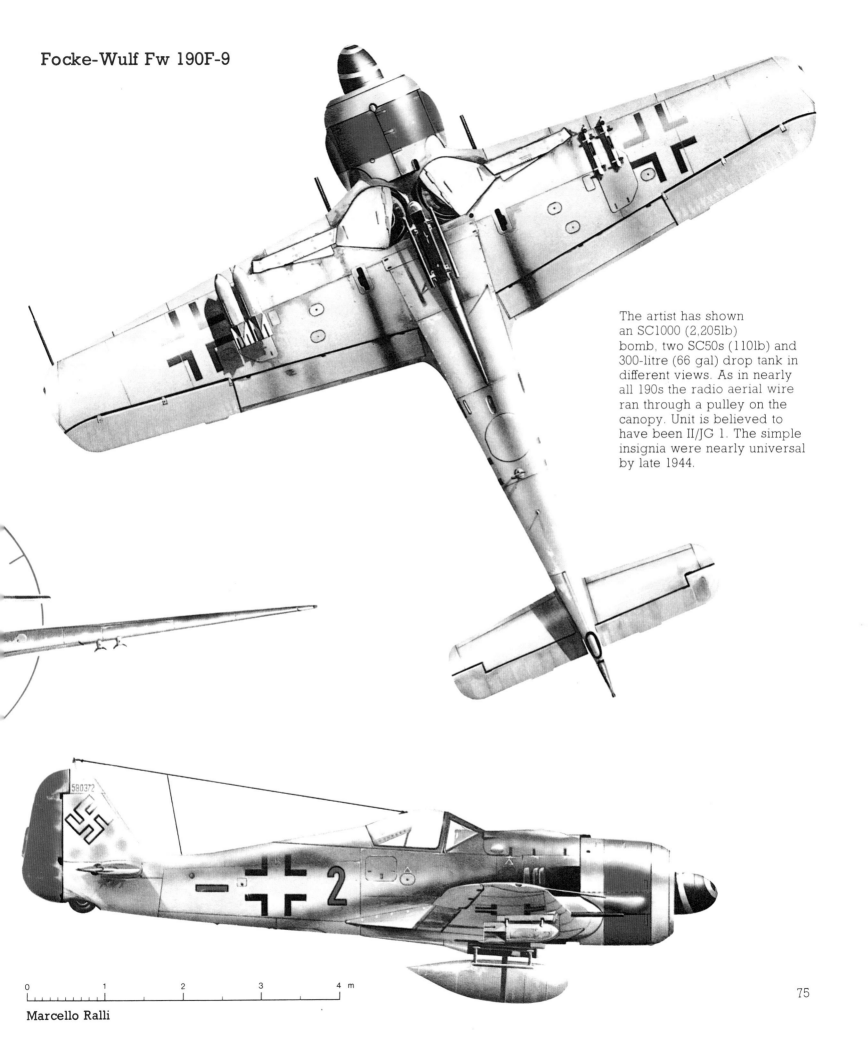

The artist has shown an SC1000 (2,205lb) bomb, two SC50s (110lb) and 300-litre (66 gal) drop tank in different views. As in nearly all 190s the radio aerial wire ran through a pulley on the canopy. Unit is believed to have been II/JG 1. The simple insignia were nearly universal by late 1944.

580372

0   1   2   3   4 m

Marcello Ralli

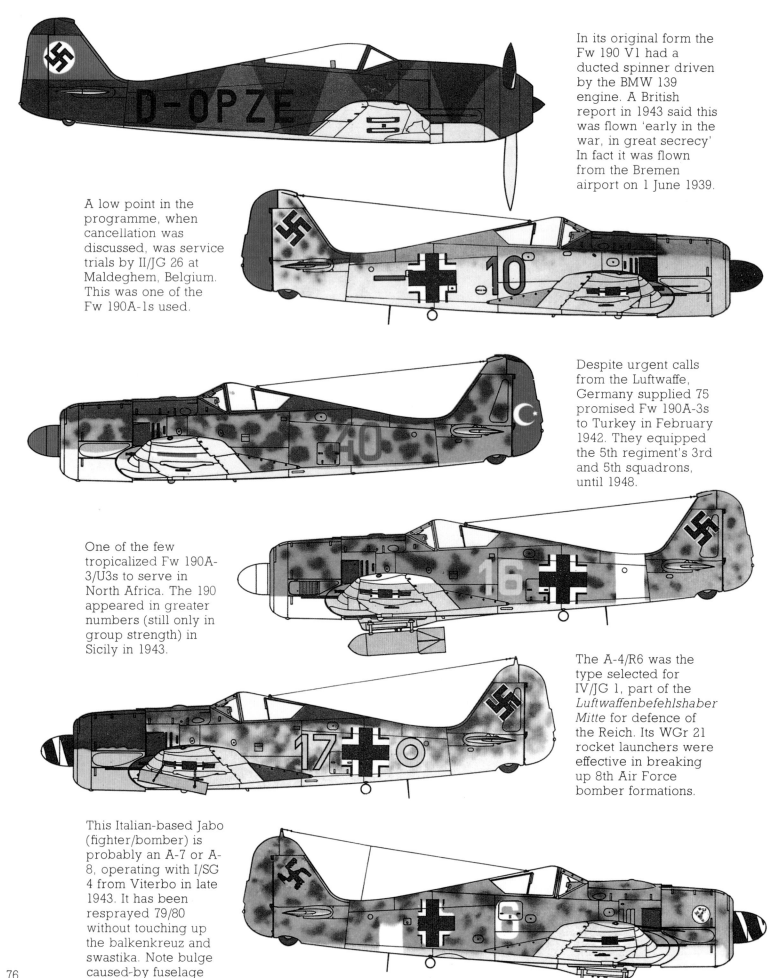

In its original form the Fw 190 V1 had a ducted spinner driven by the BMW 139 engine. A British report in 1943 said this was flown 'early in the war, in great secrecy' In fact it was flown from the Bremen airport on 1 June 1939.

A low point in the programme, when cancellation was discussed, was service trials by II/JG 26 at Maldeghem, Belgium. This was one of the Fw 190A-1s used.

Despite urgent calls from the Luftwaffe, Germany supplied 75 promised Fw 190A-3s to Turkey in February 1942. They equipped the 5th regiment's 3rd and 5th squadrons, until 1948.

One of the few tropicalized Fw 190A-3/U3s to serve in North Africa. The 190 appeared in greater numbers (still only in group strength) in Sicily in 1943.

The A-4/R6 was the type selected for IV/JG 1, part of the *Luftwaffenbefehlshaber Mitte* for defence of the Reich. Its WGr 21 rocket launchers were effective in breaking up 8th Air Force bomber formations.

This Italian-based Jabo (fighter/bomber) is probably an A-7 or A-8, operating with I/SG 4 from Viterbo in late 1943. It has been resprayed 79/80 without touching up the balkenkreuz and swastika. Note bulge caused by fuselage MG131s.

Focke-Wulf Fw 190 and Ta 152

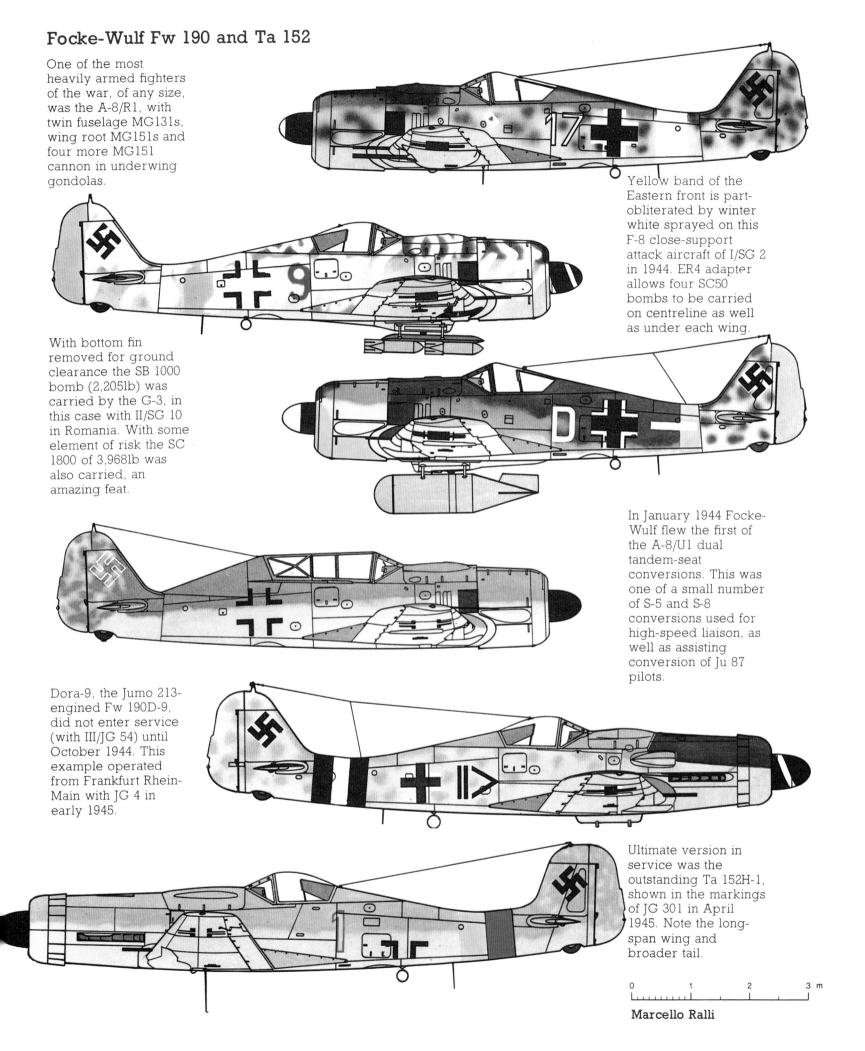

One of the most heavily armed fighters of the war, of any size, was the A-8/R1, with twin fuselage MG131s, wing root MG151s and four more MG151 cannon in underwing gondolas.

With bottom fin removed for ground clearance the SB 1000 bomb (2,205lb) was carried by the G-3, in this case with II/SG 10 in Romania. With some element of risk the SC 1800 of 3,968lb was also carried, an amazing feat.

Dora-9, the Jumo 213-engined Fw 190D-9, did not enter service (with III/JG 54) until October 1944. This example operated from Frankfurt Rhein-Main with JG 4 in early 1945.

Yellow band of the Eastern front is part-obliterated by winter white sprayed on this F-8 close-support attack aircraft of I/SG 2 in 1944. ER4 adapter allows four SC50 bombs to be carried on centreline as well as under each wing.

In January 1944 Focke-Wulf flew the first of the A-8/U1 dual tandem-seat conversions. This was one of a small number of S-5 and S-8 conversions used for high-speed liaison, as well as assisting conversion of Ju 87 pilots.

Ultimate version in service was the outstanding Ta 152H-1, shown in the markings of JG 301 in April 1945. Note the long-span wing and broader tail.

0   1   2   3 m

Marcello Ralli

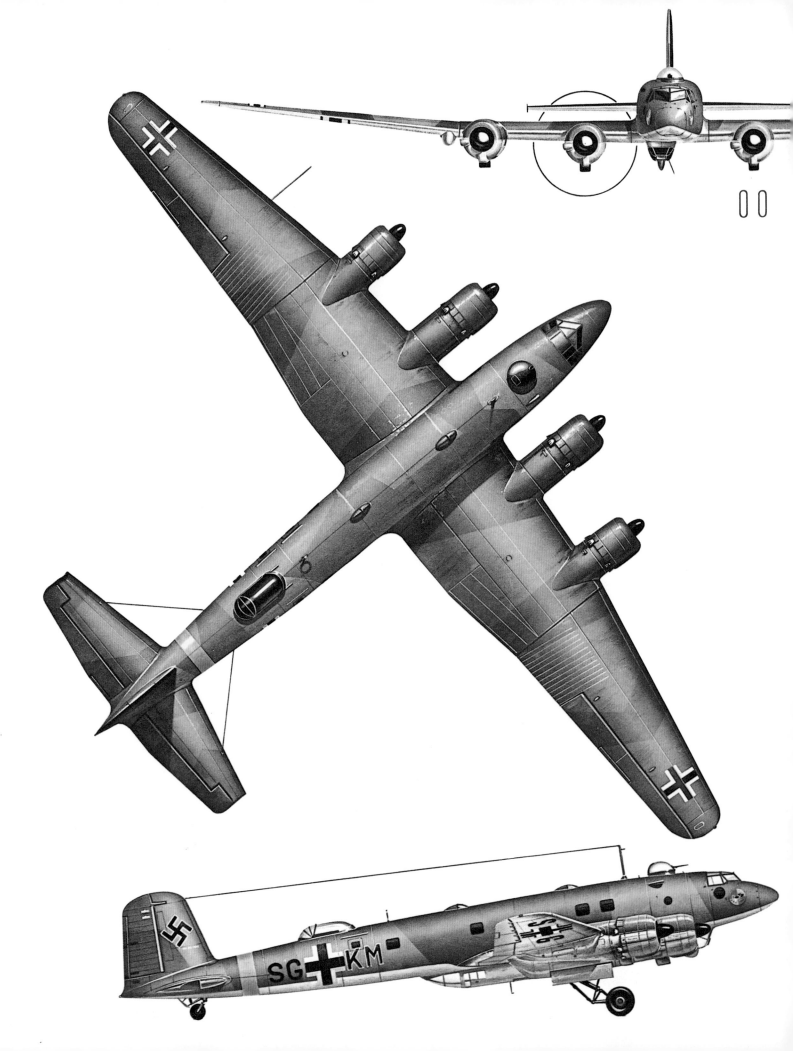

Focke-Wulf Fw 200C-3 Condor

One of the few non-operational
Condors built in 1941, this Fw
200C-3 was one of the first of
the structurally strengthened
and more powerful series
which at least gave a
semblance of fitness for
purpose to an otherwise
inadequate aircraft. Though it
wears the yellow band of the
Eastern theatre it was
assigned to B 36
Blindflugschule (instrument
flying school), and appears to
have armament removed
except for the low-drag Fw 19
turret behind the flight deck.

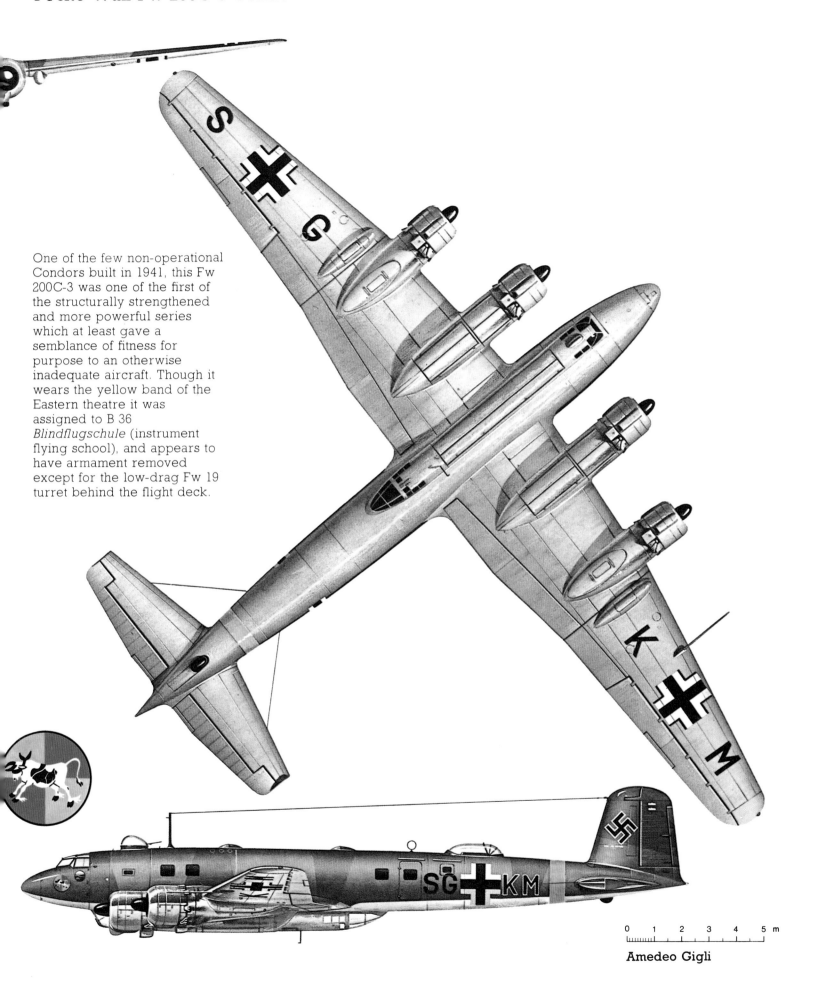

0 1 2 3 4 5 m

Amedeo Gigli

Built as D-ASVX *Thüringen* for Lufthansa, this Condor, works number 021, was the first of the three Fw 200C-0 transports for the Luftwaffe. With some of the six later C-0s, which were armed, it took part in the Norwegian campaign.

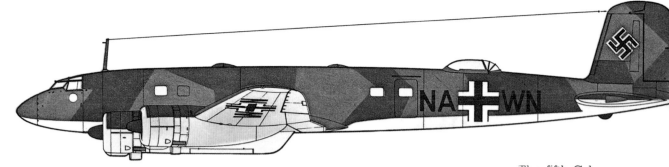

The fifth C-1, one of the last batch built at Bremen, not only had bomb racks under the outer nacelles but also the under-wing racks introduced on the third C-1. All went to KG 40.

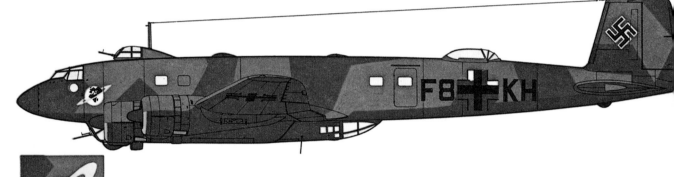

This C-2, built at Cottbus, was an interim machine with the original structure and engines but introducing properly faired-in bomb racks. KG 40's emblem is inset.

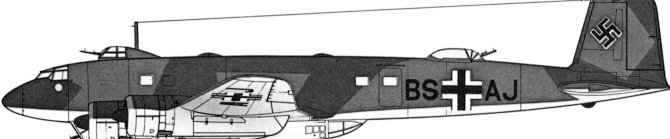

This C-3 was one of the few Condors that survived to build up an impressive tally of victims, recorded on the rudder. It was assigned to III/KG 40, with aircraft name *Neptun*.

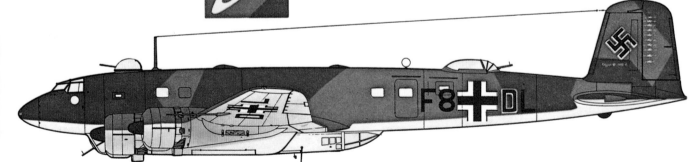

Another aircraft of B-36 (see drawings on previous pages), this time a fully armed C-3/U3. The yellow Eastern front band was applied for use at Stalingrad.

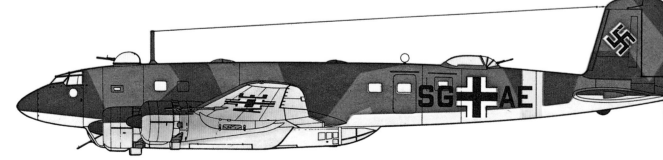

Focke-Wulf Fw 200C Condor

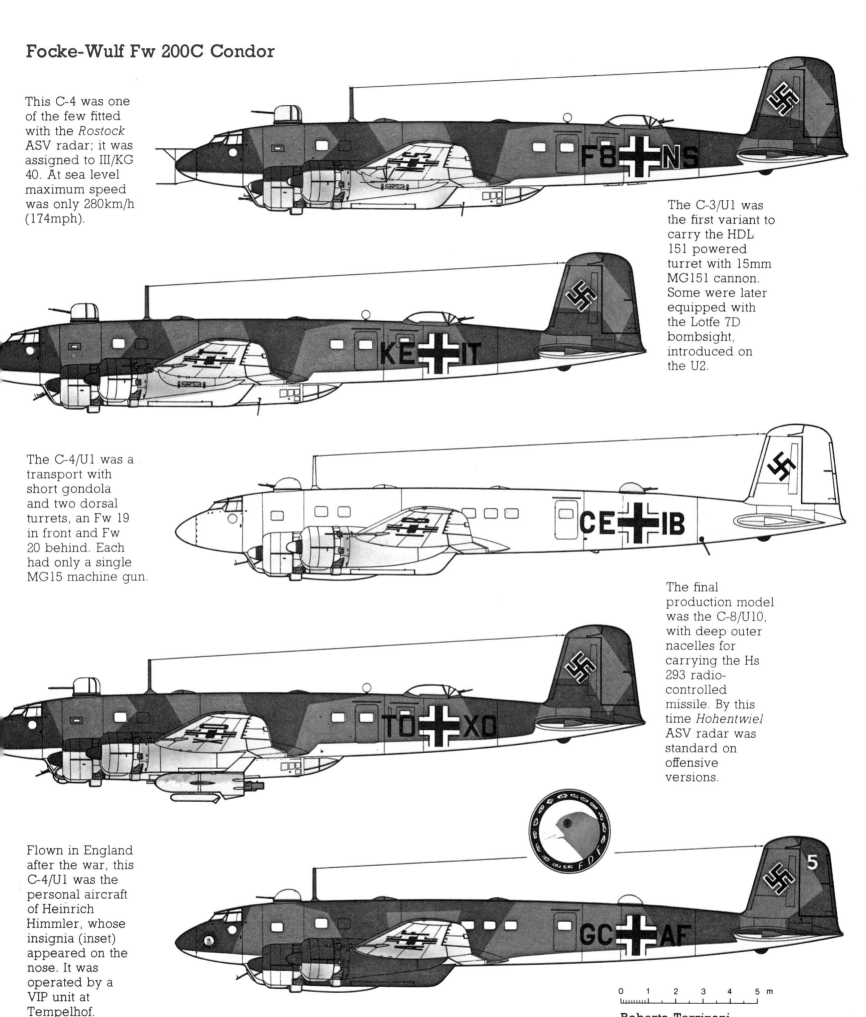

This C-4 was one of the few fitted with the *Rostock* ASV radar; it was assigned to III/KG 40. At sea level maximum speed was only 280km/h (174mph).

The C-3/U1 was the first variant to carry the HDL 151 powered turret with 15mm MG151 cannon. Some were later equipped with the Lotfe 7D bombsight, introduced on the U2.

The C-4/U1 was a transport with short gondola and two dorsal turrets, an Fw 19 in front and Fw 20 behind. Each had only a single MG15 machine gun.

The final production model was the C-8/U10, with deep outer nacelles for carrying the Hs 293 radio-controlled missile. By this time *Hohentwiel* ASV radar was standard on offensive versions.

Flown in England after the war, this C-4/U1 was the personal aircraft of Heinrich Himmler, whose insignia (inset) appeared on the nose. It was operated by a VIP unit at Tempelhof.

0 1 2 3 4 5 m

Roberto Terrinoni

Focke-Wulf Fw 200C Condor

Described by Winston Churchill as 'The Scourge of the Atlantic', and responsible for sinking or crippling many Allied ships (one unit alone sank 363,000 tons (368,800 tonnes) in six months), the Fw 200C Condor was a mere improvisation, prone to suffer catastrophic structural failure, and built only in small numbers. Seldom were more than 8 ready for action at once.

Kurt Tank directed the design of the Fw 200 in 1936 to meet a need by Lufthansa for a passenger and mail aircraft capable of transatlantic operation. The prototype flew on 27 July 1937, and just over a year later (when several Condors were in airline service) made headlines by flying non-stop to New York from Berlin, and then back, followed by flying a round trip to Tokyo. Several export orders were gained, a Japanese order secretly stipulating one Condor delivered for maritime reconnaissance. This was not delivered before the start of World War 2, but the engineering work was useful when the Luftwaffe realized it had no long-range aircraft to attack distant British shipping.

Oberst Edgar Petersen was ordered to form a long-range anti-ship unit, and the Condor appeared the only answer, in view of the delay to the He 177. Accordingly six of ten pre-production Luftwaffe Condors, designated Fw 200C-0, were hastily completed with improvised bomb racks and gun positions and issued to a new unit, I/KG 40, from April 1940. Little was done to strengthen the basic civil airframe, the only major changes being to use long-chord engine cowlings and twin-wheel main landing gears. Even the production Fw 200C-1, of which 26 were made in 1940, differed only in having a long ventral gondola under the fuselage with a gun at each end, the bomb load being hung under the outer engine nacelles and outer wings.

The gross imperfections of the early Fw 200C series were obvious. Defensive armament was wholly inadequate, there was no armour except on the first-pilot's seat, fuel lines were unprotected on the underside and the navigator had to climb into the gondola and aim the bombs using a Revi gunsight, dropping a concrete-filled bomb of full 500kg weight to check the sight readings before making a bombing run in earnest. What made the aircraft effective, however, was the near nakedness to attack of nearly all Allied merchant ships. One of the early victims was the liner *Empress of Britain*, bombed and set on fire on 26 October 1940. The captain of this Condor was Bernhard Jope who later led the the Do 217 wing with guided missiles, III/KG 100.

In 1941 the Fw 200C-2 introduced scalloped outer nacelles to fit the bombs, and by July the largely re-engineered C-3 followed, with much greater weight and military load, strengthened structure and different engines and armament. In February 1942 the C-4 introduced radar, the ultimate standard being FuG 200 Hohentwiel as also carried by some Ju 88s and 188s. The large HDL151 front turret became standard, and much useful equipment was added, but before many missions could be flown in increasingly dangerous Allied skies all available Condors were rushed to the Stalingrad area to act as transports, often also making bombing raids by night. By this time the sophisticated Lotfe 7D bombsight was fitted, enabling accurate bombing to be made from medium to high levels.

In 1943 the Condor's heyday was over. It made one last effort in versions equipped to launch and guide the Hs 293A missile. The ultimate production version was the C-8, with deep outer nacelles for the missiles and an extended gondola. The C-6 was a designation for earlier versions modified to carry the missile. Manufacture of Condors ceased in early 1944, and the aircraft that had survived into this year – though by now quite refined and combat-ready machines – were increasingly unable to survive in the face of Allied fighters and heavily armed ships. Almost all Condor missions from D-Day (6 June 1944) onwards were for transport, the task for which the aircraft had originally been designed.

COUNTRY OF ORIGIN Germany.

CREW Usually 7.

TOTAL PRODUCED Military C-series, 276.

DIMENSIONS Wingspan 32·85m (107ft 9½in); length 23·46m (76ft 11¾in); wing area 118·85m² (1,279ft²).

WEIGHTS Empty, **C-0**: 11300kg (24,911lb), **C-3/U4**: 12950kg (28,550lb); maximum loaded, **C-0**: 17500kg (38,580lb), **C-3/U4**: 22700kg (50,044lb).

ENGINES Four nine-cylinder radials. Versions up to **C-2**: 830hp BMW 132H; **C-3** and subsequent: 1,200hp BMW Bramo Fafnir 323R-2.

MAXIMUM SPEED Up to **C-3**: typically 360km/h (224mph), **C-4** onwards: 330km/h (205mph).

SERVICE CEILING Typical 5790m (19,000ft).

RANGE Typical, with maximum internal fuel: 4440km (2,759 miles).

MILITARY LOAD **C-0**: three 7·92mm MG15 fired from turret behind flight deck, rear dorsal position and rear ventral hatch; four 250kg (551lb) bombs carried externally. **C-1**: added 20mm MG FF at front of gondola and rear gun was moved to rear of gondola. **C-3**: 15mm MG151 in upper forward turret, 20mm MG151 in front of gondola, two MG15 from beam windows, bomb load of two 500kg (1,102lb), two 250kg (551lb) and (in gondola) 12 of 50kg (110lb). **C-6, C-8**: two Hs 293 missiles instead of bombs, guns generally unchanged.

Grumman TBF and TBM Avenger

On 4 June 1942 six new TBF-1 Avenger torpedo bombers roared into the air from the flight deck of USS *Hornet*, furiously engaged in the first Battle of Midway. Only one came back, and that was merely a flying heap of scrap with one crewman dead and another injured. Yet the TBF was destined to do to the Japanese seapower what the same manufacturer's F6F did to his airpower.

It is fortunate indeed that the US Navy decided to issue a specification for a new torpedo bomber in early 1940. Even as it was, the lumbering old TBD (Douglas Devastator), which had seemed so modern in 1935, was the only torpedo aircraft available until mid-1942, by which time the Japanese forces had swarmed over one-quarter of the globe. Back in 1940 there had not seemed any particular need for urgency, but Grumman Aircraft Engineering Corporation was noted for producing good aircraft quickly. Under chief engineer Bill Schwendler the design of the TBF got under way rapidly after the award of a contract on 8 April 1940, and the XTBF-1 flew on 1 August 1941.

Though the company had never built an offensive aircraft it created a wholly sound machine with a tough airframe, generous wing with the patented skewed hinges so that it folded alongside the fuselage, internal bay for torpedo or other ordnance, good low-speed qualities, plenty of fuel and even a powered dorsal turret. Production aircraft appeared in January 1942, and in March of that year the first of successive contracts was placed with Eastern Aircraft, a powerful group set up by General Motors to build Navy aircraft, which from November 1942 delivered a near-identical model known as the TBM. In early 1944 Grumman ceased making the TBF, after delivering 2,290, all subsequent Avengers being produced by Eastern.

It had been intended to standardize on the R-2600-10 engine in the TBF-2, but this was dropped and most Avengers were Eastern's TBM-3 model. This had the most powerful of the wartime R-2600 versions, strengthened wings for increased gross weights, and with reinforcement for carrying a centimetric radar scanner or rockets. Many TBM-3 versions had no dorsal turret, though in wartime most retained the original armament. Britain's Fleet Air Arm relied on the Avenger as its chief carrier-based torpedo aircraft (for it was dramatically better than the Barracuda and more survivable than the willing Swordfish) and operated 37 TBFs and 921 TBMs, originally naming them Tarpon. The RNZAF received 63 TBMs. Avengers were used in all parts of the Pacific, south-east Asia and the India/Burma theatre, lack of Japanese ships eventually resulting in missions being almost exclusively against land targets with bombs and rockets. Interception by Japanese fighters became increasingly rare, but on one famous occasion the ace Saburo Sakai mis-identified a TBF, closed on it and was nearly killed by fire from the turret.

Among many special-purpose wartime versions the most important were the TBF-1CP for photo-reconnaissance (with a Trimetrogon triple camera fan for simultaneous vertical and oblique coverage), the -1D with special radar, the -1E with APS-6/ASV radar, the all-weather -1J and the searchlight-equipped -1L, most of which had Eastern TBM equivalents. At the end of the war turrets were progressively removed in more extensive conversions, one important type being the TBM-3R COD (Carrier On-board Delivery) transport, with a cargo hold and seven seats, and the remarkable harbingers of the future, the TBM-3E and -3W.

The -3E was the first specialized ASW (anti-submarine warfare) aircraft to carry modern sensors and operate from a carrier. The -3W was the first aircraft to carry an early-warning radar in service; with the PB-1W (B-17) it tested and then in 1945 became operational with the APS-20 radar derived from 'Project Cadillac', whose belly radome looked grotesquely large. Post-war, later radar-equipped W-2 models were paired with the S and S-2 in hunter-killer teams serving in the ASW role.

COUNTRY OF ORIGIN USA.

CREW Usually 3.

TOTAL PRODUCED 9,836.

DIMENSIONS Wingspan 16·51m (54ft 2in); length 12·192m (40ft 0in); wing area 45·52m² (490ft²).

WEIGHTS Empty, **TBF-1**: 4572kg (10,080lb), **TBM-3**: 4918kg (10,842lb); maximum loaded, **TBF-1**: 7214kg (15,905lb), **TBM-3**: 8278kg (18,250lb).

ENGINE Wright R-2600 14-cylinder double-row Cyclone; **-1**: 1,700hp R-2600-8; **-3**: 1,900hp R-2600-20.

MAXIMUM SPEED Both versions: 443km/h (275mph).

SERVICE CEILING **-1**: 6828m (22,400ft); **-3**: 9174m (30,100ft).

RANGE On internal fuel, both: about 1770km (1,100 miles).

MILITARY LOAD **-1**: One fixed forward-firing 7·62mm (0·30in) (**-1C**: two 12·7mm/0·5in), one 12·7mm (0·5in) in turret and one 7·62mm (0·30in) ventral; bomb/torpedo load of 726kg (1,600lb); **-3**: two forward-firing 12·7mm (0·5in), 12·7mm (0·5in) in turret, 7·62mm (0·30in) or 12·7mm (0·5in) ventral; bomb/torpedo load of 907kg (2,000lb).

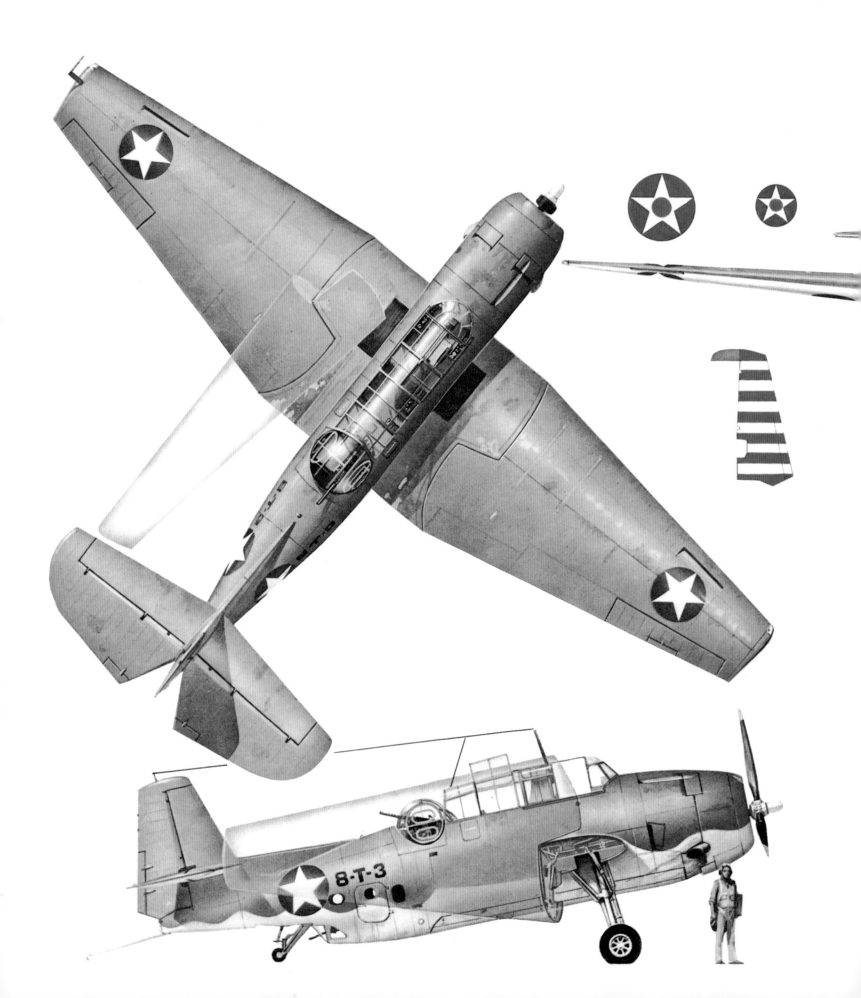

Grumman Avenger TBF-1

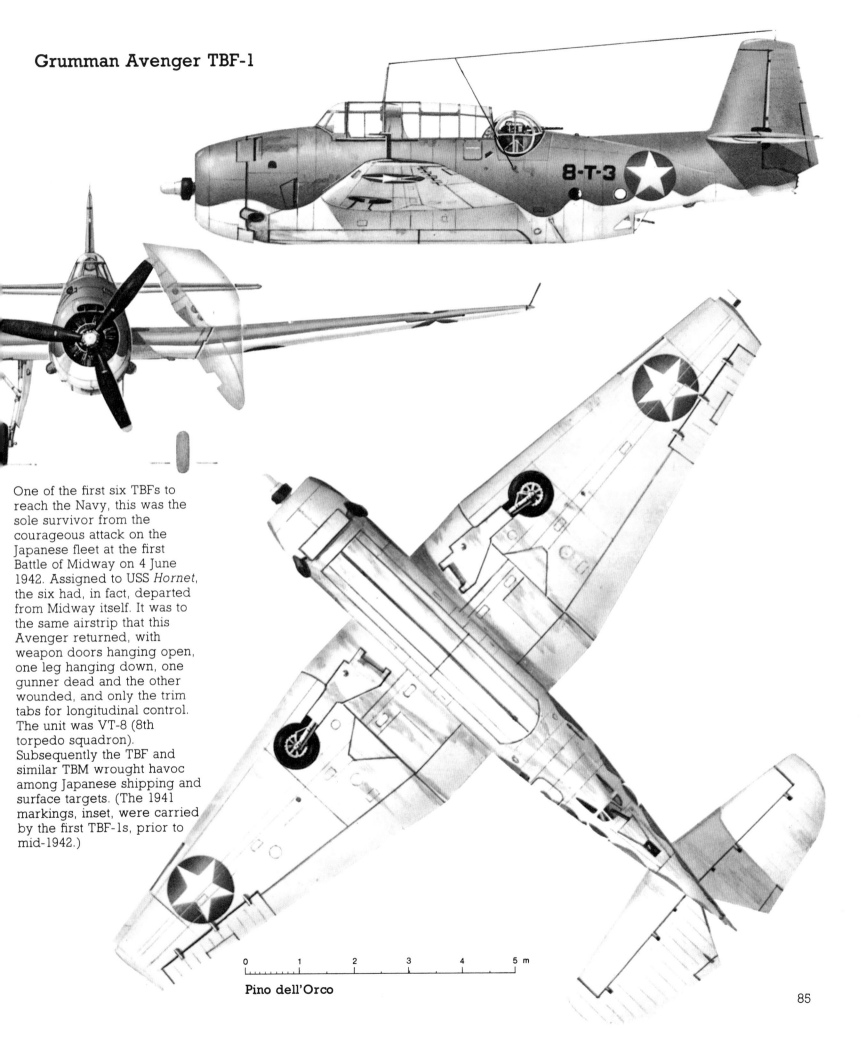

One of the first six TBFs to reach the Navy, this was the sole survivor from the courageous attack on the Japanese fleet at the first Battle of Midway on 4 June 1942. Assigned to USS *Hornet*, the six had, in fact, departed from Midway itself. It was to the same airstrip that this Avenger returned, with weapon doors hanging open, one leg hanging down, one gunner dead and the other wounded, and only the trim tabs for longitudinal control. The unit was VT-8 (8th torpedo squadron). Subsequently the TBF and similar TBM wrought havoc among Japanese shipping and surface targets. (The 1941 markings, inset, were carried by the first TBF-1s, prior to mid-1942.)

8-T-3

0   1   2   3   4   5 m

Pino dell'Orco

85

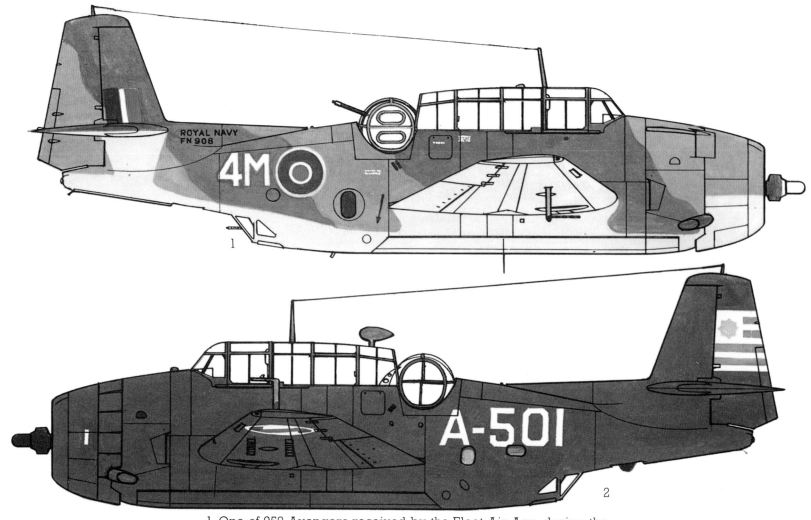

1 One of 958 Avengers received by the Fleet Air Arm during the war, this Mk I was one of the early deliveries initially known as the Tarpon. It was a Grumman-built TBF-1B, fitted with ASV radar but otherwise similar to the original production model.

2 This Avenger was supplied in 1946 to the Servicio Aeronautica de la Marina of Uruguay, where the type remained in service until at least 1956. A TBM-1C, with 12·7mm (0·5in) wing guns and D/F loop, it was assigned to the Escuela de Especialización Aeronaval on the Plate estuary.

3 A much more extensive post-war modification resulted in the anti-submarine search/attack TBM-3E as used by the Royal Canadian Navy. Rebuilt by Fairey Aviation of Canada, it had a large two-man tactical compartment with raised roof, MAD (magnetic-anomaly detection) gear and considerably modified equipment.

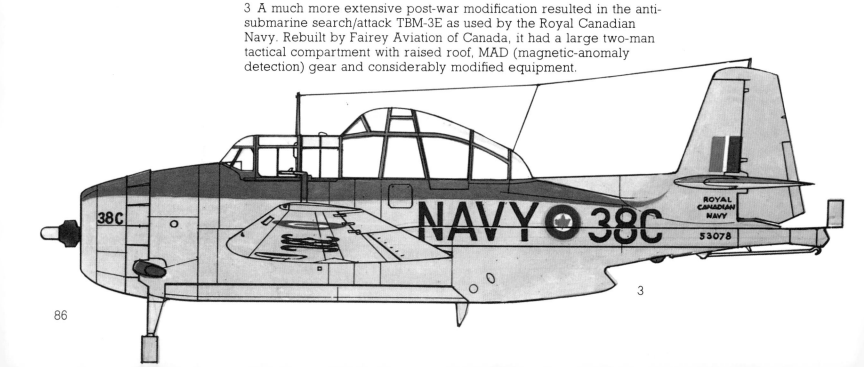

Grumman TBF
and TBM Avenger

RB

242   ═★═ NAVY

RB 242

h-2342

342   飛上自衛隊

4 The TBM-3R was a post-war rebuild for the COD (Carrier On-board Delivery) transport mission, with a rear cabin for either seven passengers or more than 680kg (1,500lb) of urgent cargo. This example was assigned to the Logistic Air Fleet Wing, Atlantic-Continental, serving CVA-43 *Coral Sea*.

5 From 1954 the Japanese maritime self-defence force (Kaijo Jeitai) used two special sub-types of the TBM-3S and 3S-2 for anti-submarine warfare, paired with the radar-equipped -3W-2. This -3S operated with the Sasebo district from Kanoya.

6 Typical of the post-war radar-equipped rebuilds, this TBM-3W-2 served aboard the light carrier *Karel Doorman* of the Royal Netherlands Navy. None of the post-war models retained wartime defensive armament, and the 3W carried nothing but APS-20 radar.

117   **16** ● **11**

0   1   2   3 m

Pino dell'Orco

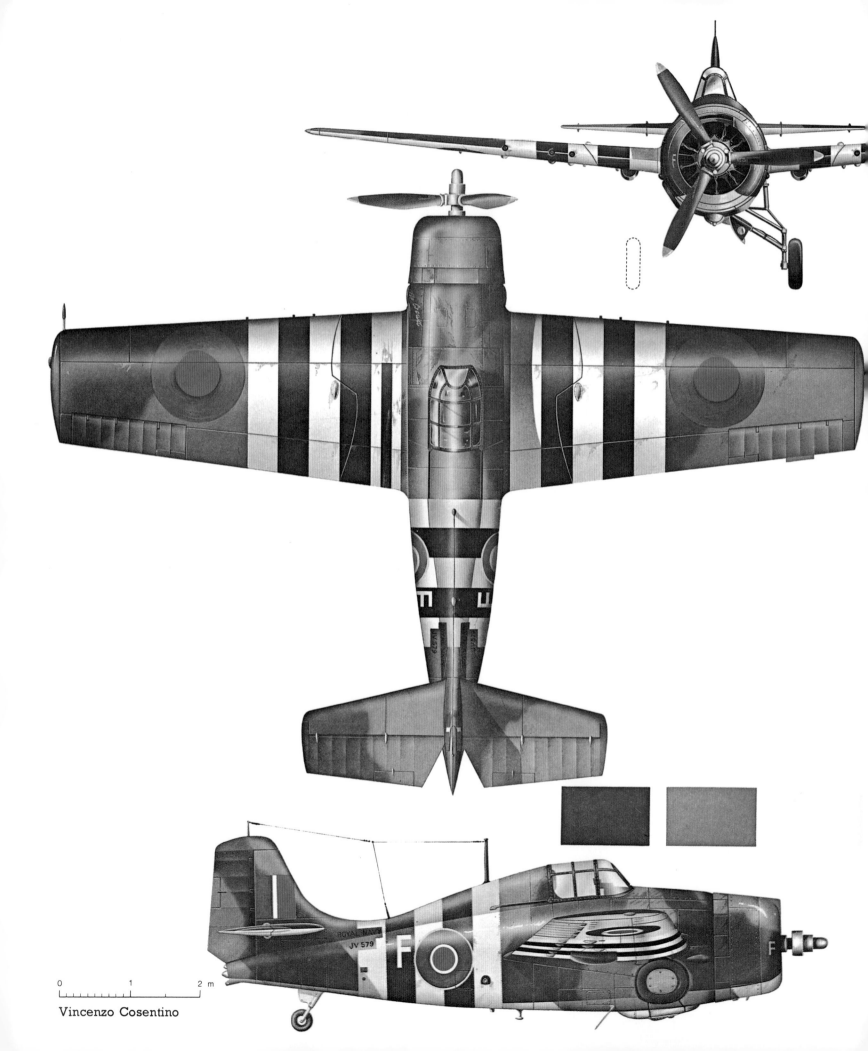

Vincenzo Cosentino

Grumman Wildcat V

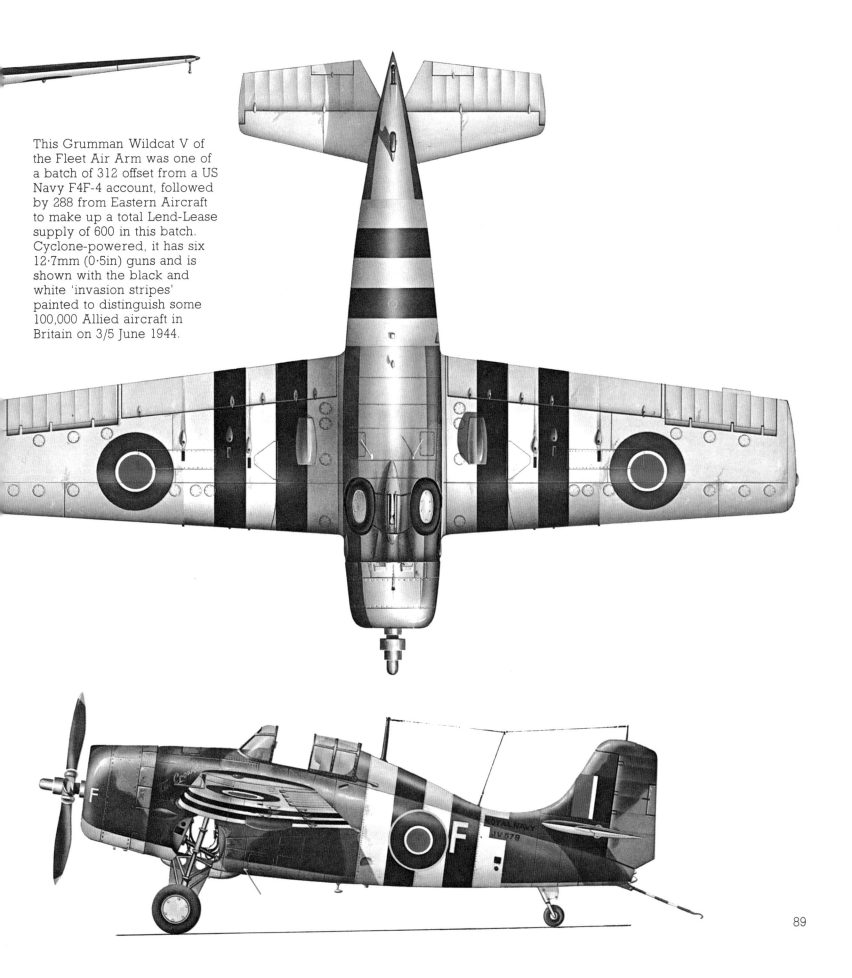

This Grumman Wildcat V of the Fleet Air Arm was one of a batch of 312 offset from a US Navy F4F-4 account, followed by 288 from Eastern Aircraft to make up a total Lend-Lease supply of 600 in this batch. Cyclone-powered, it has six 12·7mm (0·5in) guns and is shown with the black and white 'invasion stripes' painted to distinguish some 100,000 Allied aircraft in Britain on 3/5 June 1944.

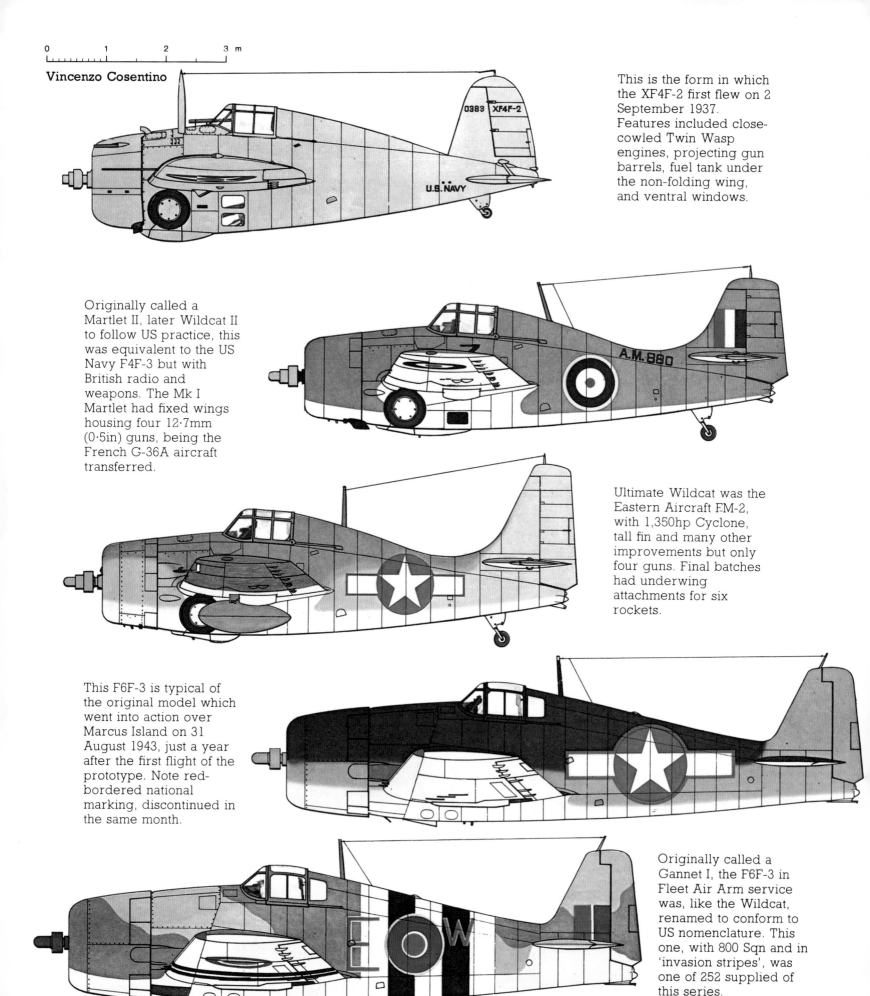

Vincenzo Cosentino

This is the form in which the XF4F-2 first flew on 2 September 1937. Features included close-cowled Twin Wasp engines, projecting gun barrels, fuel tank under the non-folding wing, and ventral windows.

Originally called a Martlet II, later Wildcat II to follow US practice, this was equivalent to the US Navy F4F-3 but with British radio and weapons. The Mk I Martlet had fixed wings housing four 12·7mm (0·5in) guns, being the French G-36A aircraft transferred.

Ultimate Wildcat was the Eastern Aircraft FM-2, with 1,350hp Cyclone, tall fin and many other improvements but only four guns. Final batches had underwing attachments for six rockets.

This F6F-3 is typical of the original model which went into action over Marcus Island on 31 August 1943, just a year after the first flight of the prototype. Note red-bordered national marking, discontinued in the same month.

Originally called a Gannet I, the F6F-3 in Fleet Air Arm service was, like the Wildcat, renamed to conform to US nomenclature. This one, with 800 Sqn and in 'invasion stripes', was one of 252 supplied of this series.

Grumman F4F, F6F and F8F

By late 1944 the US Navy had over 7,000 combat-ready Hellcats looking like this, the F6F-5 being almost indistinguishable from this -3 model. Trials were flown with a torpedo and also with the centreline tank plus two 454kg (1,000lb) bombs.

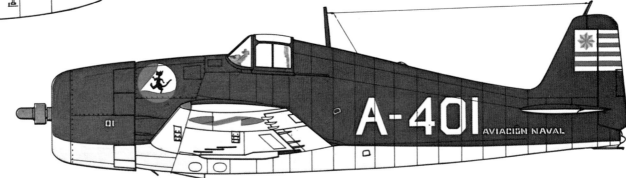

Probably the last user of the Hellcat was the Uruguayan Servicio Aeronautica de la Marina, which kept its last F6F-5s in front-line service until 1961. The Dash-5 had spring-tab ailerons, more armour, improved cowling and, like some -3s, no windows behind the canopy.

This Bearcat was one of a batch with modified fuel system, designated F8F-1D, supplied in 1948–50 to the French Armée de l'Air and used in Indo-China. This example served there with GC II/21 (previously GC II/9) *Auvergne* from October 1953 until March 1955.

One of the 129 F8F-1 Bearcats supplied to the Thai Air Force in 1954 (100 Dash-1Ds, the rest being 1Bs with original fuel system). This one served with the 2nd Fighter/Bomber Wing.

After the departure of the French most of the Armée de l'Air F8F-1Ds eventually passed to the air force of South Vietnam, appearing in VNAF markings of this time during the American attempt to preserve that state's independence. This Bearcat served with VNAF No 514 Sqn.

Grumman F4F, F6F and F8F

Though it was only formed in 1930 the Grumman company went straight into the challenging business of carrier-based fighters for the US Navy, and soon built an impressive reputation. By 1935 it was ready to tackle a stressed-skin monoplane, then a bold concept for an aircraft of this category. The original plan had been to build another biplane, but a Brewster monoplane (which became the F2A) showed its superiority. In consequence Grumman planned a superior monoplane, which flew as the XF4F-2 in September 1937. After much further development this led to the XF4F-3, the Grumman G-36, flown on 12 February 1939. From this stemmed the most important Allied naval fighter of the first half of World War 2.

Features of the F4F included a rotund but finely streamlined fuselage, unusual mid-wing of severely rectangular shape and generous area, skewed hinges to fold the wings alongside the fuselage, upper surface outwards, and typical Grumman landing gears retracting upwards into the fuselage. Though further effort was needed to perfect the tail and other details, the basic F4F was a winner. With a two-stage supercharger it was faster than the land-based Hawk 75, and the big wing gave it exceptional manoeuvrability.

France's Aéronavale placed the first order, for 100 G-36As, in March 1939. The company was already tooling for production, and in August the US Navy followed with an order for 54 F4F-3s. Delivery of both versions began in February 1940, but the entire French order was diverted to the British Fleet Air Arm, which named the aircraft Martlet I. All-French instruments and equipment were fitted to the first batch, but FAA units began to receive the Martlet in July 1940, ahead of the US Navy, and they shot down a Ju 88 on Christmas Day, 1940. Massive British orders were augmented by Lend-Lease supplies, while the US Navy and Marine Corps orders also multiplied. At Pearl Harbor the F4F-3 and -3A were the only Navy and Marine fighters, and five of them at Wake Island scored many victories before going down to sheer weight of numbers.

Subsequently no fewer than 7,816 F4Fs of several versions were built, all eventually receiving the US name of Wildcat. Except for the first 1,549 all were FM-1 or -2 versions built by Eastern Aircraft, which also built the TBM. Most F4F versions had the 1,200hp Twin Wasp engine but the mass-produced FM-2 had the 1,350hp Cyclone and taller fin. These nimble machines were aboard almost all the escort carriers in 1944-5.

Sudden need for an even better naval fighter after Pearl Harbor was met by the bigger and much more powerful F6F, which had been ordered in June 1941. First flown with R-2600 engine on 26 June 1942, the XF6F-1 was promptly re-engined with the powerplant that became standard, flying as the XF6F-3 on 30 July. So fast and successful was development that the first production F6F-3 flew on 4 October 1942, and ten had left the line in a new factory at Bethpage. Deliveries began to USS *Essex* in early 1943, a mere 18 months after the first contract!

Like its ancestor the F6F had a squarish wing of generous area, but this time it was almost low-mounted and the main gears folded backwards hydraulically to lie in the centre wing, the wheels rotating on the legs. To a remarkable degree the F6F, aptly named Hellcat, was so right that the only modifications were small. Apart from the -3 the only significant model was the -5, with improved cowling and provision for heavy ordnance loads. Though not as fast as the F4U Corsair which soon joined it in battle, the tough and manoeuvrable F6F at last wrested command of the air from the Japanese. F6Fs were credited with 4,947 of the total 6,477 victories by all US Navy carrier-based units, to which can be added 209 by shore-based aircraft and several hundred by the 1,182 Hellcats of the British Fleet Air Arm.

In August 1944 Grumman flew the first of the marvellously nimble F8F Bearcat family. Squadrons just failed to see action in World War 2, but the F8F was important post-war.

COUNTRY OF ORIGIN USA.

CREW 1.

TOTAL PRODUCED 12,275 (note, all data refer to F6F Hellcat).

DIMENSIONS Wingspan 13·06m (42ft 10in); length 10·24m (33ft 7in); wing area 31·03m² (334ft²).

WEIGHTS Empty, **-3**: 4101kg (9,042lb), **-5**: 4190kg (9,238lb); maximum loaded, **-3**: 6000kg (13,228lb), **-5**: 6991kg (15,413lb).

ENGINE Pratt & Whitney R-2800 Double Wasp 18-cylinder radial; **early -3**: 2,000hp R-2800-10, **late -3 and all -5**: R-2800-10W with water-injection rating of 2,200hp.

MAXIMUM SPEED Both versions, without tank or bombs: 612km/h (380mph).

SERVICE CEILING Both versions: 11430m (37,500ft).

RANGE **-3** without drop tank: 1755km (1,090 miles), **-5**: 1521km (945 miles).

MILITARY LOAD Normal armament six 12·7mm (0·5in) Browning machine guns; late F6F-5 often had two inboard guns replaced by 20mm cannon. **F6F-5**: underwing racks for six 127mm (5in) rockets, plus centre-section pylons for two 454kg (1,000lb) bombs or other stores.

Hawker Hurricane

Hawker Aircraft, at Kingston near London, were heirs to the Sopwith Aviation Company, builders of some of the greatest fighting scouts of World War 1. Under Sydney Camm, chief engineer and then technical director, it created a succession of fine military biplanes between the wars. Then, in 1935, the first Hawker monoplane flew. Though soon outmoded technically, it was tough, serviceable, highly manoeuvrable and easy to repair, and it stayed in production almost to the end of World War 2. In all theatres of that conflict it did sterling service, but its greatest achievement was in the Battle of Britain.

Like most of the British aircraft industry, Hawker were reluctant to move into the new era of stressed-skin construction. The period 1932–4 was marked by several other revolutions in thought, concerning steam-cooled engines, armament (since 1918 unchanged at two Vickers machine guns) and a dozen other factors. After looking at a so-called Fury Monoplane, which would have been outclassed by 1939, Camm planned the new fighter around a new Rolls-Royce engine using conventional cooling, and made it generous in size to fit small grass fields and turn almost as tightly as the preceding generation of biplanes. He used traditional steel tube, aluminium stringers and ribs, wood details and, over most of the aircraft, fabric skin. But in the thick outer wings he put the requested new armament of eight machine guns, and added flaps, retractable landing gear and a sliding canopy. The prototype flew on 6 November 1935, and thanks to the company's bold decision to tool-up to make 1,000, before any were ordered, hundreds were available at the outbreak of war.

Though slower than the Bf 109E, and disgracefully handicapped by its wooden fixed-pitch propeller, the Mk I gave a good account of itself in the Battle for France. By August 1940 Hurricanes equipped 32 RAF squadrons (compared with 18½ of Spitfires), and newer deliveries had stressed-skin wings and constant-speed propellers. It was by far the most important destroyer of German bombers, and even tackled the 109 on fairly level terms. Many operated by night and, as output swelled from Hawker, Gloster and Canada, the more powerful Mk II entered production with more weapons including bombs and cannon.

From 1941 the Hurricane served mainly in the overseas areas, including the Soviet Union. It was the natural choice for conversion into a carrier-based fighter, and was also the type chosen for the CAM (catapult-armed merchantman) ships which boosted the morale of the harassed convoys and also shot down five Condors. In North Africa the introduction of a mark with two 40mm guns showed that countries other than the Soviet Union were building aircraft to pierce the heaviest tanks.

Experiments took place for stretching the range, including overload take-offs with an extra (biplane) upper wing, which could be released in flight, and towing behind RAF bombers. In the Soviet Union, where RAF No 151 Wing had fought as a unit in 1941–2, numerous Hurricanes operated on fixed skis in winter, while a different ski was common on Canadian versions. Many hundreds of various marks served with Allied air forces and also with Finland, Ireland, Iraq, Turkey and Romania.

Though, surprisingly, a folding-wing Sea Hurricane was never built, the Fleet Air Arm used Sea Hurricanes alongside the Wildcat as leading fighters until late 1943. By this time all British production was of the Mk IV variety, with 'universal' wings similar in principle to those introduced to the Spitfire, able to be equipped with any of the available range of guns, drop tanks, bombs or rockets. Since 1941 the emphasis had been on low-altitude multi-role operations, and unlike the Spitfire the Hurricane used Merlins from both British and American sources tailored to high power at sea level. Considerable numbers of Hurricanes pioneered night fighting, at first without and, from mid-1941, with airborne radar. It was an almost ideal aircraft for this purpose, but official opinion was against single-seaters in this role.

COUNTRY OF ORIGIN Great Britain.

CREW 1.

TOTAL PRODUCED 14,533, of which 1,451 were built by CanCar (plus equivalent of 1,000 as spares, not included in total) and 2 by Avions Fairey, Belgium.

DIMENSIONS Wingspan 12·192m (40ft 0in); length, **Mk I**: 9·55m (31ft 5in), later: 9·81m (32ft 2½in); wing area 23·97m² (257·5ft²).

WEIGHTS Empty, I: 2260kg (4,982lb), IIC: 2566kg (5,657lb); maximum loaded, I: 3397kg (7,490lb), IIC: 3742kg (8,250lb), IV: 3856kg (8,500lb).

ENGINE Rolls-Royce Merlin vee-12 liquid-cooled; I: Merlin III, 1,030hp; II: Merlin XX, 1,280hp; IV: Merlin 24 or 27, 1,620hp; Canadian **MK X, XI, XII**: Packard V-1650-1, 1,300hp (Merlin 28, 29).

MAXIMUM SPEED I: 519km/h (322mph), later: typically 531km/h (330mph) except Sea Hurricane rather less and IID only 460km/h (286mph).

SERVICE CEILING All versions, about 10365m (34,000ft).

RANGE I: 813km (505 miles), IIC: without drop tanks 740km (460 miles).

MILITARY LOAD I: Eight 7·7mm (0·303in) Browning machine guns, each with 333 rounds; **Belgian I**: four 12·7mm (0·5in) FN-Browning; IIA: eight 7·7mm (0·303in) and two 227kg (500lb) bombs or drop tanks; IIB: 12 7·7mm (0·303in) and bombs; IIC: four 20mm Hispano and bombs; IID: two 40mm Vickers S, plus two 7·7mm (0·303in) to assist aiming; IV: all Mk II options plus eight 27kg (60lb) rockets.

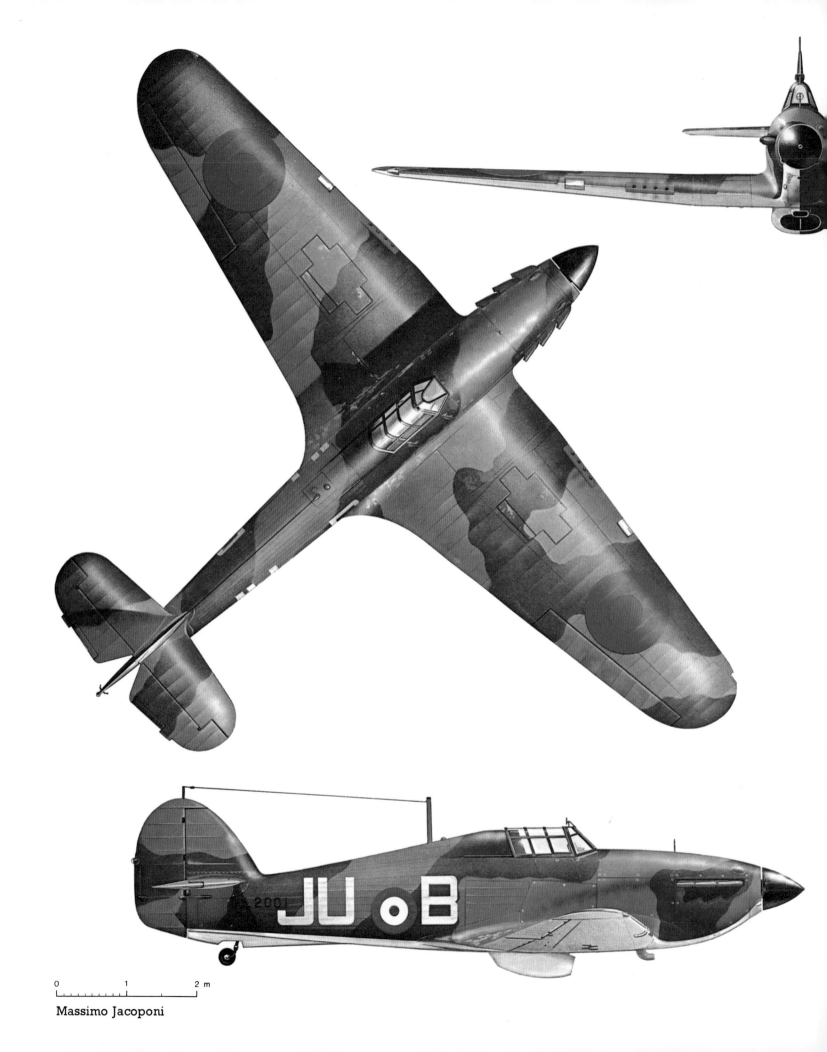

Massimo Jacoponi

Hawker Hurricane I

This Hurricane I is one of the original production batch of 600 which were already in production at Kingston before any contract was placed! It was delivered in 1938 to No 111 Sqn at Northolt, and is illustrated after being fitted with a three-blade variable-pitch propeller (first seen on L1980) and painted in the strange half-black half-white underside of 1939. The gun ports were normally covered with a strip of fabric, attached by red dope, through which the guns fired to leave large holes as seen here. This aircraft has a ring and bead sight.

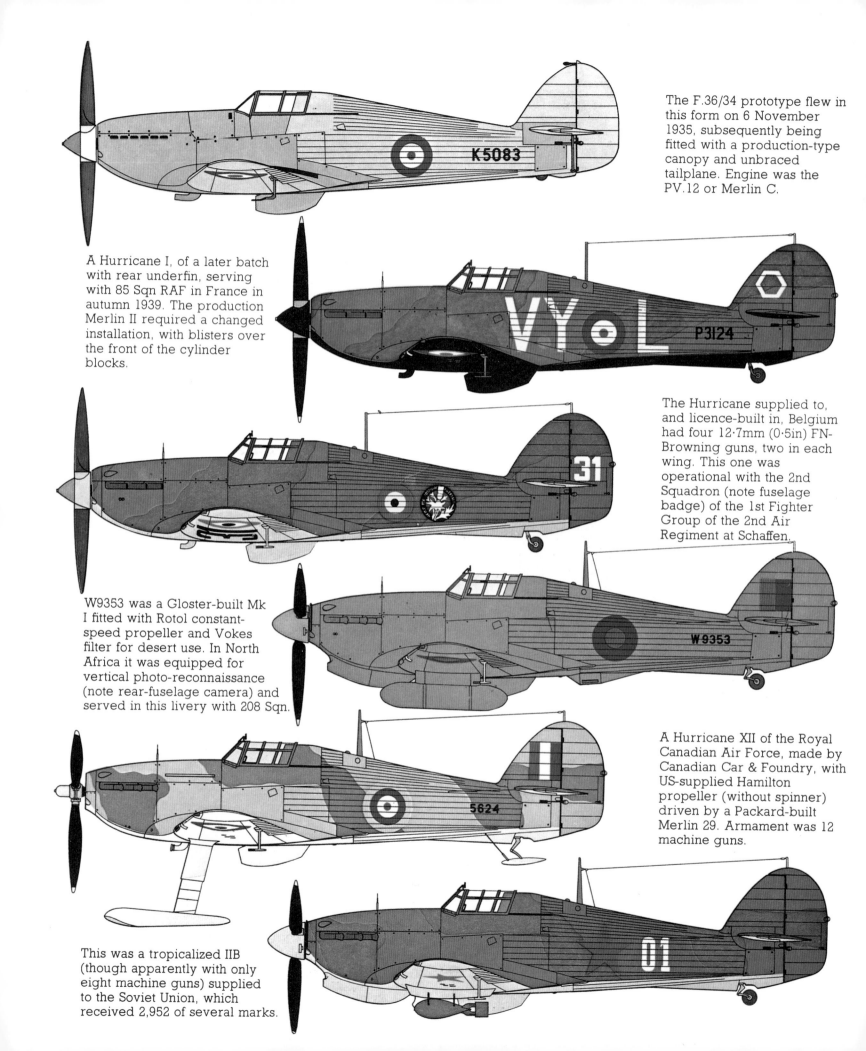

The F.36/34 prototype flew in this form on 6 November 1935, subsequently being fitted with a production-type canopy and unbraced tailplane. Engine was the PV.12 or Merlin C.

A Hurricane I, of a later batch with rear underfin, serving with 85 Sqn RAF in France in autumn 1939. The production Merlin II required a changed installation, with blisters over the front of the cylinder blocks.

The Hurricane supplied to, and licence-built in, Belgium had four 12·7mm (0·5in) FN-Browning guns, two in each wing. This one was operational with the 2nd Squadron (note fuselage badge) of the 1st Fighter Group of the 2nd Air Regiment at Schaffen.

W9353 was a Gloster-built Mk I fitted with Rotol constant-speed propeller and Vokes filter for desert use. In North Africa it was equipped for vertical photo-reconnaissance (note rear-fuselage camera) and served in this livery with 208 Sqn.

A Hurricane XII of the Royal Canadian Air Force, made by Canadian Car & Foundry, with US-supplied Hamilton propeller (without spinner) driven by a Packard-built Merlin 29. Armament was 12 machine guns.

This was a tropicalized IIB (though apparently with only eight machine guns) supplied to the Soviet Union, which received 2,952 of several marks.

Hawker Hurricane

The Royal Navy livery was one of the 80-odd modifications needed to turn a Hurricane I, in this case built by Gloster, into a Sea Hurricane I, used aboard escort carriers despite the non-folding wings from early 1942. Propeller was a Rotol.

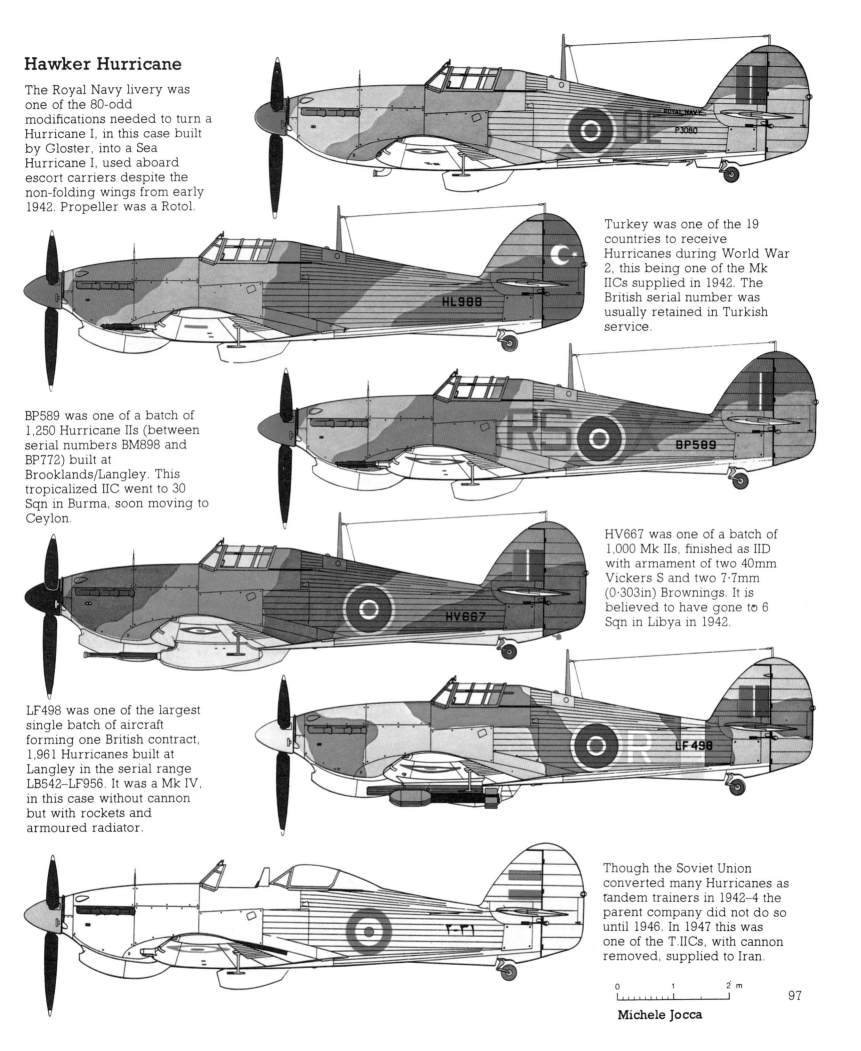

Turkey was one of the 19 countries to receive Hurricanes during World War 2, this being one of the Mk IICs supplied in 1942. The British serial number was usually retained in Turkish service.

BP589 was one of a batch of 1,250 Hurricane IIs (between serial numbers BM898 and BP772) built at Brooklands/Langley. This tropicalized IIC went to 30 Sqn in Burma, soon moving to Ceylon.

HV667 was one of a batch of 1,000 Mk IIs, finished as IID with armament of two 40mm Vickers S and two 7·7mm (0·303in) Brownings. It is believed to have gone to 6 Sqn in Libya in 1942.

LF498 was one of the largest single batch of aircraft forming one British contract, 1,961 Hurricanes built at Langley in the serial range LB542–LF956. It was a Mk IV, in this case without cannon but with rockets and armoured radiator.

Though the Soviet Union converted many Hurricanes as tandem trainers in 1942–4 the parent company did not do so until 1946. In 1947 this was one of the T.IICs, with cannon removed, supplied to Iran.

0   1   2 m

Michele Jocca

97

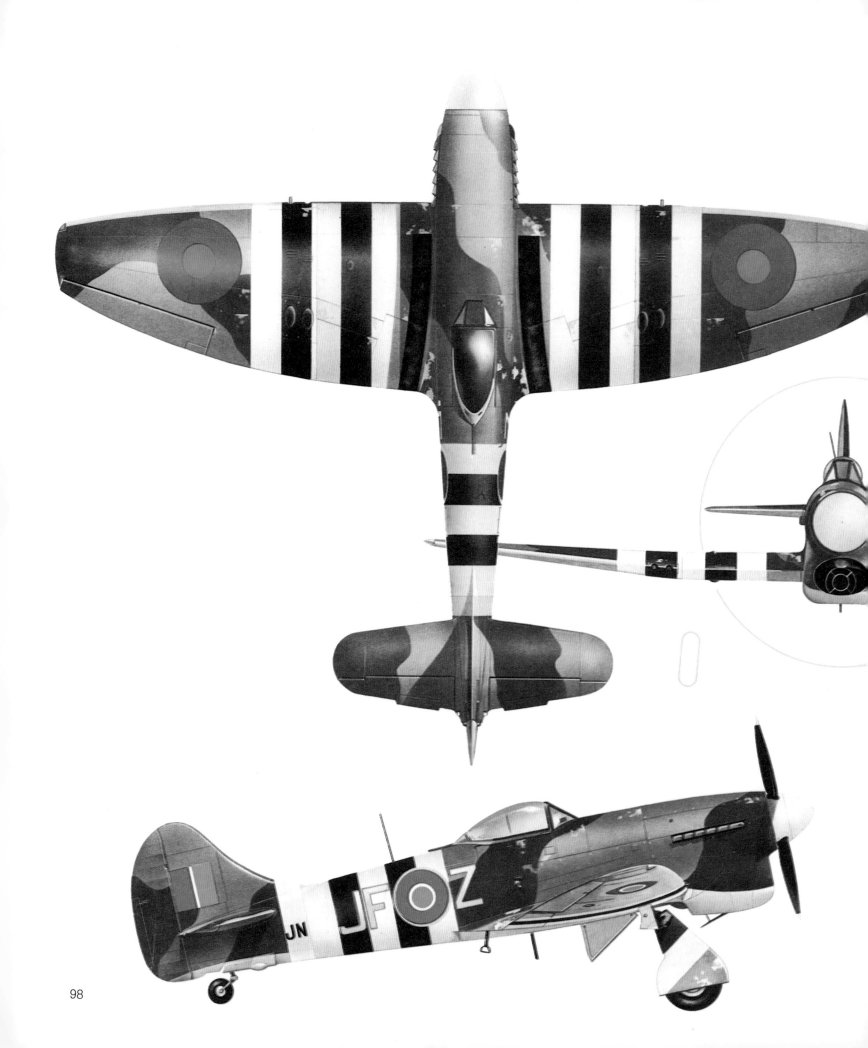

Hawker Tempest V

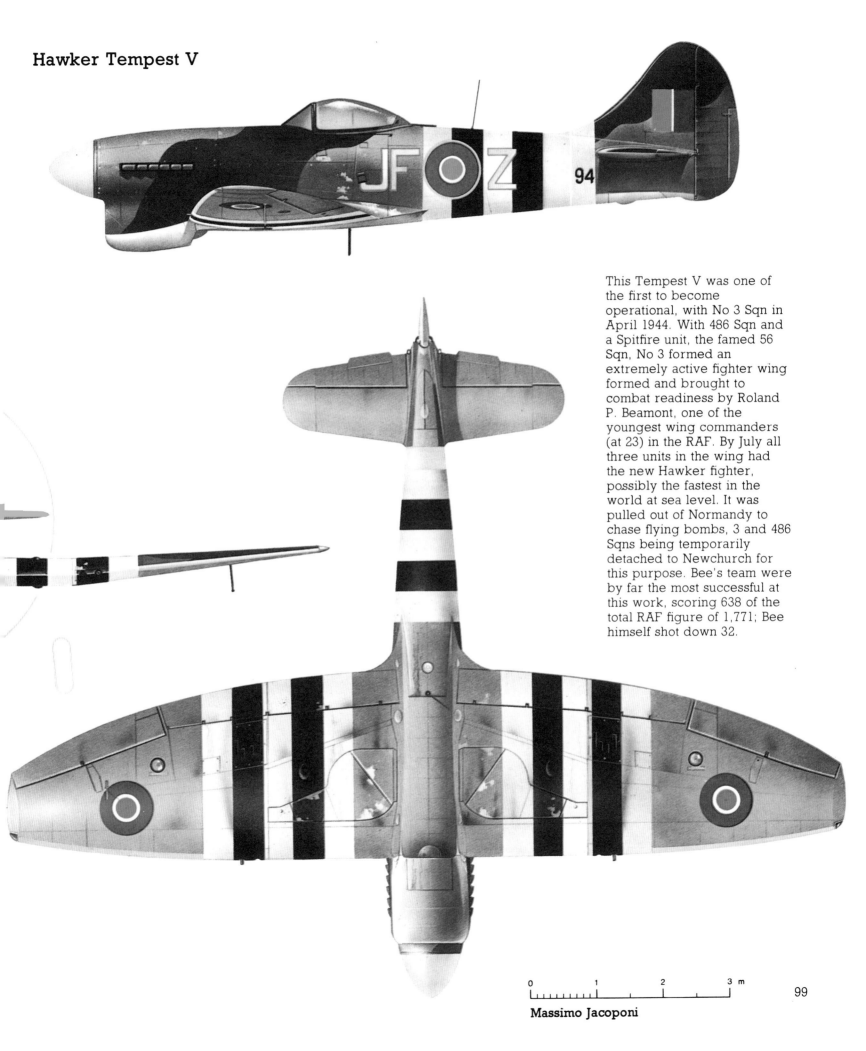

This Tempest V was one of the first to become operational, with No 3 Sqn in April 1944. With 486 Sqn and a Spitfire unit, the famed 56 Sqn, No 3 formed an extremely active fighter wing formed and brought to combat readiness by Roland P. Beamont, one of the youngest wing commanders (at 23) in the RAF. By July all three units in the wing had the new Hawker fighter, possibly the fastest in the world at sea level. It was pulled out of Normandy to chase flying bombs, 3 and 486 Sqns being temporarily detached to Newchurch for this purpose. Bee's team were by far the most successful at this work, scoring 638 of the total RAF figure of 1,771; Bee himself shot down 32.

0   1   2   3 m

Massimo Jacoponi

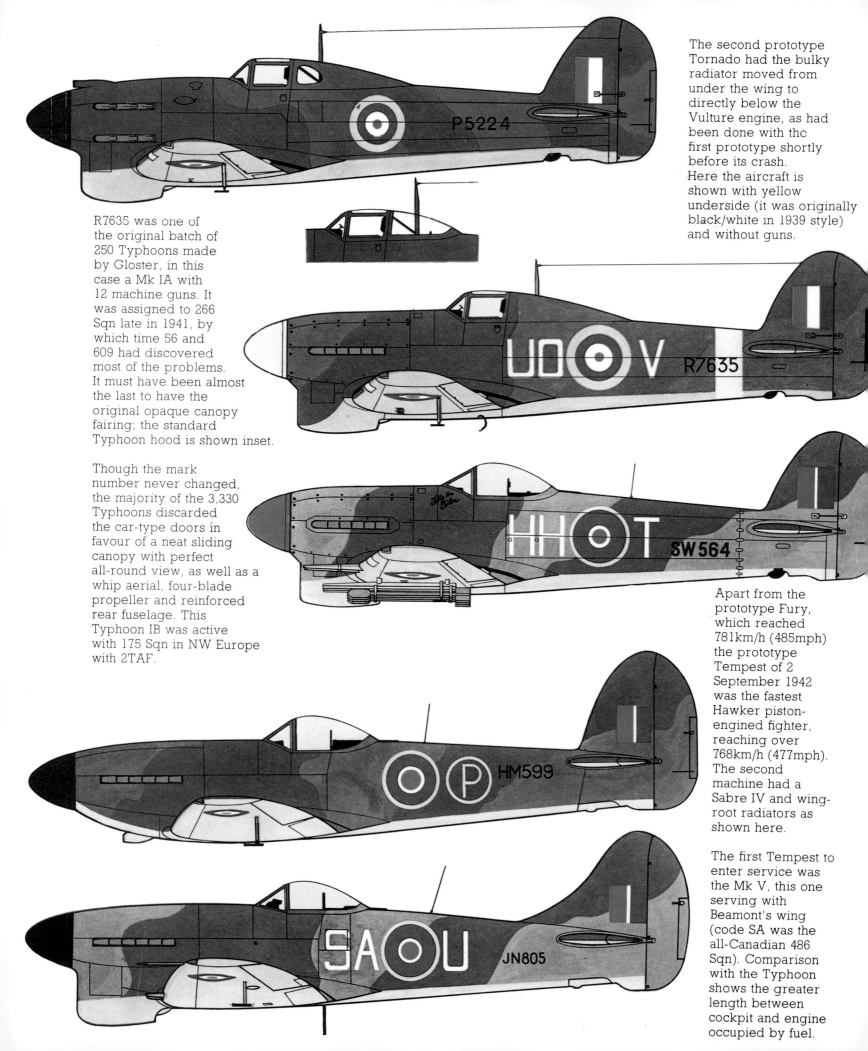

The second prototype Tornado had the bulky radiator moved from under the wing to directly below the Vulture engine, as had been done with the first prototype shortly before its crash. Here the aircraft is shown with yellow underside (it was originally black/white in 1939 style) and without guns.

R7635 was one of the original batch of 250 Typhoons made by Gloster, in this case a Mk IA with 12 machine guns. It was assigned to 266 Sqn late in 1941, by which time 56 and 609 had discovered most of the problems. It must have been almost the last to have the original opaque canopy fairing; the standard Typhoon hood is shown inset.

Though the mark number never changed, the majority of the 3,330 Typhoons discarded the car-type doors in favour of a neat sliding canopy with perfect all-round view, as well as a whip aerial, four-blade propeller and reinforced rear fuselage. This Typhoon IB was active with 175 Sqn in NW Europe with 2TAF.

Apart from the prototype Fury, which reached 781km/h (485mph) the prototype Tempest of 2 September 1942 was the fastest Hawker piston-engined fighter, reaching over 768km/h (477mph). The second machine had a Sabre IV and wing-root radiators as shown here.

The first Tempest to enter service was the Mk V, this one serving with Beamont's wing (code SA was the all-Canadian 486 Sqn). Comparison with the Typhoon shows the greater length between cockpit and engine occupied by fuel.

Hawker Typhoon and Tempest

After the war the Tempest VI remained briefly in service, in this case with 8 Sqn at Aden Khormaksar. By 1947 most Sabre-Tempests were relegated to target-towing.

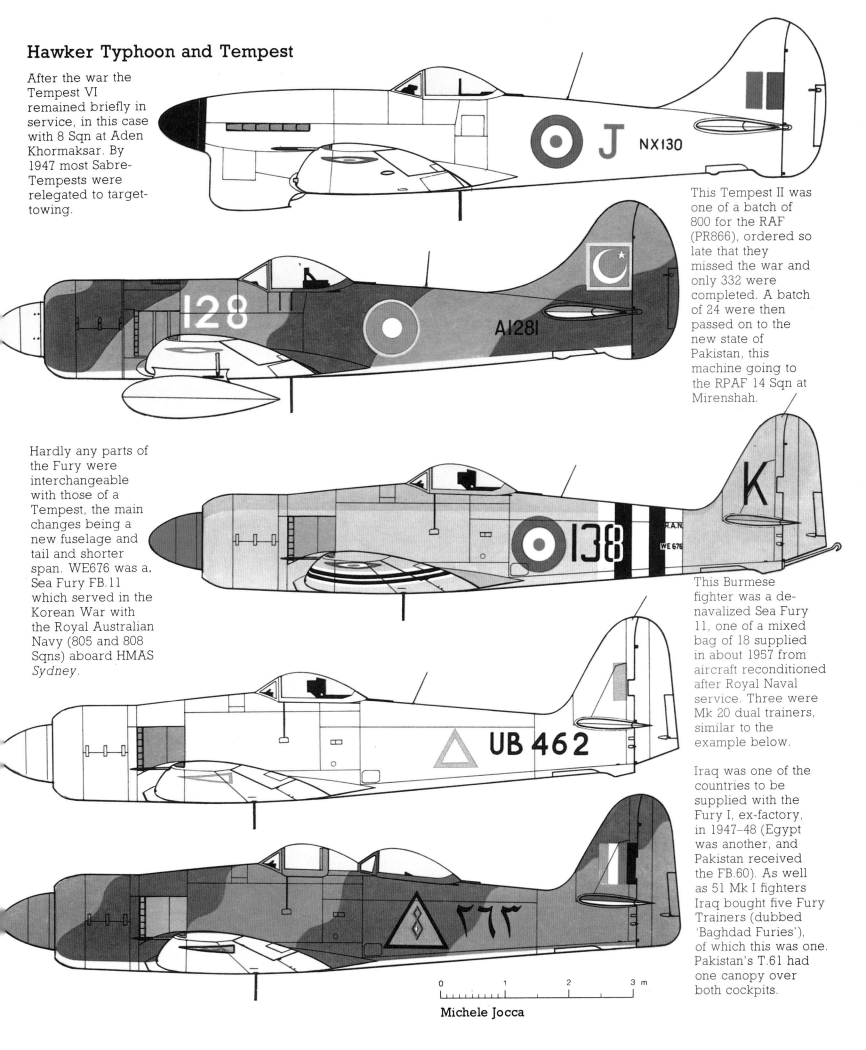

This Tempest II was one of a batch of 800 for the RAF (PR866), ordered so late that they missed the war and only 332 were completed. A batch of 24 were then passed on to the new state of Pakistan, this machine going to the RPAF 14 Sqn at Mirenshah.

Hardly any parts of the Fury were interchangeable with those of a Tempest, the main changes being a new fuselage and tail and shorter span. WE676 was a Sea Fury FB.11 which served in the Korean War with the Royal Australian Navy (805 and 808 Sqns) aboard HMAS *Sydney*.

This Burmese fighter was a de-navalized Sea Fury 11, one of a mixed bag of 18 supplied in about 1957 from aircraft reconditioned after Royal Naval service. Three were Mk 20 dual trainers, similar to the example below.

Iraq was one of the countries to be supplied with the Fury I, ex-factory, in 1947–48 (Egypt was another, and Pakistan received the FB.60). As well as 51 Mk I fighters Iraq bought five Fury Trainers (dubbed 'Baghdad Furies'), of which this was one. Pakistan's T.61 had one canopy over both cockpits.

Michele Jocca

Hawker Typhoon and Tempest

From 1936 the British government gradually accepted the need to rearm, and soon money was flowing at an unprecedented rate. As well as production, this benefited new development such as stressed-skin construction and a surprising number of radically new aero-engines in the 2,000hp class. Both advances were implicit in the Air Ministry F. 18/37 specification for a fighter to succeed the Hurricane. Camm's team at Hawker Aircraft submitted proposals in July 1937, and the company later went ahead with an 'N' fighter powered by the complex Sabre engine and an 'R' powered by the Rolls-Royce Vulture, the letters being the initials of the engine suppliers. This could have led to a formidable fighter by 1940–1, but instead the R aircraft, called Tornado, collapsed with failure of the engine programme and the N very nearly failed to make the grade.

The Tornado flew on 6 October 1939, with provision for 12 machine guns. The first N-type, named Typhoon, followed on 24 February 1940. Handling was bad, there were many other snags and before long the tail came off in flight. Gloster were assigned Typhoon production, but though a so-called production Mk IA flew in May 1941 the engine was unreliable, and there were still many shortcomings. Performance at height was a great disappointment, and the type was saved from cancellation only because it was able to catch low-level hit-and-run raiders. Even then the first units, 56 and 609 Sqns, suffered numerous failures of the engine and rear fuselage. Not until the end of 1942 did the Typhoon begin to mature as a reliable aircraft, and then its good qualities – seen from the start by W/Cdr R.P. Beamont of 609 – became generally apparent.

It was extremely fast, tough and capable, and its unplanned bomb load was doubled and then doubled again. By D-Day the RAF had 26 combat-ready squadrons, and they then made a tremendous contribution to victory in the West by ranging over the battlefront destroying everything that moved. The most famous exploit was the virtual elimination of German armour in the Falaise Gap and at Avranches, using rockets, but among many other operations was a pinpoint attack on an army HQ. Early models had a fixed canopy and radio mast, with car-type door on each side, but the last 90% had a neat bubble canopy giving all-round vision.

Such was the performance of the Typhoon, especially in a dive, that locally the air speed could reach the speed of sound. Little was then known of the phenomenon of compressibility, but Camm concluded it was the cause of the Typhoon's buffeting and nose-heaviness at high speeds, and judged the answer to be a thinner wing. In 1941 design commenced, and the first Typhoon II, by then renamed Tempest I, was ordered into production in August 1942. In fact, the first of the new breed to fly, on 2 September 1942, was the Tempest V; and this was also the first to enter service, in April 1944.

The thinner wing had a semi-elliptic shape rather like that of a Spitfire, and because of its reduced interior volume much of the fuel had to be moved to a new tank in the fuselage ahead of the cockpit. This in turn led to a dorsal fillet on the fin, and there were many other changes. Tempest Vs were available in numbers in time to chase flying bombs from mid-June 1944, and their quality in low-level work can be gauged from the fact that the Newchurch wing alone (commanded by Beamont) destroyed 638 of the RAF's total of 1,771 missiles shot down. After teething troubles with the propeller and engine the Tempest earned a superb reputation.

After delivering 100 Mk V Tempests the Hawker company continued with the Tempest V Series 2, with short-barrel cannon housed entirely within the wing. One aircraft had 40mm guns, and another a low-drag annular radiator. Two later marks, the VI, with more powerful Sabre VA engine, and the II, were just too late to see war service. The II, powered by the Bristol Centaurus radial, was by far the smoothest and quietest of the family, and became a standard post-war type along with the even faster Sea Furies.

COUNTRY OF ORIGIN Great Britain.

CREW 1.

TOTAL PRODUCED **Typhoon**: 3,330; **Tempest**: 1,401, including post-war.

DIMENSIONS Wingspan, **Typhoon**: 12·67m (41ft 7in), **Tempest**: 12·497m (41ft 0in); length, **Ty**: 9·73m (31ft 11in), **Te**: 10·26m (33ft 8in); wing area, **Ty**: 25·92m² (279ft²); **Te**: 28·057m² (302ft²).

WEIGHTS Empty, **Ty**: 4010kg (8,840lb), **Te V**: 4082kg (9,000lb); maximum loaded, **Ty**: 6341kg (13,980lb), **Te V**: 5897kg (13,000lb).

ENGINE All wartime versions, one Napier Sabre 24-cylinder H-form sleeve-valve; **Ty**: 2,180hp Sabre IIA; **Te V**: 2,200hp Sabre IIB.

MAXIMUM SPEED **Ty**: 664km/h (412mph), **Te V**: 700km/h (435mph).

SERVICE CEILING **Ty**: 10730m (35,200ft), **Te V**: 11125m (36,500ft).

RANGE With drop tanks, **Ty**: 1577km (980 miles), **Te V**: 2462km (1,530 miles).

MILITARY LOAD Four 20mm Hispano cannon; two 454kg (1,000lb) bombs, eight 27kg (60lb) rockets or other stores.

Heinkel He 111

Born at the time of Nazi ascendancy to power in 1934, the shapely Heinkel bomber, designed by Walter and Siegfried Günther – initially as a civil airliner – was the best bomber in the Spanish Civil War, and demolished countless ground targets in the first year of World War 2. Then it went on to drone harshly over the Balkans, North Africa, Soviet Union and Italy; but the awaited newer replacements never arrived. By 1944 the He 111, after hundreds of modifications in a fruitless search for ways to stave off obsolescence, was still soldiering on in the face of ever more numerous and deadly enemies.

From the start the He 111 had a modern stressed-skin structure, with very broad wings of elliptical shape matching the unusual tail. Alongside various civil examples the A-series bombers were built with three manually aimed machine guns and a bomb-load of 1000kg (2,205lb) in eight vertical cells. Most were underpowered, but the B and D series showed far better performance with the new Daimler-Benz engine, and Heinkel constructed a new factory of breathtaking size at Oranienburg solely to make this bomber.

In 1937, when Heinkels over Spain were mistakenly convincing the Luftwaffe they could operate with little escort and with just the three light machine guns for defence, the F-model went into production with a new straight-edged wing. By 1939 this in turn had been succeeded by the P, with a totally glazed nose with offset gun cupola, ventral gondola instead of a retractable 'dustbin', and much heavier bomb load. This was joined just before the start of World War 2 by the H-series, with Jumo engines, destined to remain in production until manufacture of all aircraft other than fighters was abandoned in the autumn of 1944.

During 1940 extra guns were added at the beam windows, and sometimes a 20mm cannon was mounted in the front of the gondola for attacking shipping. In 1940–1 the lumbering Heinkel sought refuge from British fighters by attacking at night, and dropped about 75% of the tonnage that fell on Britain in 'the Blitz'. By 1942, when most KG (bomb wings) were on the Eastern front, torpedo-carrying versions appeared and wrought havoc among some of the convoys sent to the Soviet Union. Variants appeared with radar, balloon-cable fenders, grenade launchers to deter hostile fighters, and a great variety of special radio and counter-measures equipment.

In 1942 the unique He 111Z appeared. Difficulty with using three Bf 110 fighters as tugs for the giant Me 321 glider led to this mating of two He 111s by a common centre wing with a fifth engine on the centreline. Z stood for Zwilling (twin), and there was a pilot in each nose, though that on the right had no throttle levers. This strange aircraft proved troublefree, but the various impressive gliderborne operations never happened.

By 1944, after three years of wholly unexpected increasing production, the H-20 entered production with the more powerful Jumo 213 engine, though this was unable to confer anything like the performance needed for operations over Western Europe. What the broad-winged Heinkel could do was lift heavy loads, including the monster 2·5-tonne (2·46 UK ton) bomb, largest in the Luftwaffe. The 111 was used in numerous trials programmes, and the H-12 entered service carrying two Hs 293 missiles, guided by radio command from the bomber, though the latter was too vulnerable to hang about for long keeping the weapon lined up with its target.

By mid-1944 most survivors were being used for transport and odd jobs, but one unfortunate wing, KG 3, was given the task of air-launching the Fi 103 flying bomb. This extremely tricky operation involved attaching a bomb under one wing root and creeping along just above the waves. Launch of bombs by night against London and Southampton began in July 1944 but casualties were very high, and after a few final flings against targets in northern England was abandoned. The Spanish air force continued to use Merlin-powered locally built versions until 1960.

COUNTRY OF ORIGIN Germany.

CREW Early: 4; **from P,H**: 5.

TOTAL PRODUCED Over 7,300, plus 10 He 111Z, about 60 He 111H-3 by SET, Romania, and 130 of various models by CASA, Spain.

DIMENSIONS Wingspan 22·6m (74ft 1¾in); length, early: 17·5m (57ft 5in), **P,H**: 16·4m (53ft 9½in); wing area, early: 87·6m² (942·9ft²), **P,H**: 86·5m² (931ft²).

WEIGHTS Empty, **E-3**: 6818kg (15,031lb), **P-4**: 7980kg (17,593lb), **H-16**: 8680kg (19,136lb); maximum loaded, **E-3**: 9600kg (21,164lb), **P-4**: 13480kg (29,718lb), **H-16**: 14000kg (30,865lb).

ENGINES Early: two BMW VI6Z vee-12, 660hp; **B**: 950hp DB600CG inverted vee-12; **E**: 1,010hp Junkers Jumo 211A-1 inverted-vee-12; **P**: 1,100hp DB601A-1; **H (most), Z**: 1,350hp Jumo 211F-1; **H-21, H-23**: 1,750hp Jumo 213E-1.

MAXIMUM SPEED All approximately 415km/h (258mph) except heavily loaded P about 322km/h (200mph).

SERVICE CEILING **E**: about 7000m (22,970ft), **P**: 4500m (14,765ft), **H**: typically 6700m (21,980ft).

RANGE Typical of all models: 1950km (1,212 miles).

MILITARY LOAD **A**: three 7·92mm MG15 aimed from nose, dorsal position and retractable ventral 'dustbin'; bomb-load 1000kg (2,205lb). **B**: same guns, bomb-load 1500kg (3,307lb). **E**: same guns, bomb-load 2000kg (4,410lb). **P**: one MG15 in nose, one fixed firing ahead, one dorsal, two in beam windows, one at rear of ventral gondola and (some models) one fixed firing aft from tail; bomb load 2000kg (4,410lb) internal and (max overload) two 500kg (1,102lb) under bomb doors. **H**: extremely varied, but typically 20mm MG FF and MG15 in nose, MG15 or twin 7·92mm MG81 in each beam window, 13mm MG131 dorsal (turret from H-16 onwards), twin MG81 at rear of gondola.

Amedeo Gigli

Heinkel He 111H-22

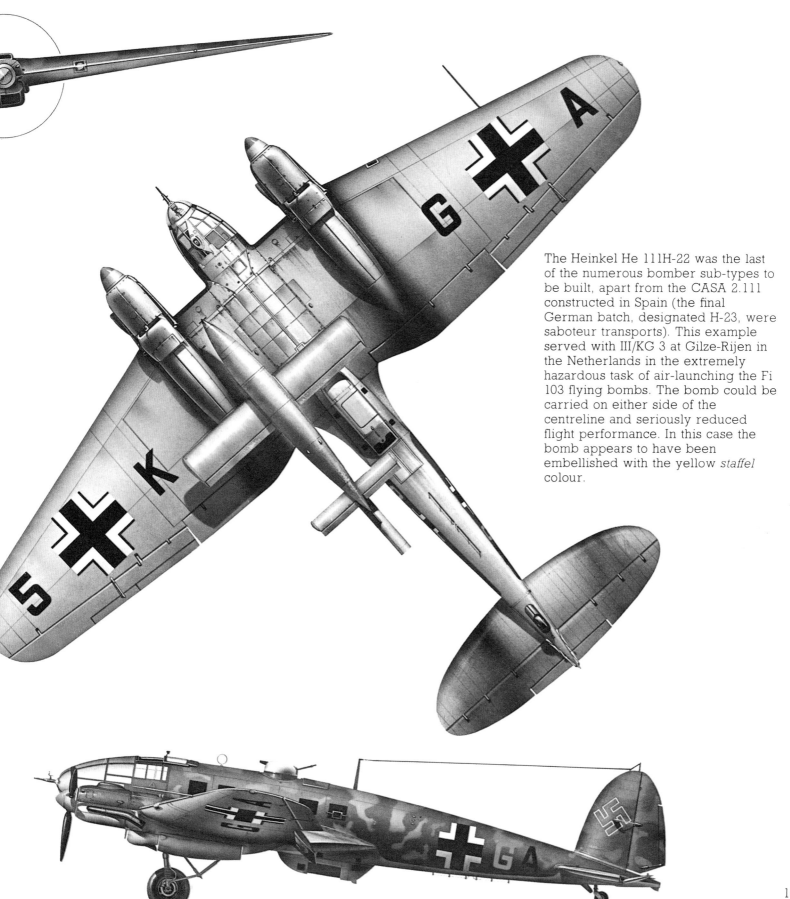

The Heinkel He 111H-22 was the last of the numerous bomber sub-types to be built, apart from the CASA 2.111 constructed in Spain (the final German batch, designated H-23, were saboteur transports). This example served with III/KG 3 at Gilze-Rijen in the Netherlands in the extremely hazardous task of air-launching the Fi 103 flying bombs. The bomb could be carried on either side of the centreline and seriously reduced flight performance. In this case the bomb appears to have been embellished with the yellow *staffel* colour.

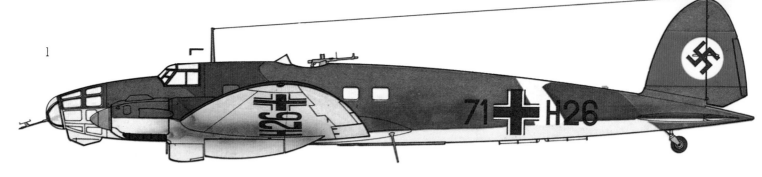

1, 2 Two views of one of the first really satisfactory models, the He 111B-2, with fully supercharged DB600C engines and auxiliary underwing radiators, which entered service with KG 154 in late 1937.

3 He 111E-1 of the Legion Kondor's K/88, which in August 1938 became part of 10-G-25 at Léon. The Spanish kept a few E-1s, and the E-4 with bombs carried internally and externally, until about 1954.

4 An He 111H-2 of 4/KG 26 in Sicily in 1942 (Lion badge of KG 26 inset).

5 This H-6 captured from the Luftwaffe at Castel Benito was used as a hack by RAF 260 Sqn.

6 One of the few Luftwaffe aircraft to wear both white and yellow theatre bands was this H-6, personal transport of Feldmarschall Kesselring.

7 With the S.M.79 the H-6 was an excellent torpedo bomber, able to carry two LT F5b torpedoes externally.

8 One of the H-6s of II/KG 4 which in April 1941 operated in temporary Iraqi colours fomenting trouble in that area until recalled to attack the Soviet Union in June.

9 The H-8 was a modified H-3 or H-5 with a clumsy fender intended to allow it to penetrate British balloon barrages. British bombers had neat cartridge-operated cable cutters on the leading edges.

10 Powered by the Merlin 500-20, the CASA C-2111D was the final production bomber (followed, as in Germany, by a troop-carrier, the C-2111E). Spanish Air Force markings.

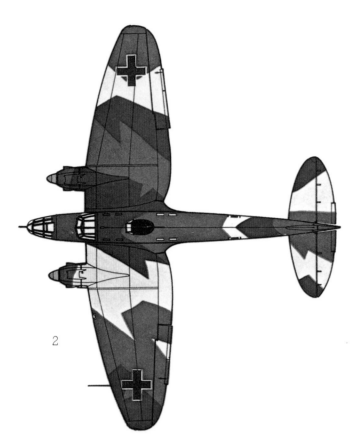

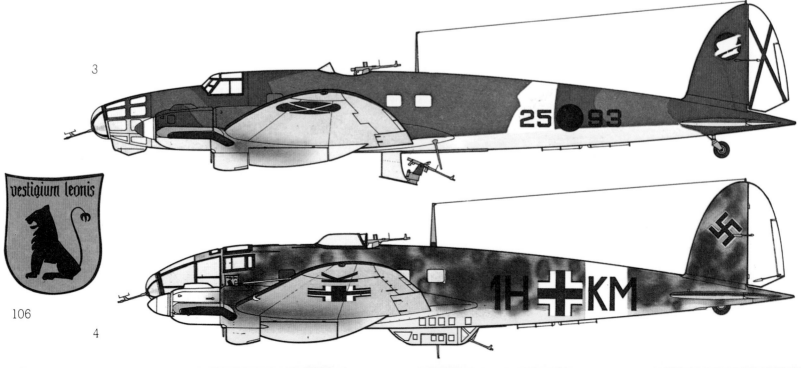

vestigium leonis

Heinkel He 111

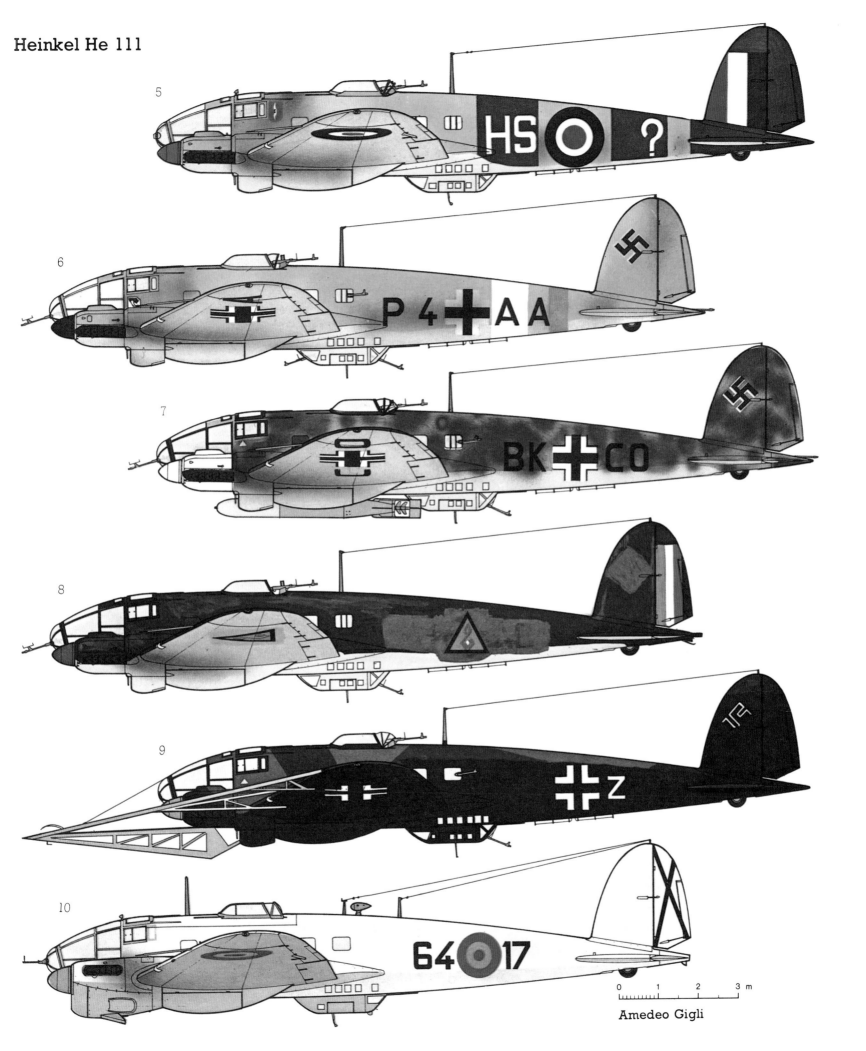

5

6   P4✠AA

7   BK✠CO

8

9   ✠Z

10   64●17

Amedeo Gigli

0 1 2 3 m

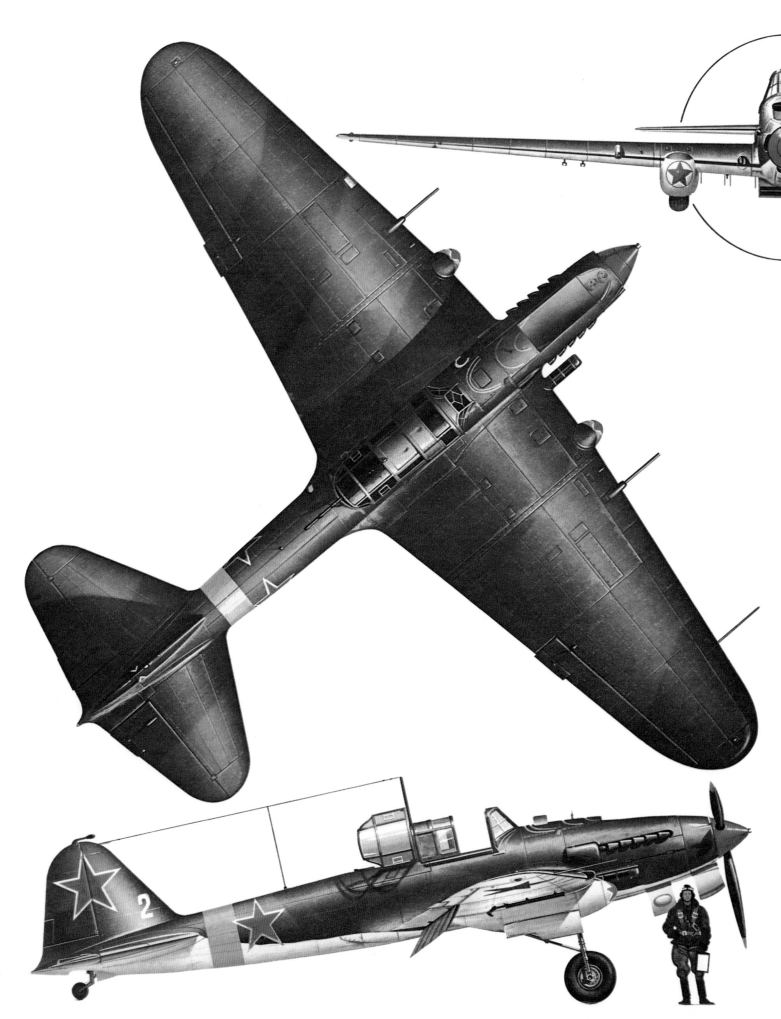

Ilyushin Il-2M3 Stormovik

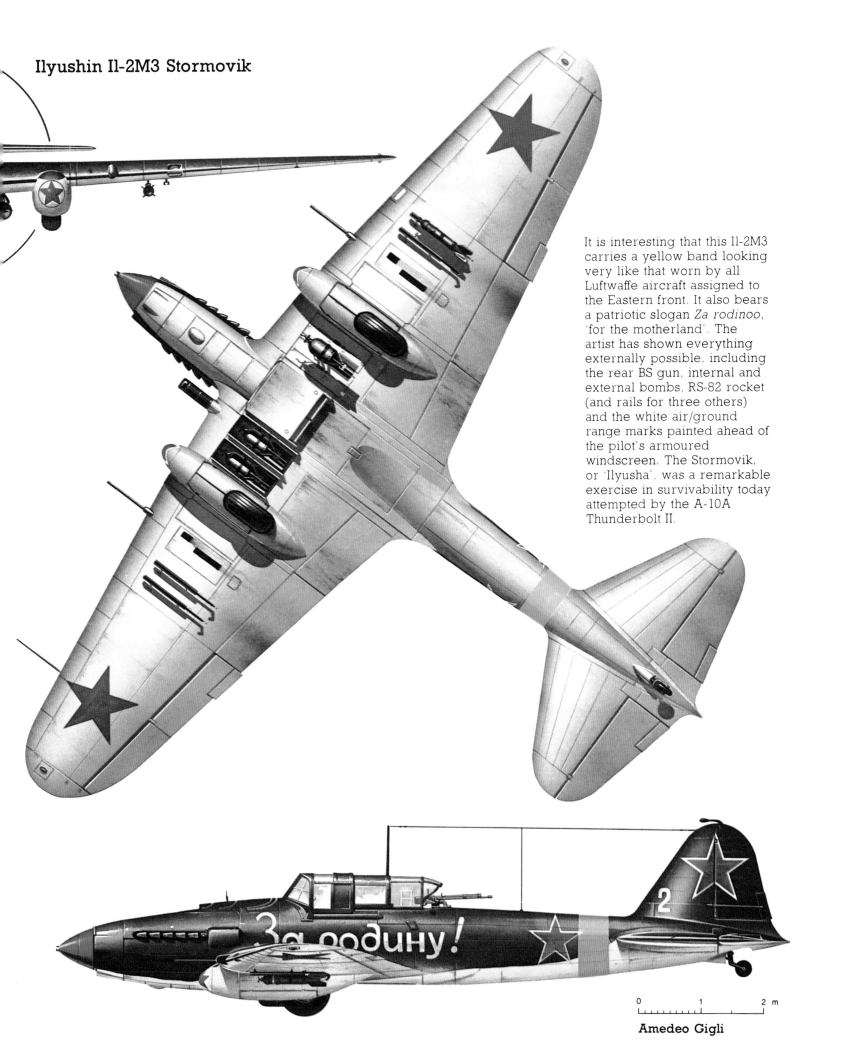

It is interesting that this Il-2M3 carries a yellow band looking very like that worn by all Luftwaffe aircraft assigned to the Eastern front. It also bears a patriotic slogan *Za rodinoo*, 'for the motherland'. The artist has shown everything externally possible, including the rear BS gun, internal and external bombs. RS-82 rocket (and rails for three others) and the white air/ground range marks painted ahead of the pilot's armoured windscreen. The Stormovik, or 'Ilyusha', was a remarkable exercise in survivability today attempted by the A-10A Thunderbolt II.

За родину!

0   1   2 m

Amedeo Gigli

A production Il-2 of the
first series, with two
20mm ShVAK cannon
and two 7·62mm (0·30in)
ShKAS machine guns,
and the eight RS-82
rockets that were such a
surprise to Britain
(though the same
weapon had figured in
many public manoeuvres
for years).

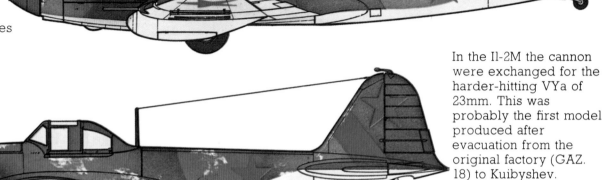

In the Il-2M the cannon
were exchanged for the
harder-hitting VYa of
23mm. This was
probably the first model
produced after
evacuation from the
original factory (GAZ.
18) to Kuibyshev.

In August 1942 the
decision was taken to
produce the Il-2M3,
tested as a prototype in
March. This model, with
AM-38F engine and a
12·7mm (0·5in) BS rear
gun, reached troops in
October. The rockets in
this example are the
increased-calibre RS-132
type.

An Il-2M3 in winter garb.
This sub-type, produced
from May 1943, had NS-
37 cannon of 37mm
calibre, in an installation
much better than the
lash-up of 37mm guns on
the Ju 87G.

The M3 served with a
Guards regiment during
the Battle for Berlin.
Variants seldom
illustrated included the
Il-2U trainer and Il-2T
torpedo bomber.

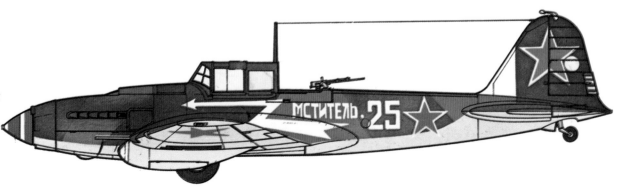

Ilyushin Il-2 and 10 Stormovik

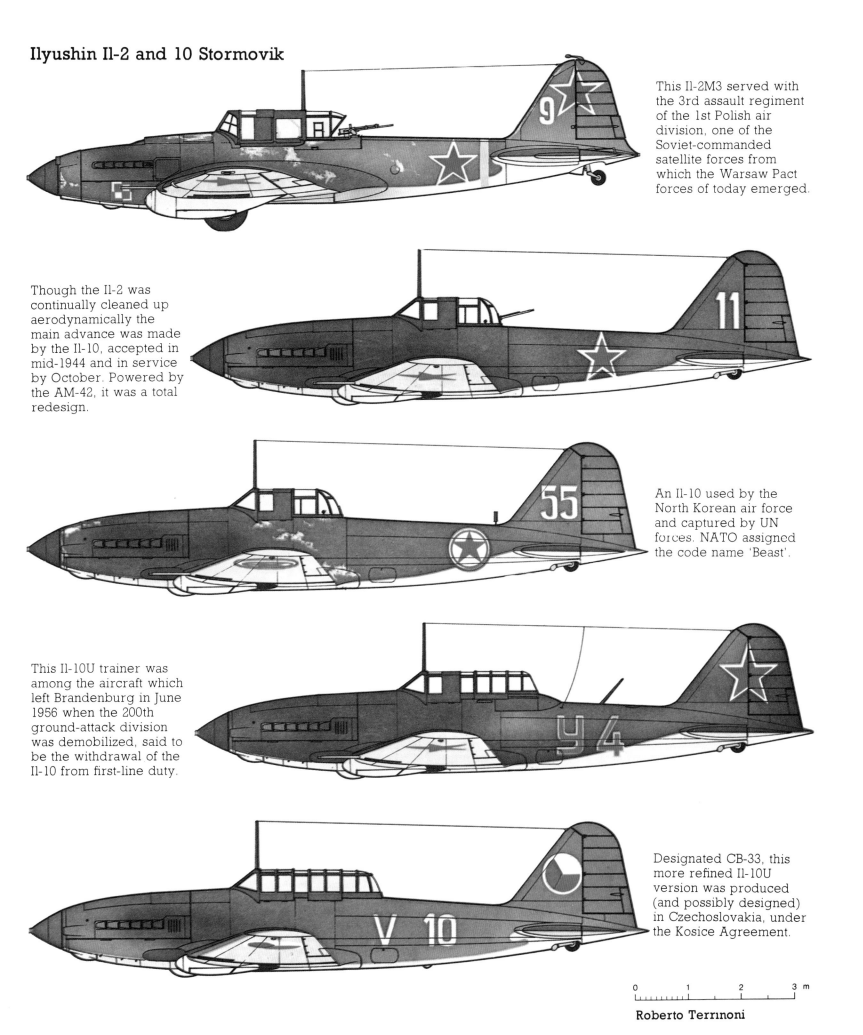

This Il-2M3 served with the 3rd assault regiment of the 1st Polish air division, one of the Soviet-commanded satellite forces from which the Warsaw Pact forces of today emerged.

Though the Il-2 was continually cleaned up aerodynamically the main advance was made by the Il-10, accepted in mid-1944 and in service by October. Powered by the AM-42, it was a total redesign.

An Il-10 used by the North Korean air force and captured by UN forces. NATO assigned the code name 'Beast'.

This Il-10U trainer was among the aircraft which left Brandenburg in June 1956 when the 200th ground-attack division was demobilized, said to be the withdrawal of the Il-10 from first-line duty.

Designated CB-33, this more refined Il-10U version was produced (and possibly designed) in Czechoslovakia, under the Kosice Agreement.

0   1   2   3 m

Roberto Terrinoni

Ilyushin Il-2 and 10 Stormovik

One of the first new stressed-skin monoplanes to join the RAF in the late 1930s was the Fairy Battle light bomber, but it proved to be a death-trap and was hastily withdrawn from operational squadrons. A few years later, the Soviet Union introduced an aircraft almost identical in shape, size, performance and role. It differed in small degrees, notably in having heavy cannon firing ahead, an accurate rocket to kill hostile armour and, above all, exceptional armour protection. Unlike the Battle, it played a central role in World War 2, and was described by Stalin as 'as necessary to the Red Army as air and bread'. So many were built that the total exceeds that for any other aircraft in history.

The Soviet government issued a requirement for a specialized anti-tank aircraft in 1935, which resulted in the VIT-1, the most heavily armed aircraft of its day. This did not enter service, partly because the battery of heavy guns threw the aircraft off-target, and nothing was done until in late 1938 the specification was hastily reissued. Ilyushin's design bureau then produced the BSh-2 prototype, flown on 30 December 1939. After re-engining with a much more powerful engine this was ordered into production in March 1941, beating a rival Sukhoi design, and squadrons began to form just before the German invasion of the Soviet Union on 22 June.

A single-seater, the production Il-2 had an engine just powerful enough to enable it to carry a good fuel load and heavy armament as well as the 700kg (1,543lb) of steel armour which, forming the main structure of vital areas, protected the cockpit and engine. Large numbers were soon over the battlefront, and units worked out tactics for knocking out Panzer formations without suffering too many casualties themselves, or being fooled by such ruses as tanks igniting harmless but impressive flares and smoke canisters. Armament was increased by introduction of a new 23mm gun, and in October 1942 the longstanding problem of rear defence was met by the Il-2M3 with a rear gunner behind the pilot.

A little later, in good time for the great Battle of Kursk in the summer of 1943, the calibre of the main guns was raised to 37mm, sufficient to pierce the thick armour of even the Panther and Tiger tanks. Popularly called the Stormovik (more precisely 'Shturmovik'), the Il-2 was affectionately called Ilyusha by its crews. Squadrons engaged in every kind of tactical air warfare, dropping bombs of many kinds, laying smoke screens, and even undertaking front-line reconnaissance. Many Il-2U dual-control models were built, originally in the shops of the Naval Aviation which was a large-scale user of the Il-2. From this stemmed a rather inefficient transport version, and it even became common practice to carry a passenger in each landing-gear well, the pilot having to remember to leave the wheels down!

Casualties among Il-2 units must have been heavy to both fighters and ground fire, though there are abundant records of successful combats with Bf 109s. The main attribute of this remarkable aircraft was certainly survivability, with firepower a close second, qualities resurrected in Pentagon conferences in the 1960s that led to today's exact counterpart, the American A-10 Thunderbolt II.

Total production of the Il-2 averaged about 1,200 per month, and by mid-1944 had reached about 36,000. A year earlier Ilyushin had begun design of a successor, which looked similar but in fact was a new aircraft. Whereas parts of the Il-2 were wood, the new model was all light-alloy, and the engine installation, radiators and landing gear were new, the latter having wheels turned 90° to lie flush inside the wings. Cockpit armour was extended aft to enclose a powered dorsal turret with 20mm gun, yet overall drag compared with the Il-2 was cut by nearly half. Designated Il-10 the production model began to reach combat units in October 1944, and large numbers were in action by VE-Day. The Il-10 raised total production of Ilyushin tactical machines to a reported 42,330.

COUNTRY OF ORIGIN Soviet Union.

CREW Early: 1; Il-2M3 and subsequent: 2.

TOTAL PRODUCED Il-2: about 36,000 (believed 36,163); Il-10: about 6,330.

DIMENSIONS Wingspan, -2: 14·6m (47ft 10⅞in), -10: 13·9m (45ft 7in); length, -2: 11·65m (38ft 2¾in), -2M3: 12·0m (39ft 4½in), -10: 12·2m (40ft 0¼in); wing area, -2: 38·5m² (414·4ft²).

WEIGHTS Empty, -2: about 3250kg (7,165lb), -2M3: about 3400kg (7,495lb), -10: about 3500kg (7,716lb); maximum loaded, typical -2,-2M3: 5872kg (12,945lb), -10: 6336kg (13,968lb).

ENGINE Mikulin vee-12 liquid-cooled, -2: 1,300hp AM-38; -2M3: 1,750hp AM-38F; -10: 2,000hp AM-42.

MAXIMUM SPEED -2: 415km/h (258mph); -2M3: 425km/h (264mph); -10: 501km/h (311mph).

SERVICE CEILING Typical of all: 6500m (21,325ft).

RANGE -2,-2M3: typically 600km (373 miles), -10: 650km (405 miles).

MILITARY LOAD -2: two 20mm ShVAK and two 7·62mm (0·30in) ShKAS fixed firing ahead, underwing racks for four RS-82 82mm rockets and internal wing cells for four 100kg (220lb) bombs; late -2: ShVAK exchanged for 20mm VYa; -2M3: two VYa, two ShKAS or 37mm SP-37, 12·7mm (0·5in) BS in rear cockpit, bomb-load of 600kg (1,323lb); -10: 2/4 VYa or 2/4 23mm NS-23, sometimes plus two ShKAS, dorsal turret with 20mm VYa, bomb-load of 1000kg (2,205lb).

Junkers Ju 52/3m

Like most of the famous warplanes of the wartime Luftwaffe the Ju 52/3m was designed long before World War 2 and was increasingly obsolescent throughout the conflict; yet, like the other types, it had to be kept in production and soldiered on to the bitter end.

Professor Hugo Junkers was one of the pioneers of both the cantilever (unbraced) monoplane and the all-metal aeroplane. A notable feature of his designs was the use of corrugated skin, which at some penalty in increased drag made the whole airframe exceptionally robust and well suited to military operation in extremely harsh environments.

In October 1930 the prototype Ju 52 showed what could be achieved by a scaled-up version of the patented Junkers wing. An outstanding feature was the so-called double-wing technique of full-span flaps and ailerons hinged just below and behind the wing proper. With these, the aircraft could rise off the ground almost as soon as the throttles were opened.

Only five Ju 52s were built, because in May 1932 the first Ju 52/3m (three engines instead of one) showed much better performance. The same basic size as the Ju 52, the 3m version had its wing engines at right angles to the tapered wing, so that they were oddly toed outwards. Numerous types of engine were fitted, but by far the most important in German-operated machines were different sub-types of BMW 132. They usually drove simple Junkers two-blade Duralumin propellers.

Virtually all the early production aircraft were civil transports, and soon established a high reputation that made them by far the best-selling European airliner. In 1935 the openly resurrected Luftwaffe adopted the Ju 52/3mg3e as a standard bomber-transport. Vertical bomb bays with a total capacity of 1500kg (3,307lb) were built into the mid-fuselage, ahead of and behind a glazed bomb-aiming fairing and a 'dustbin' containing a gunner and 7·92mm MG15 machine gun. A second MG15 could be fired from an open position above the rear fuselage.

As soon as the Spanish Civil War broke out the 3mg3e and 3mg4e (with small changes including a tailwheel instead of a skid) were supplied in numbers to the insurgent Nationalists and were instrumental in bringing across the 13,962 troops airlifted from Morocco which enabled the Nationalists to consolidate their initially precarious position. The big Junkers also carried out numerous important bombing raids, the first by German aircraft since 1918.

After the start of World War 2 production was augmented by a factory in Hungary and the Amiot and SNCASO organizations in France, the latter gradually taking over the bulk of production. Successive sub-types introduced large cargo doors, autopilot, improved engines, glider coupling, augmented defensive armament and many other details, and special-purpose models included floatplane, ambulance and minesweeping versions. Altogether 4,845 were delivered on German account by 1945, and these provided more than nine-tenths of the total German wartime airlift capability. Without an aircraft like the Ju 52 the Norwegian, Crete, Tunisian and Eastern Front campaigns would have been impossible.

By 1938 the German airline Deutsche Lufthansa was talking with Junkers about a modern successor, and this emerged as the Ju 252 in 1941. Much larger and more powerful, it had smooth stressed skin, seated 35 and incorporated a large *Trapoklappe* (rear ramp door). This could have replaced the Ju 52/3m in production, but in 1942 Junkers was told to see whether the 252 could be redesigned to use low-powered BMW-Bramo 323 Fafnir engines in a redesigned wooden airframe. Effectively this so delayed matters that the definitive Ju 352 did not fly until October 1943 and made little contribution to the war.

Post-war the French Ju 52/3m, called the AAC.1, remained in production until 1947, and the final 170 were CASA 352-L multi-role transports, designated T.2B by the Spanish air force.

COUNTRY OF ORIGIN Germany.

CREW Usual flight crew of 3 or 4.

TOTAL PRODUCED Unknown, but in excess of 4,845.

DIMENSIONS Wingspan 29·25m (95ft 11½in); length 18·90m (62ft 0in); wing area 110·5m² (1,189·4ft²).

WEIGHTS Empty, **3mg3e**: 5720kg (12,610lb), **3mg7e**: 6500kg (14,330lb); maximum loaded, **3e**: 10500kg (23,148lb), **7e**: 11000kg (24,250lb).

ENGINES **3mg3e**: Three 725hp BMW 132A-3 nine-cylinder radials; **3mg5e**: 830hp BMW 132T-2; (late-production **3mg8e** onwards) 830hp BMW 132Z.

MAXIMUM SPEED (all sub-types, typical) 270km/h (168mph) at sea level, 282km/h (175mph) at 1500m (4,920ft).

SERVICE CEILING (typical of all) 5900m (19,360ft).

RANGE (typical on standard fuel) 1100km (684 miles).

MILITARY LOAD Seating for up to 18 equipped troops or maximum cargo load of 2000kg (4,409lb); very varied armament usually including one manually aimed 7·92mm MG15 or 13mm MG131 in dorsal position, two MG15 beam guns aimed through side windows and sometimes cockpit-roof cupola with MG15 or dorsal turret with 20mm MG151 or MG15 in hatch at rear of cargo floor.

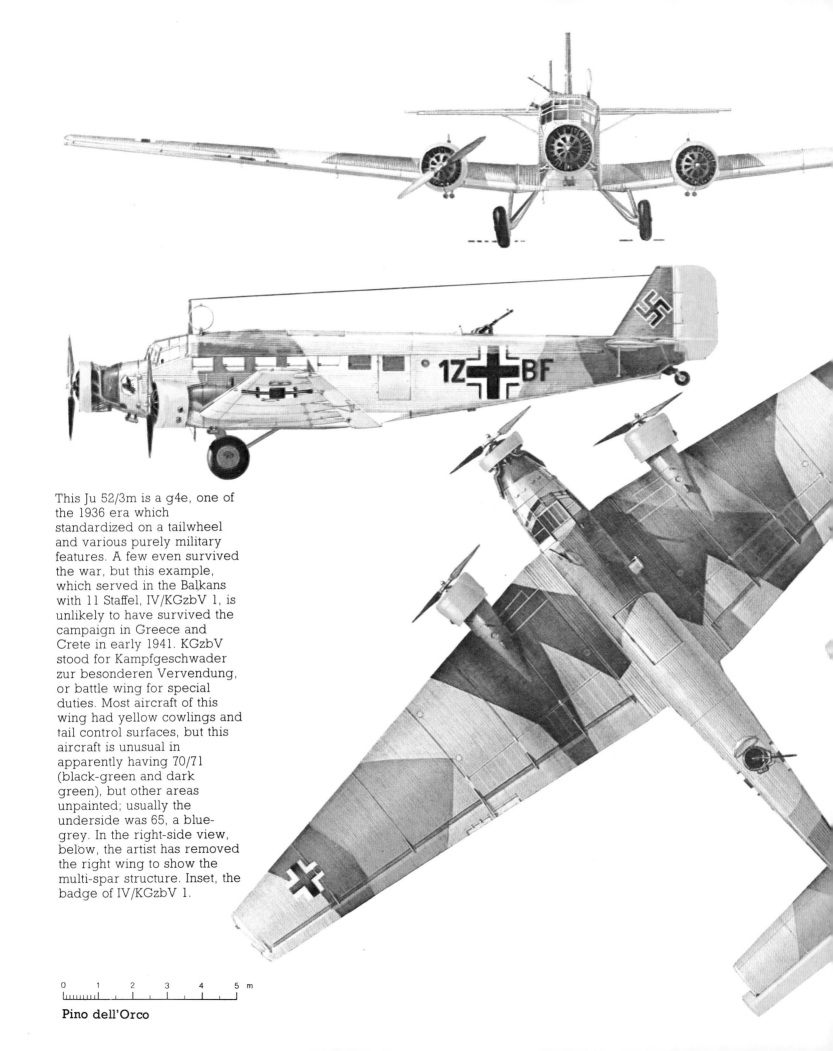

This Ju 52/3m is a g4e, one of the 1936 era which standardized on a tailwheel and various purely military features. A few even survived the war, but this example, which served in the Balkans with 11 Staffel, IV/KGzbV 1, is unlikely to have survived the campaign in Greece and Crete in early 1941. KGzbV stood for Kampfgeschwader zur besonderen Verwendung, or battle wing for special duties. Most aircraft of this wing had yellow cowlings and tail control surfaces, but this aircraft is unusual in apparently having 70/71 (black-green and dark green), but other areas unpainted; usually the underside was 65, a blue-grey. In the right-side view, below, the artist has removed the right wing to show the multi-spar structure. Inset, the badge of IV/KGzbV 1.

0   1   2   3   4   5   m

Pino dell'Orco

Junkers Ju 52/3mg4e

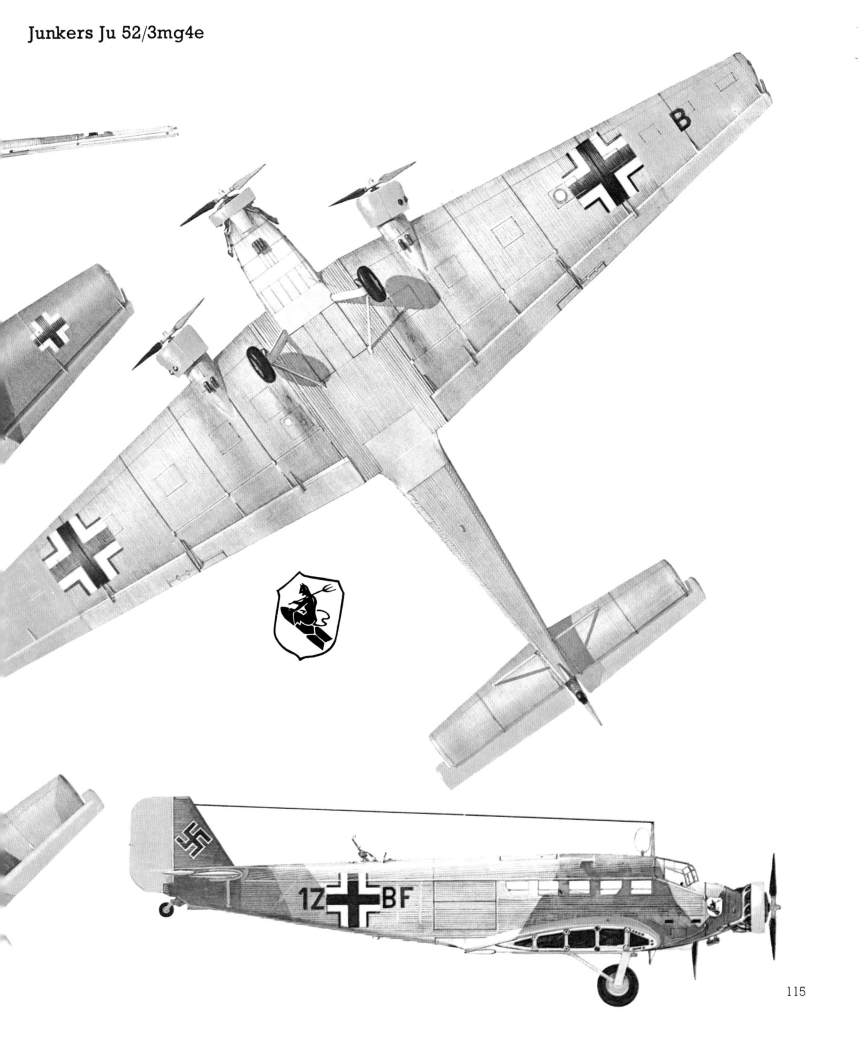

115

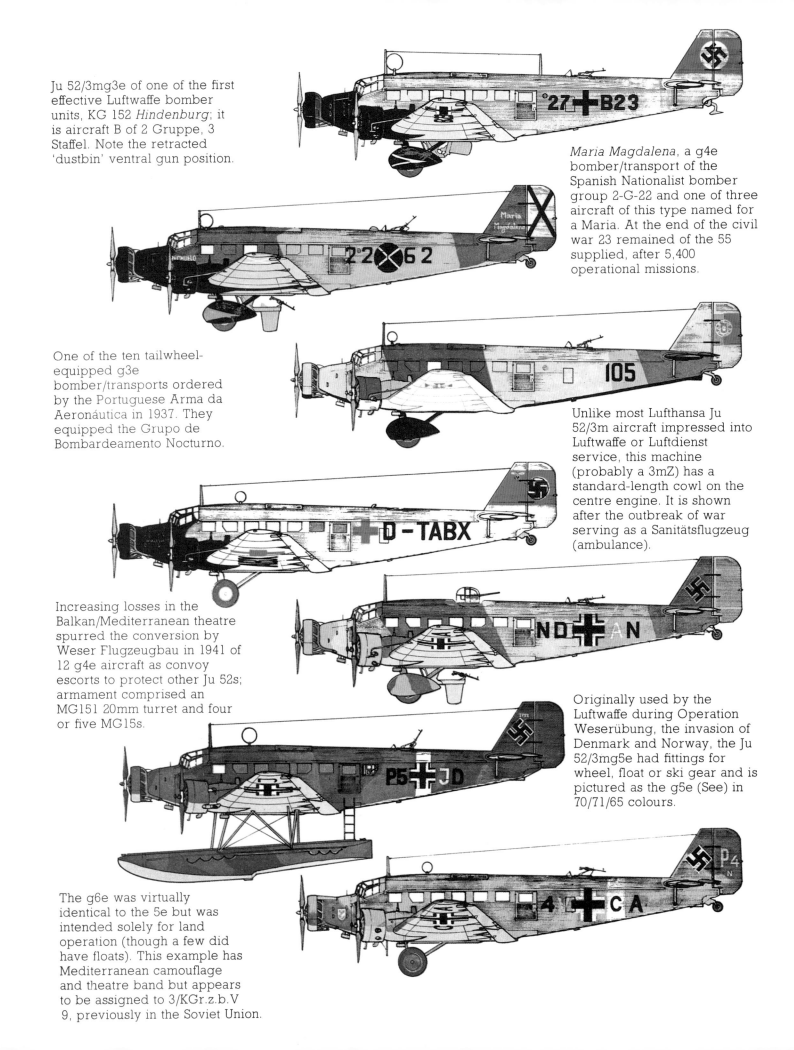

Ju 52/3mg3e of one of the first effective Luftwaffe bomber units, KG 152 *Hindenburg*; it is aircraft B of 2 Gruppe, 3 Staffel. Note the retracted 'dustbin' ventral gun position.

Maria Magdalena, a g4e bomber/transport of the Spanish Nationalist bomber group 2-G-22 and one of three aircraft of this type named for a Maria. At the end of the civil war 23 remained of the 55 supplied, after 5,400 operational missions.

One of the ten tailwheel-equipped g3e bomber/transports ordered by the Portuguese Arma da Aeronáutica in 1937. They equipped the Grupo de Bombardeamento Nocturno.

Unlike most Lufthansa Ju 52/3m aircraft impressed into Luftwaffe or Luftdienst service, this machine (probably a 3mZ) has a standard-length cowl on the centre engine. It is shown after the outbreak of war serving as a Sanitätsflugzeug (ambulance).

Increasing losses in the Balkan/Mediterranean theatre spurred the conversion by Weser Flugzeugbau in 1941 of 12 g4e aircraft as convoy escorts to protect other Ju 52s; armament comprised an MG151 20mm turret and four or five MG15s.

Originally used by the Luftwaffe during Operation Weserübung, the invasion of Denmark and Norway, the Ju 52/3mg5e had fittings for wheel, float or ski gear and is pictured as the g5e (See) in 70/71/65 colours.

The g6e was virtually identical to the 5e but was intended solely for land operation (though a few did have floats). This example has Mediterranean camouflage and theatre band but appears to be assigned to 3/KGr.z.b.V 9, previously in the Soviet Union.

Junkers Ju 52/3m

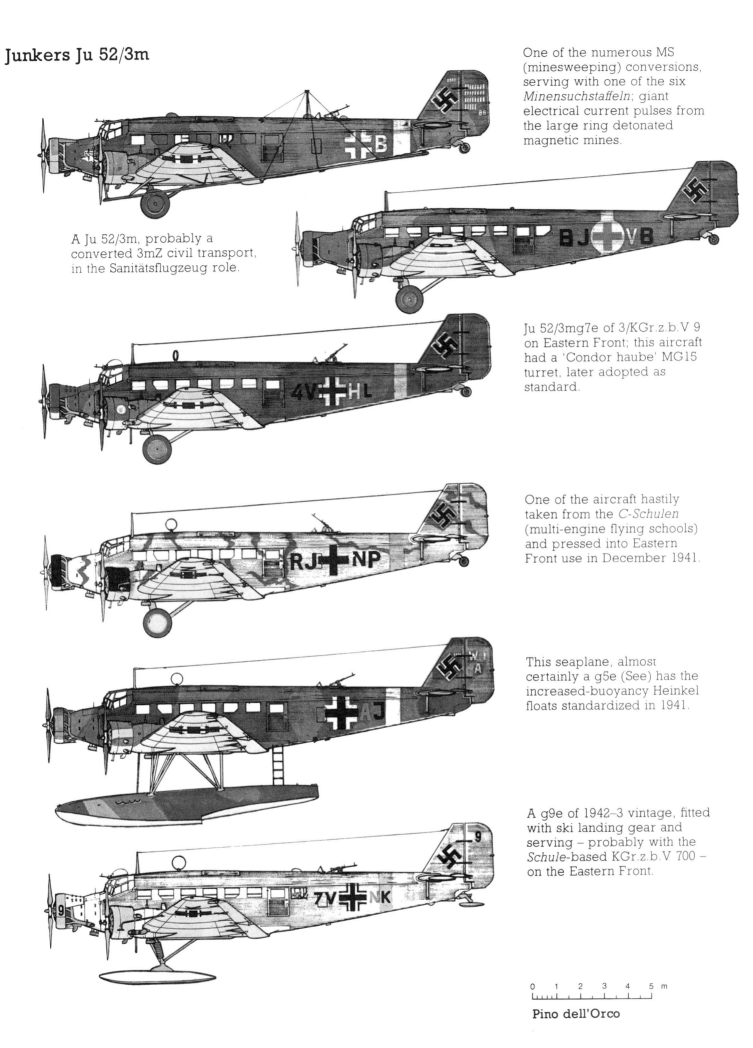

One of the numerous MS (minesweeping) conversions, serving with one of the six *Minensuchstaffeln*; giant electrical current pulses from the large ring detonated magnetic mines.

A Ju 52/3m, probably a converted 3mZ civil transport, in the Sanitätsflugzeug role.

Ju 52/3mg7e of 3/KGr.z.b.V 9 on Eastern Front; this aircraft had a 'Condor haube' MG15 turret, later adopted as standard.

One of the aircraft hastily taken from the *C-Schulen* (multi-engine flying schools) and pressed into Eastern Front use in December 1941.

This seaplane, almost certainly a g5e (See) has the increased-buoyancy Heinkel floats standardized in 1941.

A g9e of 1942–3 vintage, fitted with ski landing gear and serving – probably with the *Schule*-based KGr.z.b.V 700 – on the Eastern Front.

0 1 2 3 4 5 m

Pino dell'Orco

117

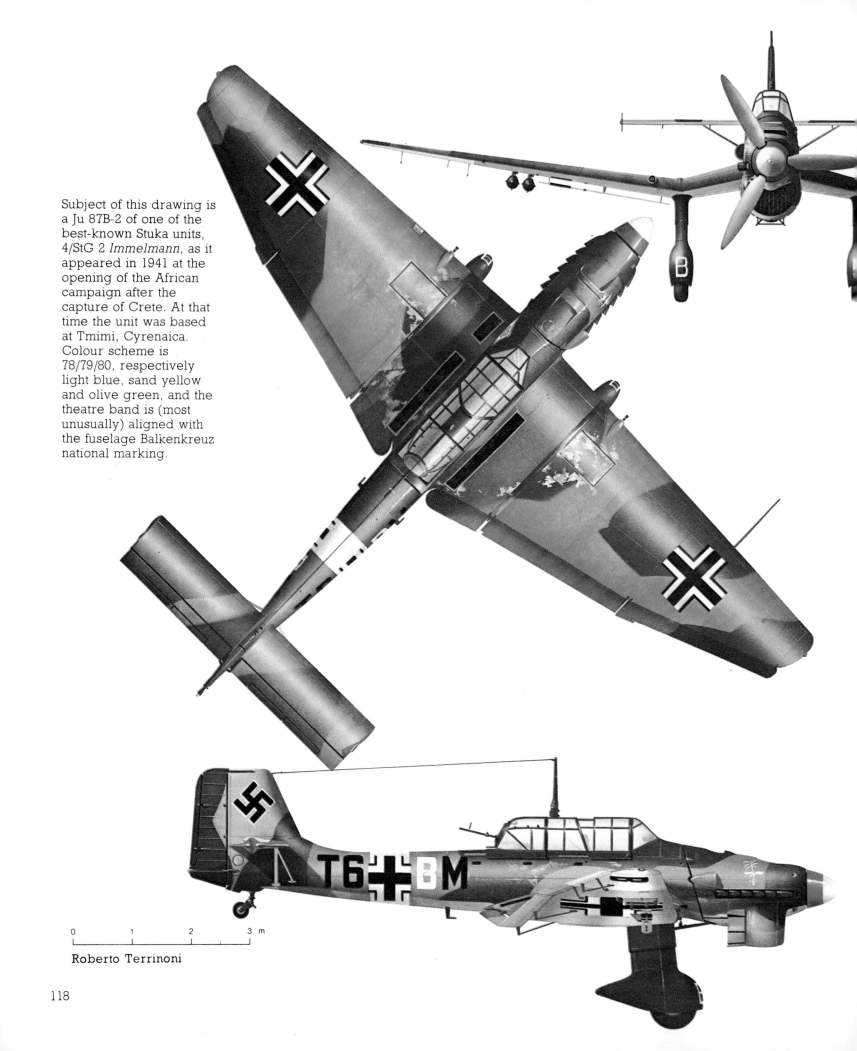

Subject of this drawing is a Ju 87B-2 of one of the best-known Stuka units, 4/StG 2 *Immelmann*, as it appeared in 1941 at the opening of the African campaign after the capture of Crete. At that time the unit was based at Tmimi, Cyrenaica. Colour scheme is 78/79/80, respectively light blue, sand yellow and olive green, and the theatre band is (most unusually) aligned with the fuselage Balkenkreuz national marking.

T6+BM

0   1   2   3 m

Roberto Terrinoni

Junkers Ju 87B-2

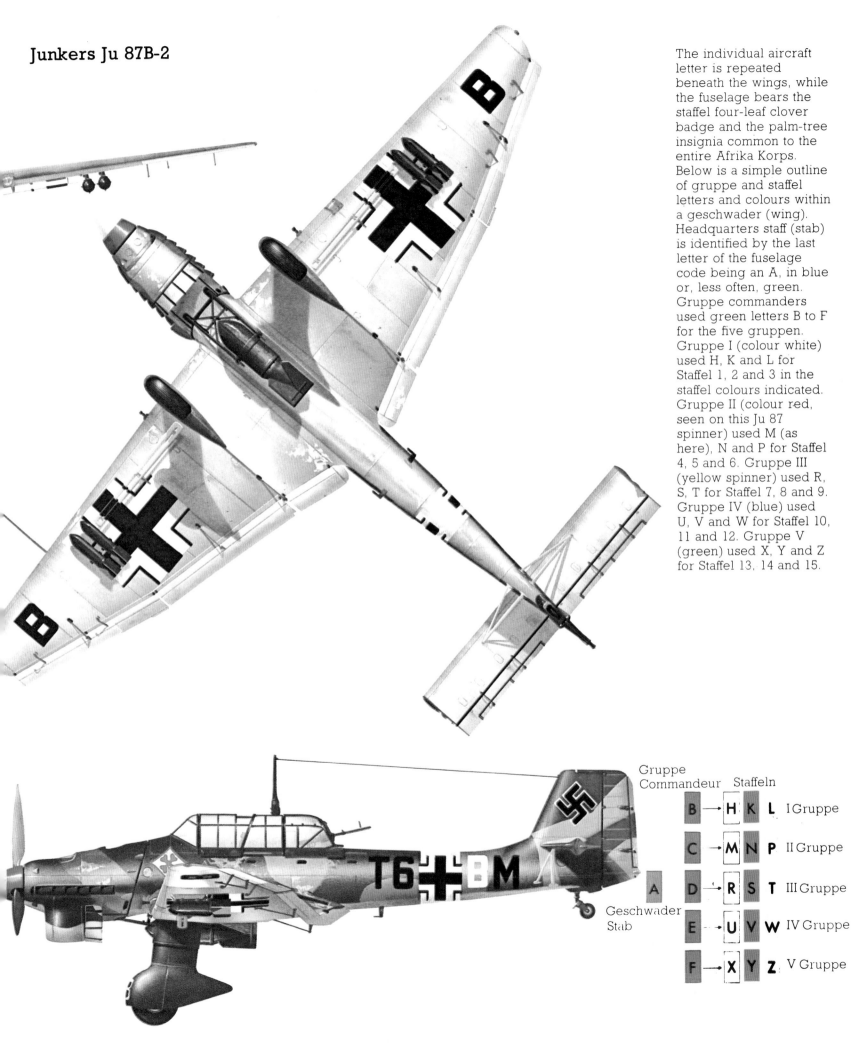

The individual aircraft letter is repeated beneath the wings, while the fuselage bears the staffel four-leaf clover badge and the palm-tree insignia common to the entire Afrika Korps. Below is a simple outline of gruppe and staffel letters and colours within a geschwader (wing). Headquarters staff (stab) is identified by the last letter of the fuselage code being an A, in blue or, less often, green. Gruppe commanders used green letters B to F for the five gruppen. Gruppe I (colour white) used H, K and L for Staffel 1, 2 and 3 in the staffel colours indicated. Gruppe II (colour red, seen on this Ju 87 spinner) used M (as here), N and P for Staffel 4, 5 and 6. Gruppe III (yellow spinner) used R, S, T for Staffel 7, 8 and 9. Gruppe IV (blue) used U, V and W for Staffel 10, 11 and 12. Gruppe V (green) used X, Y and Z for Staffel 13, 14 and 15.

Gruppe
Commandeur   Staffeln

B → H K L   I Gruppe

C → M N P   II Gruppe

A   D → R S T   III Gruppe
Geschwader
Stab   E → U V W   IV Gruppe

F → X Y Z   V Gruppe

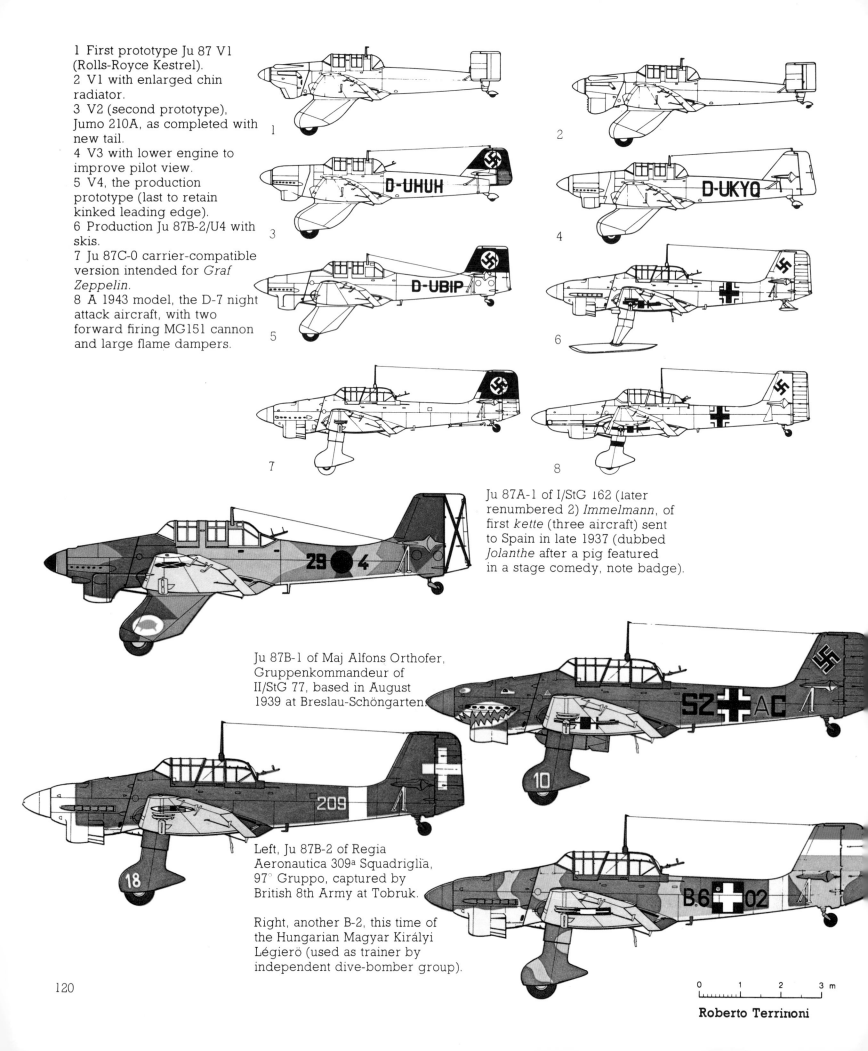

1 First prototype Ju 87 V1 (Rolls-Royce Kestrel).

2 V1 with enlarged chin radiator.

3 V2 (second prototype), Jumo 210A, as completed with new tail.

4 V3 with lower engine to improve pilot view.

5 V4, the production prototype (last to retain kinked leading edge).

6 Production Ju 87B-2/U4 with skis.

7 Ju 87C-0 carrier-compatible version intended for *Graf Zeppelin*.

8 A 1943 model, the D-7 night attack aircraft, with two forward firing MG151 cannon and large flame dampers.

Ju 87A-1 of I/StG 162 (later renumbered 2) *Immelmann*, of first *kette* (three aircraft) sent to Spain in late 1937 (dubbed *Jolanthe* after a pig featured in a stage comedy, note badge).

Ju 87B-1 of Maj Alfons Orthofer, Gruppenkommandeur of II/StG 77, based in August 1939 at Breslau-Schöngarten.

Left, Ju 87B-2 of Regia Aeronautica 309ª Squadriglïa, 97° Gruppo, captured by British 8th Army at Tobruk.

Right, another B-2, this time of the Hungarian Magyar Királyi Légierö (used as trainer by independent dive-bomber group).

120

Roberto Terrinoni

Junkers Ju 87

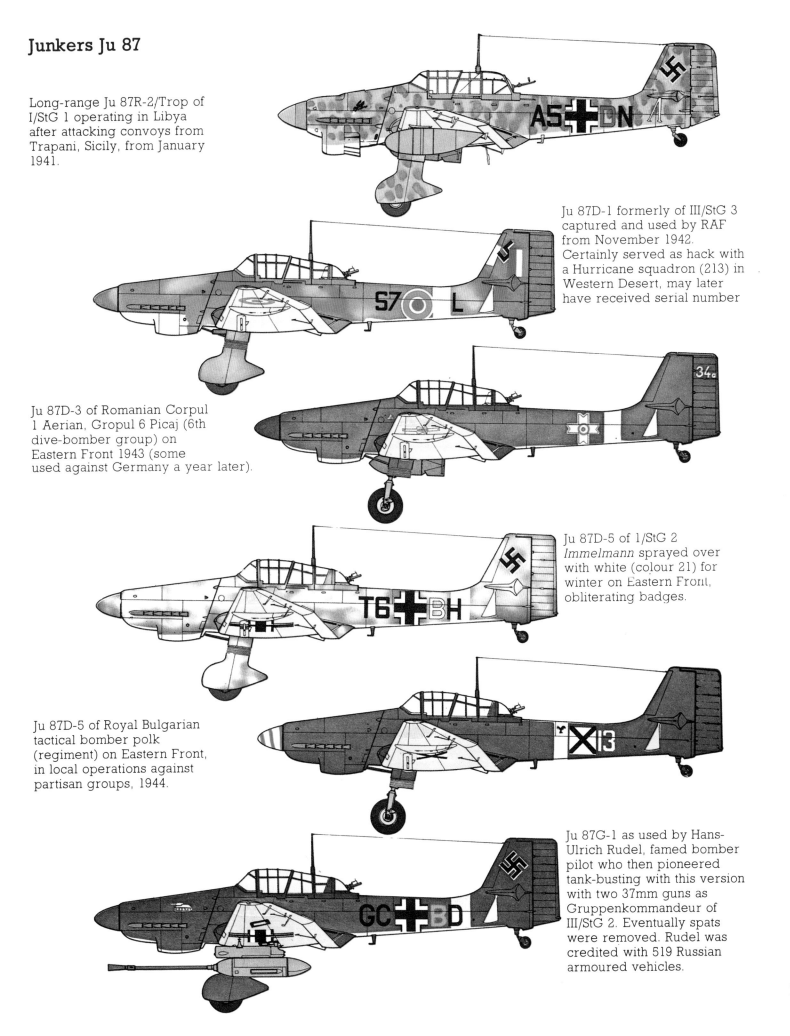

Long-range Ju 87R-2/Trop of I/StG 1 operating in Libya after attacking convoys from Trapani, Sicily, from January 1941.

Ju 87D-1 formerly of III/StG 3 captured and used by RAF from November 1942. Certainly served as hack with a Hurricane squadron (213) in Western Desert, may later have received serial number

Ju 87D-3 of Romanian Corpul 1 Aerian, Gropul 6 Picaj (6th dive-bomber group) on Eastern Front 1943 (some used against Germany a year later).

Ju 87D-5 of 1/StG 2 *Immelmann* sprayed over with white (colour 21) for winter on Eastern Front, obliterating badges.

Ju 87D-5 of Royal Bulgarian tactical bomber polk (regiment) on Eastern Front, in local operations against partisan groups, 1944.

Ju 87G-1 as used by Hans-Ulrich Rudel, famed bomber pilot who then pioneered tank-busting with this version with two 37mm guns as Gruppenkommandeur of III/StG 2. Eventually spats were removed. Rudel was credited with 519 Russian armoured vehicles.

Junkers Ju 87

No aircraft in history was ever more feared, nor accomplished more, when conditions were right for its use, than the Junkers Ju 87, universally called the Stuka though this is actually just the abbreviation for a dive bomber (of any kind) in German. At one time, in the first two years of World War 2, thousands of these bent-wing machines were striking terror into the hearts not only of helpless civilians but also seasoned troops and warship crews. Then, as soon as command of the air was disputed, the dreaded Stuka became almost a sitting duck, and though production was maintained and even increased until near the end of the war these aircraft seldom operated in their design role again.

German experts had never lost an interest in dive bombers kindled in World War 1, and Junkers built a prototype designated K.47 at their Swedish plant in 1928 to explore possibilities. This assisted the design of the aircraft that in 1934 was planned as the definitive Luftwaffe dive bomber to replace the interim machine that matured as the Hs 123 biplane. Karl Pohlmann led the design team, and the rather ungainly prototype Ju 87, powered by a British Kestrel engine, flew in late 1935. Tail failure caused redesign and delay, but in November 1936 the pre-production Ju 87A-0 emerged from the Dessau factory, and the following year the Sturzkampfgeschwader Immelmann was in business. Later in the year three Ju 87A-1s were sent to the Legion Kondor in Spain, and such was the precision of their bombing that they had a tremendous effect on the Republican forces. Perhaps for the first time it was possible in all except the worst weather to put a heavy bomb exactly on a crossroads, a bridge or other target.

All 87s were modern stressed-skin machines with the Junkers double-wing flap/aileron system and, in all dive-bomber versions, hinged dive brakes under the outer wings. The engine and propeller had automatic controls, and an auto-trimmer made the aircraft tail-heavy as the pilot rolled over into his dive, lining up red lines on the cockpit side window (choice of 60°, 75° or 80°) with the horizon and aiming at the target with the sight for the fixed gun. The heavy bomb was swung down clear of the propeller on crutches prior to release. It was normal to pull out at the lowest safe height, and many Stukas were lost in 1937-8 either through pilot black-out or because mist hid the ground and caused error of judgement.

By the start of World War 2 the standard Stuka was the Ju 87B, with much greater power, heavier load and all-round improved performance. In the 27-day Polish campaign these aircraft had an effect that can be called shattering, and their exploits included virtual elimination of an entire infantry division at Poitrkow railway station, destruction of all major ships of the Polish navy except two which escaped, and accurate bombing of Polish forces 100m (330ft) ahead of German troops. In April 1940 the long-range Ju 87R played a main role in Operation *Weser* in Norway, sinking several important Allied warships, and virtually the entire StG (Stukageschwader) force participated in the drive through the Low Countries and France in May. But from July RAF fighters curtailed and then halted operations over England.

By late 1940 the Stukas were pressing south through Yugoslavia to Greece, Crete and Libya, while June 1941 saw the much more capable Ju 87D on the Eastern Front where most 87s were concentrated. No longer a dive bomber, the later Ju 87s served as low-level close-support aircraft with heavy armour and many weapons, as glider tugs and, thanks largely to the amazing exploits and persistence of Hans-Ulrich Rudel, as the Ju 87G series of tank-busters armed with two 37mm Flak 18 (BK 3,7) guns each with a clip of six rounds. By this time spats had vanished from the wheels, and in winter skis were often fitted. Production continued right up to the final time when, in September 1944, all production was stopped except for fighters. Like so many Luftwaffe aircraft the 87 had had to carry on because nothing arrived to replace it.

COUNTRY OF ORIGIN Germany.

CREW Almost always 2.

TOTAL PRODUCED Believed to be 5,709.

DIMENSIONS Wingspan, all versions up to **D-1**: 13·8m (45ft 3¼in), later 15·0m (49ft 2½in); length, up to **D-1**: 11·13m (36ft 5in), later: 11·5m (37ft 8¾in); wing area up to **D-1**: 31·95m² (343ft²), later: 33·68m² (363ft²).

WEIGHTS Empty **Ju 87A**: 2268kg (5,000lb), **B-1**: 2762kg (6,090lb), **D-7**: 3939kg (8,683lb); maximum loaded, **A**: 3400kg (7,496lb), **B-1**: 4336kg (9,560lb), **D-7**: 6607kg (14,565lb).

ENGINES One Junkers inverted-vee 12-cylinder, **A**: 640hp Jumo 210Ca; **B-1**: 1,200hp Jumo 211Da; **D-7**: 1,500hp Jumo 211P.

MAXIMUM SPEED **A**: 285km/h (177mph); **B-1**: 383km/h (238mph); **D-7**: 399km/h (248mph).

SERVICE CEILING Usually about 7500m (24,600ft) except later versions at maximum weight reduced to 4730m (15,520ft).

RANGE All versions about 1000km (620 miles) with maximum fuel, except R about 1800km (1,100 miles).

MILITARY LOAD **A**: One fixed 7·92mm MG17 and one 7·92mm MG15 in rear cockpit, plus 250kg (551lb) bomb; **B**: two fixed MG17, one MG15 and 500kg (1,102lb) bomb; **D**: two MG17, twin 7·92mm MG81 in rear cockpit and bomb load up to 1800kg (3,968 lb).

Junkers Ju 88

Built in much greater quantity than any other twin-engined warplane of its day, the Ju 88 was one of the few combat aircraft in history to have excelled at a wide range of tasks. Like the Mosquito it was an exceptional fighter and an exceptional bomber, and also served as a torpedo carrier, missile platform, tank buster, and in many other roles including transport and pilotless missile. Again like so many other famous combat aircraft its versatility simply stemmed from the sheer excellence of the basic design, and had nothing to do with far-sighted officials or clever strategic planning.

Originally the Ju 88 was a *Schnellbomber* (fast bomber) carrying only a modest load and with just a single machine gun for defence. Two brilliant Americans were hired to assist in creating a truly advanced stressed-skin airframe, and the prototype flew on 21 December 1936. It took 2½ years of intensive further development to produce the pre-production Ju 88A-0 bomber, and KG 30, the first Luftwaffe unit with the production A-1 version, was only just forming as World War 2 began. Features of this version included a compact crew compartment (it was thought that having all crew-members in close contact improved morale), an extremely heavy bomb load (three times that originally demanded) carried both internally and on four racks under the inner wing, exceptionally tall landing gears with big tyres suitable for soft fields carried on oleo legs sprung by stacks of steel rings which intermeshed, and turning 90° on these legs to lie flat inside the nacelles, and large slatted dive brakes hinged under the outer wings. These brakes gave trouble, and because of the extreme structural loads when flying at maximum weight the early versions had a long take-off run and were prohibited from dive bombing or making sharp manoeuvres.

These restrictions were rectified in subsequent versions, and the A-5 arrived in time to display its remarkable power of manoeuvre in the Battle of Britain. Engine power increased, armament was greatly (if hastily) augmented, and in the first really satisfactory model, the A-4 (delayed beyond the A-5 by unavailability of its improved engine), the wing was increased in span. At this early date the engine nacelles were already so designed that either a liquid-cooled engine (with the coolant radiators in a ring round the front) or an air-cooled radial could be installed without difficulty.

In 1940 the B-0 series searched for a better crew compartment and, fitted with the excellent BMW radial at first, led to the Ju 188 and thence to the 388, which were outstanding multi-role machines in their own right. Neither, however, ever supplanted the 88, production of which was stable at about 2,000 a year in 1940–3, and from 1940 was increasingly augmented by long-range fighter versions. The first Ju 88C fighter had flown as early as July 1939 but it was not until mid-1942 that definitive radar-equipped C-versions were in production, followed by the radial-engined R and, in 1944, the outstanding Ju 88G with the larger tail of the 188.

The Ju 88G family were certainly the best Luftwaffe night fighters used in quantity and carried so many night sensing devices that they could home on heavy bombers at will, a few expert crews destroying as many as six aircraft in one long mission.

Another model coming into service at the start of 1944 was the S, a high-speed bomber which went back to the original specification in relying more on speed than defensive firepower. Internal fuel cut into the bomb load, and in some S-models the bombs went into a large wooden box on the underside of the fuselage. Another of the versions with a large ventral box was the P-series with heavy cannon for use against tanks. To the end of the war the 88 was one of the very few Luftwaffe aircraft that occasionally dared to fly at high speed over Britain, and on New Year's day 1945 88s led the *Bodenplatte* raid by fighter-bombers against Allied airfields in Western Europe. But Hitler's knockout blow with *Mistel* explosive-packed 88s never came about.

COUNTRY OF ORIGIN Germany.

CREW From 2–6 depending on version.

TOTAL PRODUCED About 14,980.

DIMENSIONS Wingspan **A-0** to **A-3**: 18·36m (60ft 2¾in), all subsequent: 20·0m (65ft 7½in); length most: 14·39m (47ft 2¾in), G-series with radar and tail-warning: 16·36m (53ft 8in); wing area (except A-0/A-3) 53·5m² (576ft²).

WEIGHTS Empty **A-1**: 7700kg (16,975lb), **A-4**: 9860kg (21,737lb); maximum loaded **A-1**: 10360kg (22,840lb), **A-4**: 14000kg (30,865lb), **G-7b**: 14675kg (32,353lb).

ENGINES **A-1**: two Junkers Jumo 211B inverted-vee 12-cylinder each rated at 1,200hp; **A-4**: Jumo 211J of 1,350hp (also used in many other versions); many **C, G** and **S** versions: BMW 801G 18-cylinder radials each rated at 1,730hp; alternative for late production: 1,776hp (2,040hp with special boost) Jumo 213A or 213E.

MAXIMUM SPEED Most: 450km/h (280mph), typical **S**: 610km/h (379mph), best **G** without flame dampers: 650km/h (404mph).

SERVICE CEILING Most: 8000m (26,250ft), (**S** with power boost: 11580m (38,000ft)).

RANGE Great variation but most A-series about 1770km (1,100 miles).

MILITARY LOAD **Most bombers**: 28 bombs of 50kg (110lb) internal plus up to four 500kg (1,102lb) external, or two torpedoes or many other loads; more than 200 variations of armament including 7·92mm MG17 or MG81 fixed or free-firing ahead from cockpit, twin MG81 or single 13mm MG131 or 20mm MG FF firing from nose, two or four 7·92mm MG15 or MG81 firing to upper rear and twin MG15 or MG81 firing to lower rear; **C, R and G fighters**: many combinations of cannon, a standard G-series fit being six 20mm MG151, four fixed firing ahead from ventral tray and two firing upwards at about 80 .

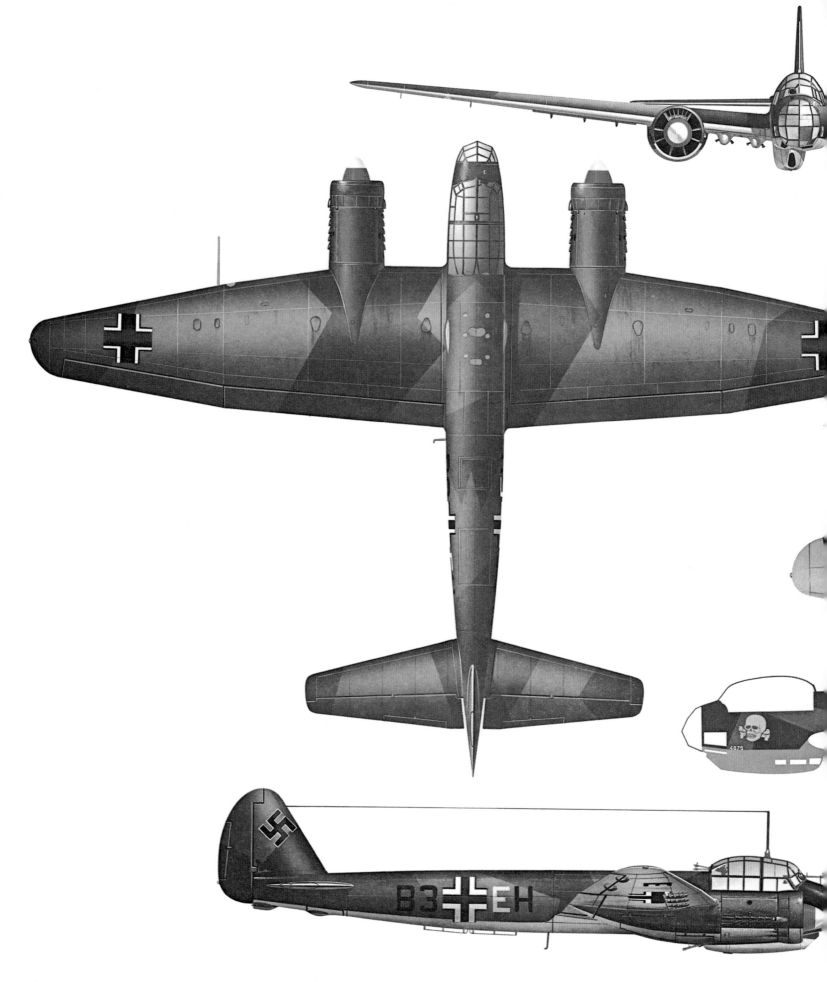

Junkers Ju 88A-5

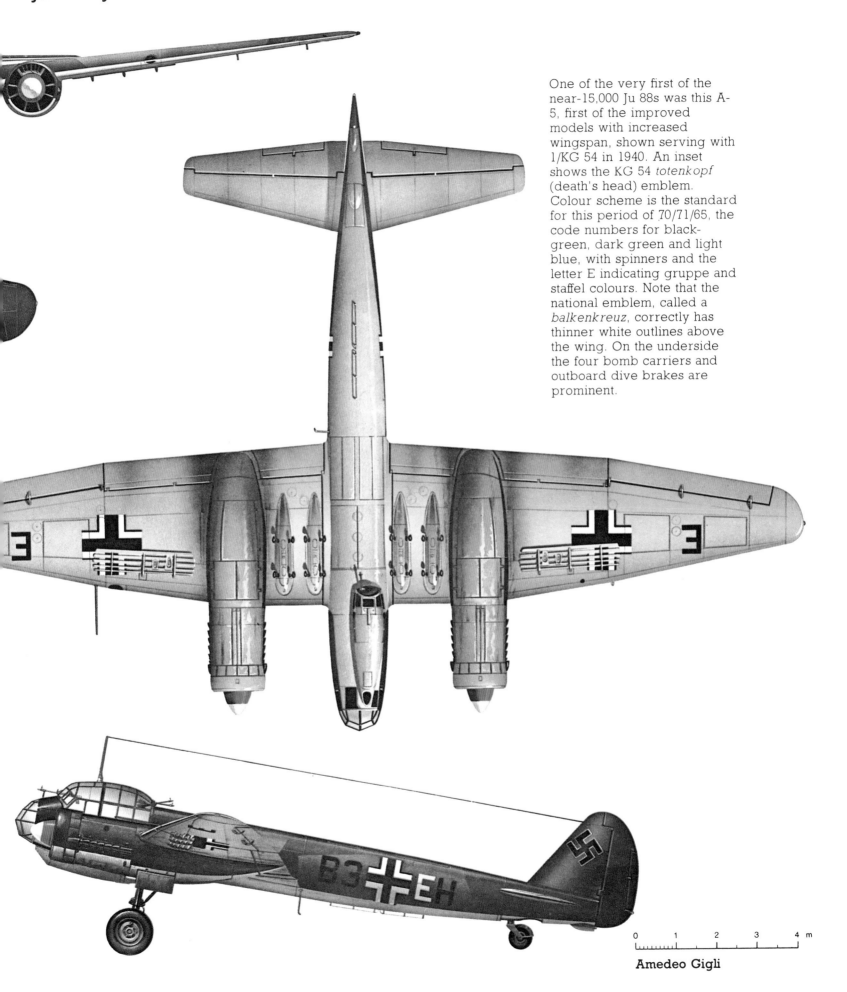

One of the very first of the near-15,000 Ju 88s was this A-5, first of the improved models with increased wingspan, shown serving with 1/KG 54 in 1940. An inset shows the KG 54 *totenkopf* (death's head) emblem. Colour scheme is the standard for this period of 70/71/65, the code numbers for black-green, dark green and light blue, with spinners and the letter E indicating gruppe and staffel colours. Note that the national emblem, called a *balkenkreuz*, correctly has thinner white outlines above the wing. On the underside the four bomb carriers and outboard dive brakes are prominent.

0   1   2   3   4 m

Amedeo Gigli

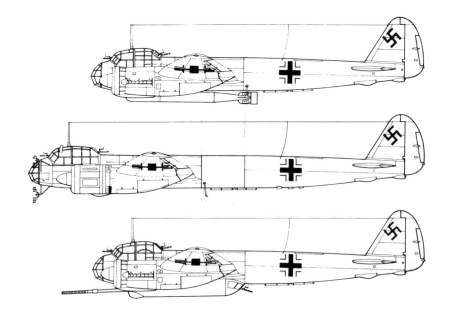

The Ju 88A-17 was one of the torpedo-carrying sub-types in the prolific A-series, with two LT F5bs.

At the end of bomber development in 1944 the Ju 88H-1 appeared, with extra fuel and cameras (plus Hohentwiel radar). Later H versions were intended as fighter/bomber leadships.

First prototype of the Ju 88P-1 with the Kwk 39 gun of 75mm, replaced in production (which was limited) by the Pak 40.

First long-span version in service was the A-5, in this case operated by III/KG 30 from Aalborg after the invasion of Denmark.

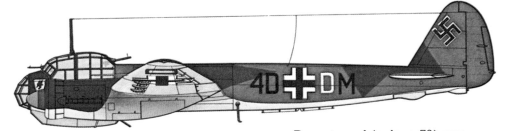

Desert sand (colour 79) was the original tropical finish, seen on this A-4/Trop of 1/LG 1 at Benghazi in 1942. This geschwader, which also used the A-9 and -10, bore the brunt of Ju 88 action in the Mediterranean.

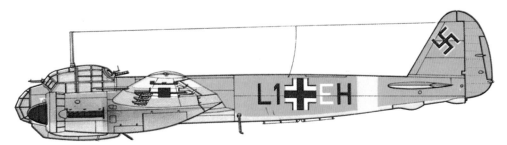

An old A-4, probably ex-Luftwaffe, with the Hungarian 4th Bomber Regiment on the Eastern Front in 1943. Unlike the similar machines used by Finland and Romania, they were never used against Germany.

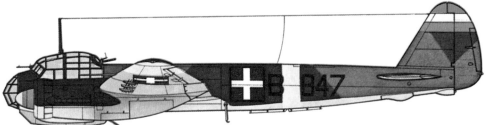

The A-14 anti-shipping aircraft, with 20mm MG FF in front of the gondola, used by Capt J. Saarinen of the Finnish 44th LeLv. He was killed in 1944, before the unit changed sides after the cease-fire of 4 September.

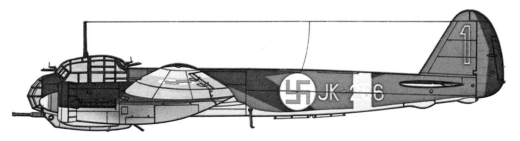

Junkers Ju 88

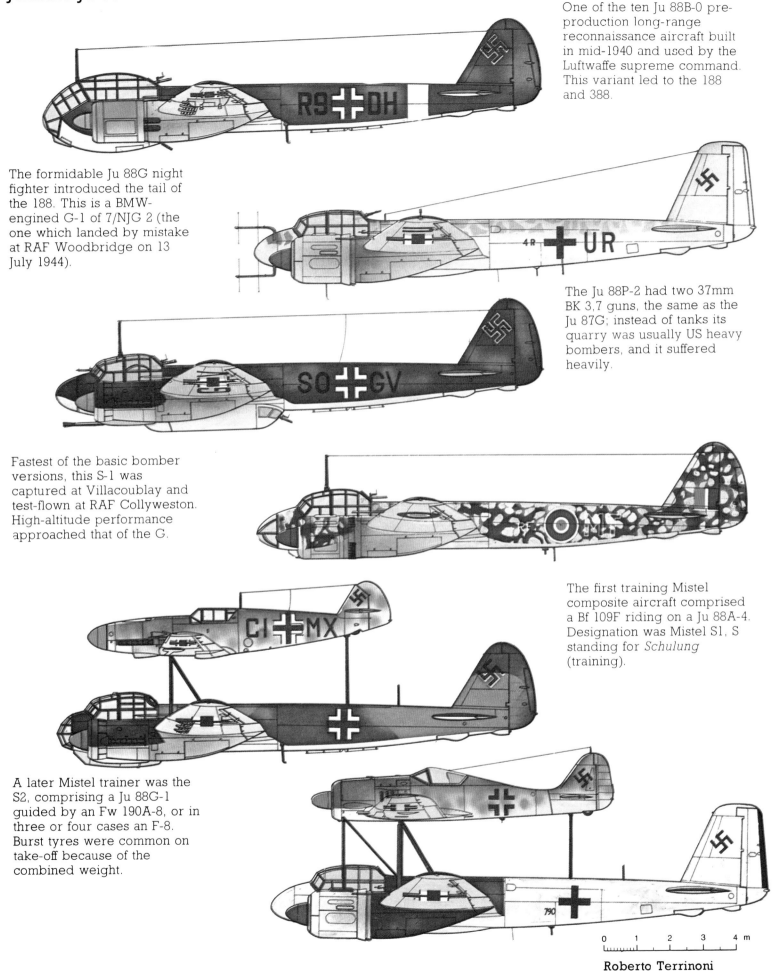

One of the ten Ju 88B-0 pre-production long-range reconnaissance aircraft built in mid-1940 and used by the Luftwaffe supreme command. This variant led to the 188 and 388.

The formidable Ju 88G night fighter introduced the tail of the 188. This is a BMW-engined G-1 of 7/NJG 2 (the one which landed by mistake at RAF Woodbridge on 13 July 1944).

The Ju 88P-2 had two 37mm BK 3,7 guns, the same as the Ju 87G; instead of tanks its quarry was usually US heavy bombers, and it suffered heavily.

Fastest of the basic bomber versions, this S-1 was captured at Villacoublay and test-flown at RAF Collyweston. High-altitude performance approached that of the G.

The first training Mistel composite aircraft comprised a Bf 109F riding on a Ju 88A-4. Designation was Mistel S1, S standing for *Schulung* (training).

A later Mistel trainer was the S2, comprising a Ju 88G-1 guided by an Fw 190A-8, or in three or four cases an F-8. Burst tyres were common on take-off because of the combined weight.

Roberto Terrinoni

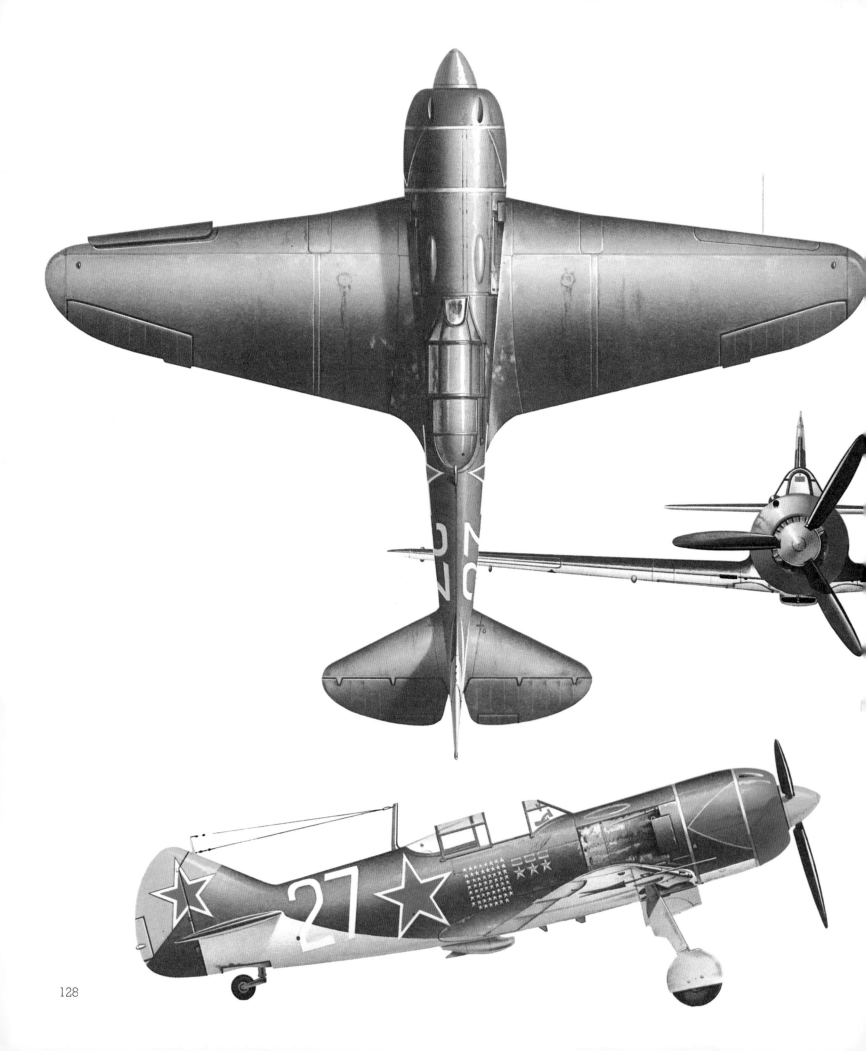

Lavochkin La-7

Displayed in the Moscow Museum of the Soviet armed forces, this La-7 was the last fighter flown in World War 2 by the top-scoring Soviet ace, whose name is usually rendered in English as Kozhedub or Kojedub. Ivan N. Kozhedub did not shoot down an enemy aircraft until 5 July 1943, when he was flying an La-5. (Previously he had, against his wishes, been kept on as an instructor.) On 2 May 1944 he was given an La-5FN with special presentation insignia and this took his score to 47 in mid-July. He then switched to this La-7, which appears to have been one of those fitted with only two guns.

Amedeo Gigli

Essentially the LaG-5 or
LaGG-5 was a LaGG-3
re-engined with the M-82
or M-82F radial. Despite
bad workmanship and
deeper problems it had
the makings of a
splendid fighter.

The La-5FN of
V.I. Popkov, who scored
41 confirmed victories in
the closing months of the
European war. By
February 1943 all
engines were of the
more powerful FN type.

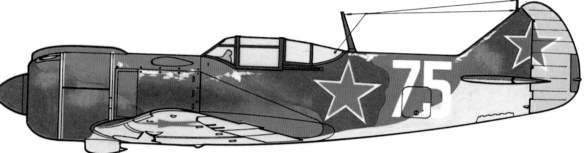

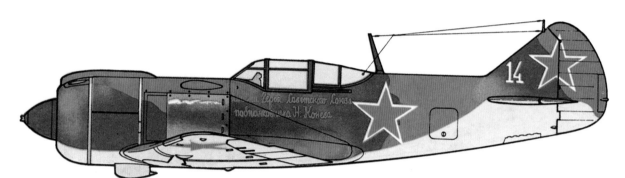

This was the La-5FN
flown by Ivan Kozhedub
during summer 1944. It is
inscribed 'In the name of
Hero of the Soviet Union
Lt-Col N. Konyev'

This La-5 was flown by L.
Valousek of the 1st
Czech fighter regiment,
which was integrated
with Soviet operations in
the Tri Duby area,
during the September
1944 Slovak revolt.

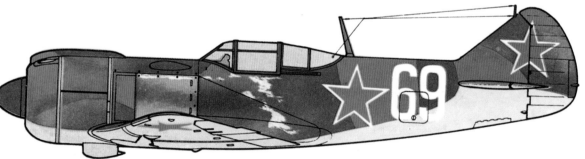

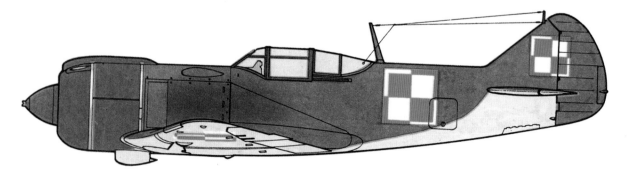

This La-5FN was not
allowed to wear Polish
markings until after the
war, though several
Polish units had operated
the type from the end of
1943.

Lavochkin LaGG-3 to La-11

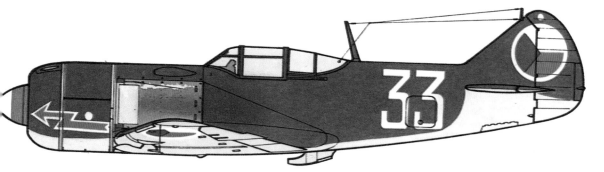

An La-7 of the Czech air division, repainted in national markings after the end of the war. In contrast, the La-7 in the national air museum in Prague wears Russian insignia.

In the La-7UTI dual trainer the rudder chord was considerably increased and the oil cooler returned to the same position as in the La-5.

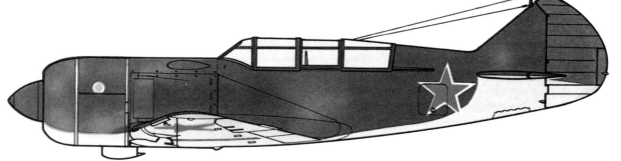

This La-7 has two underwing ramjets, similar to those fitted to a pair of La-9 fighters which took part in the Armed Forces Day flying display at Tushino in 1945. A number of La-7s and -9s actually saw service with a liquid rocket in the tail.

This is the La-7 in the Prague museum, restored in Russian markings even though the same aircraft saw active service with the 1st Czech mixed air division.

Final model in the publicly known series of Lavochkin piston-engined fighters was the outstanding La-11. Too late for the Great Patriotic War (WW2), it saw wide service with Communist countries. This one made a forced landing at Tullinge, Sweden, in May 1949.

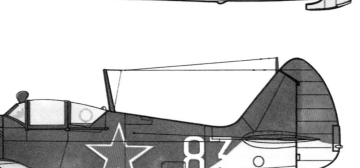

Roberto Terrinoni

Lavochkin LaGG-3 to La-11

Little is known of S.A. Lavochkin prior to his teaming up with V.P. Gorbunov and M.I. Gudkov in 1938 to create a new fighter to meet an important specification. All the submissions to this specification were relatively small machines powered by the large and heavy water-cooled engines then the most powerful available in the Soviet Union. Another factor shared by all the submissions known in the West was elimination of light alloys wherever this was practicable. Such aluminium-based materials were likely to be in short supply in emergency, whereas steel and wood were plentiful. This inevitably resulted in aircraft a little less efficient, but able to be built quickly in extremely large numbers. Lavochkin's new fighter was almost all-wood, using advanced multiply curvature and bonding techniques. It flew on 30 March 1939.

After many changes the production model, called LaGG-1, was delivered from late 1940. It was a little slower than its MiG and Yak rivals, but had fair manoeuvrability and exceptional ability to survive combat damage. Handling shortcomings were rectified by early 1941 in the LaGG-3, with many small changes including wing slats. Later in 1941 LaGG-3s appeared with fresh armament options, an internally balanced rudder, retractable tail-wheel and, in winter, retractable ski landing gear. The final major change was to pipe the wing for drop tanks.

In late 1941 Lavochkin's team fitted a LaGG-3 of the latest type with a powerful radial engine. The result was a great success, performance being transformed and especially at high altitudes. It was no mean achievement to instal the big engine in the low-drag way that later became common in other countries. The new aircraft went into production at once as the LaG-5 while further modifications resulted within weeks in the La-5 (Gorbunov and Gudkov having retired or been dismissed) with the boosted F-series engine and cut-down rear fuselage to improve pilot view. By late 1942 the La-5 was being called 'the wooden saver of Stalingrad'; Lavochkin was given a Stalin Prize and his bureau

moved into the gigantic Aircraft Factory No 21 where each successive batch of 1,000 fighters had improvements.

By March 1943 a more powerful FN-series engine, with direct fuel-injection, was being fitted, distinguished by the long supercharger duct above the cowling. An intensive effort was mounted to reduce weight, and light-alloy was substituted for wood in the wing spars (later, elsewhere), though the resulting extra space was not used for fuel. Throughout 1943 the La-5FN was used in as many units as the Yaks, and it scored in outstanding all-round performance and manoeuvrability, gained at the expense of rather lighter armament than the opposing German fighters. The La-5UTI was a trainer, with rear instructor cockpit, F-series engine, reduced tankage and a single gun.

During 1943 production switched to the aesthetically more attractive La-7, in which the big upper inlet duct was removed and the supercharger and oil-cooler fed by ram inlets in the wing roots and under the rear fuselage. Armament was increased, though continued efforts at weight-saving resulted in reduction in fuel capacity and increases in light-alloy structure. By late 1943 the La-7 was probably the best dogfighter in service in the world, and it was selected by almost all the Soviet aces. As before, the La-7UTI was a single-gun dual trainer, and the La-7R was an experimental version with a liquid rocket engine in the tail. There were other versions, some of which led to the next-generation La-9.

Again, this increased the proportion of light alloy, which was now close to 100%. Though superficially resembling an La-7 with square-cut wings and tailplane, the -9 was actually a new design that had no part betraying LaGG ancestry. Among the more obvious changes were a new cockpit and canopy, vertical tail, engine installation and armament. Deliveries began in late 1944 but the -9 saw only limited action before VE-Day. After the war, with the -5FN, -7 and their trainer versions, it equipped many communist air forces.

COUNTRY OF ORIGIN Soviet Union.

CREW 1, except UTI versions 2.

TOTAL PRODUCED **LaGG-1**: over 500; **LaGG-3**: about 7,000; **LaG-5, La-5**: about 2,000; **La-5FN**: about 15,000; **La-7**: believed 5,753; **La-9**: probably about 2,500.

DIMENSIONS Wingspan 9·8m (32ft 1$\frac{7}{8}$in), except **La-9**: 10·6m (34ft 9$\frac{1}{3}$in); length, **LaGG**: 8·87m (29ft 1$\frac{1}{4}$in); **La-5**: 8·5m (27ft 10$\frac{5}{8}$in); **La-7**: believed as -9; **La-9**: 9·2m (30ft 1in); wing area 17·5m^2 (188·36ft^2), except -9 unknown.

WEIGHTS Empty, **LaGG-3**: 2620kg (5.776lb): **La-5FN**: 2800kg (6,173lb); **-7**: 2638kg (5,816lb); maximum loaded, **-3**: 3300kg (7,275lb), **-5FN**: 3360kg (7,407lb), **-7**: 3400kg (7,495lb).

ENGINE **LaGG-1**: Klimov M-105P vee-12 rated at 1,050hp; **-3**: M-105PF, 1,240hp; **-5**: 1,330hp Shvetsov M-82A 14-cylinder radial; **-5FN, -7**: 1,700hp M-82FN; **-9**: 1,850hp ASh-82FNV.

MAXIMUM SPEED **-3**: 560km/h (348mph); **-5**: 626km/h (389mph); **-5FN**: 647 km/h (402mph); **-7**: 680km/h (422·5mph); **-9**: 690km/h (429mph).

SERVICE CEILING **-3**: 9000m (29,529ft); **-5FN**: 10000m (32,800ft); **-7**: 10500m (34,450ft).

RANGE **-3**: 650km (404 miles); **-5, -5FN**: 700km (435 miles); **-7**: 635km (395 miles); **-9**: 1725km (1,072 miles).

MILITARY LOAD **LaGG-1, -3**: very varied but usually one 20mm ShVAK plus one or two 12·7mm (0·5in) BS plus six RS-82 rockets or two 50kg (110lb) and four 25kg (55lb) bombs. **La-5, 5FN**: usually two 20mm ShVAK plus bomb-load of 150kg (331lb). **La-7**: three 20mm ShVAK plus six RS-82 or two 100kg (220lb) bombs. **La-9**: four 20mm ShVAK or 23mm NR-23.

Lockheed P-38 Lightning

Called 'fork-tailed devil' by the Luftwaffe, the unique P-38 was designed to meet a far-sighted US Army specification of February 1937 which called for a speed of 360mph (579km/h) at medium height and an endurance at this speed of one hour. The Lockheed 22, the company's first purely military design, was a radical concept posing high risks, with two of the new Allison engines, ducts leading to and from turbochargers in the tops of the long tail booms, further pipes linking the engines to coolant radiators on the sides of the booms, and a battery of guns in the nose of the small central nacelle. The first prototype, accepted by the Army as the XP-38, flew on 27 January 1939. It soon shattered all US transcontinental records in a startlingly fast flight to New York, but was destroyed on arrival.

Three months later 13 test aircraft were ordered, but before the first of these flew the British ordered 667 of an export version. Inexplicably, the British requested removal of the turbochargers and the counter-rotation of the 'handed' propellers, and Lockheed's prediction of poor performance was amply fulfilled, the RAF rejecting the resulting inferior aircraft. All the RAF contributed was the name, Lightning.

In August 1941 the USAAF received the first true production P-38D, with many detail changes. This tough but shapely machine incorporated a laminar-flow wing, Fowler flaps, intercoolers in the leading edges, a pull-out step at the rear tip of the nacelle for climbing aboard, and a comfortable cockpit with aileron control wheel instead of a stick. The P-38 was probably the quietest fighter in history, the exhaust merely whispering out of the turbo exits. It was extremely forgiving, and could be mishandled in many ways, but the rate of roll was too slow for it to excel as a dogfighter.

By 1942 the F model introduced racks under the inner wings for tanks or bombs, and a version of the F introduced the F-5 series of unarmed photo-reconnaissance models. The G added more power and a new radio, but the H of September 1942 changed to an even more powerful version of the engine and increased the external bomb load. In August 1943, when production had greatly increased, a demand for more range was met in the J by adding fuel for an extra hour in the leading edge. This meant moving the intercoolers to below the spinners, together with the oil coolers, but here the latter were too efficient and, usually as a result of the oil becoming too sluggish, engine failure or turbo overspeed caused far more losses than combat. To improve manoeuvrability later J models had hydraulically boosted ailerons and small powered dive flaps under the centre section. One of the enduring shortcomings was inadequate cockpit heating, and most P-38s flew at high altitude.

There were many modifications, including examples with skis, the redesigned XP-49 with different engines, and a large number of bombing leadship variants equipped either with 'Mickey' BTO (bombing through overcast) radar or with a Norden sight and bombardier in a glazed nose.

Most numerous of all versions was the one in production at VJ-Day, the P-38L. This had the most powerful wartime Allison engines and introduced underwing attachments for rockets. Numerous L models were completed as F-5E and G photographic aircraft, and 75 were rebuilt after delivery as P-38M night fighters for use in the Pacific. This version had ASH radar in an undernose pod worked by an operator seated in a confined space just behind the pilot.

Lightnings were never great fighters in the close-combat sense, but they combined numerous good qualities and were among the best long-range interceptors of the war. The first kill was an Fw 200C shot down in August 1942 by a P-38F from Iceland. The P-38 subsequently served in Western Europe, throughout the Mediterranean, Far East and Pacific. Top P-38 exponent was Maj Richard Bong, who scored 40 in the Pacific. In this theatre the P-38 undertook one of the most remarkable missions of the entire war: the interception at extreme range of the aircraft conveying Adm Yamamoto.

COUNTRY OF ORIGIN USA.

CREW Fighters, 1; some other versions, 2.

TOTAL PRODUCED 9,942.

DIMENSIONS Wingspan 15·85m (52ft 0in); length, all fighter versions: 11·53m (37ft 10in); wing area 30·43m² (327·5ft²).

WEIGHTS Empty, **F**: 5563kg (12,265lb); **J**: 5797kg (12,780lb); maximum loaded, **F**: 8165kg (18,000lb), **J**: 9798kg (21,600lb).

ENGINES Two Allison V-1710 vee-12 liquid-cooled engines driving handed (opposite-rotation) propellers; **F**: 1,225hp V-1710-49/53; **G,J**: 1,425hp -88/91; **L**: 1,600hp -111/113.

MAXIMUM SPEED **F**: 636km/h (395mph); **G**: 644km/h (400mph); **H**: 650km/h (404mph); **J,L**: 676km/h (420mph).

SERVICE CEILING **D** to **G**: 11890m (39,000ft), **H** to **L**: 13410m (44,000ft).

RANGE **D,F,G,H**: 1448km (900 miles) on internal fuel, 2816km (1,750 miles with drop tanks on F,G,H); **J,L**: 1891km (1,175 miles) on internal fuel, 3637km (2,260 miles) with drop tanks.

MILITARY LOAD **D**: one 37mm cannon and four 12·7mm (0·5in); **E**: cannon changed to 20mm; **F**: racks added for two tanks, 454kg (1,000lb) bombs, torpedo or smoke apparatus; **H,J**: improved M2C cannon and pylons restressed for two bombs of 726kg (1,600lb); **L**: extra option of rockets under outer wings, at first row of 10 each side later replaced by single attachment for 7 each side.

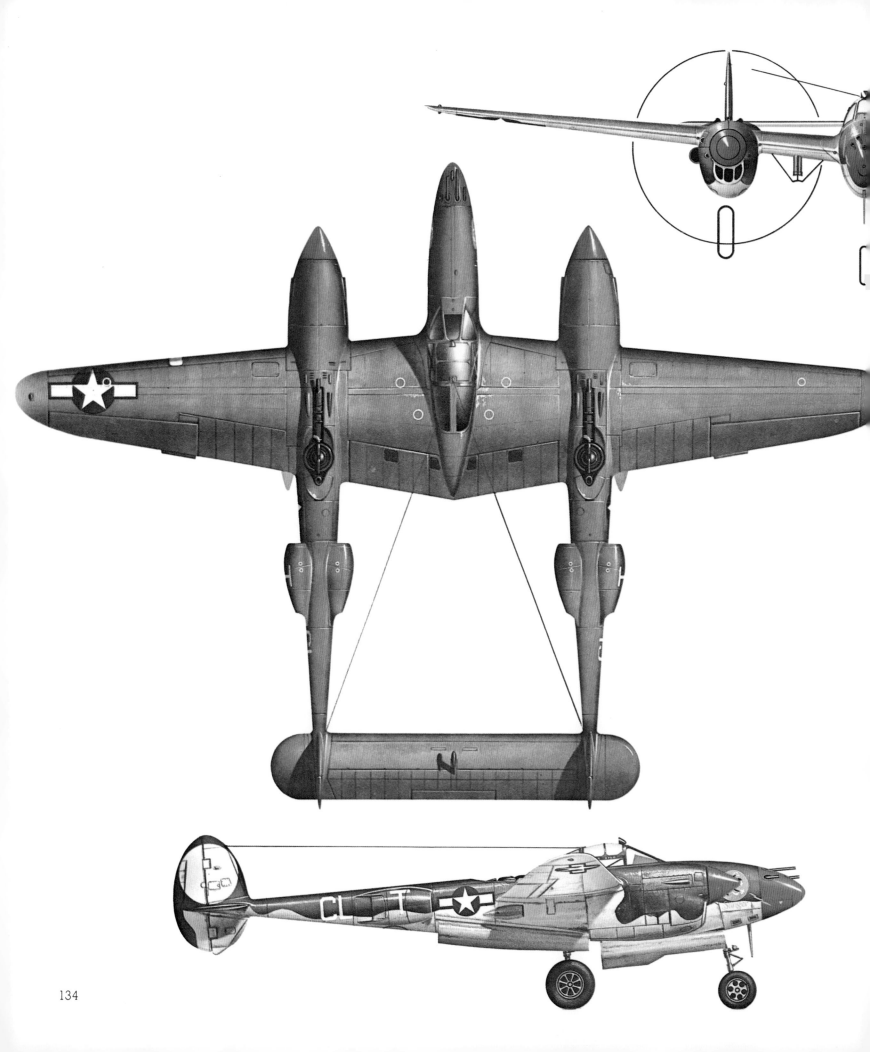

Lockheed P-38J Lightning

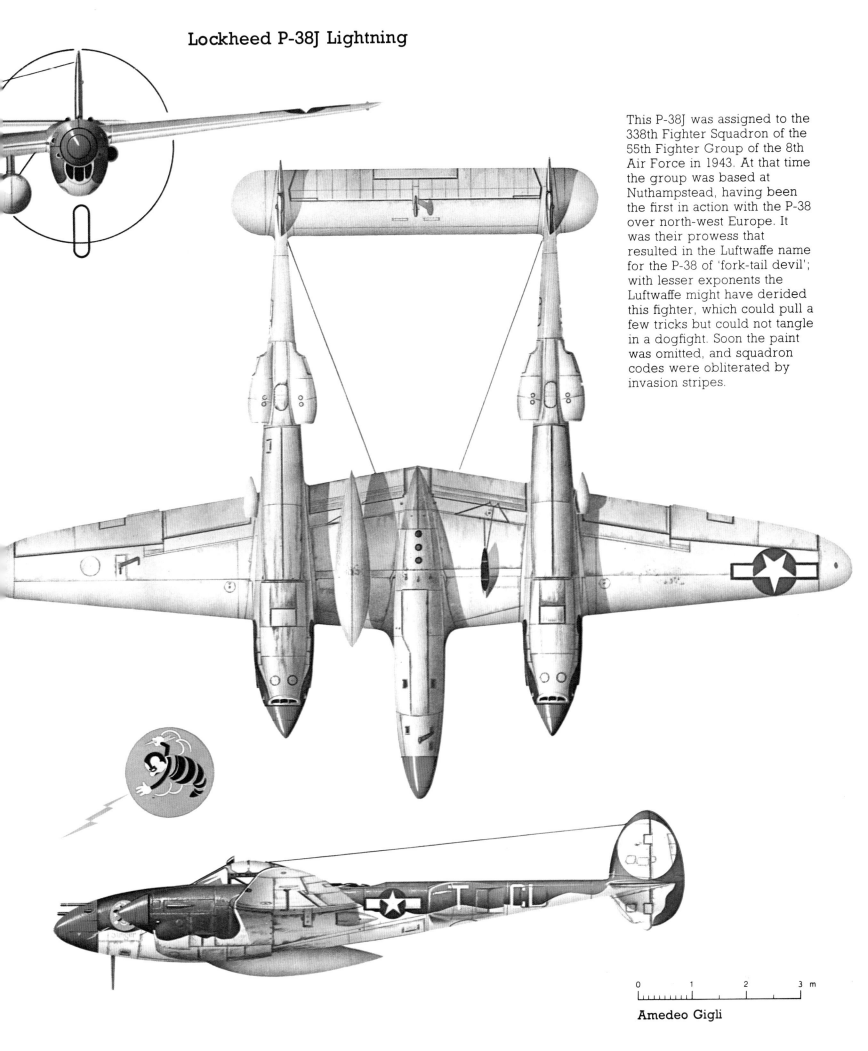

This P-38J was assigned to the 338th Fighter Squadron of the 55th Fighter Group of the 8th Air Force in 1943. At that time the group was based at Nuthampstead, having been the first in action with the P-38 over north-west Europe. It was their prowess that resulted in the Luftwaffe name for the P-38 of 'fork-tail devil'; with lesser exponents the Luftwaffe might have derided this fighter, which could pull a few tricks but could not tangle in a dogfight. Soon the paint was omitted, and squadron codes were obliterated by invasion stripes.

Amedeo Gigli

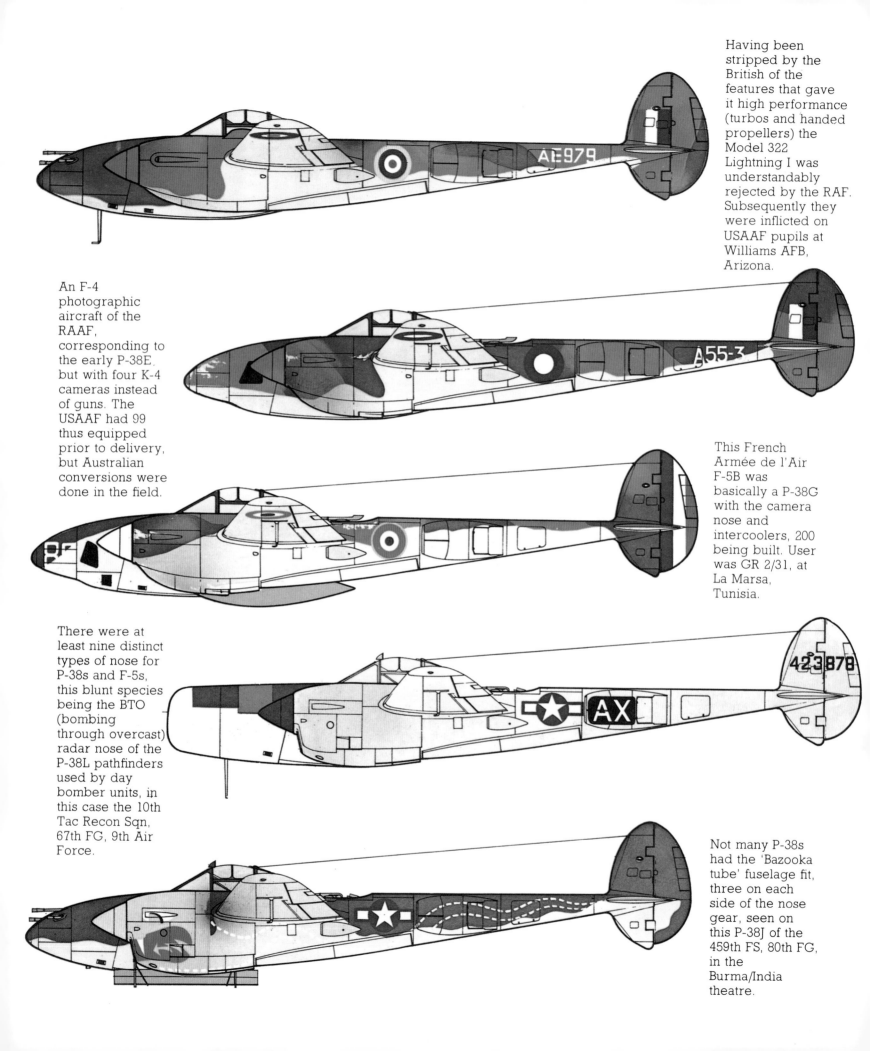

Having been stripped by the British of the features that gave it high performance (turbos and handed propellers) the Model 322 Lightning I was understandably rejected by the RAF. Subsequently they were inflicted on USAAF pupils at Williams AFB, Arizona.

An F-4 photographic aircraft of the RAAF, corresponding to the early P-38E, but with four K-4 cameras instead of guns. The USAAF had 99 thus equipped prior to delivery, but Australian conversions were done in the field.

This French Armée de l'Air F-5B was basically a P-38G with the camera nose and intercoolers, 200 being built. User was GR 2/31, at La Marsa, Tunisia.

There were at least nine distinct types of nose for P-38s and F-5s, this blunt species being the BTO (bombing through overcast) radar nose of the P-38L pathfinders used by day bomber units, in this case the 10th Tac Recon Sqn, 67th FG, 9th Air Force.

Not many P-38s had the 'Bazooka tube' fuselage fit, three on each side of the nose gear, seen on this P-38J of the 459th FS, 80th FG, in the Burma/India theatre.

Lockheed P-38 Lightning

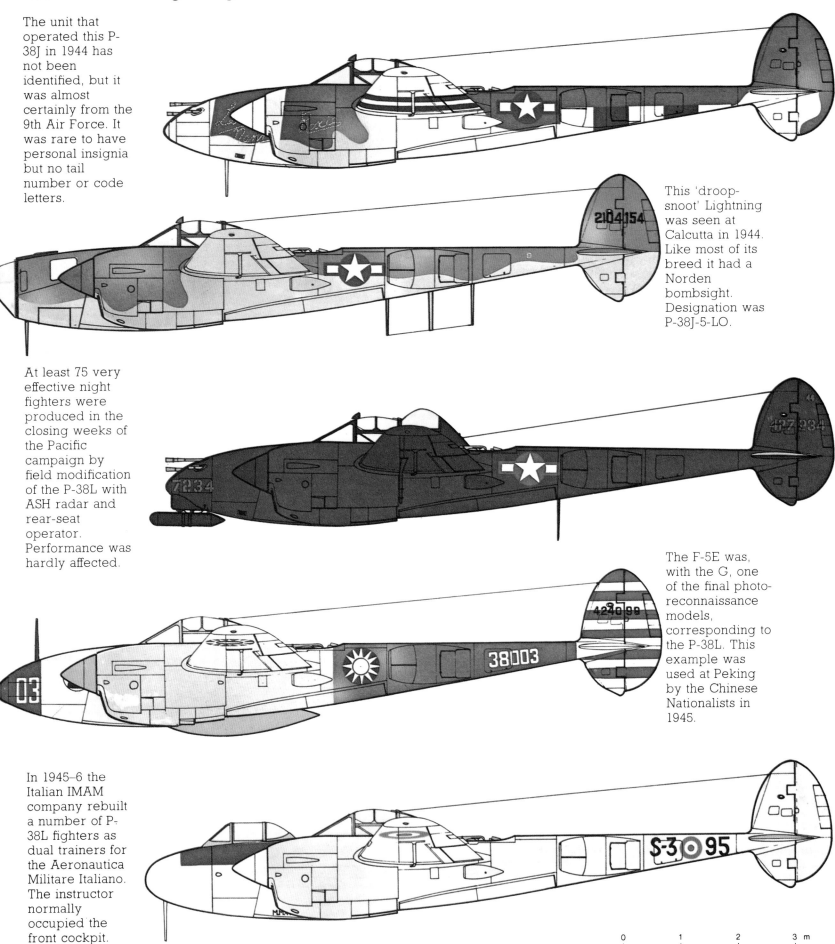

The unit that operated this P-38J in 1944 has not been identified, but it was almost certainly from the 9th Air Force. It was rare to have personal insignia but no tail number or code letters.

This 'droop-snoot' Lightning was seen at Calcutta in 1944. Like most of its breed it had a Norden bombsight. Designation was P-38J-5-LO.

At least 75 very effective night fighters were produced in the closing weeks of the Pacific campaign by field modification of the P-38L with ASH radar and rear-seat operator. Performance was hardly affected.

The F-5E was, with the G, one of the final photo-reconnaissance models, corresponding to the P-38L. This example was used at Peking by the Chinese Nationalists in 1945.

In 1945–6 the Italian IMAM company rebuilt a number of P-38L fighters as dual trainers for the Aeronautica Militare Italiano. The instructor normally occupied the front cockpit.

0   1   2   3 m

Roberto Terrinoni

This Messerschmitt Bf 109E-4/N/Trop is typical of the final batches of the 'Emil' (109E series), with DB 601N engine and pointed spinner. It is seen serving with 1/JG 27, the unit famed, and at one time named, for Lt H.-J. Marseille, who scored 158 victories including 151 against the RAF in North Africa before suffering engine failure (not in combat) and striking the tailplane on bailing out in September 1942. Marseille flew 'yellow 14', while this is 'white 3'. Note the belly bomb/tank fitting, and tropical filter on the left-side air inlet.

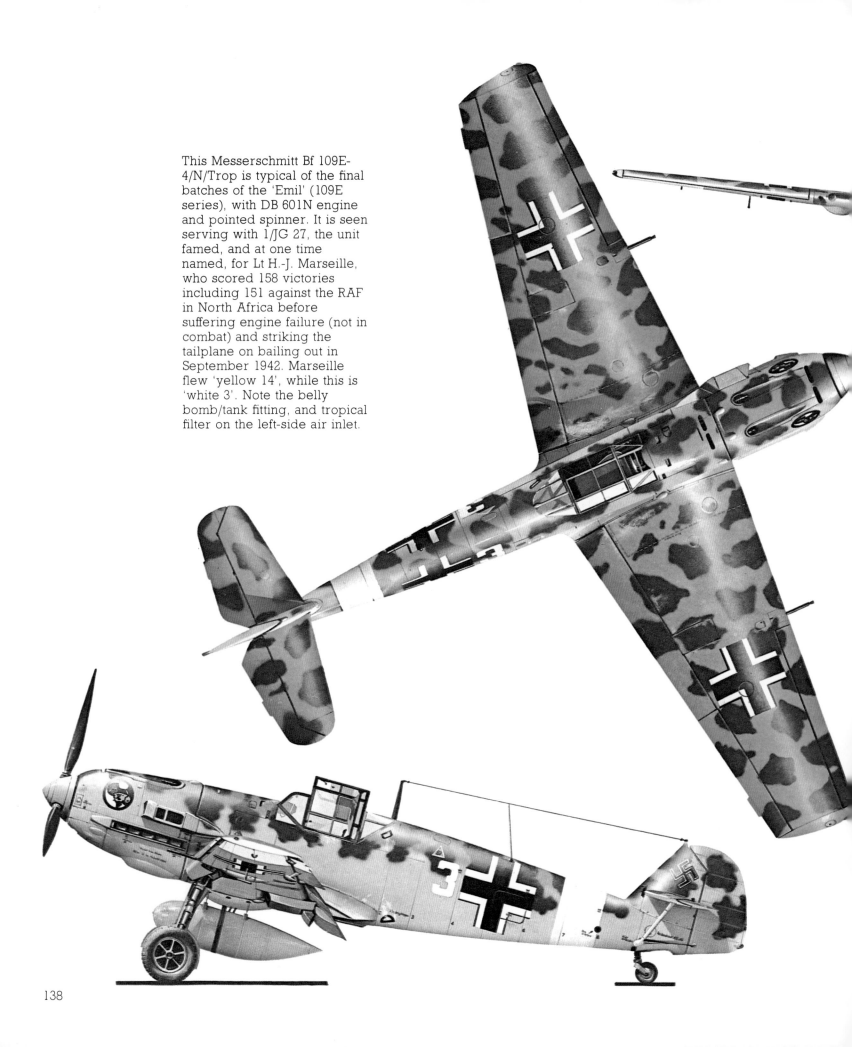

Messerschmitt Bf 109E-4/N/Trop

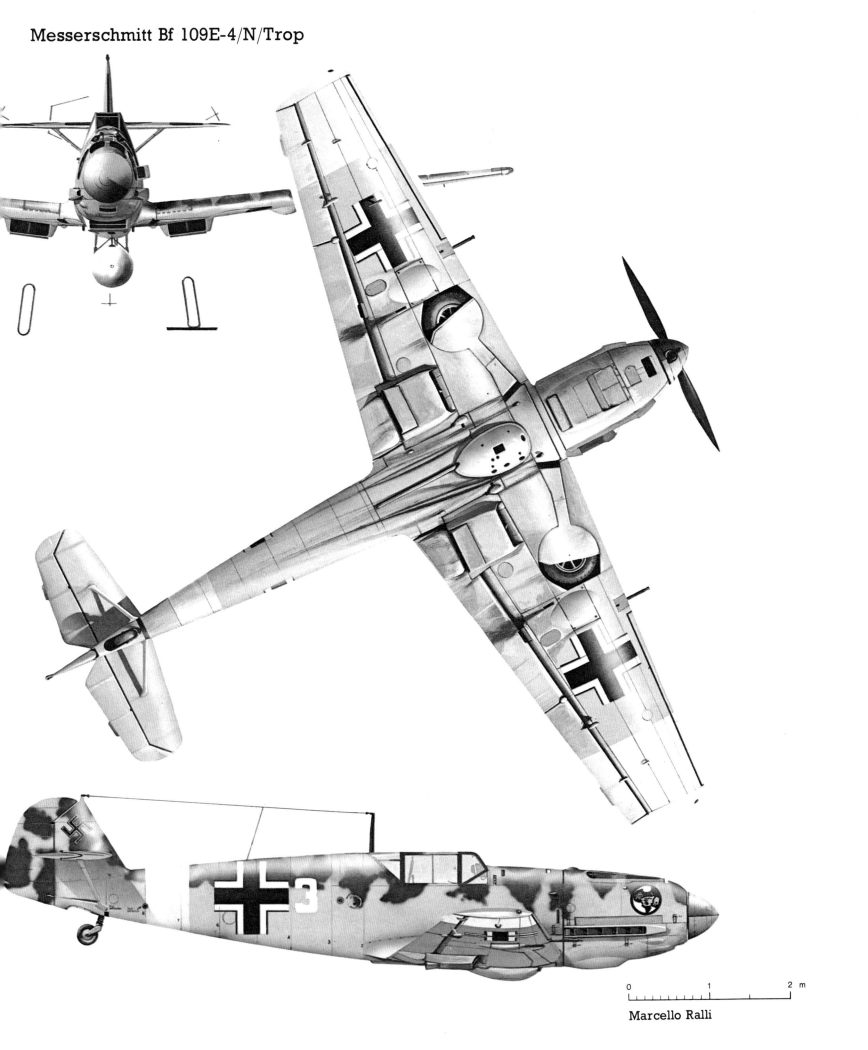

Marcello Ralli

0   1   2 m

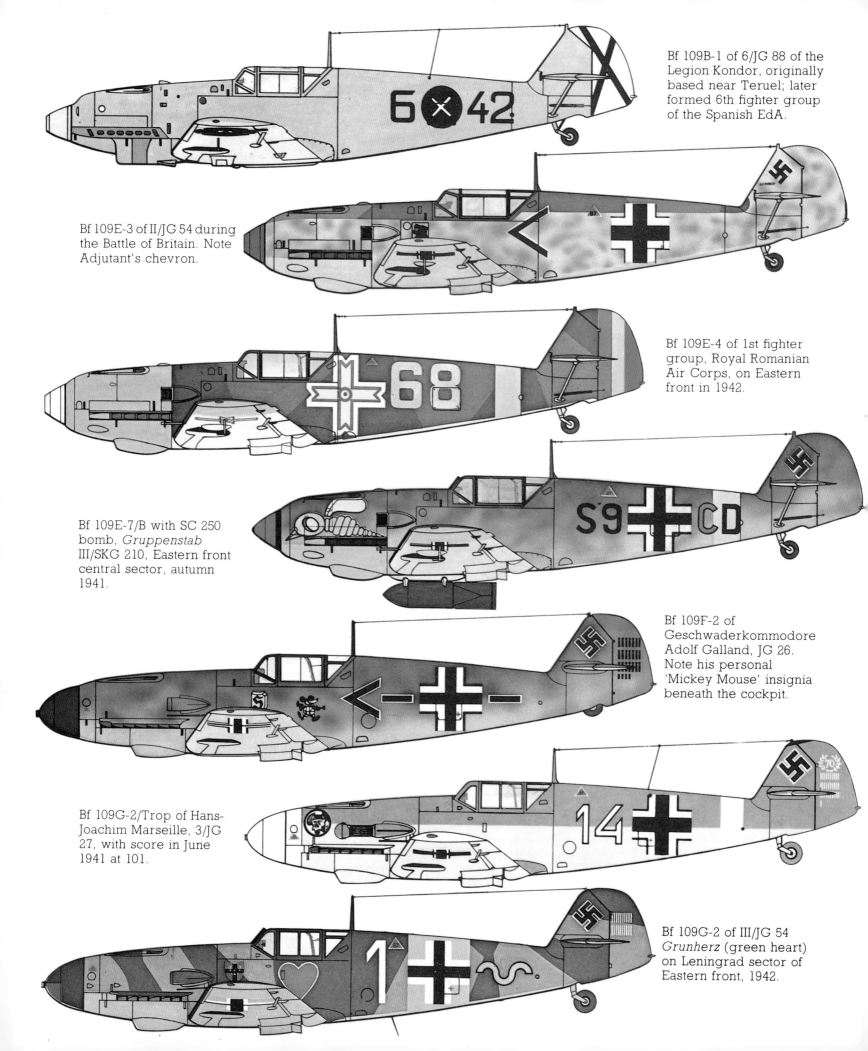

Bf 109B-1 of 6/JG 88 of the Legion Kondor, originally based near Teruel; later formed 6th fighter group of the Spanish EdA.

Bf 109E-3 of II/JG 54 during the Battle of Britain. Note Adjutant's chevron.

Bf 109E-4 of 1st fighter group, Royal Romanian Air Corps, on Eastern front in 1942.

Bf 109E-7/B with SC 250 bomb, *Gruppenstab* III/SKG 210, Eastern front central sector, autumn 1941.

Bf 109F-2 of Geschwaderkommodore Adolf Galland, JG 26. Note his personal 'Mickey Mouse' insignia beneath the cockpit.

Bf 109G-2/Trop of Hans-Joachim Marseille, 3/JG 27, with score in June 1941 at 101.

Bf 109G-2 of III/JG 54 *Grunherz* (green heart) on Leningrad sector of Eastern front, 1942.

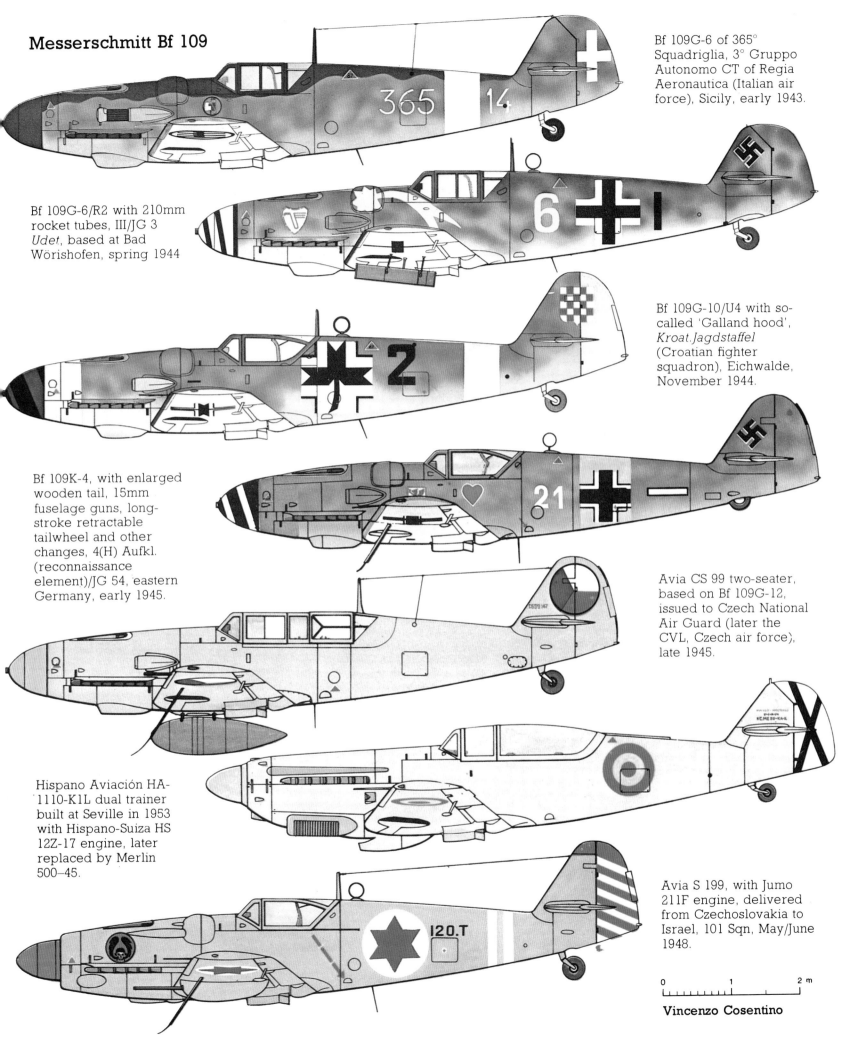

Messerschmitt Bf 109

Bf 109G-6 of 365°
Squadriglia, 3° Gruppo
Autonomo CT of Regia
Aeronautica (Italian air
force), Sicily, early 1943.

Bf 109G-6/R2 with 210mm
rocket tubes, III/JG 3
Udet, based at Bad
Wörishofen, spring 1944

Bf 109G-10/U4 with so-
called 'Galland hood',
Kroat.Jagdstaffel
(Croatian fighter
squadron), Eichwalde,
November 1944.

Bf 109K-4, with enlarged
wooden tail, 15mm
fuselage guns, long-
stroke retractable
tailwheel and other
changes, 4(H) Aufkl.
(reconnaissance
element)/JG 54, eastern
Germany, early 1945.

Avia CS 99 two-seater,
based on Bf 109G-12,
issued to Czech National
Air Guard (later the
CVL, Czech air force),
late 1945.

Hispano Aviación HA-
1110-K1L dual trainer
built at Seville in 1953
with Hispano-Suiza HS
12Z-17 engine, later
replaced by Merlin
500–45.

Avia S 199, with Jumo
211F engine, delivered
from Czechoslovakia to
Israel, 101 Sqn, May/June
1948.

0   1   2 m

Vincenzo Cosentino

Messerschmitt Bf 109

Produced in greater numbers than any other fighter before or since, the Bf 109 was a strange enigma. One of its greatest puzzles was its continuance in ever-increasing production at a time when it was so full of shortcomings that it would have been judged unacceptable to most other air forces. Throughout its life its attributes were small size, toughness, serviceability and excellent armament. Average pilots found the mass-produced G-model, built from 1942 onwards, no easy mount to master; but in the hands of a true expert it was deadly. Several 109-equipped JG (fighter wings) had 1,000 victories before 1942, and some went on to exceed 7,000.

In 1934 Professor Willi Messerschmitt was extremely unpopular with the Nazis, and was curtly told he would receive no production order for the new fighter he was building. Flown in early September 1935, the Bf 109 was the most advanced fighter in the world. Its features included stressed-skin construction, a highly loaded wing with flaps and full-span slats, neat outward-retracting landing gear far ahead of the centre of gravity, and a hinged canopy on the cockpit. The whole machine had a rakish appearance utterly unlike the nimble open-cockpit biplanes that filled the brains of the fighter experts. Even Ernst Udet, soon to head Luftwaffe procurement, said 'That thing will never make a fighter!' But a few months later he admitted the Messerschmitt, by an outcast company which had no experience of military aircraft, was simply fantastic.

So dominant was the 109 that it formed virtually the entire single-seat fighter force of the Luftwaffe at the start of World War 2. Blooded in Spain in 1937, it had progressed by 1939 to the outstanding new 109E version, combining heavy armament with the best available engine – one of the features of the latter being direct fuel-injection which eliminated icing and allowed negative-g manoeuvres without the engine spluttering or cutting out as it did on fighters of other nations. On the other hand, the 109 became increas-

ingly difficult to fly as speed was increased. In tight turns the slats flicked open and closed, jerking the pilot off his aim, and the extremely heavy ailerons were made even more difficult by the pilot's posture in the narrow cockpit of the 109.

By mid-1940 the E-series was carrying bombs or reconnaissance cameras, and special equipment included skis, tropical filters for sand, overload tanks and power-boost systems. At the end of 1940 the F appeared with more power, different armament, a rounded wing and many other changes, resulting in what most pilots considered the best 109. It should have been the last, but absence of a successor resulted in the 109G, first delivered in early 1942. With a bigger and heavier engine, boosted by either MW50 (methanol/water) or GM-1 (nitrous oxide) the G soon became standard, augmented by a profusion of field kits for weapons and special role equipment. Production kept climbing, and, despite the G ('Gustav' to its pilots) being extremely unsatisfactory in many respects, it was built in ever-greater quantity to the end of the war, joined near the close by the K which had the so-called Galland hood giving better vision (used by most late-model Gs), taller wooden tail and many other refinements.

Fighters assigned to Defence of the Reich were used by day, with rocket projectors and other missiles to break up US bomber formations, and by night with simple navaids and using the freelance *Wilde Sau* (wild boar) technique which dispensed with almost everything but pilot vision. The 109G served with all Axis air forces on the Eastern and Italian fronts, and was exported to Switzerland and Spain. The latter country manufactured a succession of post-war versions with Hispano-Suiza and Rolls-Royce engines. An even stranger cross-breed was the Czech Avia S 199, produced post-war from existing 109 parts but engined with ex-bomber Jumo 211s. The result was an almost unflyable fighter, which was nevertheless made in numbers and sold to Israel.

COUNTRY OF ORIGIN Germany.

CREW 1, except for rare dual trainer.

TOTAL PRODUCED German production in 1944–5 is impossible to assess accurately because hundreds of wings or fuselages were taken from bombed factories and built into fresh machines, but overall total including Spain and Czech post-war output is estimated at 35,000.

DIMENSIONS Wingspan, up to E: 9.85m (32ft 4½in), F onwards: 9.92m (32ft 6½in); length, E: 8.64m (28ft 4in), F: 8.84m (29ft 0¼in), G,K: 8.85m (29ft 0½in); wing area, up to E: 16.17m² (176.5ft²), F onwards: 16.2m² (174.38ft²).

WEIGHTS Empty, E-3: 2125kg (4,685lb), G-6: 2673kg (5,893lb); maximum loaded, E-3: 2685kg (5,919lb), G-6: 3400kg (7,496lb).

ENGINE Inverted-vee 12-cylinder; B,C: 635hp Junkers Jumo 210D or Ga; D: 1,000hp Daimler-Benz DB600Aa; E: 1,150 or 1,175hp DB601A or Aa, 1,200hp DB601N or 1,300hp DB601E; F: DB601E; G: 1,475hp DB605A or other version up to 1,800hp with special boost; K: 1,550hp DB605ASCM, 2,000hp with boost.

MAXIMUM SPEED B,C: 470km/h (292mph), D: 520km/h (323mph), E: 560/570km/h (348/354mph), F: 624km/h (388mph), G: depending on weapon fit, 569/690km/h (353/428mph), K: 729km/h (452mph).

SERVICE CEILING E: typically 10500m (34,450ft), F onwards: typically 12000m (39,372ft).

RANGE All versions, on internal fuel, approximately 700km (435 miles).

MILITARY LOAD B: three 7.92mm MG17; C: four MG17; D: 20mm MG FF and two MG17; E: two/three MG FF and two MG17, later also bombs up to 250kg (551lb); F: 15mm MG151 or 20mm MG151 and two MG17; G: early sub-types 20mm MG151 and two MG17, plus bombs to 500kg (1,102lb) or other stores, later variants 30mm MK108 (often three), two 13mm MG131, often 20mm MG151 in underwing gondolas; K: various, eg 30mm MK103 or MK108 and two 15mm MG151.

Messerschmitt Bf 110

During the 1930s one of several fundamental fighter debates concerned the long-range escort. Generally assumed to be twin-engined, and have a crew of two, such aircraft were to accompany bombers into enemy territory and protect them from interception. Apart from Britain, most nations equipped themselves with such machines. But in the stern test of battle their inability to dogfight put them at a grave disadvantage. The only reason the RAF regretted omitting such machines – a gap temporarily filled by an inadequate attempt to convert Blenheim bombers – was that they were ideal candidates for radar-equipped night fighters, something not dreamed of when the big fighters were planned.

In the Luftwaffe the category was called a *Zerstörer* (destroyer). The BFW company flew the prototype Bf 110 on 12 May 1936, and though extremely underpowered with two 730hp Jumo 210Ga engines the first production version of July 1938 carried heavy armament and was apparently the basis for a truly outstanding warplane. By 1939 the definitive 110C was at last in production with the long-awaited DB601 engine, and the general expectation was that it would simply carve a swathe through any enemy airspace. Goering said to his new *Zerstörergruppen*, 'You will be like Hannibal's cavalry protecting his elephants; the bombers are my elephants.' They were the élite of the Luftwaffe.

In Poland it was recognized that new tactics would be needed to overcome the Bf 110C's limited manoeuvrability, but the aircraft had proved extremely useful in many roles. In Norway in April 1940 they accomplished much, and a force of 350 cut through opposition in the West in May. But in the high summer it was a different story; ZG units were decimated over Britain, and on occasion the escorts had to be protected by the Bf 109! This did not seem important, as the Me 210 was about to replace the 110; but when the new aircraft proved a failure the 110 had to be kept in production in a succession of improved versions. It received new radio, extra tan-

kage, bomb racks, different guns, cameras, night-fighter radar, a third seat for a radar operator (in a few sub-types four men were crammed in) and a host of other add-ons often supplied as a field conversion kit.

From September 1940 it avoided Britain, but ranged over the Balkans, Crete, North Africa, the Eastern Front, and as a major night fighter, over Germany itself. Even in the later versions, which were burdened with more than a ton of extra equipment and handicapped by large exhaust flame-dampers, performance was sufficient for an *experte* to destroy several RAF heavy bombers in one night. The top-scorer, Heinz-Wolfgang Schnaufer, notched up a tally of 121. At all times the 110 was docile and extremely pleasant to fly, unlike the Me 210 and 410. Production of this basically obsolescent aircraft was actually increased each year until 1944, long after it was planned to have been replaced.

The first really big increase in weight had come in early 1941 with the long-range tanks, drop tanks and bombs of the D-series. With the E and F there were small increases in power, insufficient to match the great proliferation of weapons and equipment which in some F-versions included the first examples of *Schräge Musik* (jazz) upward-firing cannon and Lichtenstein radar with an aerodynamically degrading array of dipole aerials projecting ahead of the nose.

By mid-1942 the urgent need for a much better 110 (to replace its missing replacement) had resulted in the G-series, with bigger engine, re-engineered structure and systems, larger fins and rudders and many engine-installation improvements. Like the 109 and 190, versions were equipped with a succession of special weapons for use against American bombers by day and quite different equipment for use by night. Night fighters operated in constant fear of the RAF Mosquito intruders, while the day interceptors carried so many rocket tubes and heavy guns they were almost helpless against the American escorts.

COUNTRY OF ORIGIN Germany.

CREW At first 2, later 3 or 4.

TOTAL PRODUCED Reported as 5,873, 6,050 (believed the most accurate) and 6,150.

DIMENSIONS Wingspan, all major variants: 16·25m (53ft 3¾in): length **C**: 12·1m (39ft 8½in): **D-3,E-2**: 12·7m. (41ft 8in): most other versions, excluding radar: as C: with radar, 13·05m (42ft 9¾in): wing area 38·5m² (413·4ft²).

WEIGHTS Empty **C-1**: 4425kg (9,755lb): **G-2**: 5100kg (11,243lb): **G-4b**: about 5800kg (12,787lb): maximum loaded, **C-1**: 6750kg (14,880lb): **G-2,G-4b**: up to 10045kg (22,145lb).

ENGINES Two Daimler-Benz inverted-vee-12: **C,D**: 1,100hp DB601A-1: **E**: 1,200hp DB601N: **F**: 1,350hp DB601F: **G**: 1,475hp DB605B-1.

MAXIMUM SPEED All normal versions, clean: about 550km/h (342mph).

SERVICE CEILING Most: about 10000m (32,800ft), except clean **E,F**: 10900m (35,760ft) and late G-series night fighters 8000m (26,250ft).

RANGE **C**: typically 775km (480 miles): **D,E,F**: on internal fuel, typically 1200km (745 miles): **G**: internal fuel, 900km (560 miles): in all cases extended by drop tanks.

MILITARY LOAD **C**: two 20mm MG FF, four 7·92mm MG17, one 7·92mm MG15 in rear cockpit: **E**: various including fuselage racks for two 1000kg (2,205lb) bombs: **F**: some night fighters added two 30mm MK108 in ventral tray: **G**: extremely variable, but rear defence now twin 7·92mm MG81 and forward-firing guns usually two 20mm MG151, often augmented by two MK108 and with option of *Schräge Musik* inclined installation of two MK108 as first fitted to F-4/U1. Many models carried two 210mm rocket tubes and G-2/R4 was fitted with a 37mm BK 3,7 Flak 18 gun primarily for use against heavy day bombers.

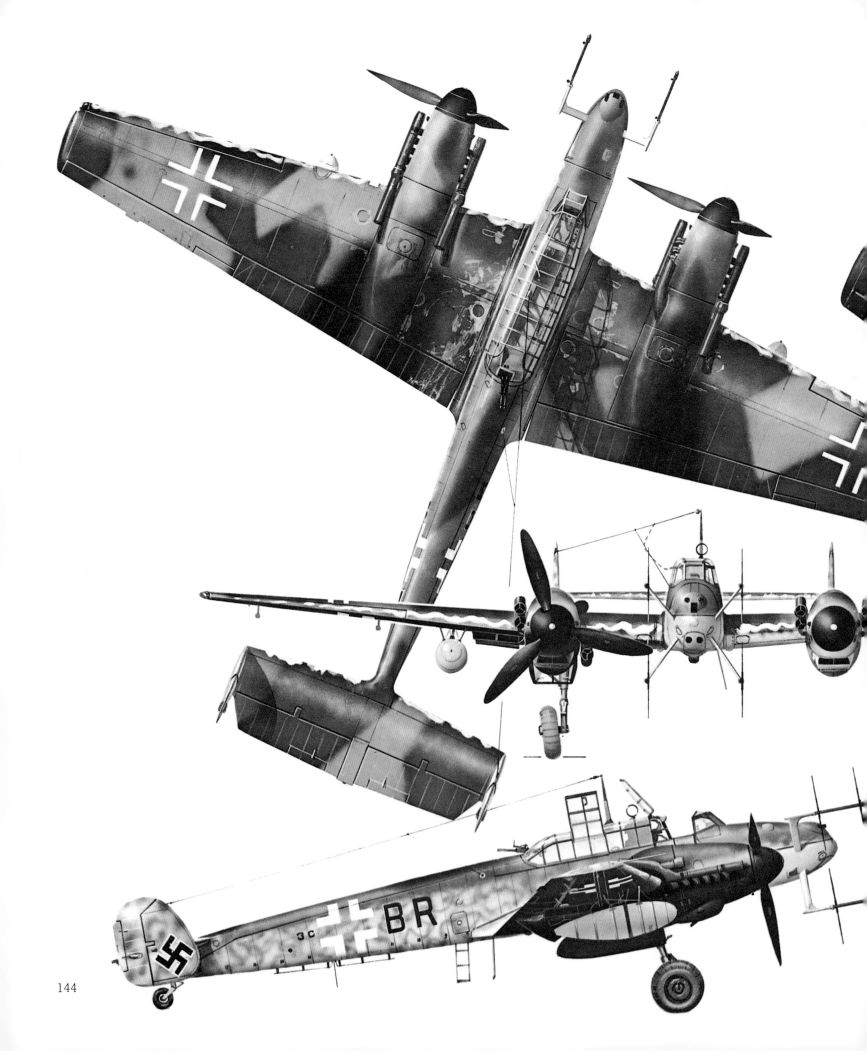

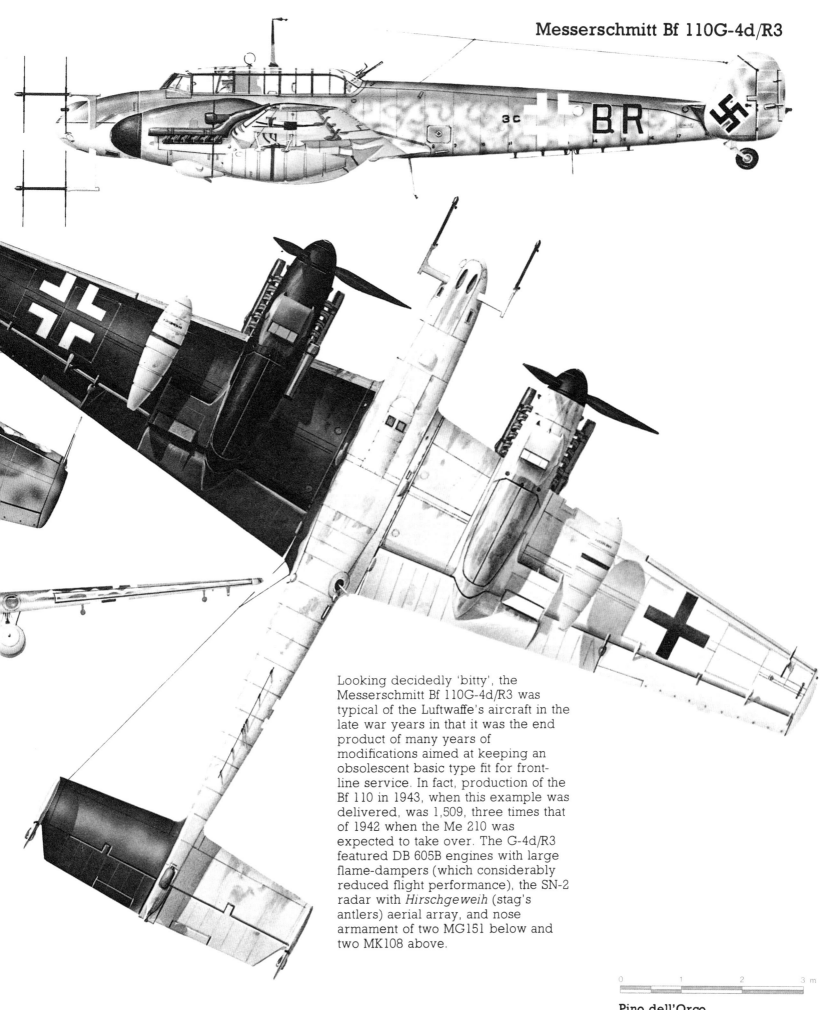

Messerschmitt Bf 110G-4d/R3

BR

Looking decidedly 'bitty', the Messerschmitt Bf 110G-4d/R3 was typical of the Luftwaffe's aircraft in the late war years in that it was the end product of many years of modifications aimed at keeping an obsolescent basic type fit for front-line service. In fact, production of the Bf 110 in 1943, when this example was delivered, was 1,509, three times that of 1942 when the Me 210 was expected to take over. The G-4d/R3 featured DB 605B engines with large flame-dampers (which considerably reduced flight performance), the SN-2 radar with *Hirschgeweih* (stag's antlers) aerial array, and nose armament of two MG151 below and two MK108 above.

0   1   2   3 m

Pino dell'Orco

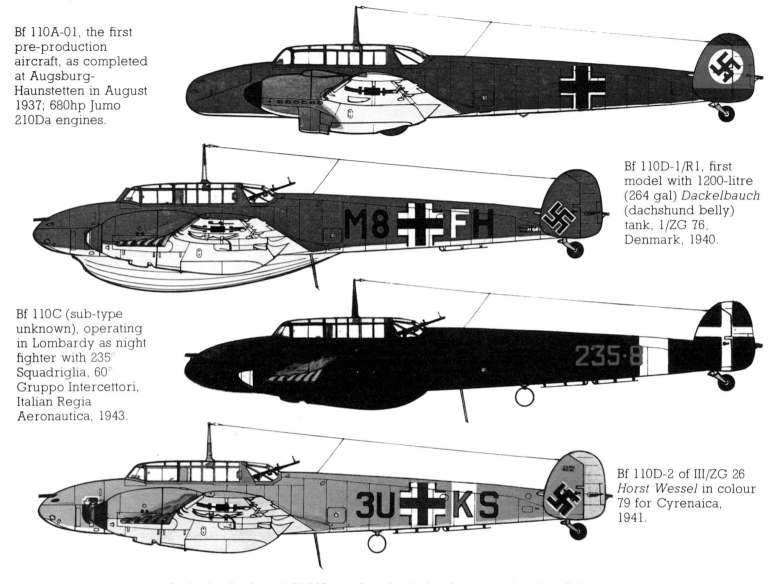

Bf 110A-01, the first pre-production aircraft, as completed at Augsburg-Haunstetten in August 1937; 680hp Jumo 210Da engines.

Bf 110D-1/R1, first model with 1200-litre (264 gal) *Dackelbauch* (dachshund belly) tank, 1/ZG 76, Denmark, 1940.

Bf 110C (sub-type unknown), operating in Lombardy as night fighter with 235° Squadriglia, 60° Gruppo Intercettori, Italian Regia Aeronautica, 1943.

Bf 110D-2 of III/ZG 26 *Horst Wessel* in colour 79 for Cyrenaica, 1941.

Insignia of selected Bf 110 geschwader (wings), gruppen and staffels.

1 1/ZG 76.
2 5/ZG 76.
3 I/ZG 76.
4 I/ZG 52.
5 1/NJG 3.
6 Erprobungsgruppe 210 (later SKG 210).
7 II/ZG 76 *Haifisch*.
8 Original badge of Nachtjagdverband (night fighter force).
9 V/JG 5; 7,10,13 *Dachshund-staffeln*.
10 KG 55.
11 II/ZG 26.
12 I/ZG 26 (later other units), *Ringelpitz*.
13 ZG 26 *Horst Wessel*.
14 III/ZG 76.
15 ZG 1 *Wespen*.
16 7/ZG 26.
17 4/14(H) Aufkl. reconnaissance group *Munchausen*.
18 Unidentified gruppe of ZG 26.

Messerschmitt Bf 110

Bf 110D-2 of 4/ZG 76 *Haifisch* (shark) detached to Iraq in May 1941 and temporarily in Iraqi colours.

Bf 110D-3 with dinghy in extended rear fuselage and DB 601N engines, III/ZG 76, Balkans/Greece, spring 1941.

Bf 110F (probably an F-2) with *Spanner* infra-red night-detection sensor for hostile aircraft exhausts, V/JG 5 on Finnish sector of Eastern front, 1942.

Bf 110G-2/R3 with four Wfr.Gr.210 rocket tubes, II/ZG 76, Grossenhain, 1944, used primarily in day bomber interceptor role.

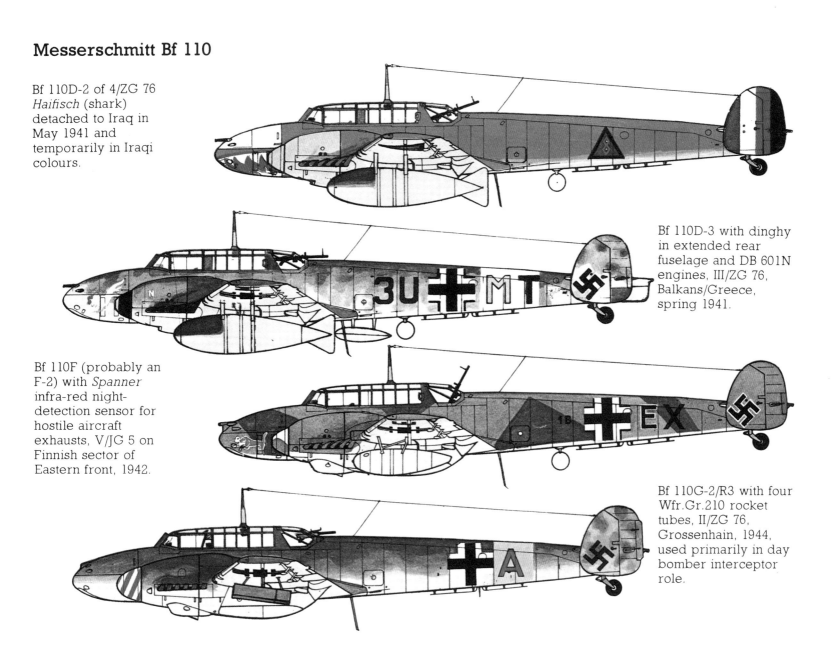

Nose of G-4/U5 with single-pole aerial array of FuG 212 Lichtenstein C-1.

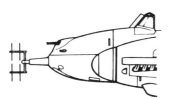

Nose of unidentified G-4 variant with SN-2 radar and twin long-barrel cannon with flash-hiders (possibly MG 151) in the upper position. Probably experimental installation on G-4c/R4.

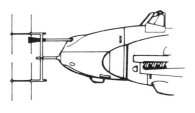

Bf 110G-4b of III/NJG 1, March–October 1944 (probably aircraft of Gruppenkommandeur Martin Drewes), with SN-2 radar and also C-1 FuG 212 retained to permit closure to visual range.

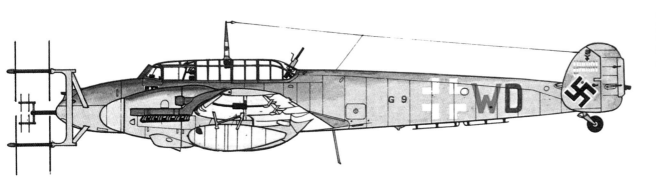

0   1   2   3 m

Pino dell'Orco

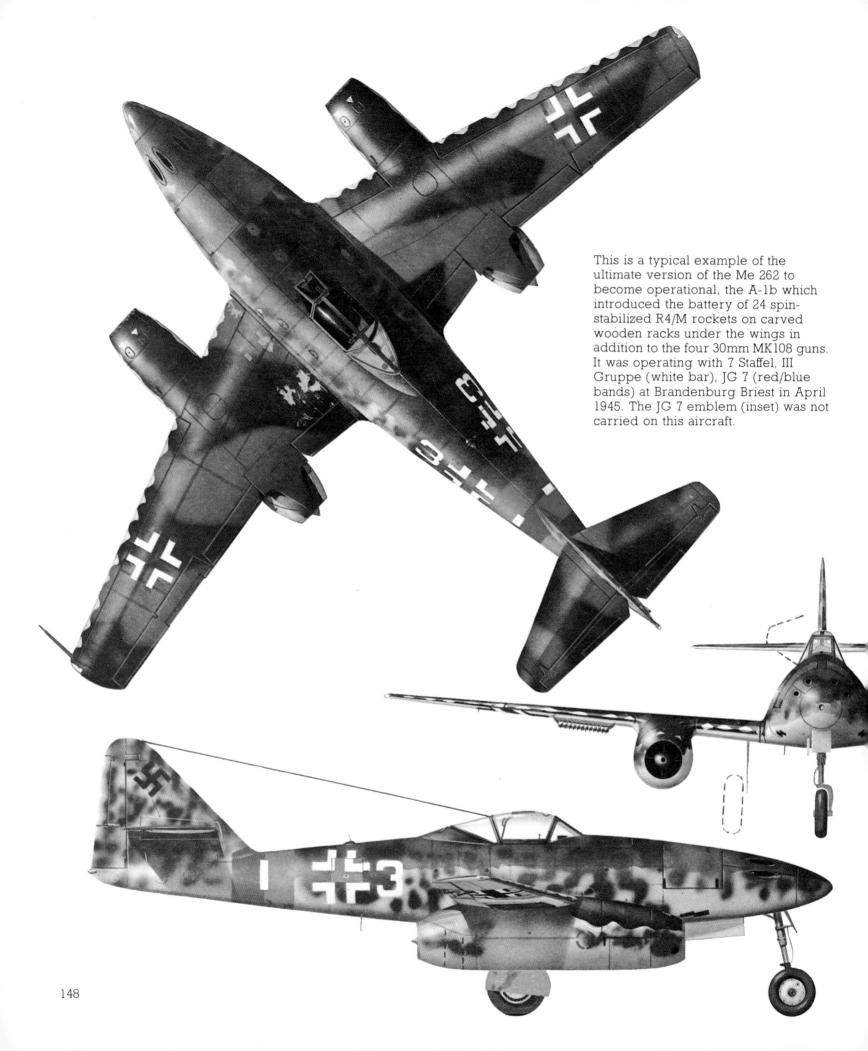

This is a typical example of the ultimate version of the Me 262 to become operational, the A-1b which introduced the battery of 24 spin-stabilized R4/M rockets on carved wooden racks under the wings in addition to the four 30mm MK108 guns. It was operating with 7 Staffel, III Gruppe (white bar), JG 7 (red/blue bands) at Brandenburg Briest in April 1945. The JG 7 emblem (inset) was not carried on this aircraft.

Messerschmitt Me 262A-1b

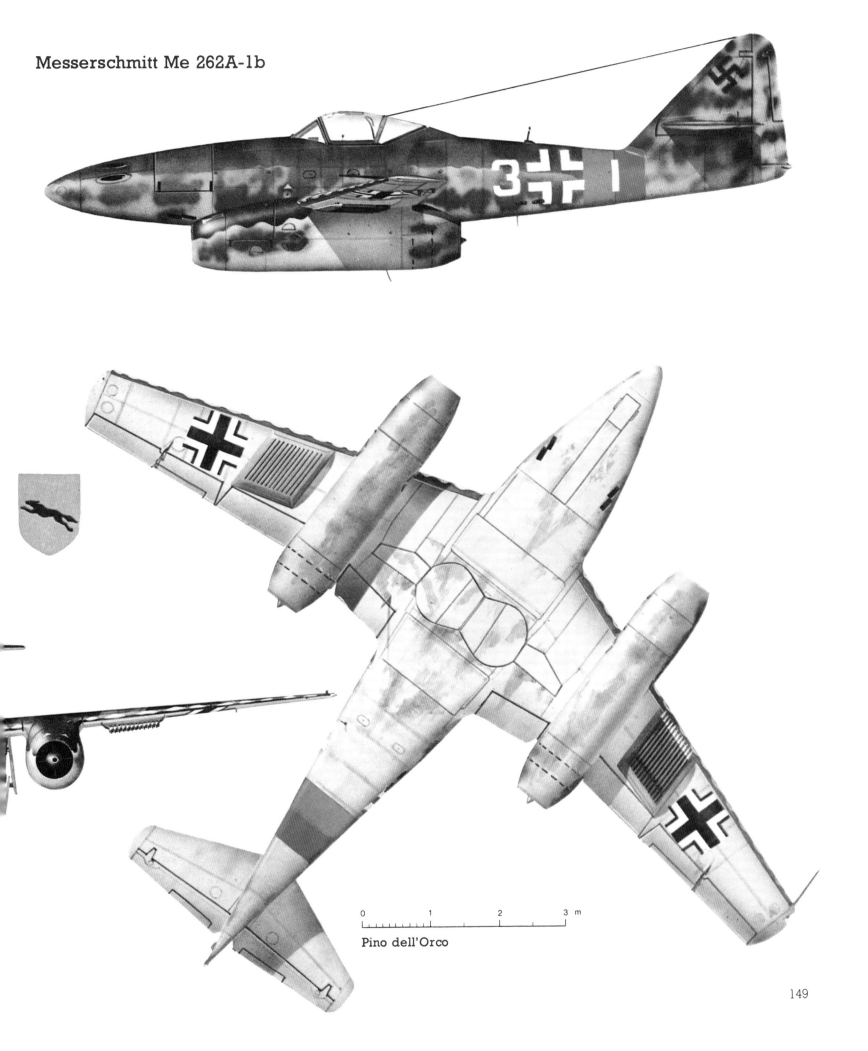

Pino dell'Orco

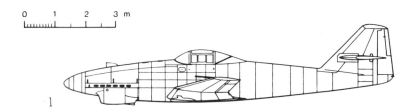

1 Me 262 V1 as first flown on 18 April 1941 with no power save a 700hp Jumo 210Ga piston engine. Flown on 25 March 1942 with two BMW 003 turbojets added.

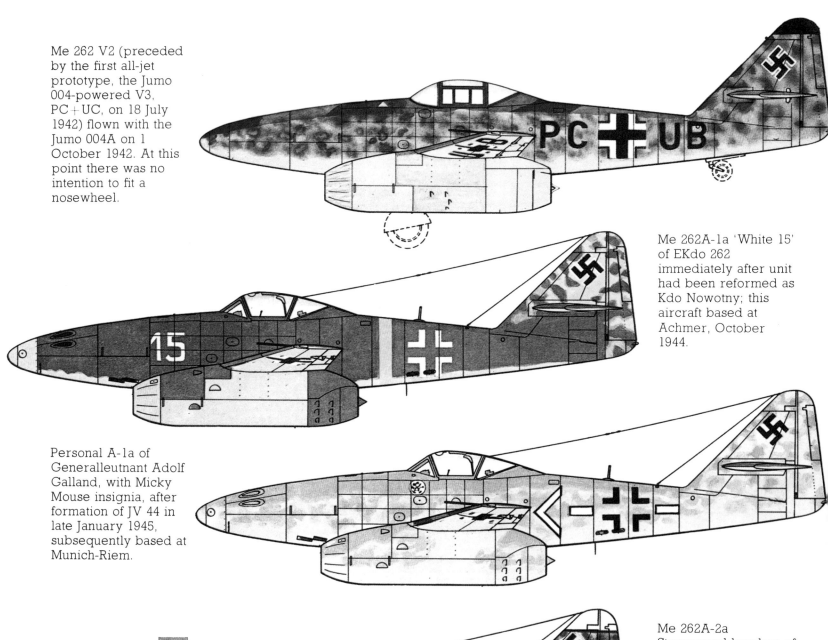

Me 262 V2 (preceded by the first all-jet prototype, the Jumo 004-powered V3, PC+UC, on 18 July 1942) flown with the Jumo 004A on 1 October 1942. At this point there was no intention to fit a nosewheel.

Me 262A-1a 'White 15' of EKdo 262 immediately after unit had been reformed as Kdo Nowotny; this aircraft based at Achmer, October 1944.

Personal A-1a of Generalleutnant Adolf Galland, with Micky Mouse insignia, after formation of JV 44 in late January 1945, subsequently based at Munich-Riem.

Me 262A-2a Sturmvogel bomber of 1/KG 51 *Edelweiss* (geschwader emblem shown inset), nucleus of which had converted to this aircraft as Kdo Schenck in August 1944.

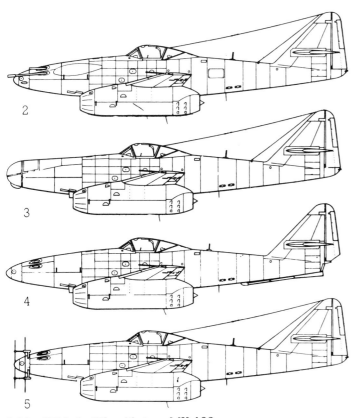

2

3

4

5

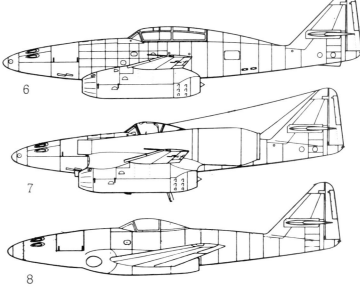

6

7

8

2 Me 262A-1a/U1 with two MK 108,
two MK 103 and two MG 151.
3 A-2a/U2 with bomb-aimer in nose
with Lotfe 7H sight.

4 C-1a Heimatschutzer I with Walter
R II-211/3 (HWK 509) rocket.
5 A-1a tested at Rechlin in October
1944 with SN-2 radar.
6 B-1a dual conversion trainer,
usually flown with two drop tanks.
7 Proposal for development with two
ramjets, probably to be developed
by DFS; not proceeded with.
8 Proposal for swept-wing
development with buried engines;
not proceeded with.

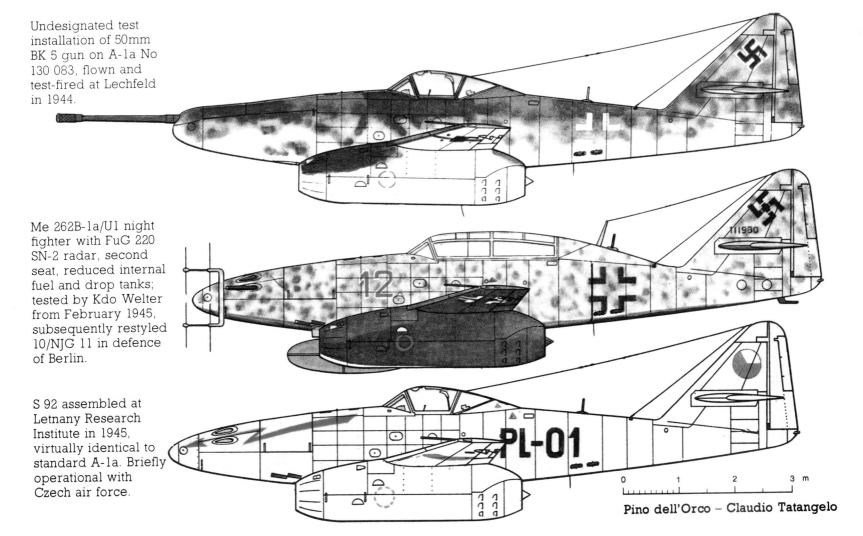

Undesignated test
installation of 50mm
BK 5 gun on A-1a No
130 083, flown and
test-fired at Lechfeld
in 1944.

Me 262B-1a/U1 night
fighter with FuG 220
SN-2 radar, second
seat, reduced internal
fuel and drop tanks;
tested by Kdo Welter
from February 1945,
subsequently restyled
10/NJG 11 in defence
of Berlin.

S 92 assembled at
Letnany Research
Institute in 1945,
virtually identical to
standard A-1a. Briefly
operational with
Czech air force.

0 1 2 3 m

Pino dell'Orco – Claudio Tatangelo

Messerschmitt Me 262

The Messerschmitt Me 262 is generally called 'the first jet fighter'; it is also popularly believed it would have made a much bigger and earlier impact on the war but for Hitler's personal insistence it be produced as a bomber. Neither is quite true. There are several other aircraft – the He 280, Bell P-59A and Meteor I – which have at least an equal claim to have been the first jet fighter; and the pacing item in the 262 programme was the engine, not any decision by Hitler. What is beyond dispute is that the 262 was a technical achievement of the greatest magnitude, and the only turbojet fighter to have any influence on the war.

In August 1938 Whittle's turbojet was not something officials cared to be associated with, but in Germany Messerschmitt AG was entrusted with the design of a new fighter to use two of the axial turbojets then under development at BMW. By 1940 the Junkers Jumo 004 had overtaken the smaller BMW unit, but in the event the first Me 262 was ready far ahead of the engines and it was rebuilt to fly with a piston engine (Jumo 210) in the nose on 18 April 1941. On 25 March 1942 a hair-raising flight was made with this aircraft fitted with two BMW003 turbojets; these promptly failed, and the piston engine just managed to bring the machine back to a landing. But on 18 July 1942 test-pilot Wendel made a perfect flight in the third prototype, fitted with the Junkers engine, after discovering he had to touch the brakes to get the tail up.

In April 1943 Adolf Galland flew the fourth prototype and soon reported that in his view all fighters except the Fw 190 should be terminated, the available capacity being used to build the 262, unofficially called Schwalbe (swallow). More fuel was needed, and this demanded a tricycle landing gear which was also desirable from the viewpoints of handling and ground erosion. On 2 November 1943 a special organization was formed to speed this potentially vital military aircraft, and on the same day Goering visited Messerschmitt and told him that all Hitler wanted to know was if it could carry bombs. There followed months of vacillation, Hitler flying into a rage at the slow progress and Junkers failing to make the engine reliable.

The 004B engine was finally released for production in June 1944, but by this time the resources behind it, and the 262, were considerable. The first Me 262A-1a fighter – to no small degree produced without Hitler's knowledge – was delivered to special test unit EKdo 262 in July 1944, by which time the first Meteors were with 616 Sqn, RAF. Unlike the British jet the 262 had an advanced airframe and offered a tremendous margin of performance over all other fighters (except the dangerous point-defence Me 163B Komet, which had a rocket). In contrast to the Bf 109G the 262 was a beautiful machine to fly, but many problems remained, including basic engine unreliability and short life, the near-impossibility of formation flying because of engine-handling limitations, and a slight aiming problem because of a tendency to yaw.

The first jet in action is unrecorded but two F-5 Lightnings and a PR Mosquito were claimed by EKdo 262 during July 1944, and on 25 July an RAF Mosquito crew managed to evade repeated firing passes. In August a detachment of KG 51 became operational with several of the A-2a bomber version, and on 28 August one of these was shot down by P-47s near Brussels. On 3 October the Kommando Nowotny was formed to operate the A-1a, and though it achieved many successes it lost two aircraft to Lt Urban L. Drew's P-51 on 7 October, and Nowotny himself was killed a month later.

Late in 1944 JG 7 scored many kills, but also suffered many losses, and though the four big-calibre guns had immense firepower their low muzzle velocity and constant jamming were grave drawbacks. There were several special weapon fits, listed in the data, and about half the aircraft delivered were A-2a Sturmvogels, which failed to cause the predicted havoc to Allied surface targets. A handful of interim night-fighter 262B-1a/U1s saw service in 1945.

COUNTRY OF ORIGIN Germany.

CREW 1, except B-series: 2.

TOTAL PRODUCED Accepted figure for completions is 1,433, not including small number assembled in Czechoslovakia post-war as S 92 and two-seat CS 92.

DIMENSIONS Wingspan 12·48m (40ft 11½in); length, **A-series**: 10·6m (34ft 9½in), **B-series**: 11·8m (38ft 9in); wing area 21·7m² (234ft²).

WEIGHTS Empty, **A-1a**: 4418kg (9,740lb); **A-2a**: 4500kg (9,921lb); maximum loaded, **A-1a**: 6394kg (14,096lb), **A-2a**: 7085kg (15,619lb).

ENGINES Two Junkers Jumo 004B-1, -2 or -3 single-shaft axial-flow turbojets each rated at 900kg (1,980lb) static thrust.

MAXIMUM SPEED **A-1a**: 866km/h (538mph); **A-2a**, with bombs: 750km/h (466mph).

SERVICE CEILING **A-1a**: 11450m (37,565ft); **A-2a**, with bombs: 10025m (32,890ft).

RANGE **A-1a**, high altitude: 1050km (650 miles).

MILITARY LOAD **A-1a**: four 30mm MK108 cannon; **A-1a/U1**: two 30mm MK103, two MK108 and two 20mm MG151; **A-1b**: as A-1a plus 24 spin-stabilized R4/M 50mm rockets; **A-2a**: as A-1a plus two 250kg (551lb) bombs; **B-1a**: as A-1a; **B-2a**: as A-1a plus two *Schräge Musik* MK108 mounted obliquely behind cockpit; **D**: SG500 Jagdfaust with 12 inclined mortar barrels in nose; **E**: 50mm MK114 gun or 48 R4/M rockets in nose.

Mitsubishi G4M Betty

In all their war planning the Japanese recognized the vast distances over which they wished to deploy their power. The Imperial Navy issued a 12-Shi (1937) specification for a new land-based bomber able to carry a heavy torpedo or bomb load over a range of nearly 3,000 miles (4800km). Had the Mitsubishi company been given a free hand they could have met this need with a four-engined aircraft that would probably have been first-class. But their design staff, led in this programme by Kiro Honjo; was flatly overruled by the Navy, which insisted on twin engines. As a result, the G4M was a cripplingly severe compromise suffering from near-fatal shortcomings. In particular, it caught fire so easily when shot at that US Navy pilots knew it as 'the one-shot lighter'.

The prototype flew in October 1939. At this early stage Mitsubishi were instructed to adapt the bomber for escort duties, with greatly increased gun armament and a crew of ten. Considerable development effort was wasted on this proposal, and 30 of the escorts, designated G6M, were actually test-flown, before the Yokosuka flight-test air corps, which had been behind the project, admitted it could not be accomplished. The 30 aircraft eventually became troop transports.

In December 1940 a second G4M1 bomber managed to reach the flight-test stage, followed by 13 more by March 1941. Though the extremely severe weight and space problems encountered in meeting the need for long range eliminated the provision of armour protection, or self-sealing tanks, the basic G4M was a most efficient aircraft which met almost all the Navy requirements. It was officially adopted in April 1941, and the first production batches began operating against targets in China in June 1941.

More than 120 were available at the time of Pearl Harbor, and on 10 December G4M1 bombers were involved in sinking the British capital ships *Prince of Wales* and *Repulse*, 26 of the new machines being used together with 60 of the still far more numerous Mitsubishi G3M. Production by the Nagoya factory proceeded at a high rate, so that by the spring of 1942 few G3Ms were still operating in front-line units. On the whole the G4M was very popular, because real fighter opposition had yet to be encountered. It was called Hamaki (cigar), for obvious reasons; the Allies bestowed the code-name Betty, in conformity with the policy of using girls' names for bombers. (The true designation was then unknown in the West.)

As 1942 progressed the G4M1 encountered ever-increasing opposition over New Guinea and northern Australia, and took a series of almost annihilating encounters during the Solomons campaign in August. By March 1942 Mitsubishi was working urgently on temporary remedial measures, which soon resulted in the G4M1 Model 12 with slightly better over-target height and fuel-tank rubber/sponge sheets and fire-suppression (but still no armour). In November 1942 the first of a largely redesigned G4M2 family flew. This had a laminar wing with rounded tips, larger horizontal tail, more powerful engines, better armament and additional fuel; after the 65th aircraft doors were added to the bomb bay.

Production of the G4M1 continued until 1944, due to a shortage of the high-power engines, but eventually all production, including that at the added Okayama factory, centred upon further-improved G4M2 Model 22A, B and C with various armament fits. In the final year of the war the G4M2 was by far the most important Navy land-based bomber, often making almost suicidal attacks against Allied ships, and the G4M2e being the carrier aircraft for the MXY7 Ohka piloted rocket missile.

Back in November 1942 the desperate need for a properly protected G4M led to a third major variant, the G4M3, first flown in January 1944. Range was abandoned, and full armour and self-sealing were incorporated, along with a tail turret copied from the American B-26, a dihedral tailplane and other modifications. Hardly any of the 60 built got into service.

COUNTRY OF ORIGIN Japan.

CREW Usually 7.

TOTAL PRODUCED 2,446, including 1,230 G4M1 and 1,154 G4M2.

DIMENSIONS Wingspan 25·0m (82ft 0¼in); length, **M1,M2**: 20·0m (65ft 7½in); **M3**: 19·5m (63ft 11¾in); wing area: 78·125m² (840·93ft²).

WEIGHTS Empty, **M1**: 6800kg (14,991lb), **M2**: 8160kg (17,990lb); maximum loaded, **M1**: 9500kg (20,944lb), **M2**: 12500kg (27,558lb).

ENGINES Two Mitsubishi MK4 Kasei 14-cylinder two-row radials; **M1**: 1,530hp Kasei 11 or 15; **M2**: 1,800 or 1,825hp Kasei 21, 25 or 25b.

MAXIMUM SPEED **M1**: 428km/h (266mph); **M2**: 438km/h (272mph).

SERVICE CEILING **M2**: 8950m (29,365ft).

RANGE **M1**: maximum 6033km (3,749 miles); **M2**: maximum 6059km (3,765 miles); **M3**: maximum 4336km (2,694 miles).

MILITARY LOAD **M1**: 800kg (1,764lb) bombs or torpedo, three hand-aimed 7·7mm Type 92 machine guns and tail position with 20mm Type 99. **M2**: very varied, but 1000kg (2,205lb) bombs or torpedo, Type 92 in nose, two Type 99 beam, Type 99 dorsal and Type 99 tail usual armament.

Mitsubishi G4M1 Betty

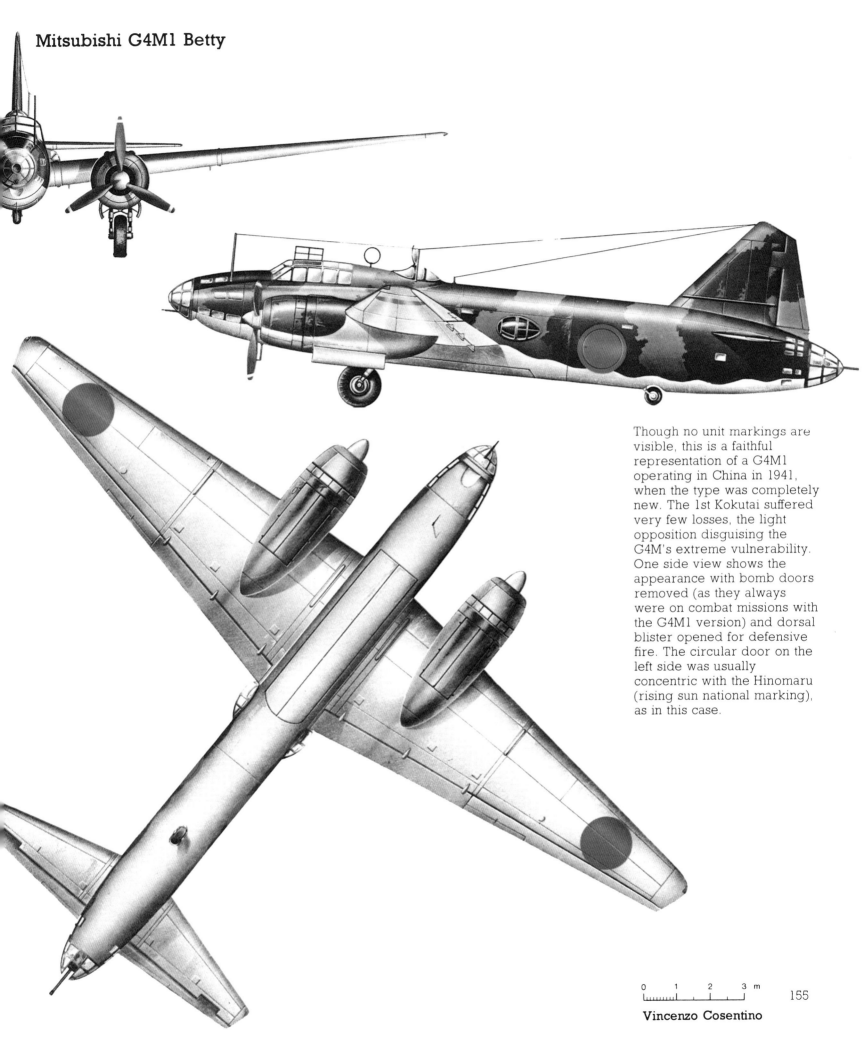

Though no unit markings are visible, this is a faithful representation of a G4M1 operating in China in 1941, when the type was completely new. The 1st Kokutai suffered very few losses, the light opposition disguising the G4M's extreme vulnerability. One side view shows the appearance with bomb doors removed (as they always were on combat missions with the G4M1 version) and dorsal blister opened for defensive fire. The circular door on the left side was usually concentric with the Hinomaru (rising sun national marking), as in this case.

0   1   2   3 m

155

Vincenzo Cosentino

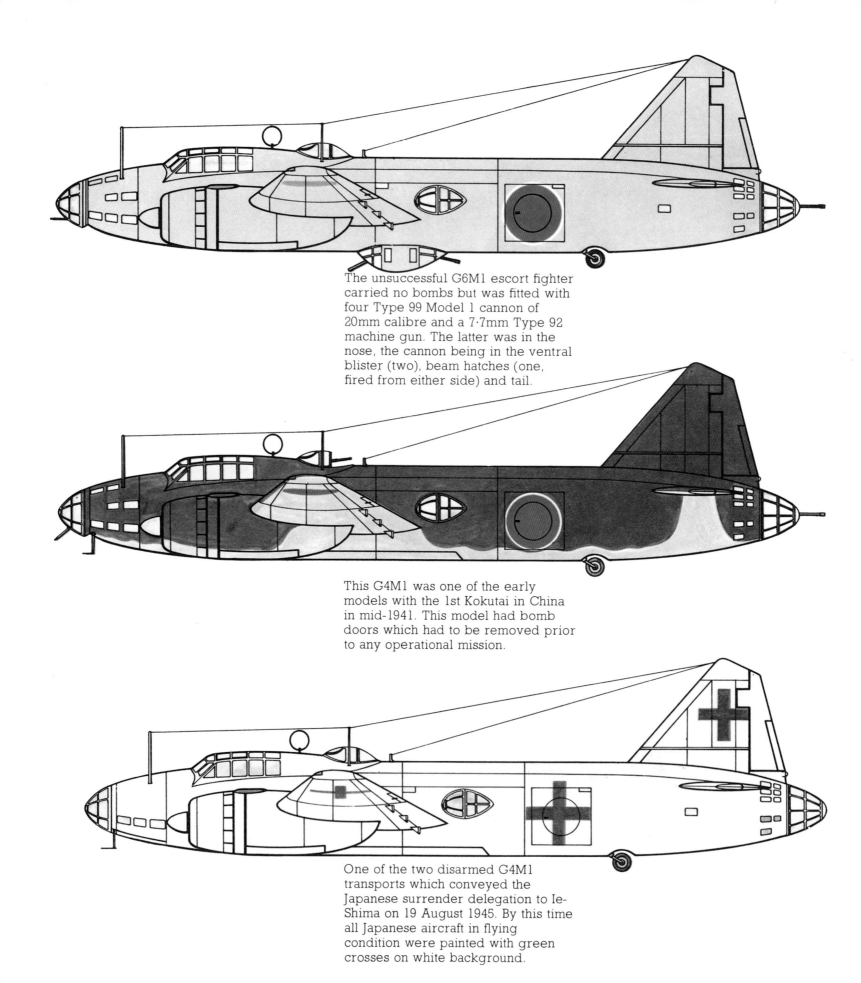

The unsuccessful G6M1 escort fighter carried no bombs but was fitted with four Type 99 Model 1 cannon of 20mm calibre and a 7·7mm Type 92 machine gun. The latter was in the nose, the cannon being in the ventral blister (two), beam hatches (one, fired from either side) and tail.

This G4M1 was one of the early models with the 1st Kokutai in China in mid-1941. This model had bomb doors which had to be removed prior to any operational mission.

One of the two disarmed G4M1 transports which conveyed the Japanese surrender delegation to Ie-Shima on 19 August 1945. By this time all Japanese aircraft in flying condition were painted with green crosses on white background.

Mitsubishi G4M Betty

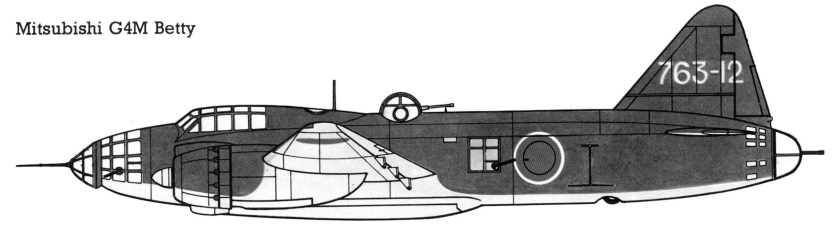

A G4M2a of the 763rd Kokutai
discovered in the Philippine islands
in late 1944. This example had ASV
radar with dipole aerials on the nose
and rear fuselage. The G4M2 did
have hinged doors on a bulged
weapon bay.

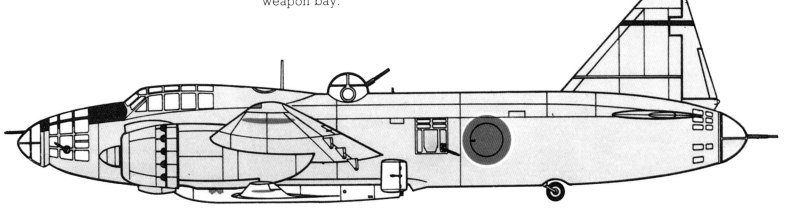

The G4M2e was the special sub-type
designed to carry the MXY-7 Ohka
piloted rocket missile, which fitted
into the modified doorless weapon
bay. The carrier aircraft was sluggish
and vulnerable until the missile had
been released.

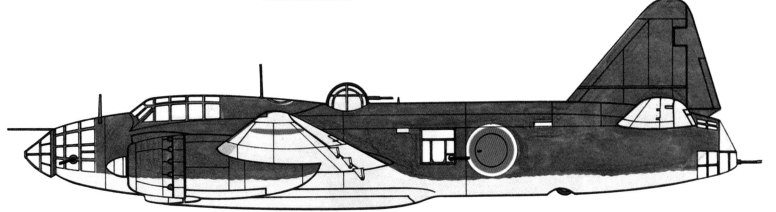

The final production version was the
G4M3, with considerably shorter
range but much better protection, a
new tail turret and tailplane with
dihedral. Only 60 were completed
before the end of the war.

Vicenzo Cosentino

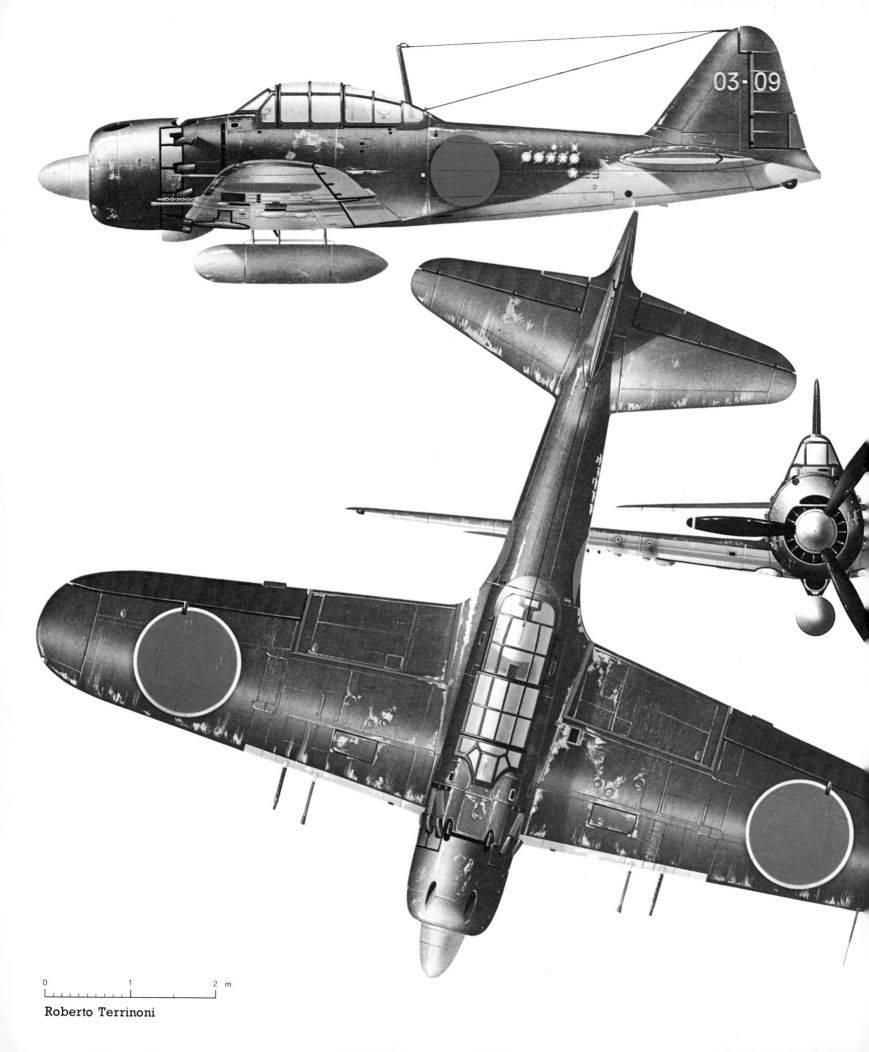

Roberto Terrinoni

03-09

0 1 2 m

Mitsubishi A6M5c Zero

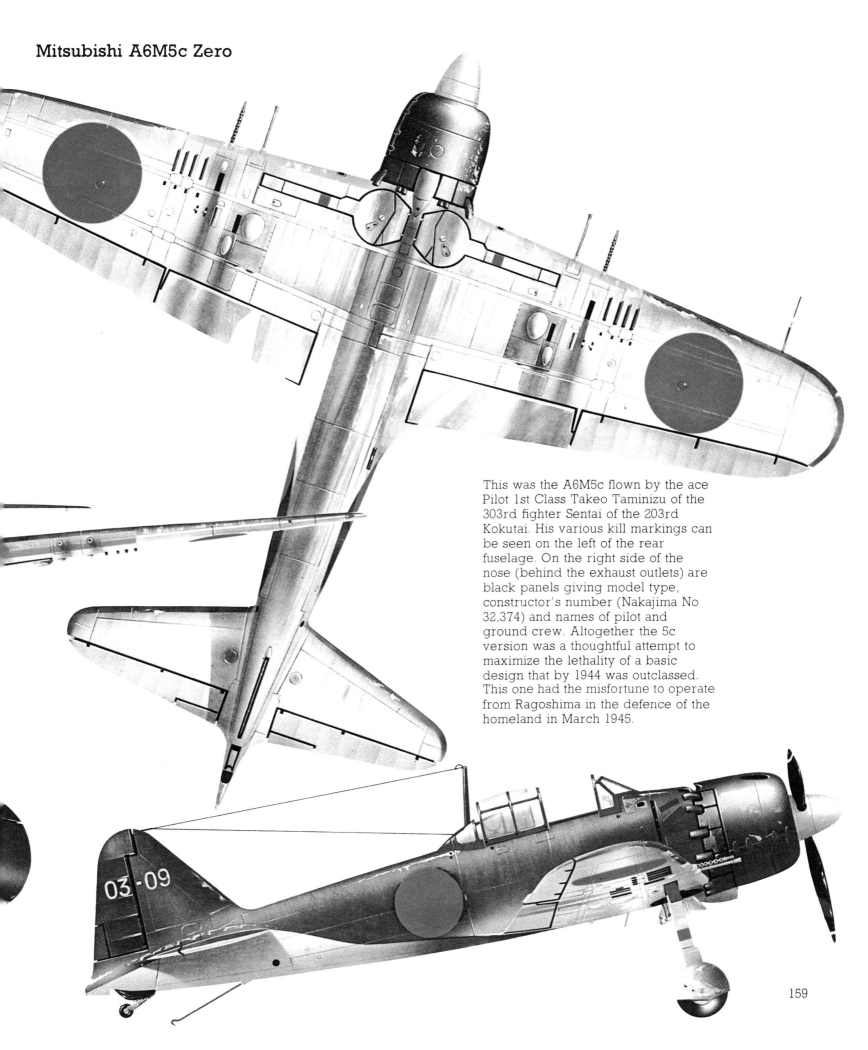

This was the A6M5c flown by the ace Pilot 1st Class Takeo Taminizu of the 303rd fighter Sentai of the 203rd Kokutai. His various kill markings can be seen on the left of the rear fuselage. On the right side of the nose (behind the exhaust outlets) are black panels giving model type, constructor's number (Nakajima No 32,374) and names of pilot and ground crew. Altogether the 5c version was a thoughtful attempt to maximize the lethality of a basic design that by 1944 was outclassed. This one had the misfortune to operate from Ragoshima in the defence of the homeland in March 1945.

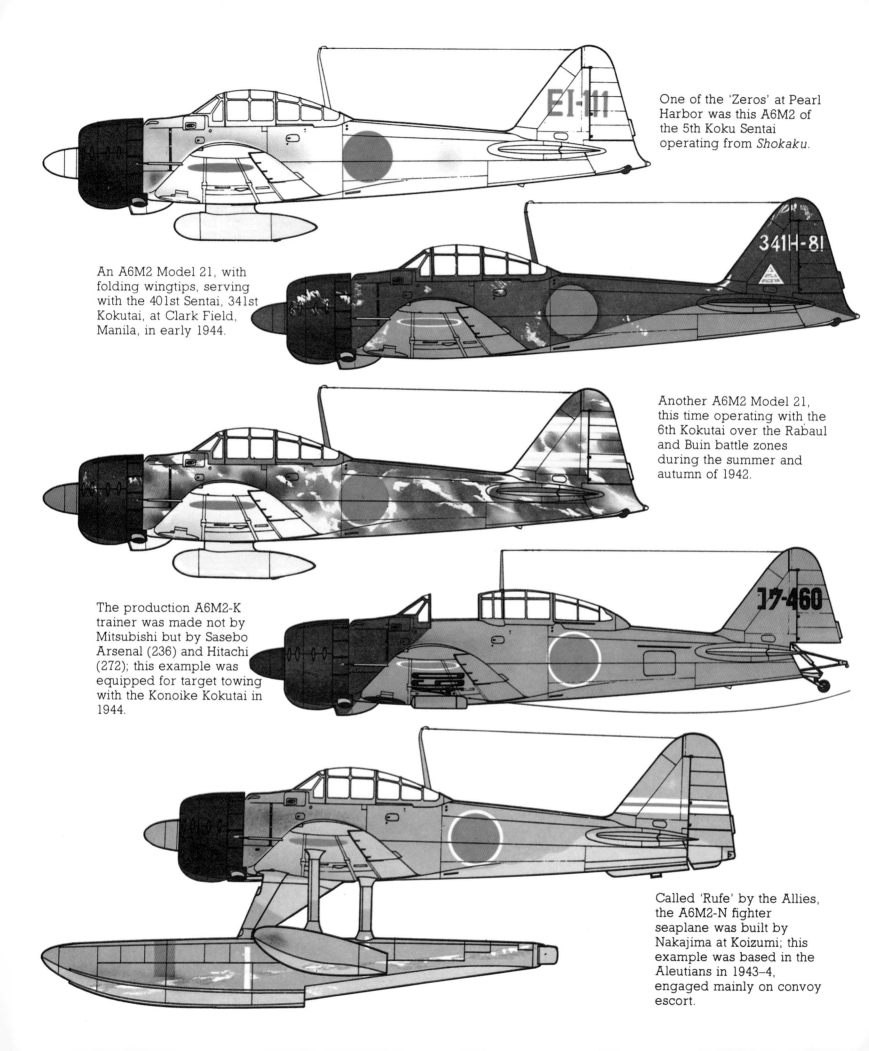

One of the 'Zeros' at Pearl Harbor was this A6M2 of the 5th Koku Sentai operating from *Shokaku*.

An A6M2 Model 21, with folding wingtips, serving with the 401st Sentai, 341st Kokutai, at Clark Field, Manila, in early 1944.

Another A6M2 Model 21, this time operating with the 6th Kokutai over the Rabaul and Buin battle zones during the summer and autumn of 1942.

The production A6M2-K trainer was made not by Mitsubishi but by Sasebo Arsenal (236) and Hitachi (272); this example was equipped for target towing with the Konoike Kokutai in 1944.

Called 'Rufe' by the Allies, the A6M2-N fighter seaplane was built by Nakajima at Koizumi; this example was based in the Aleutians in 1943–4, engaged mainly on convoy escort.

Mitsubishi A6M Zero

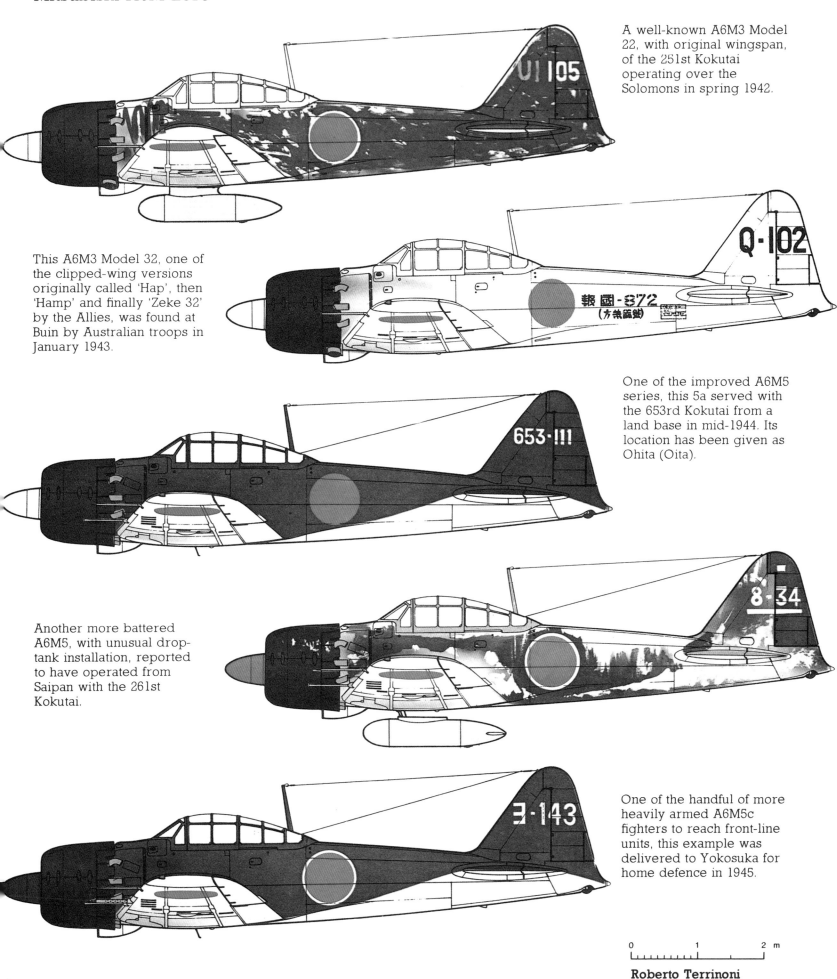

A well-known A6M3 Model 22, with original wingspan, of the 251st Kokutai operating over the Solomons in spring 1942.

This A6M3 Model 32, one of the clipped-wing versions originally called 'Hap', then 'Hamp' and finally 'Zeke 32' by the Allies, was found at Buin by Australian troops in January 1943.

One of the improved A6M5 series, this 5a served with the 653rd Kokutai from a land base in mid-1944. Its location has been given as Ohita (Oita).

Another more battered A6M5, with unusual drop-tank installation, reported to have operated from Saipan with the 261st Kokutai.

One of the handful of more heavily armed A6M5c fighters to reach front-line units, this example was delivered to Yokosuka for home defence in 1945.

0   1   2 m

Roberto Terrinoni

Mitsubishi A6M Zero

Like Britain's Spitfire, the fighter popularly called the *Rei-sen* (Zero) became symbolic of a nation, its designer became famous, and it mirrored the fortunes of the rising sun which within four years had set. In widespread service long before Pearl Harbor, it failed to become known to Allied commanders. Thanks to a combination of excellent manoeuvrability and firepower it easily disposed of the motley collection of Allied aircraft at first sent against it, while its tremendous range allowed it to appear over distant battlefronts and give Allied commanders the belief there must be several times as many Zeros as there actually were. This is no mean achievement when it is remembered the A6M, unlike most of its early adversaries, had to operate from carriers.

Its immediate predecessor was the Mitsubishi A5M, a beautiful little fighter with extraordinary manoeuvrability that, in enormous and bloody battles over central Asia in 1937–40, enabled it to beat nimble biplanes of the Soviet Union. To replace it, the Imperial Navy issued a 12-Shi (1937) specification for a faster, longer-ranged fighter carrying two cannon as well as the two machine guns of the A5M, yet with manoeuvrability as good as that of the much lighter earlier fighter. It was as great a challenge as any design team has faced, but under chief engineer Jiro Horikoshi, Mitsubishi created a masterpiece. At least, it was a masterpiece until it had to fight for its life; then its basically light construction made it vulnerable.

The first A6M1 prototype flew on 1 April 1939. After fitting a three-blade constant-speed propeller the aircraft met or surpassed all requirements except maximum speed. Once a more powerful engine, made by the rival Nakajima company, had been fitted the A6M2 was regarded as outstanding in every respect. In July 1940 the Navy sent 15 to fight in China, and by September 1941 they had shot down 99 for the loss of two (neither a victim of air combat). Small changes, including folding wingtips, were introduced during 1940, and the Kokutais (naval air corps) not only worked up to fighting proficiency but took great care to learn how to cruise with maximum fuel economy, so that with a drop tank a sortie of nine hours could be flown – unheard-of for a high-performance monoplane fighter, let alone a carrier-based one.

At Pearl Harbor the Imperial Navy had 328 A6M2s in service, and in a matter of days these had swept away effective air opposition from Hawaii to Ceylon. It was a traumatic shock to the Allies, who later called the A6M Zeke. Soon the clipped-wing A6M3 appeared, to be code-named Hap, hastily changed to Hamp (because of 'Hap' Arnold, USAAF Chief of Staff) and then, when its true identity was appreciated, to Zeke 32. But by this time, in July 1942, four Japanese carriers had been sunk at Midway, and most A6Ms subsequently operated from land.

Like major Luftwaffe types the A6M had to soldier on because its replacements never arrived. It was especially outclassed at high altitude, and after abortive trials with the turbocharged A6M4 the A6M5 entered production at Mitsubishi and Nakajima in mid-1943. A mere interim stop-gap, this slightly better machine remained in production almost to the end of the war. Its main features were smaller but thicker-skinned wings, for faster diving, and separate engine exhaust stacks for small thrust assistance. Progressively better armament combinations were fitted, but in combat with an F6F or F4U the results of either pilot hitting the other were one-sided; the only positive thing that could be said of the Zero at this stage of the war was that in the hands of a skilful pilot it could manoeuvre as well as most of its opponents.

From October 1944 many Zeros were used up in suicide missions with bombs of up to 250kg (551lb) attached. Few A6M7 or powerful A6M8 were built, but Nakajima, which had manufactured most of the Zeros, delivered 327 of the A6M2-N floatplane version in 1941–3 (called Rufe by the Allies) and other companies made 515 of the A6M2-K and 5-K trainer versions.

COUNTRY OF ORIGIN Japan.

CREW 1, except 2-K, 5-K trainers: 2.

TOTAL PRODUCED Basic **A6M** fighter: believed to be 10,449; **K** trainers: 515; **N** seaplanes: 327.

DIMENSIONS Wingspan, **A6M2, 2-K, 2-N**: 12·0m (39ft 4½in), subsequent: 11·0m (36ft 1$\frac{1}{16}$in); length, **2,3**: 9·06m (29ft 8$\frac{11}{16}$in); **5**: 9·12m (29ft 11¼in); **2-K**: 9·15m (30ft 0¼in); **2-N**: 10·1m (33ft 1⅝in); wing area, **2, 2-K, 2-N**: 22·44m² (241·54ft²); **3**: 21·53m² (231·75ft²); **5**: 21·3m² (229·27ft²).

WEIGHTS Empty, **2**: 1680kg (3,704lb); **2-K**: 1819kg (4,010lb); **2-N**: 1912kg (4,215lb); **3**: 1807kg (3,984lb); **5**: 1876kg (4,136lb); maximum loaded, **2**: 2796kg (6,164lb); **2-K**: 2627kg (5,792lb); **2-N**: 2880kg (6,349lb); **3**: 2544kg (5,609lb); **5**: 2733kg (6,025lb).

ENGINE Production versions, Nakajima Sakae 14-cylinder two-row radial; **2, 2-K, 2-N**: 940hp NK1C Sakae 12; **3,5**: 1,130hp NK1F Sakae 21. A6M6 and 7 had 1,130hp Sakae 31 and A6M8 the 1,560hp Mitsubishi MK8P Kinsei 62, which Mitsubishi had wanted to introduce years earlier.

MAXIMUM SPEED **2**: 533km/h (331mph); **2-K**: 476km/h (296mph); **2-N**: 436km/h (271mph); **3**: 544km/h (338mph); **5**: 565km/h (351mph).

SERVICE CEILING **2**: 10000m (32,810ft); **2-N**: reported as 2, but bound to be lower; **3**: 11050m (36,250ft); **5**: 11740m (38,520ft).

RANGE **2**: 3100km (1,926 miles); **2-N**: 1782km (1,107 miles); **3**: 2380km (1,479 miles); **5**: 1922km (1,194 miles).

MILITARY LOAD Standard: two 20mm Type 99 and two 7·7mm Type 97, plus two 60kg (132lb) bombs; **2-K**: cannon deleted; **5b**: fuselage guns changed to one Type 97 and one 13·2mm Type 3; **5c,6c,7**: one Type 3 in fuselage, and two Type 99 and two Type 3 in wings.

North American B-25 Mitchell

Though not famous enough to be known to the general public, the B-25 was supplied to almost every Allied air force in World War 2, and served on every front. It was made in a succession of versions which eventually bristled with as many weapons as the four-engined heavies, and total output was greater than for any other American medium bomber.

North American Aviation only began as an aircraft constructor in early 1935, and in 1938 accepted a major challenge in designing a prototype for an Army medium-bomber competition, the NA-40. This flew with Twin Wasp engines in January 1939, but in the same month the Army issued a revised specification to which the company submitted a modified and more powerful design, the NA-62. In August 1939 an order was placed for 184, when the NA-62 was still only on paper (the rival Martin 179 was also ordered as the B-26 Marauder), and the first B-25 flew on 19 August 1940.

It was less ambitious than the B-26, having a lower wing-loading, conventional instead of circular-section fuselage and not quite such powerful engines. By 1941 the Inglewood factory had delivered 24 B-25s, and then followed with 40 B-25As with armour and self-sealing tanks, and 119 B-25Bs with the tail gun replaced by a dorsal turret and two-gun retractable ventral barbette. In 1941 larger orders were placed for the B-25C from Inglewood and identical D from a new factory at Kansas City, this series having increased fuel capacity and revised equipment. Deliveries began in January 1942, the RAF calling the B-25B Mitchell I, and the C and D the Mk II, while larger numbers were supplied to the Soviet Union.

On 18 April 1942 Lt-Col Jimmy Doolittle led 16 B-25Bs in an epic morale-boosting raid from the heaving deck of USS *Hornet* (the B-25 was never designed for such a take-off) over Tokyo, with subsequent landings in China, the Soviet Union or by parachute. Experience showed heavy nose armament to be needed for low-level attack in the Pacific, especially on ships, and

175 were modified in the field with ten 12·7mm (0·5in) guns firing ahead. Then followed the B-25G with Army 75mm gun, which was soon replaced by the much more heavily armed H, the first to have revised rear armament and a dorsal turret just behind the cockpit.

By 1944 production was concentrated on the J, produced with either a glazed nose for a navigator/bombardier or a solid nose with a battery of heavy machine guns. The J was manufactured at a rapid rate at both factories until July 1944 when output was stopped at Inglewood (which concentrated thereafter on the P-51) and balanced by continual increases in production at Kansas City. In the RAF the J was designated Mitchell III, while from January 1943 the Navy received 248 Hs and 252 Js as the PBJ-1H and -1J respectively. Usually the glazed-nose versions served as visual-bombing lead ships, though the J carried heavy forward-firing armament in the side packages which were standard on all late combat versions of the B-25 and B-26.

Though not built as such, the F-10 was a fully equipped strategic reconnaissance version, rebuilt from the B-25D and usually used for training. A multi-role pilot and crew trainer was the AT-24, large numbers of which were rebuilt from the D,C,G and J. Single examples of the XB-25E and XB-25F experimented with hot-air and electric airframe de-icing. There were a very large number of special versions, including Navy PBJ-1D, G, H and J models with torpedo, mines, depth charges and different radar installations in the nose or right wing tip. Towards the end of the war increasing numbers of B-25s were used as transports and couriers, usually stripped of armament. Wartime operators of the B-25 included the air forces of the USA, Britain, Australia, Soviet Union, China, Netherlands (East Indies), Netherlands (with RAF), Free France, Brazil, Mexico and Italy (co-belligerent air force).

After the war the B-25 remained a major type with most of these countries. In the USAAF (from 1947 USAF) most became TB-25 crew trainers.

COUNTRY OF ORIGIN USA.
CREW Glazed nose: 5; solid nose: 4.
TOTAL PRODUCED 9,816.
DIMENSIONS Wingspan 20·6m (67ft 7in); length, **B-25, A**: 16·48m (54ft 1in), **B,C,J**: 16·1m (52ft 11in), **G,H**: 15·54m (51ft 0in); wing area 56·67m² (610ft²).
WEIGHTS Empty, **B-25**: 7605kg (16,766lb), **C**: 9208kg (20,300lb). **J**: 8836kg (19,480lb); maximum loaded, **B-25**: 12388kg (27,310lb), **C**: 15422kg (34,000lb), **H,J**: 18960kg (41,800lb).
ENGINES Two Wright R-2600 Cyclone 14-cylinder two-row radials, up to **B**: 1,700hp R-2600-9; later: 1,700hp R-2600-13 or -29.
MAXIMUM SPEED **B-25, A**: 510km/h (317mph); **B**: 483km/h (300mph), **C,G,H,J**: typically 443km/h (275mph).
SERVICE CEILING All 7620m (25,000ft).
RANGE **B-25** and some **PBJ-1J**: 3219km (2,000 miles), all other versions, about 2414km (1,500 miles).
MILITARY LOAD **B-25, A**: One 7·62mm (0·30in) gun in nose, three aimed from amidships and one 12·7mm (0·5in) in tail; normal internal bomb-load 907kg (2,000lb). **B,C,D**: 7·62mm (0·30in) in nose, upper and lower powered turrets each with two 12·7mm (0·5in); normal bomb-load 1361kg (3,000lb), overload with eight 113kg (250lb) bombs external, 2359kg (5,200lb). **G**: M4 Army gun, hand-served with 21 rounds and aimed by two 12·7mm (0·5in) guns in nose; upper turret as before, lower turret often removed; bomb-load unchanged. **H**: lightweight T13E1 75mm gun, four 12·7mm (0·5in) in nose, four 12·7mm (0·5in) in packages on sides of nose, two 12·7mm (0·5in) in dorsal turret (relocated further forward), two 12·7mm (0·5in) in new manual beam positions and two 12·7mm (0·5in) in tail turret (no ventral turret); normal bomb-load 1452kg (3,200lb). **J**: Internal bomb-load up to 1814kg (4,000lb); nose, either four package guns (if nose glazed for nav/bombardier) or four package guns plus eight 12·7mm (0·5in) all firing ahead; other guns as H, thus total of 18 guns of 12·7mm (0·5in).

North American B-25J-1 Mitchell

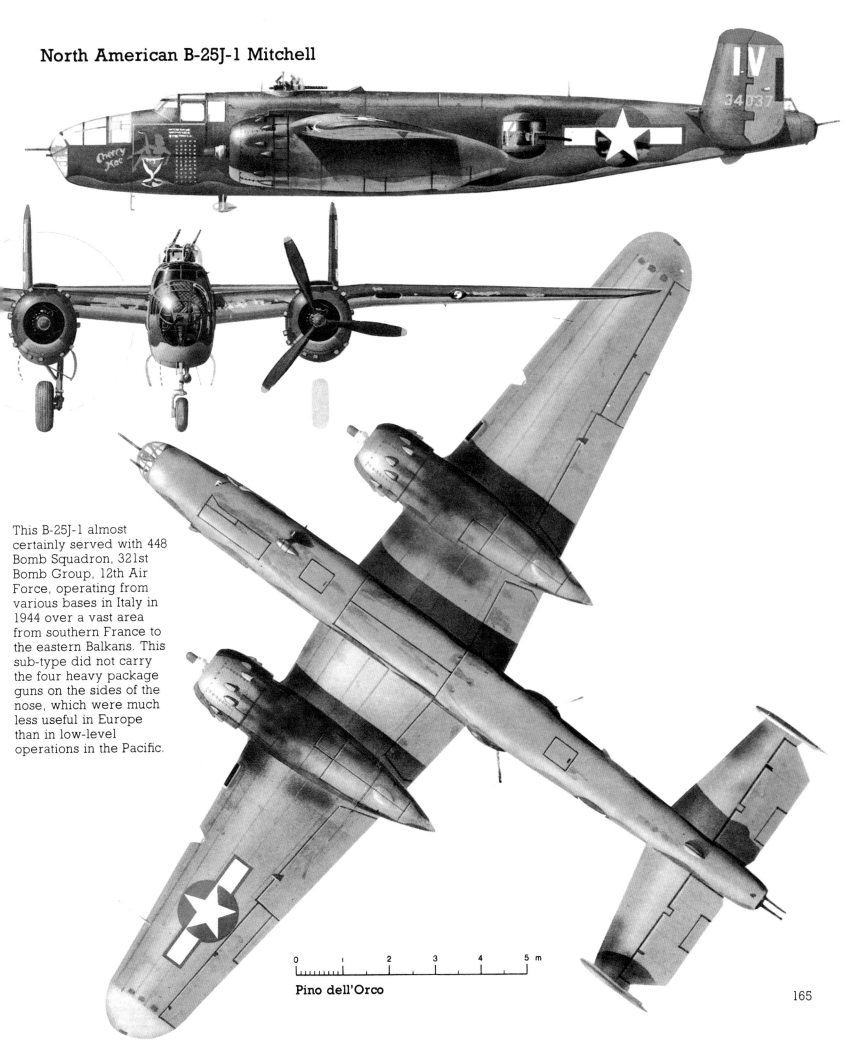

This B-25J-1 almost certainly served with 448 Bomb Squadron, 321st Bomb Group, 12th Air Force, operating from various bases in Italy in 1944 over a vast area from southern France to the eastern Balkans. This sub-type did not carry the four heavy package guns on the sides of the nose, which were much less useful in Europe than in low-level operations in the Pacific.

Pino dell'Orco

North American B-25 Mitchell

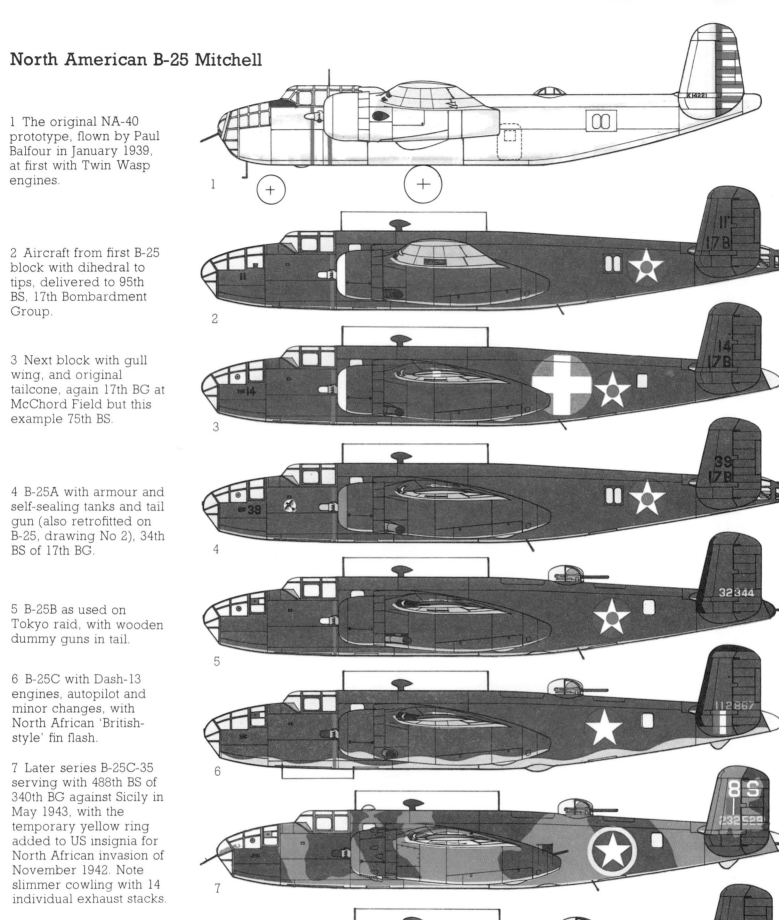

1 The original NA-40 prototype, flown by Paul Balfour in January 1939, at first with Twin Wasp engines.

2 Aircraft from first B-25 block with dihedral to tips, delivered to 95th BS, 17th Bombardment Group.

3 Next block with gull wing, and original tailcone, again 17th BG at McChord Field but this example 75th BS.

4 B-25A with armour and self-sealing tanks and tail gun (also retrofitted on B-25, drawing No 2), 34th BS of 17th BG.

5 B-25B as used on Tokyo raid, with wooden dummy guns in tail.

6 B-25C with Dash-13 engines, autopilot and minor changes, with North African 'British-style' fin flash.

7 Later series B-25C-35 serving with 488th BS of 340th BG against Sicily in May 1943, with the temporary yellow ring added to US insignia for North African invasion of November 1942. Note slimmer cowling with 14 individual exhaust stacks.

8 US Navy PBJ-1D with ventral anti-submarine radar and manually aimed tail gun, but without beam guns usually fitted.

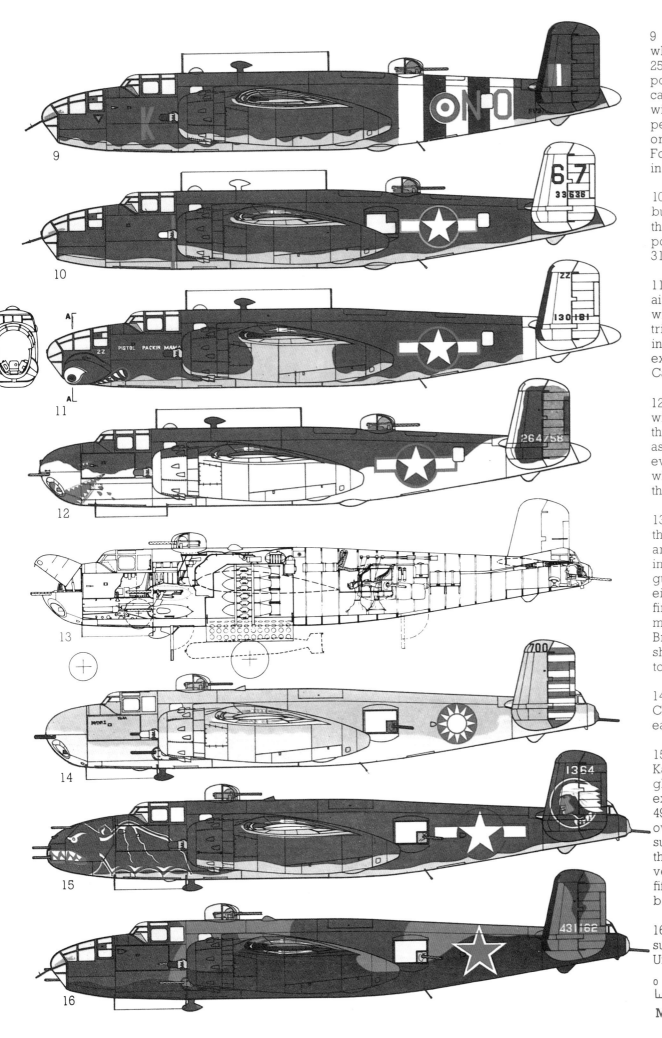

9 RAF Mitchell II, most of which were ex-USAAF B-25Cs but with beam gun positions (absent in this case); unit was 320 Sqn, with Netherlands personnel who originally operated their Fokker T.8/W seaplanes in Wales.

10 B-25D (the C model built at Kansas City) in this case with beam positions; served with 319th BG in Italy in 1943.

11 F-10 photographic aircraft, based on B-25D, with inset showing trimetrogon camera installation in nose; this example was based in Caribbean.

12 The original version with the 75mm gun was the B-25G, in this case assigned to Orlando for evaluation and trials which began there with the same gun in a B-18A.

13 Longitudinal section through the heavily armed B-25H, with much-improved T13E1 75mm gun supplemented by eight 12·7mm (0·5in) firing ahead and six more for rear defence. Broken outline shows short 907kg (2000lb) torpedo.

14 A B-25H of the Chinese air force in early 1945.

15 Most of the 4,318 Kansas-built B-25Js had a glazed nose but this example, used by the 499th BS of the 345th BG over the Philippines in summer 1944, was one of the field-modified attack versions with 'eight fifties' instead of a bombardier.

16 Standard B-25J-20 as supplied to the Soviet Union.

0 1 2 3 4 m

Marcello Ralli

North American P-51B Mustang

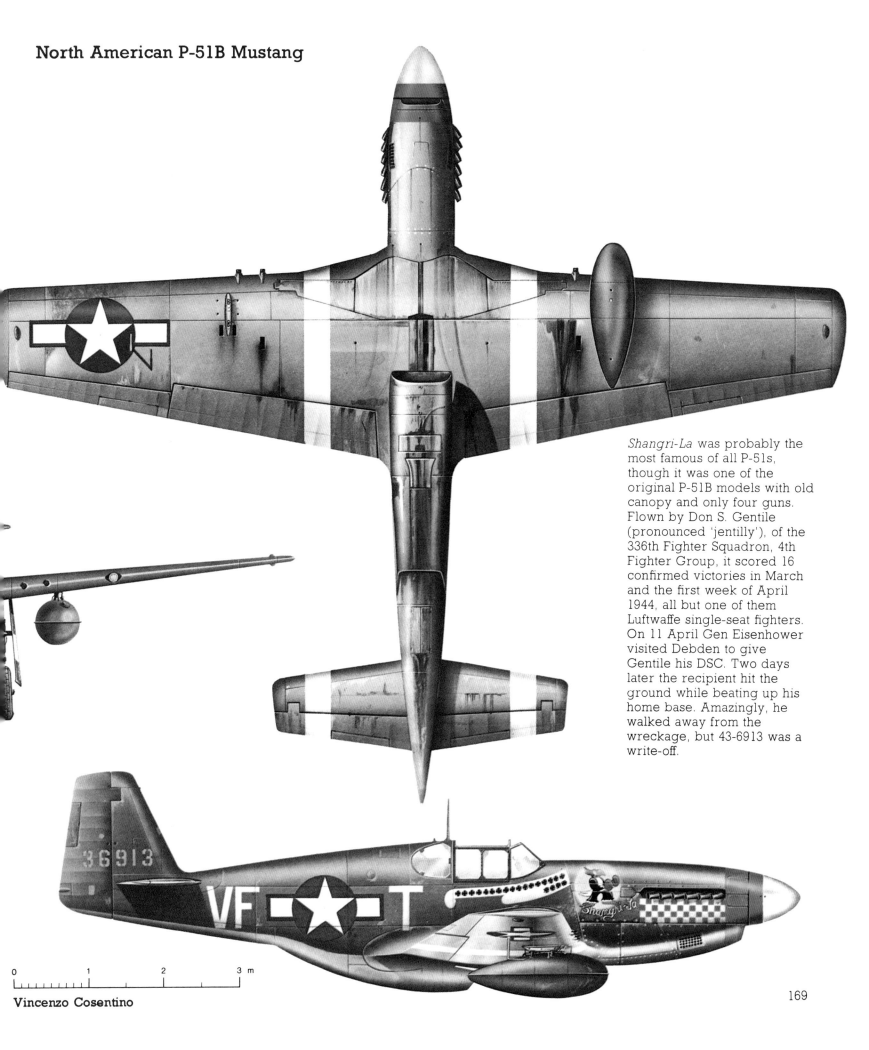

Shangri-La was probably the most famous of all P-51s, though it was one of the original P-51B models with old canopy and only four guns. Flown by Don S. Gentile (pronounced 'jentilly'), of the 336th Fighter Squadron, 4th Fighter Group, it scored 16 confirmed victories in March and the first week of April 1944, all but one of them Luftwaffe single-seat fighters. On 11 April Gen Eisenhower visited Debden to give Gentile his DSC. Two days later the recipient hit the ground while beating up his home base. Amazingly, he walked away from the wreckage, but 43-6913 was a write-off.

0   1   2   3 m

Vincenzo Cosentino

The US Army Air Corps required NAA to deliver two Mustangs without charge for evaluation. This was the second, the tenth aircraft off the line, with Wright Field insignia. It was delivered unpainted.

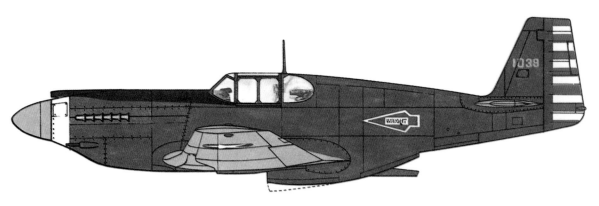

So successful were the US Army trials that 150 were ordered as the P-51 Apache (later the British name was adopted), with four M-2 cannon. The basic aircraft resembled the RAF Mk IA with four Hispano cannon.

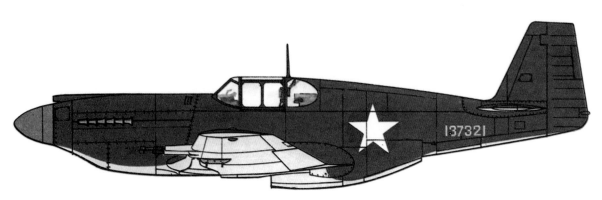

EW998 was ex-USAAF 42-83685, an A-36 attack bomber with six 12·7mm (0·5in) guns (four in the wings), bomb racks and dive brakes; it was the only one of this type on RAF charge.

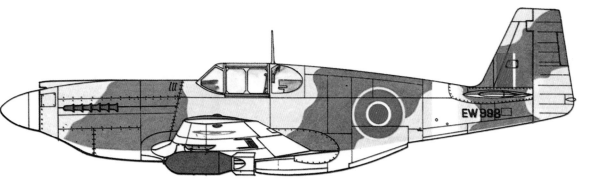

Serving with 19 Sqn RAF this Mustang III was one of those modified in Britain with a Malcolm sliding hood, a great improvement also fitted to more than 1,000 Mustangs including USAAF P-51Bs, Cs and F-6s.

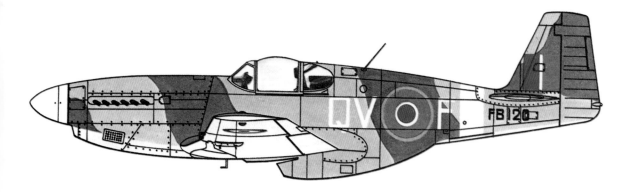

This P-51D was supplied to the Philippine Air Force and saw action against insurgent forces in 1947. The last remained in service until 1959.

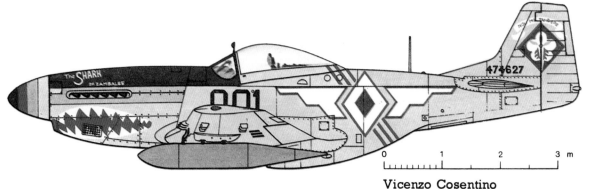

Vicenzo Cosentino

North American P-51 Mustang

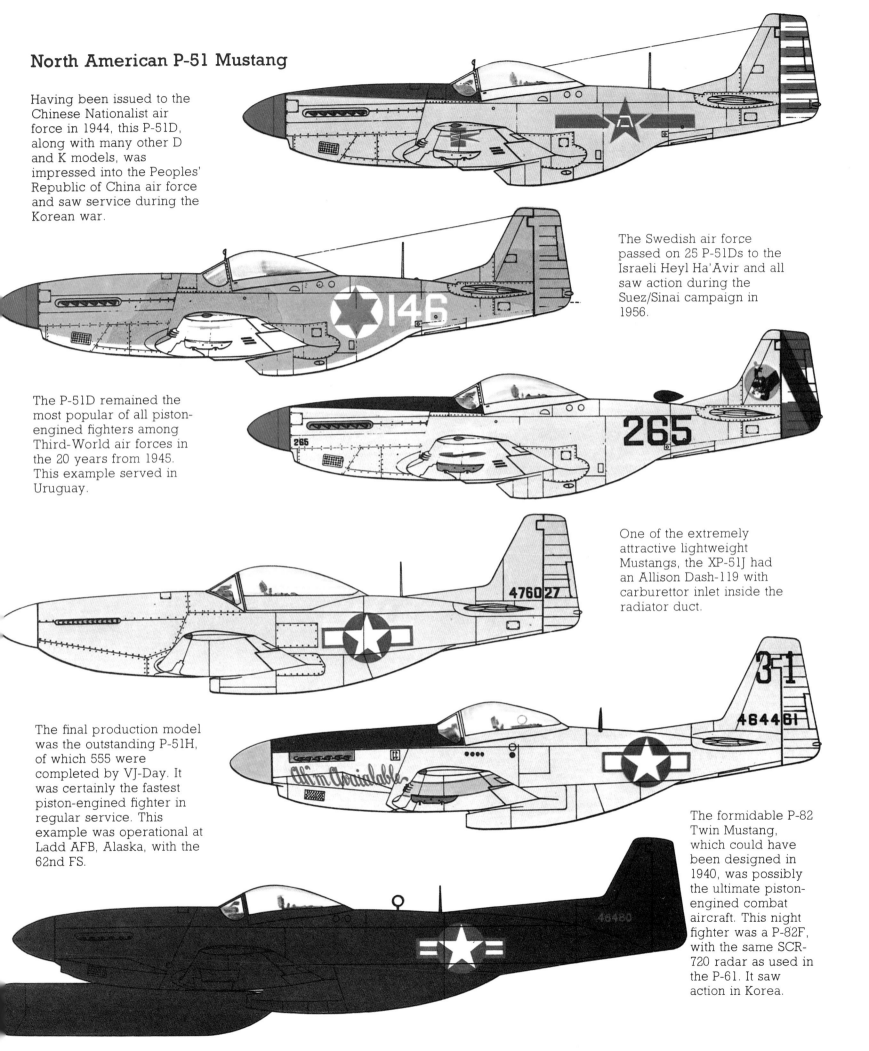

Having been issued to the Chinese Nationalist air force in 1944, this P-51D, along with many other D and K models, was impressed into the Peoples' Republic of China air force and saw service during the Korean war.

The Swedish air force passed on 25 P-51Ds to the Israeli Heyl Ha'Avir and all saw action during the Suez/Sinai campaign in 1956.

The P-51D remained the most popular of all piston-engined fighters among Third-World air forces in the 20 years from 1945. This example served in Uruguay.

One of the extremely attractive lightweight Mustangs, the XP-51J had an Allison Dash-119 with carburettor inlet inside the radiator duct.

The final production model was the outstanding P-51H, of which 555 were completed by VJ-Day. It was certainly the fastest piston-engined fighter in regular service. This example was operational at Ladd AFB, Alaska, with the 62nd FS.

The formidable P-82 Twin Mustang, which could have been designed in 1940, was possibly the ultimate piston-engined combat aircraft. This night fighter was a P-82F, with the same SCR-720 radar as used in the P-61. It saw action in Korea.

North American P-51 Mustang

Unlike most of the famous aircraft of World War 2 the P-51 Mustang had not even been thought of when the war started. It was designed extremely quickly to meet a British order, and was at first of only passing interest to the US Army. Soon, however, its outstanding qualities brought it to the very forefront, and in the final 18 months of war it was the leading US fighter in the European theatre. Not least of its many attributes was its ability to escort bombers over long distances. Goering said, 'When I saw the Mustangs over Berlin I knew the war was lost.'

Discussions between the British Air Purchasing Commission and North American Aviation began in late 1940. The British wanted NAA to build the Curtiss Hawk 87 (Kittyhawk) under licence. NAA said they could design a much better fighter and, after British counter-arguments, a contract was signed in April 1940 for a prototype NA.73. British hesitation was due to the fact NAA had never built a fighter (except the P-64 derived from a trainer), but the NA.73X prototype was a masterpiece. Rolled out in 117 days, and flown on 26 October 1940, it combined every modern aerodynamic, structural and systems advance, chief results of which were exceptional internal fuel capacity and low drag.

In April 1942 the Mustang I entered service with No 2 Sqn, RAF Army Co-operation Command, in the low-level reconnaissance role. It was obviously far better than any previous American fighter, but the low rated height of its engine resulted in poor performance above medium altitudes. Orders mounted, a September 1940 batch having specified four-cannon armament. USAAF trials soon resulted in American orders, starting with the cannon-armed P-51 and following with 500 A-36A fighter-bombers. Altogether 1,579 Allison-engined models were built, called Mks I, IA and II by the RAF, the F-6A being a photo version.

By 1942 several observers had suggested overcoming the high-altitude limitation by fitting a 60-series Merlin, and the first 'Mustang X' flew on 13 October 1942. However, only a few weeks later NAA did a totally different conversion, and this was ordered in massive numbers (2,200) before the first XP-51B flew in December 1942. Largely redesigned, the P-51B had an additional intercooler radiator and augmented coolant and oil radiators, and a large-area four-blade propeller to absorb the power at high altitude, where its all-round performance put the new variant in the very front rank.

By summer 1943 extremely large-scale production of the P-51B was in hand at Inglewood and of the identical C at Dallas, and combat wings of the 8th Air Force in England received aircraft on 1 December 1943. The key to long-range escort – a task expected to be met by a special design such as the unsuccessful XP-75 Eagle – was extra fuel capacity. More fuel in the fuselage, at the expense of tricky stability until the extra tank had been emptied, was augmented by drop tanks of 75 and finally 108 US gallons (284 and 409 litres) capacity under each wing, with which flights could be made to a target 1368km (850 miles) away, covering every point in Western Europe. Once the tanks had been emptied and dropped the P-51 could out-perform any regular Bf 109 or Fw 190.

One of the features unchanged in the P-51B was the canopy, but it was soon realized the British Malcolm sliding hood was better and this was fitted as a field modification to RAF Mustang IIIs and to many USAAF P-51Bs and Cs. Later in 1944 NAA introduced the P-51D with sliding 'bubble' canopy, cut-down rear fuselage, increased firepower and, later, bigger bomb-load plus rocket attachments. By the end of 1944 an extended dorsal fin was standard.

P-51s served with many Allied air forces. As well as the P-51K with a propeller of different make, NAA built prototypes of the P-51F and G lightweight Mustangs, from which emerged the final production model, the P-51H, a few of which saw action against Japan. The P-82 Twin Mustang, like the P-51J, was too late for war service.

COUNTRY OF ORIGIN USA.

CREW 1, though there were 2-seat conversions.

TOTAL PRODUCED 15,586, including 200 assembled by Commonwealth Aircraft in Australia, mainly from NAA components.

DIMENSIONS Wingspan 11·278m (37ft 0¼in); length, most: 9·83m (32ft 3in), **H**: 10·16m (33ft 4in); wing area, most: 21·65m² (233ft²), **H**: 21·83m² (235ft²).

WEIGHTS Empty, **Mk I, P-51**: 2996kg (6,605lb), **D**: 3232kg (7,125lb), **H**: 2977kg (6,563lb); maximum loaded, **Mk I, P-51**: 3992kg (8,800lb), **D**: 5489kg (12,100lb), **H**: 5216kg (11,500lb).

ENGINE One vee-12 liquid-cooled; **I,IA,II, P-51, A, A-36**: 1,150hp Allison V-1710-F3R or -39 (some A-36A, 1,325hp -87); all later production models: Packard V-1650 (Merlin), usually 1,520hp V-1650-3 but later **D,K**: 1,590hp -7, and **H**: 2,218hp -9.

MAXIMUM SPEED V-1710, typical: 624km/h (388mph), **B,C,D**, clean, typical: 703km/h (437mph), **H**: 784km/h (487mph).

SERVICE CEILING V-1710 versions, typically: 9144m (30,000ft), **D**: typical of later models: 12770m (41,900ft).

RANGE V-1710 models, maximum internal fuel: 1207km (750 miles); **D**, maximum fuel, typical: 3927km (2,440 miles).

MILITARY LOAD **I**: four 12·7mm (0·5in) and four 7·7mm (0·303in) Browning machine guns (two 12·7mm/0·5in under engine); **II, P-51A**: four 12·7mm (0·5in) (all in wing); **IA, P-51**: four 20mm in wing, two 227kg (500lb) bombs; **A-36A**: six 12·7mm (0·5in) (two under engine), two 227kg (500lb) bombs; **B,C** (most): four 12·7mm (0·5in), two 454kg (1,000lb) bombs; late **B,C**, all **D,K**: six 12·7mm (0·5in), two 454kg (1,000lb) bombs, plus (D only) six 127mm (5in) rockets; **H**: as D.

Petlyakov Pe-2

Until recently the dominant mission of the Soviet air forces, during World War 2 called the Voyenno-Vozdushni Sily, VVS, was close support of the Red Army. This inevitably meant a concentration of short-ranged single-engined aircraft, but one design was produced in very large numbers with great versatility and capable of long-range attack, reconnaissance and, in some versions, even fighting. It was one of the most important aircraft of World War 2, being in many respects similar to the British Mosquito, though manufactured in even greater quantity.

Vladimir M. Petlyakov had headed a major design team in the Tupolev bureau, but his work was so successful that when, in 1940, aircraft were redesignated according to their designers, he was allowed to call his aircraft 'Pe' types. By far the most important of his designs began in 1938 as the VI-100 high-altitude fighter, with pressure cabin. This was changed in 1939 to a high-altitude bomber, just after the prototype VI-100 flew. The VI-100 was extremely advanced for its day, in the context of the Soviet Union, because instead of making maximum use of wood it was entirely of metal, with stressed skin; and it incorporated extensive accessory systems, especially electrical equipment, at a time when other Soviet aircraft were deliberately made almost unbelievably simple.

The second prototype strongly resembled the VI-100 but was the PB-100 dive bomber, flown on 22 December 1939. The pressure cabin and engine turbosuperchargers were removed, and crew stations provided for pilot, nav/bombardier and radio/gunner in a fuselage of minimum cross section. From the start each of the three seats was armoured, and by the time State Acceptance Trials were completed in June 1940 the internal tanks were self-sealing. At first all bombs were carried internally in bays occupying the space between the wing spars and the rear of the engine nacelles.

Production deliveries began in August 1940, with the new designation Pe-2, and squadrons formed just before the German invasion of 22 June 1941. Handling was good, and performance so high that Hurricanes of the RAF detailed to fly as escorts found it almost impossible to keep up! By June 1942 an urgent front-line request (FT) had resulted in the Pe-2FT, with improved defensive armament, which was fitted as a modification to most of the 2,000-odd aircraft then in service. The weight of extra guns and armour caused a fall in performance, and by the end of 1942 the PF engine was fitted, as well as the new standard Soviet system of purging fuel tanks with filtered and cooled exhaust gas.

Variants included the Pe-2R with three cameras in the fuselage bomb bay, the UT dual-control trainer and, from February 1943, the M (*modifikatsi-rovanni*) with many refinements to reduce drag. Small numbers of the Pe-3 family were delivered, which were basically fighters but also included reconnaissance versions. By 1944 this and the basic bomber had led to a faster series with the VK-107 engine. The fighter prototypes were designated Pe-2VI, with heavy armament and pressure cabin. A VB-109 bomber was built with the pressure cabin, but crashed; and the high-altitude fighter was dropped because Luftwaffe high-flying threats receded.

By mid-1944 production was centred on the Pe-2M, with an enlarged fuselage bomb bay and external racks for a maximum load of 3 tonnes (6,614lb), though this was not often carried. Wing racks were recessed into the undersurface, and in most later batches the dive brakes were removed to save drag. A proportion of late-war production had VK-107 engines and increased forward-firing armament, and were designated Pe-2I (interceptor). The Pe-2 served with the air forces of Finland and, from late 1944, the Communist-organized Polish and Czech air forces. Many examples were used for test programmes, including the RD-1 acid/kerosine rocket, several turbojets, at least one ramjet and the first Russian ejection seat. The post-war NATO name was 'Buck'.

COUNTRY OF ORIGIN Soviet Union.

CREW Usually 3.

TOTAL PRODUCED Accepted figure is 11,427.

DIMENSIONS Wingspan, normal: 17·16m (56ft 3½in), **Pe-2I** and other VK-107: 18·0m (59ft 0½in); length, normal: 12·6–12·66m (41ft 4¼in–41ft 6in); wing area 40·5m² (435·9ft²).

WEIGHTS Empty, early: 5870kg (12,941lb), **M** with PF engines: 5950kg (13,117lb); maximum loaded, early: 8496kg (18,730lb), late-model **M**: 8520kg (18,783lb).

ENGINES Two vee-12 liquid-cooled, by Klimov bureau based on Hispano-Suiza design; pre-1943: 1,100hp M-105R; 1943: 1,260hp M-105PF (VK-105PF); 1944, some versions: 1,650hp VK-107A.

MAXIMUM SPEED Early, typical: 540km/h (336mph); **Pe-2M**, with PF engines: 580km/h (360mph); with VK-107A engines: 655km/h (407mph).

SERVICE CEILING All M-105 versions: typically 8800m (28,870ft); with 107A engine: 11000m (36,100ft).

RANGE With bomb load, typical: 1200km (746 miles); **Pe-2R**: 1700km (1,056 miles).

MILITARY LOAD **PB-100** and original **Pe-2**: internal bomb load of 200kg (441lb) in fuselage and 100kg (220lb) in nacelles, plus four 100kg (220lb) bombs external; defensive armament of four 7·62mm (0·30in) ShKAS, two fixed firing ahead and one aimed above and one below at rear. **Pe-2FT**: upper rear gun replaced by manual UBT turret (with aerodynamic vane to assist rotation) with 12·7mm (0·5in) BS; external racks for four 250kg or two 500kg (1,102lb) bombs. Late production **Pe-2M**: 12·7mm (0·5in) BS in turret and lower rear, two ShKAS beam guns; total bomb load of 3000kg (6,615lb) including 2000kg (4,410lb) internal.

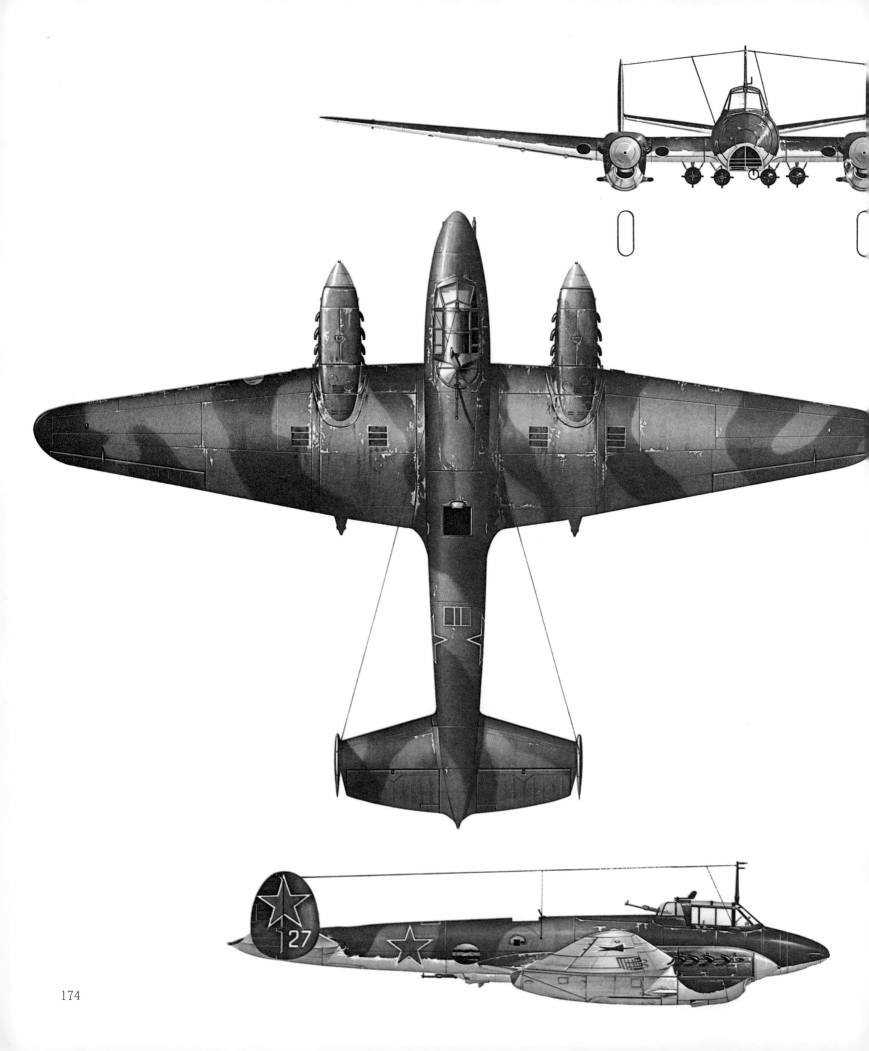

Petlyakov Pe-2

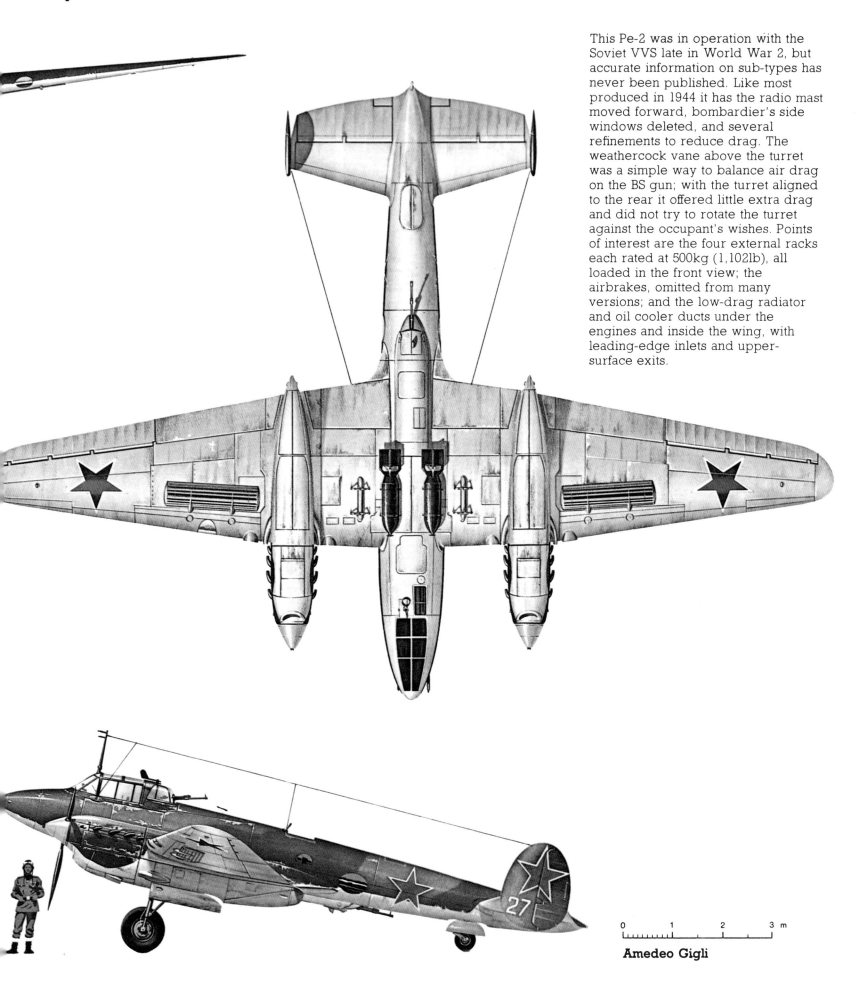

This Pe-2 was in operation with the Soviet VVS late in World War 2, but accurate information on sub-types has never been published. Like most produced in 1944 it has the radio mast moved forward, bombardier's side windows deleted, and several refinements to reduce drag. The weathercock vane above the turret was a simple way to balance air drag on the BS gun; with the turret aligned to the rear it offered little extra drag and did not try to rotate the turret against the occupant's wishes. Points of interest are the four external racks each rated at 500kg (1,102lb), all loaded in the front view; the airbrakes, omitted from many versions; and the low-drag radiator and oil cooler ducts under the engines and inside the wing, with leading-edge inlets and upper-surface exits.

0   1   2   3 m

Amedeo Gigli

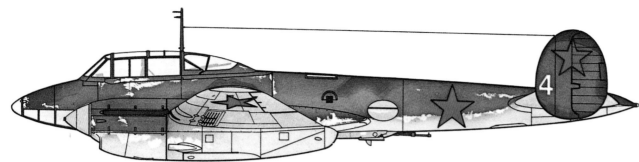

Details of Pe-2 variants have never been published. This was one of the original production series with side windows for the bomb-aimer/radio operator, M-105R engines and long crew canopy.

Seen in winter camouflage, this aircraft is again an early series but in this case with a BS gun for rear upper protection as introduced to the Il-2.

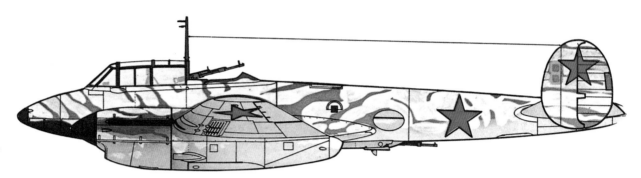

Captured by the Finns and put into service with LeLv 48, this Pe-2 had no airbrakes but was fitted with a D/F loop under the nose. Within a few weeks the Finns were Allies of the Russians and fighting the retreating Germans.

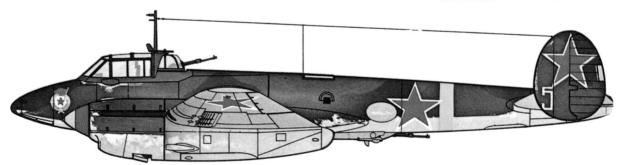

Typical of the mainstream production of 1943–4, in which time some 7,500 Pe-2s were built, this aircraft has no nose side windows but does have a turret and airbrakes. Note Guards insignia on the nose. Designation was almost certainly Pe-2FT.

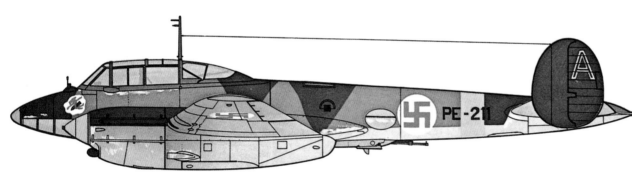

Another Pe-2 from the mid-series. The radio operator normally sat behind the pilot facing aft, but could get down to the prone bombing position under the cockpit floor. The rear gunner aimed the lower gun through a periscope.

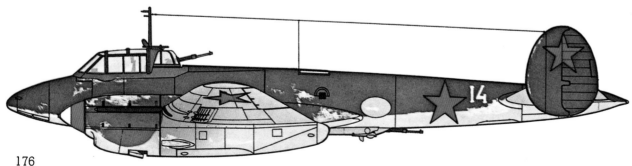

Petlyakov Pe-2

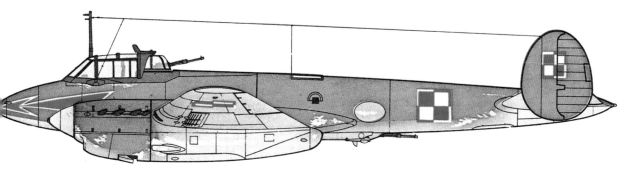

One of the later Pe-2M series with M-105PF engines, and many other changes including a forward-mounted radio mast. This example was assigned to the Communist Polish forces, later the *Polskie Wojska Lotnicze*.

This late-series M-105PF bomber is shown in markings believed to be those of the Communist Hungarian air force in the 1945–6 era. The fuselage cockade is similar to that of North Korea but with the ring colours transposed.

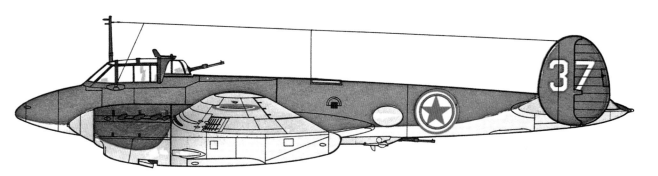

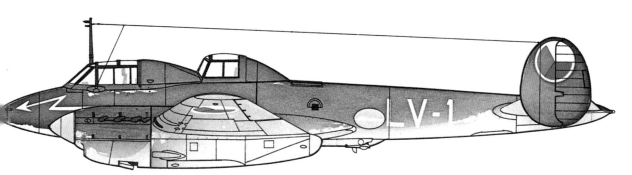

Together with the Polish PWL the Czech CL (Ceskoslovenske Letectvo) used the Pe-2FT and this dual trainer version. the Pe-2U, in the immediate post-war period. The extra rear cockpit, with rudimentary instrumentation, was occupied by the instructor.

The Pe-2VI (*vysotny istrebitel*, high-altitude fighter) was flown in prototype form in 1944, with pressurized cabin, VK-107A engines and four 20mm ShVAK cannon in the nose.

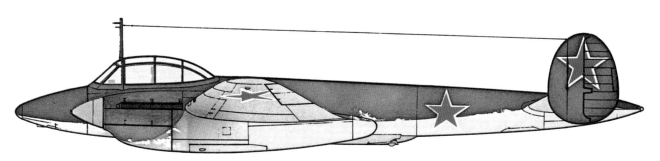

This weary Pe-2 was photographed in about 1951 engaged in ejection-seat trials, the test seat being installed above the trailing edge. Engines were PF series.

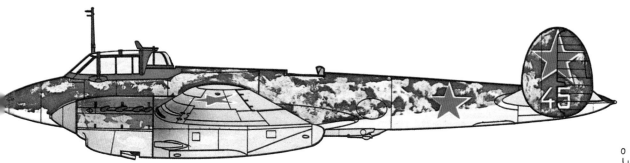

0   1   2   3 m

Roberto Terrinoni

Republic P-47D-5-RE Thunderbolt

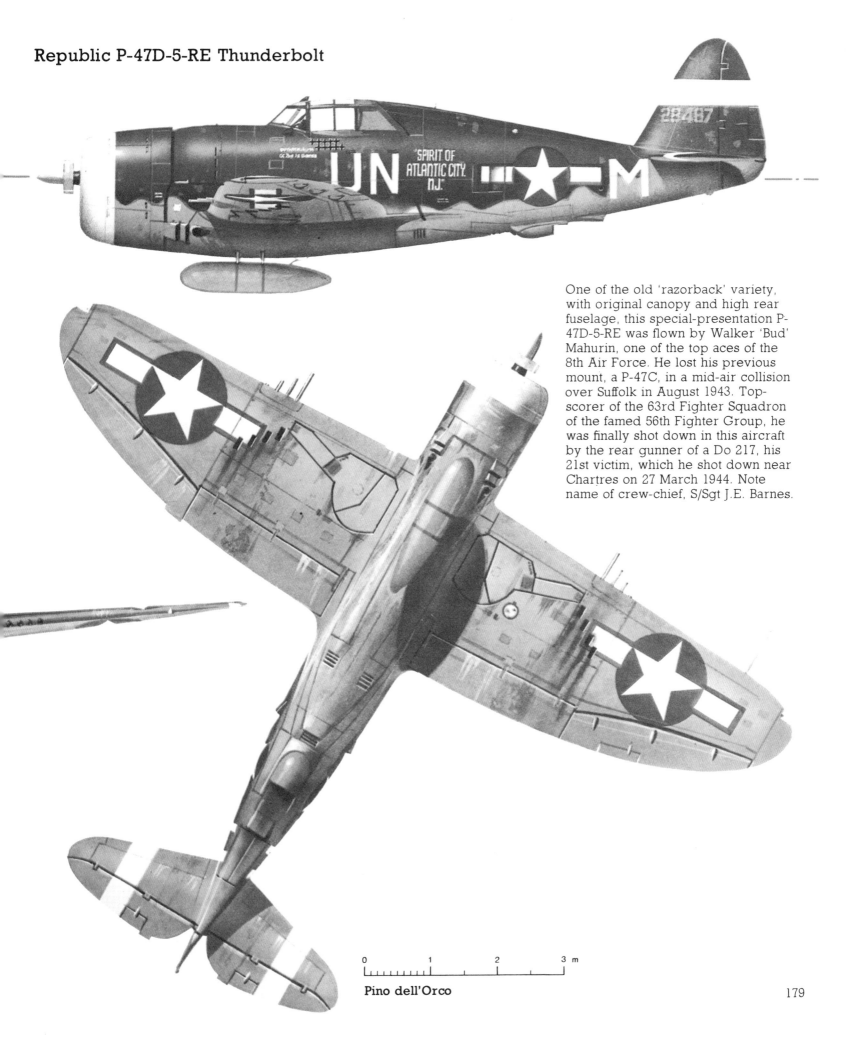

One of the old 'razorback' variety, with original canopy and high rear fuselage, this special-presentation P-47D-5-RE was flown by Walker 'Bud' Mahurin, one of the top aces of the 8th Air Force. He lost his previous mount, a P-47C, in a mid-air collision over Suffolk in August 1943. Top-scorer of the 63rd Fighter Squadron of the famed 56th Fighter Group, he was finally shot down in this aircraft by the rear gunner of a Do 217, his 21st victim, which he shot down near Chartres on 27 March 1944. Note name of crew-chief, S/Sgt J.E. Barnes.

Pino dell'Orco

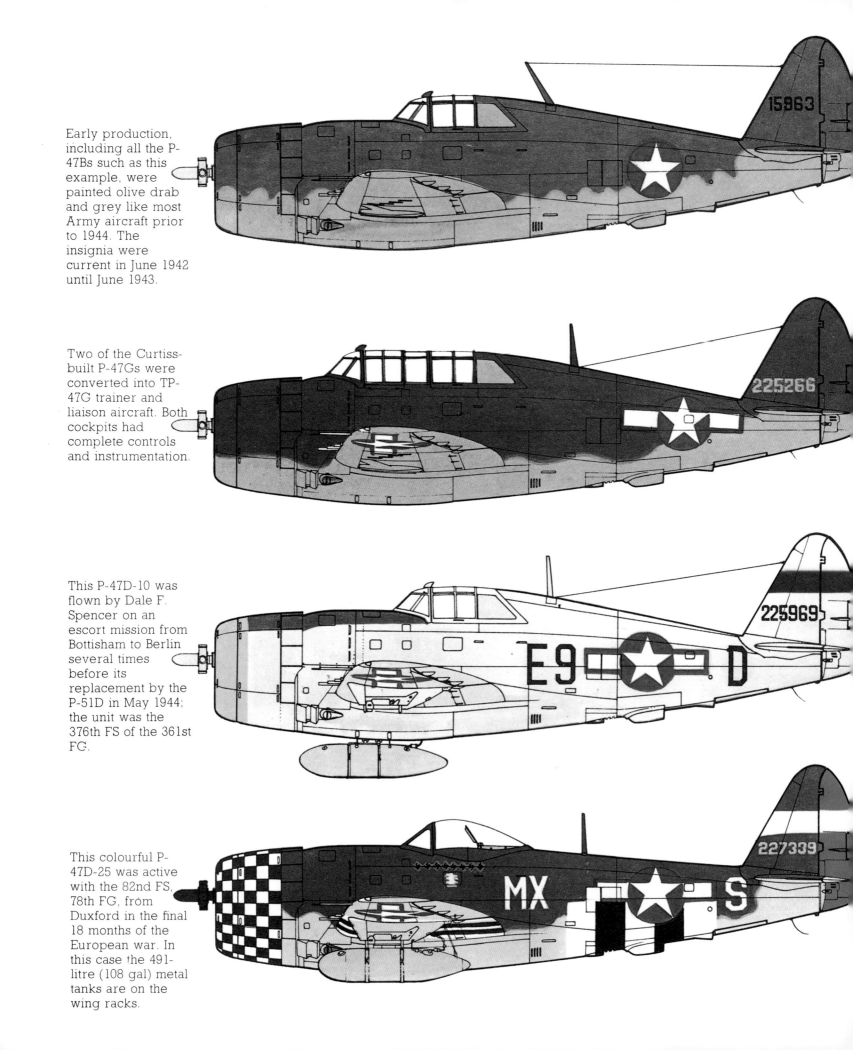

Early production, including all the P-47Bs such as this example, were painted olive drab and grey like most Army aircraft prior to 1944. The insignia were current in June 1942 until June 1943.

Two of the Curtiss-built P-47Gs were converted into TP-47G trainer and liaison aircraft. Both cockpits had complete controls and instrumentation.

This P-47D-10 was flown by Dale F. Spencer on an escort mission from Bottisham to Berlin several times before its replacement by the P-51D in May 1944; the unit was the 376th FS of the 361st FG.

This colourful P-47D-25 was active with the 82nd FS, 78th FG, from Duxford in the final 18 months of the European war. In this case the 491-litre (108 gal) metal tanks are on the wing racks.

Republic P-47 Thunderbolt

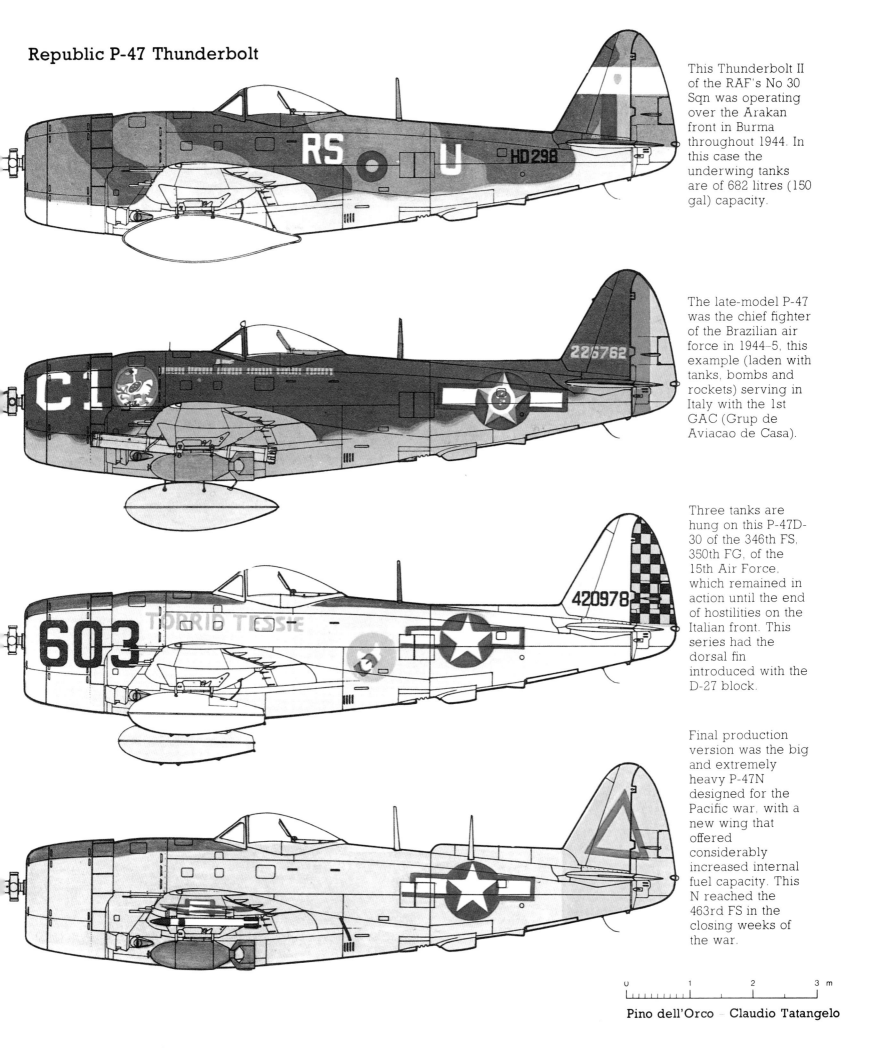

This Thunderbolt II of the RAF's No 30 Sqn was operating over the Arakan front in Burma throughout 1944. In this case the underwing tanks are of 682 litres (150 gal) capacity.

The late-model P-47 was the chief fighter of the Brazilian air force in 1944–5, this example (laden with tanks, bombs and rockets) serving in Italy with the 1st GAC (Grup de Aviacao de Casa).

Three tanks are hung on this P-47D-30 of the 346th FS, 350th FG, of the 15th Air Force, which remained in action until the end of hostilities on the Italian front. This series had the dorsal fin introduced with the D-27 block.

Final production version was the big and extremely heavy P-47N designed for the Pacific war, with a new wing that offered considerably increased internal fuel capacity. This N reached the 463rd FS in the closing weeks of the war.

Pino dell'Orco - Claudio Tatangelo

Republic P-47 Thunderbolt

The P-47 Thunderbolt was the biggest, heaviest and most expensive fighter in history to be powered by a single piston engine. As such it ran directly counter to the vehemently expressed beliefs of many experts, including such eminent designers as Kurt Tank and Alex Yakovlev; yet the record tends to support the official American view that the big fighter could carry more weapons, fly further and hit harder. Certainly more P-47s were made than any other US fighter before or since.

The P-47 was the outcome of a long evolutionary process which began with the very first Seversky designs in 1933. In 1935 Seversky flew the prototype that led to the P-35, and by 1939 the next generation had materialized as the AP-4, from which stemmed the P-43 Lancer, an important fighter/bomber of the early war period. By late 1939 a further design was ordered as the XP-47, but combat reports from Europe indicated a need for more guns and more horsepower. Chief engineer Alex Kartveli thereupon designed a scaled-up P-43 to be powered by the most powerful engine actually available (as distinct from the numerous even more powerful engines that were under development). This powerplant was boosted by a turbosupercharger under the rear fuselage, with a complex array of large pipes linking the turbo and intercooler with the engine. Even with four blades the propeller required a diameter of 3·71m (12ft 2in), in turn calling for long landing gears and pushing the heavy armament of eight 12·7mm (0·5in) guns well outboard.

Designated XP-47B, the first of these impressive new fighters flew on 6 May 1941. After conquering more than the usual run of development problems the production P-47B flew in March 1942, and by the summer of that year the crack 56th Fighter Group (later to be top scorers of the USAAF in air combat in World War 2) was forming up ready to proceed to Europe. At the 172nd aircraft the engine was moved forward 0·2m (8in) to improve stability, resulting in the designation P-47C. This also introduced a bomb or tank shackle, and

soon had a new-series engine with water injection to boost power.

By early 1943 production switched to the definitive P-47D, with refined engine, turbo and intercooler installation, more armour, increased ammunition and weapon loads and, from the -25 production block, a 'bubble' canopy. The -30 block introduced an extended dorsal fin. Production by this time was increasing rapidly, with three assembly lines: the parent plant at Farmingdale, a new factory at Evansville, Indiana, and the Curtiss-Wright company whose aircraft were designated P-47G. During the course of D-model production further improvements included a universal wing able to carry tanks, bombs or rockets, a stronger belly attachment for heavier tanks and bombs, and broad 'paddle-blade' propellers. Total output of the D model was 12,602, exceptional for a single subtype of any aircraft. This great fighter, called the 'Jug' (from Juggernaut), excelled at long-range escort, bombing and ground straffing, and served with Australia, Brazil, France, the Soviet Union and RAF as well as the USAAF.

As well as several experimental models and the planned replacement, the XP-72, Republic hastily produced the P-47M in mid-1944 to chase flying bombs over the English Channel. This was a lightened model with a specially uprated version of the engine, 130 being delivered within three weeks of design. The second of this family was fitted with a completely new wing to produce the ultra-long-range P-47N for the Pacific war. Total fuel capacity of this version was no less than 4337 litres (954 Imp gal), and among many other changes the landing gear was strengthened to match the extremely high maximum weight. Altogether the P-47 was credited with 3,752 aircraft shot down (excluding Soviet results) and 3,315 destroyed on the ground, plus 9,000 locomotives, 86,000 rail trucks, 6,000 armoured vehicles and 68,000 motor trucks. In the closing stages of the Pacific war P-47s were flying 1,677 sorties and dropping 550 tonnes (541 tons) of bombs each day.

COUNTRY OF ORIGIN USA.

CREW 1 (there were a few 2-seat conversions).

TOTAL PRODUCED 15,660.

DIMENSIONS Wingspan, most: 12·42m (40ft 9¼in), **N**: 12·98m (42ft 7in); length, **B**: 10·75m (35ft 3¼in), **C,D**: 11·02m (36ft 1¾in); **M,N**: 11·07m (36ft 4in); wing area, **B,C,D,M**: 27·87m² (300ft²), **N**: 29·91m² (322ft²).

WEIGHTS Empty, **B**: 4239kg (9,346lb), **D**: 4491–4536kg (9,900–10,000lb), **M**: 4728kg (10,423lb), **N**: 4990kg (11,000lb); maximum loaded, **B**: 6060kg (13,360lb), **D-22**: 6804kg (15,000lb), **D-25/35**: 7938kg (17,500lb), **M**: 7031kg (15,500lb), **N**: 9390kg (20,500lb).

ENGINE Pratt & Whitney R-2800 Double Wasp 18-cylinder radial; **B**: 2,000hp R-2800-21; **C**: 2,300hp -59; **D**: usually -59 with wet rating of 2,535hp; **M,N**: -57C with combat (water/methanol) rating of 2,800hp.

MAXIMUM SPEED **B**: 690km/h (429mph), **C,D**: 697km/h (433mph), **M**: 756km/h (470mph), **N**: 752km/h (467mph).

SERVICE CEILING All production types, about 12800m (42,000ft).

RANGE **B**: with drop tank 2012km (1,250 miles), **D**: maximum fuel, 3060km (1,900 miles), **M**: clean, 901km (560 miles), **N**: maximum fuel, 3782km (2,350 miles).

MILITARY LOAD Normal fixed-gun armament, eight 12·7 (0·5in) Browning M53-2, originally with 267, later 425 rounds per gun; external load, **B**: none; **C**: 227kg (500lb); **D**: 1134kg (2,500lb); **N**: 1361kg (3,000lb) including ten 127mm (5in) rockets.

Savoia-Marchetti S.M.79 Sparviero

Italian arms and accomplishments in World War 2 have often been derided. This is sometimes unfair, and the S.M.79 achieved a record in action that speaks well of its toughness and of the courage of its crews. It was by far the most important Italian offensive warplane of that conflict, and was one of the very few Italian machines to be produced in substantial quantities.

The famous company SIAI Savoia-Marchetti, which had been responsible for many bombers, airliners and flying boats, had by the 1930s come to the conclusion that the preferred number of engines for bombers and transports was three. In early 1934 its management decided that, despite the great success of a design which gave rise to the S.M.73 airliner and S.M.81 bomber and multi-role military machine, they could manufacture a more modern and faster aircraft with a more highly loaded wing and retractable landing gear. This was the S.M.79, and the prototype, with civil registration I-MAGO, flew for the first time in late October 1934. Within a few months it was re-engined with Alfa Romeo 125 units of greater power (750hp each) and quickly set an impressive list of world class records for flights combining speed, useful load and distance.

Like most Italian aircraft of the day the S.M.79 had mixed construction. The fuselage was welded from steel tubing, the covering being light alloy forward, part light alloy and part plywood on top and fabric elsewhere. The wing was all-wood, and its small size was offset by trailing-edge flaps and drooping ailerons and leading-edge slats. Over the next four years various engines were fitted for Italian and export customers, and for some countries twin-engined versions were produced. The Iraq bomber variant of 1938 had 1,000hp Fiat A.80 engines and a glazed nose for the bomb-aimer, while the Romanian version used on the Eastern Front in 1942 had 1,300hp Jumo 211 engines and was as fast as the tri-motors.

The first major production version for the Regia Aeronautica was the S.M.79-I, all types having the family name Sparviero (Hawk). Production built up fast from December 1936, and most of the early 79-I bombers served with the Aviación Legionaria in the Spanish Civil War, soon achieving an impressive reputation. The normal crew comprised two pilots side-by-side, a radio operator and flight engineer further back (the latter manning the dorsal gun) and a bomb-aimer in the lower rear compartment. The bomb-aimer had a ventral blister in which he either lay prone or else stood with his legs in two retractable fairings projecting vertically downwards. He had comprehensive instruments and his own temporary rudder control during the bombing run, plus automatic camera.

First flown in October 1939, the much more powerful 79-II was the chief wartime version, built not only by the parent company but also by Aeronautica Macchi and OM Reggiane. This ensured output that more than kept pace with attrition and enabled the Regia Aeronautica to build up a formidable Sparviero force, of which a growing proportion were Aerosiluranti (air torpedo) squadrons. These units were among the hardest-worked in the whole Mediterranean theatre, and by mid-1943 had sunk 86 Allied ships totalling 708,500 metric tonnes (697,164 UK tons).

The final production model was a highly refined machine, because, though it had less-powerful engines, the 79-III was if anything faster than earlier versions and also had a greater fuel capacity and longer range. Manufacture continued at much-reduced rate until early 1944. By this time the once-proud force of the Regia Aeronautica had been dispersed or shot down. Some Sparvieros were sequestrated on the spot by the Luftwaffe and used with German or Italian crews as regular Luftwaffe utility transports. Some served in the newly created ARSI, the air arm of the Repubblica Sociale Italiana which continued to fight on the side of the Axis. A few found their way to the Allied side and served with the Co-Belligerent Air Force against the German forces.

COUNTRY OF ORIGIN Italy.

CREW 4 or 5.

TOTAL PRODUCED About 1,350, of which just over 100 were exported.

DIMENSIONS Wingspan 21·2m (69ft 6½in); length most: 15·6m (51ft 2in), **79-III**: 16·2m (53ft 1¾in); wing area 61·7m² (664ft²).

WEIGHTS Empty **79-I**: 6800kg (14,990lb), **79-III**: 7700kg (16,975lb); maximum loaded **79-I**: 10500kg (23,148lb), **79-III**: 11400kg (25,132lb).

ENGINES Three air-cooled radials, **79-I**: 780hp Alfa Romeo 126RC34 nine-cylinder; **79-II**: 1,000hp Piaggio P.XIRC40 14-cylinder; **79-III**: 860hp Alfa Romeo 128RC18.

MAXIMUM SPEED **79-I**: 420km/h (261mph); **79-II**: 430km/h (267mph); **79-III**: 460km/h (286mph).

SERVICE CEILING All versions, about 7500m (24,600ft).

RANGE **79-I**: 1900km (1,180 miles); **79-II**: 2000km (1,242 miles); **79-III**: 2300km (1,429 miles).

MILITARY LOAD One fixed 12·7mm (0·5in) Breda-SAFAT firing ahead above cockpit (20mm in 79-III), one 12·7mm (0·5in) manually aimed from dorsal position and another aimed from rear of ventral gondola (absent from 79-III), one or two 7·7mm (0.303in) often aimed from beam windows; internal bomb load of 1200kg (2,645lb) or two externally slung 450mm torpedoes.

S.M. 79-II Sparviero

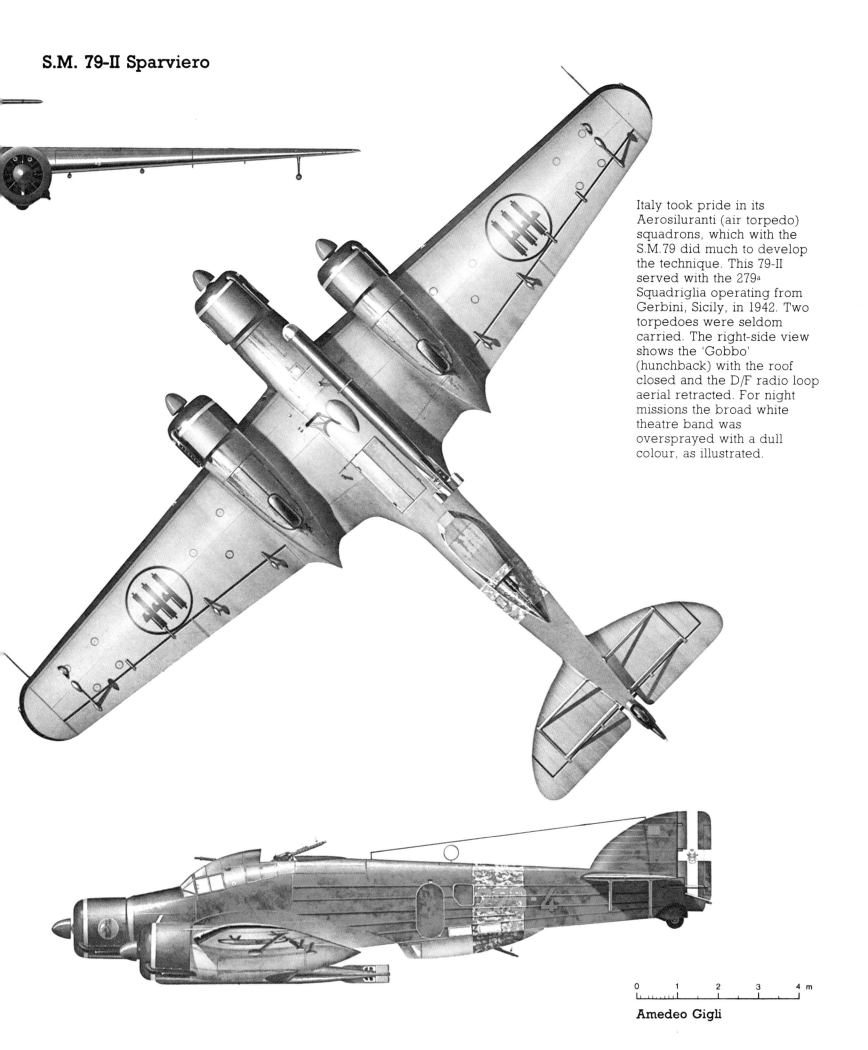

Italy took pride in its Aerosiluranti (air torpedo) squadrons, which with the S.M.79 did much to develop the technique. This 79-II served with the 279ª Squadriglia operating from Gerbini, Sicily, in 1942. Two torpedoes were seldom carried. The right-side view shows the 'Gobbo' (hunchback) with the roof closed and the D/F radio loop aerial retracted. For night missions the broad white theatre band was oversprayed with a dull colour, as illustrated.

0 1 2 3 4 m

Amedeo Gigli

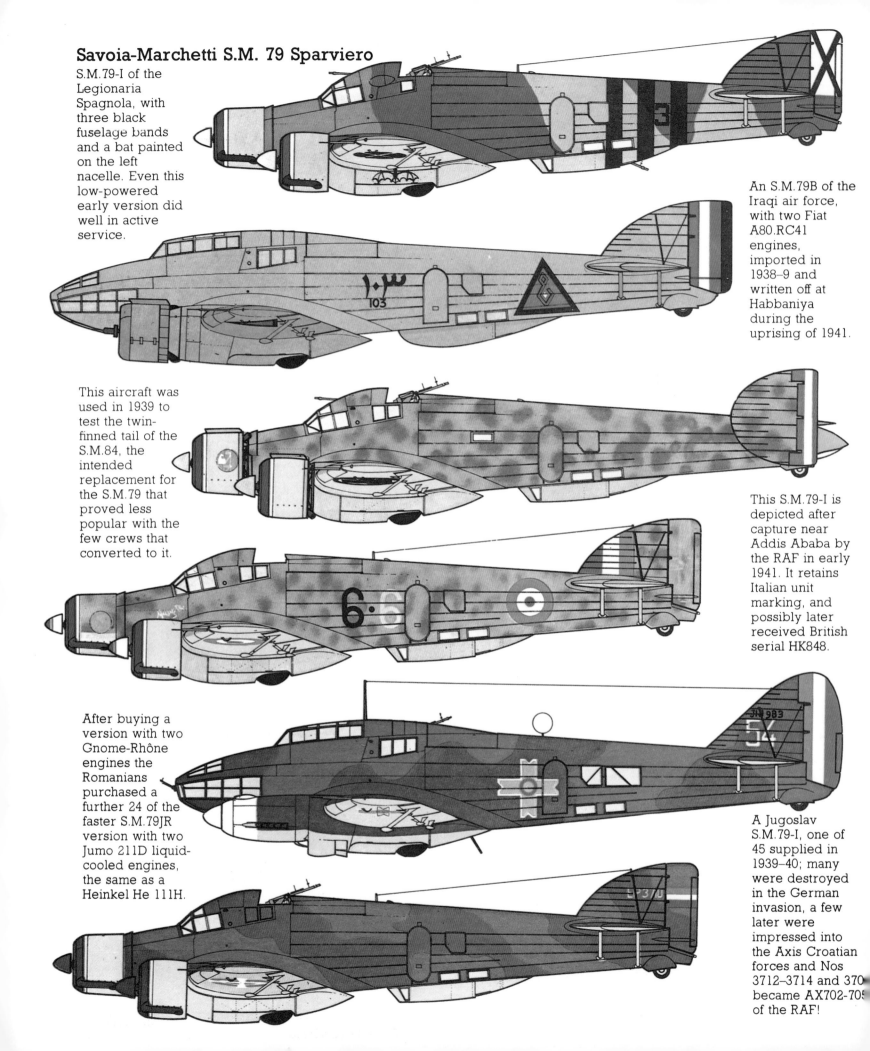

Savoia-Marchetti S.M. 79 Sparviero

S.M.79-I of the Legionaria Spagnola, with three black fuselage bands and a bat painted on the left nacelle. Even this low-powered early version did well in active service.

An S.M.79B of the Iraqi air force, with two Fiat A80.RC41 engines, imported in 1938–9 and written off at Habbaniya during the uprising of 1941.

This aircraft was used in 1939 to test the twin-finned tail of the S.M.84, the intended replacement for the S.M.79 that proved less popular with the few crews that converted to it.

This S.M.79-I is depicted after capture near Addis Ababa by the RAF in early 1941. It retains Italian unit marking, and possibly later received British serial HK848.

After buying a version with two Gnome-Rhône engines the Romanians purchased a further 24 of the faster S.M.79JR version with two Jumo 211D liquid-cooled engines, the same as a Heinkel He 111H.

A Jugoslav S.M.79-I, one of 45 supplied in 1939–40; many were destroyed in the German invasion, a few later were impressed into the Axis Croatian forces and Nos 3712–3714 and 370 became AX702-705 of the RAF!

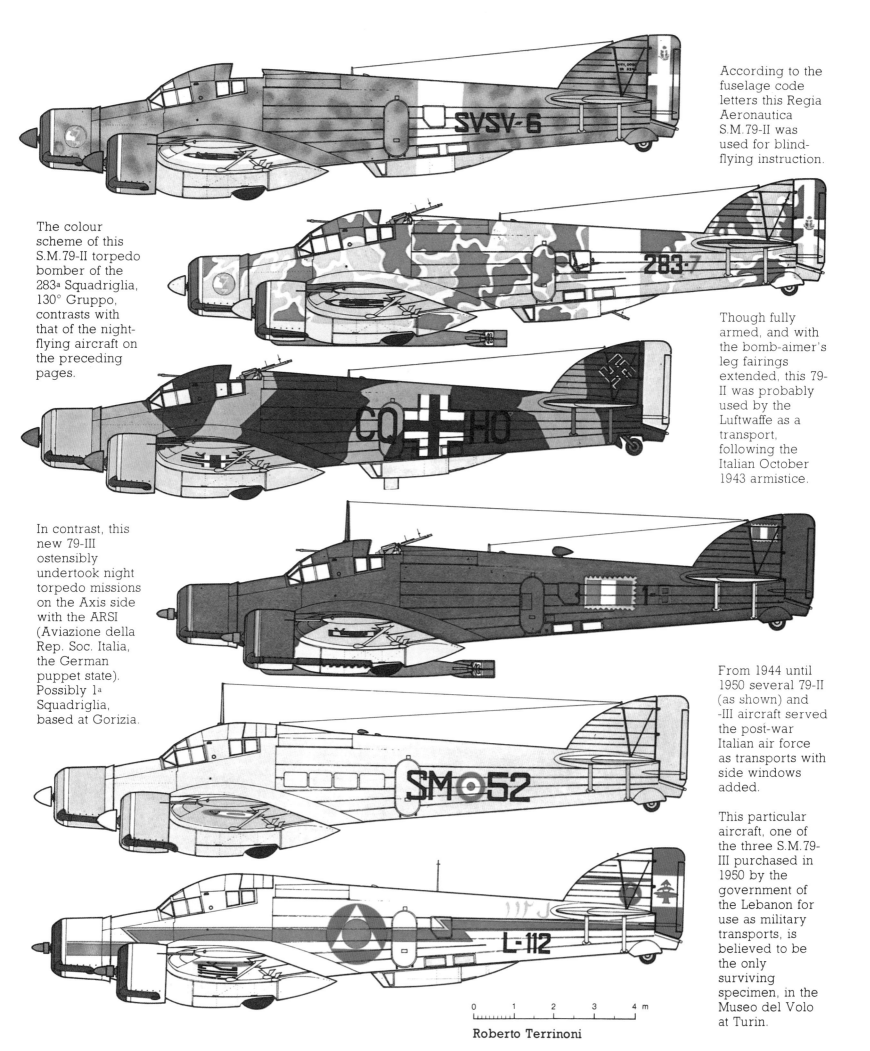

According to the fuselage code letters this Regia Aeronautica S.M.79-II was used for blind-flying instruction.

The colour scheme of this S.M.79-II torpedo bomber of the 283ª Squadriglia, 130° Gruppo, contrasts with that of the night-flying aircraft on the preceding pages.

Though fully armed, and with the bomb-aimer's leg fairings extended, this 79-II was probably used by the Luftwaffe as a transport, following the Italian October 1943 armistice.

In contrast, this new 79-III ostensibly undertook night torpedo missions on the Axis side with the ARSI (Aviazione della Rep. Soc. Italia, the German puppet state). Possibly 1ª Squadriglia, based at Gorizia.

From 1944 until 1950 several 79-II (as shown) and -III aircraft served the post-war Italian air force as transports with side windows added.

This particular aircraft, one of the three S.M.79-III purchased in 1950 by the government of the Lebanon for use as military transports, is believed to be the only surviving specimen, in the Museo del Volo at Turin.

SVSV-6

283-7

CQ+HO

SM●52

L-112

0 1 2 3 4 m

Roberto Terrinoni

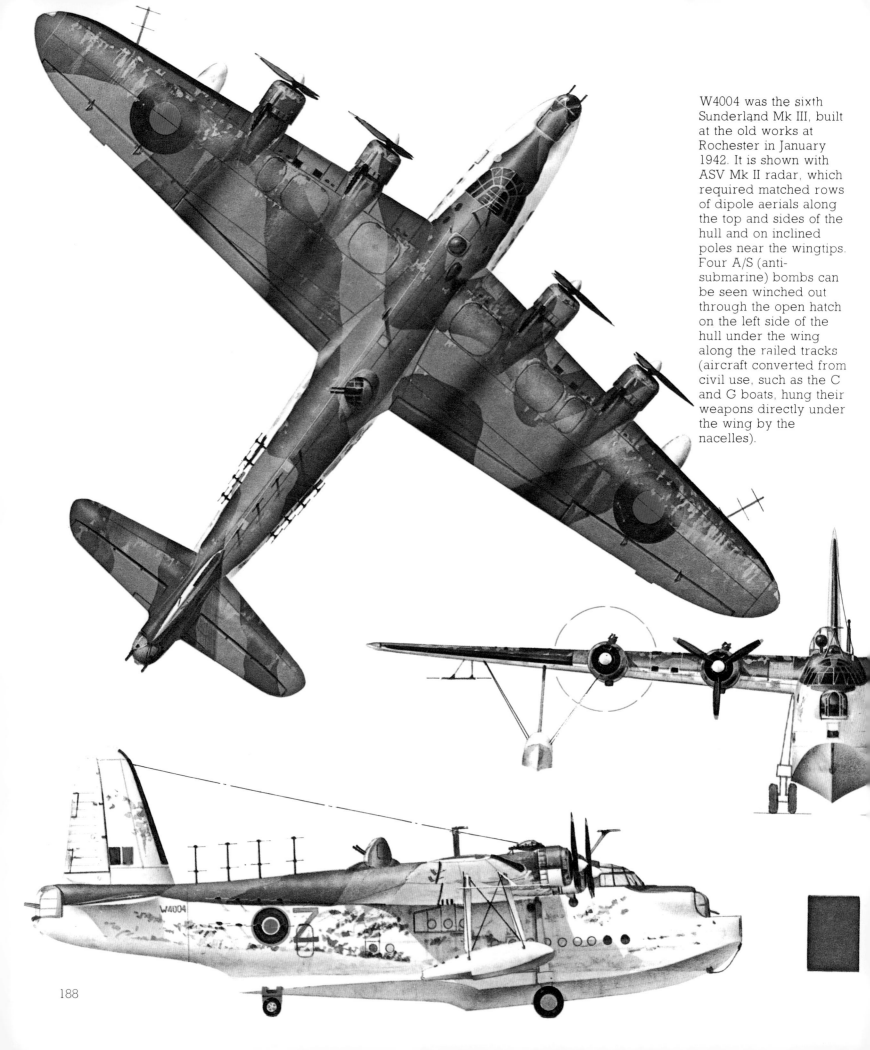

W4004 was the sixth Sunderland Mk III, built at the old works at Rochester in January 1942. It is shown with ASV Mk II radar, which required matched rows of dipole aerials along the top and sides of the hull and on inclined poles near the wingtips. Four A/S (anti-submarine) bombs can be seen winched out through the open hatch on the left side of the hull under the wing along the railed tracks (aircraft converted from civil use, such as the C and G boats, hung their weapons directly under the wing by the nacelles).

Short Sunderland Mk III

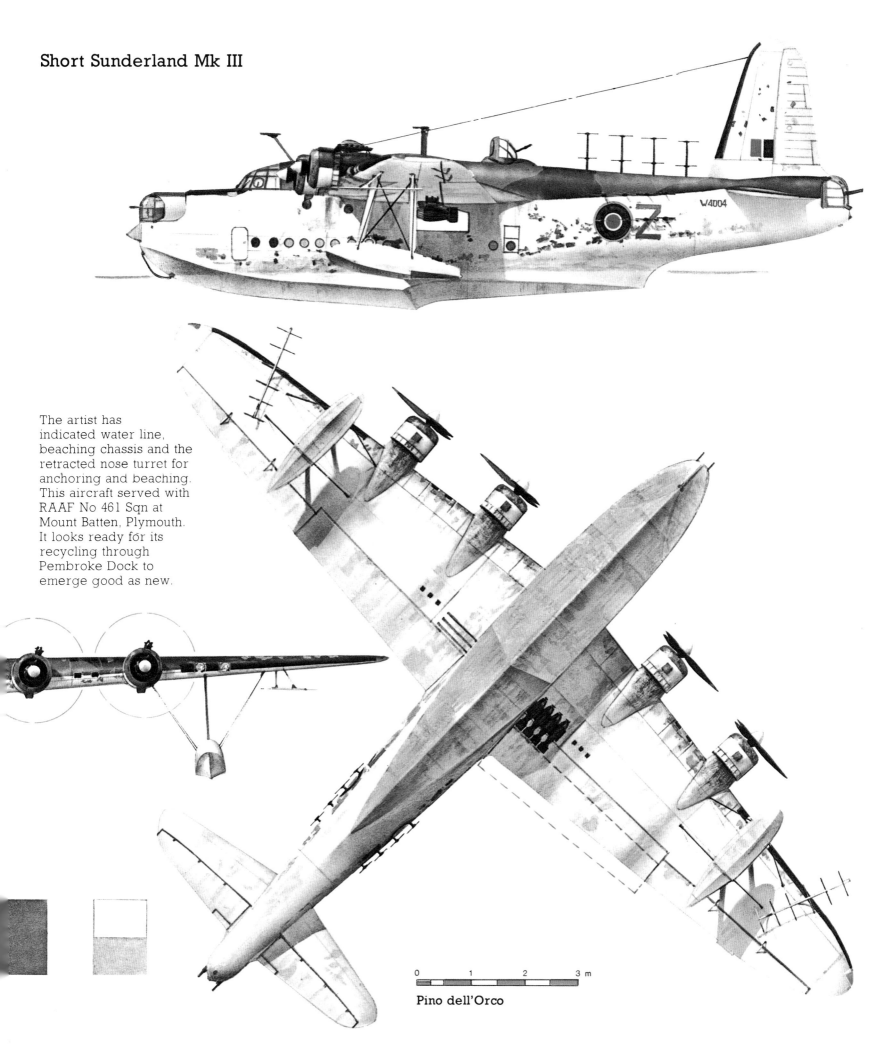

The artist has indicated water line, beaching chassis and the retracted nose turret for anchoring and beaching. This aircraft served with RAAF No 461 Sqn at Mount Batten, Plymouth. It looks ready for its recycling through Pembroke Dock to emerge good as new.

0 1 2 3 m

Pino dell'Orco

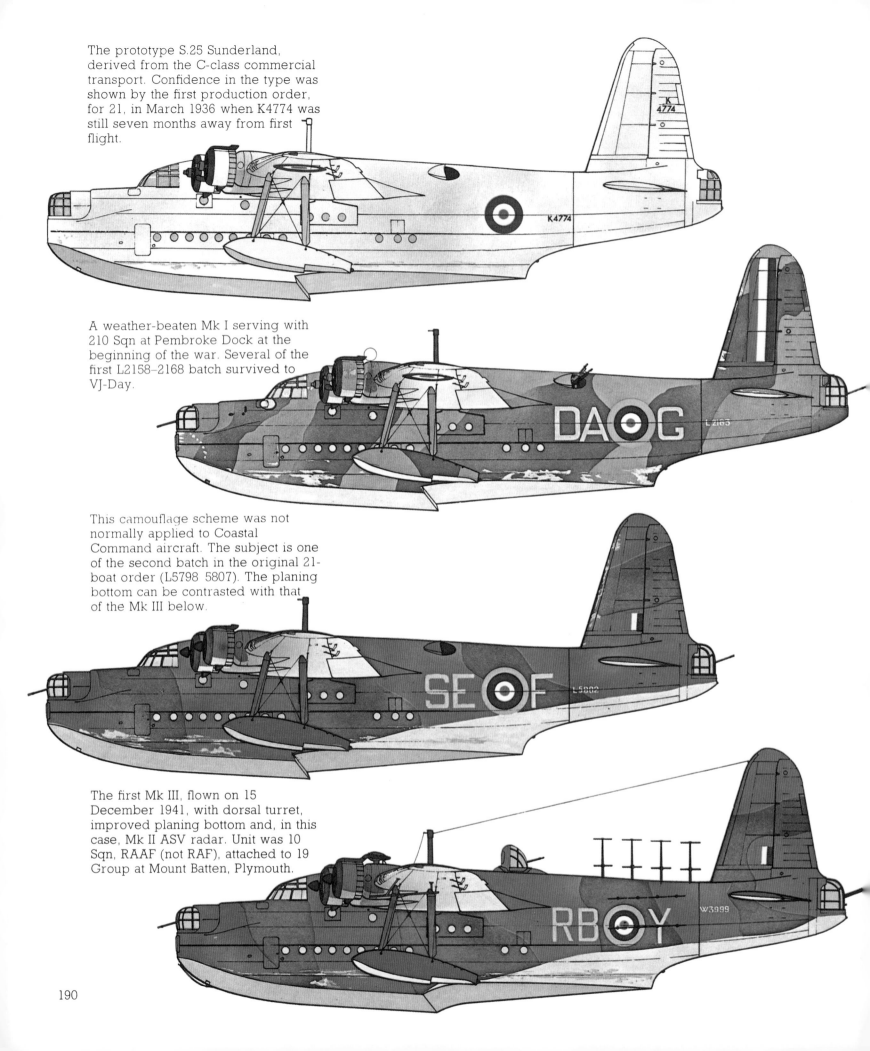

The prototype S.25 Sunderland, derived from the C-class commercial transport. Confidence in the type was shown by the first production order, for 21, in March 1936 when K4774 was still seven months away from first flight.

A weather-beaten Mk I serving with 210 Sqn at Pembroke Dock at the beginning of the war. Several of the first L2158–2168 batch survived to VJ-Day.

This camouflage scheme was not normally applied to Coastal Command aircraft. The subject is one of the second batch in the original 21-boat order (L5798 5807). The planing bottom can be contrasted with that of the Mk III below.

The first Mk III, flown on 15 December 1941, with dorsal turret, improved planing bottom and, in this case, Mk II ASV radar. Unit was 10 Sqn, RAAF (not RAF), attached to 19 Group at Mount Batten, Plymouth.

Short Sunderland

This Mk V served with RAF No 201 Sqn (code letters NS-Z) from 1944 until 1951, when it was refurbished for the French Aéronavale, with whom it operated from Dakar with Flotille 7FE.

The South African Air Force used the Sunderland until the receipt of Shackletons in 1958. The user, 35 Sqn, was then based at Congella, Durban.

Originally called Sunderland IV, the Hercules-powered Solent saw only brief service with No 201 Sqn. The example illustrated was the prototype.

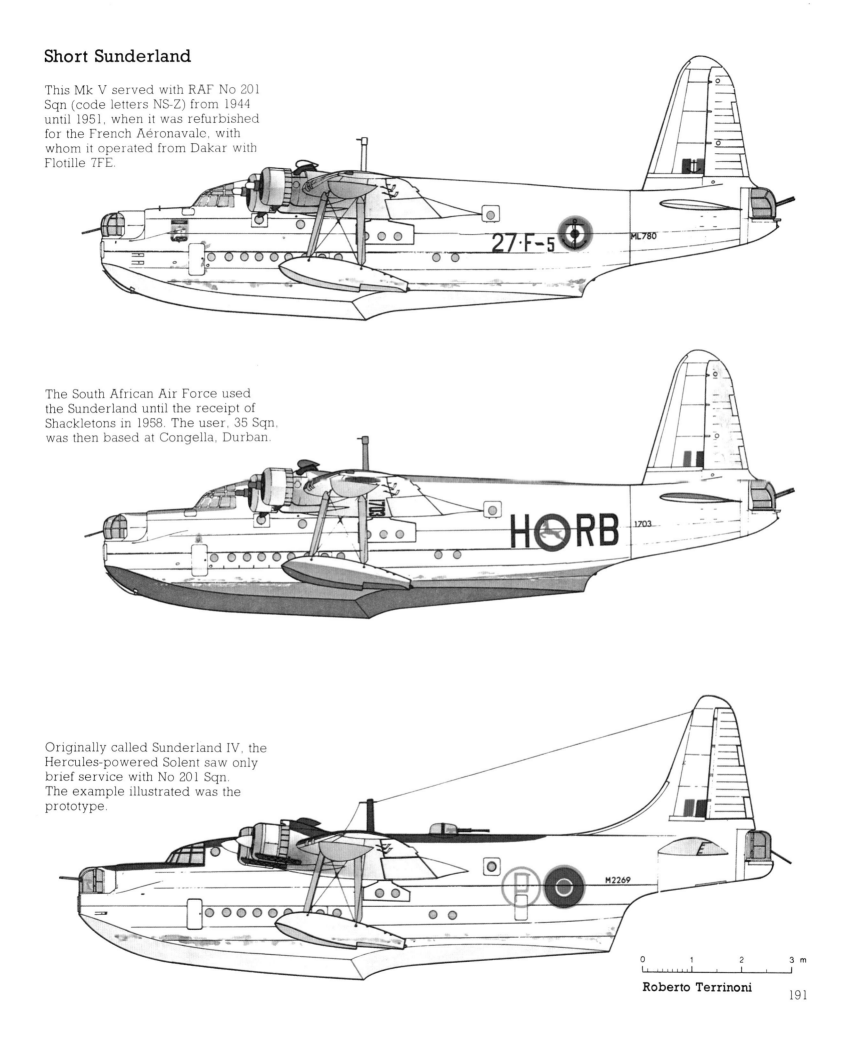

Roberto Terrinoni

Short Sunderland

Few aircraft can claim a 21-year period of service in their original combat role (though such records are becoming more common today). The Sunderland, built to the Air Ministry R.2/33 specification of 1933, was based closely on the C-class Empire flying boat, so development was swift. Compared with the civil boat the S.25 Sunderland had a re-stressed structure, different planing bottom, rear mounted flight deck, and armament in the form of two turrets, dorsal guns in hatches normally closed by sliding covers, and bombs, depth charges or other stores hung on rails under the wing and cranked outboard for release after opening hinged doors on either side of the hull.

The prototype flew on 16 October 1937, and service began with 210 and 230 Sqns in June 1938, and spread to most of the long-range patrol units at home in Coastal Command and overseas. Two weeks after the start of World War 2 a pair of Sunderlands rescued the entire crew of a torpedoed steamer, alighting on a stormy sea, while during the evacuation from Crete in 1941 one carried 87 equipped troops. At the start of the Norwegian campaign a single Sunderland, escorting a small convoy, fought off six Ju 88s, shooting one down and forcing another to land; the Luftwaffe thereafter called the boat the 'flying porcupine'. In 1943 another was attacked by eight formidable Ju 88 fighters over the Bay of Biscay, shot down three and returned to base.

Production took place at both the old Rochester works and the new Belfast factory, augmented from 1941 by Blackburn at Dumbarton. In August 1941 the Mk II introduced improved engines with two-speed blowers, and within two months replaced the dorsal guns by a power turret. By December 1941 the main production version, the Mk III, introduced a different planing bottom. By this time almost all Sunderlands had been equipped with ASV (air to surface vessel) radar, at first of the Mk II type which festooned the aircraft with dipole aerials and by 1943 of later marks with aerials housed in neat blisters under the outer wings. There were at least 12 other new equipment fits, but the Leigh searchlight was seldom carried. Kills of U-boats, sharply increased by fitting ASV radar, declined as the submarines began to use Metox receivers tuned to the aircraft radar, the usual procedure being to fight it out on the surface with batteries of 20mm and 37mm flak. In February 1943 10 Sqn Royal Australian Air Force at Plymouth fitted four machine guns to fire ahead from their Sunderlands, enabling the pilot to deter the submarine crew from manning the guns. In January 1944 an aircraft from this squadron opened fire from 1100m range and knocked out all the U-boat gunners, after which it destroyed the submarine with depth charges. (Until 1943 Sunderlands had not had powerful Torpex charges, but only 45kg and 113kg [100lb and 250lb] anti-submarine bombs, which were ineffective.)

The Sunderland IV was a major redesign embodying elements of the bigger Short G-series, and powered by 1,720hp Hercules sleeve-valve engines. Later it was renamed Seaford, but only eight were used for a short time by 201 Sqn after the war. The final mark of Sunderland, the V, differed only in having an American engine of greater power, which did much to redress the decline in performance consequent upon the considerable increase in weight that took place between the Mk I and Mk III.

Production of the Mk V continued at reduced tempo until June 1946. This tough and reliable boat subsequently had an extremely active career in the Berlin airlift, the Korean war, many difficult special assignments such as the British North Greenland Expedition, and the campaign against terrorists in Malaya. During World War 2 four of the civil S.30 C-class served as radar-equipped patrol aircraft, each with two four-gun Boulton Paul turrets (unlike those of the Sunderland), while the RAF also used three of the big G-class Hercules-engined boats, in this case with three Boulton Paul four-gun turrets, two being above the hull. All these civil conversions could carry a 907kg (2,000lb) weapon load on fixed carriers.

COUNTRY OF ORIGIN Great Britain.

CREW Usually 10.

TOTAL PRODUCED 739 (90 Mk I, 43 II, 456 III and 150 V).

DIMENSIONS Wingspan 34·38m (112ft 9½in); length 26·01m (85ft 3½in); wing area 138·14m² (1,487ft²).

WEIGHTS Empty, I: 12832kg (28,289lb), III: 14969kg (33,000lb), V: 16737kg (36,900lb); maximum loaded, I: 20729kg (45,700lb), III: 26308kg (58,000lb), V: 29484kg (65,000lb).

ENGINES Four air-cooled radials; I: 1,010hp Bristol Pegasus XXII 9-cylinder; II, III: 1,065hp Pegasus XVIII; V: 1,200hp Pratt & Whitney Twin Wasp R-1830-90B 14-cylinder.

MAXIMUM SPEED All versions, 330–343km/h (205–213mph).

SERVICE CEILING All versions, about 5182m (17,000ft).

RANGE Typically 4329km (2,690 miles) with full bomb load; Mk V: 4796km (2,980 miles).

MILITARY LOAD Mk I: offensive weapon load of up to 907kg (2,000lb) winched on rails along wings prior to release; Nash and Thompson F.N.11 nose turret with 7·7mm (0·303in) Vickers GO gun, two Vickers GO aimed by hand from hatches above hull behind wing and four 7·7mm (0·303in) Brownings in F.N.13 tail turret. II,III: ordnance load increased to maximum of 2250kg (4,960lb); nose turret, two 7·7mm (0·303in) Browning; in Mk III, F.N.7 dorsal turret with two Brownings in place of open hatch guns; some III also four fixed Brownings in nose. V: generally as III, but various armament fits up to total of 18 guns including two 12·7mm (0·5in). Brownings aimed from beam window hatches aft of trailing edge.

Supermarine Spitfire

By far the most numerous British aircraft of World War 2, and possibly the most famous fighter of all time, the Spitfire was a triumph of development of a sound basic design. The original concept, by Reginald Mitchell, matured just late enough to use the PV.12 engine (which became the Merlin) and a stressed-skin airframe. Detail design was by Joe Smith, who on Mitchell's death in 1937 became chief designer and masterminded the incredible subsequent growth in strength, power, weapons, performance and roles.

'Mutt' Summers flew the prototype at the Southampton factory on 5 March 1936. A contract was soon placed for 310 Mk Is, later multiplied and augmented by contracts for the more powerful Mk II at a 'Shadow factory' built by Lord Nuffield at Castle Bromwich near Birmingham. Early Mk I Spitfires reached 19 Sqn in June 1938. From the start handling and combat manoeuvrability were excellent, though the slower Hurricane and various biplanes could turn more tightly. By the outbreak of war the Mk IA had introduced a bulged hood, bulletproof windscreen, the extra four guns and three-blade variable-pitch propeller. The IB and IIB introduced 20mm cannon armament.

In 1941 the unarmed PR.IV photo-reconnaissance model was produced, as well as the strengthened and more powerful Mk V, which was built in larger numbers than any other. The development of standard wings resulted in suffix letters A, B and C for different armament (see data), and there were 94 Mk VAs, 3,923 VBs and 2,447 VCs. Later Vs introduced metal-skinned ailerons, bombs, drop tanks and tropical filter. Seafires for the Fleet Air Arm began with a part-navalized VB called Seafire IB and progressed to the main Merlin variant, with folding wings, the Mk III family, built in various forms by different contractors.

Appearance of the Fw 190 caused an urgent need for higher performance, to some degree met by hasty introduction of a V fitted with the 60-series engine, with two-stage supercharger and intercooler, driving a four-blade propeller and with equal-size radiators under both wings. This stop-gap Mk IX in fact persisted in production until 1944, no fewer than 5,665 being delivered. The definitive version with the new engine, the much better and more refined Mk VIII, was held back and only 1,658 were made. Both models were built in LF (low-altitude), F (medium) and HF (high) versions with clipped, standard and extended wingtips. Smaller numbers were made of the high-flying VI and VII with pressurized cockpit.

Principal photo-reconnaissance version was the shapely PR.XI, with fuel along the leading edge, and a deeper nose to house an enlarged oil tank which was needed for the long missions to targets as distant as Berlin or Prague. The last Merlin model built in quantity was the XVI, virtually an IX with Packard-built engine and usually fitted with clipped wings, pointed rudder and, from 1944, cut-down rear fuselage and bubble canopy.

Another hasty conversion was the Mk XII, in which the bigger Griffon engine was fitted to a strengthened VC with LF wings, entering service in March 1943 to chase low-level fighter/bombers and, in 1944, flying bombs. A more studied Griffon Spitfire was the XIV, based upon the VIII and fitted with the 60-series two-stage Griffon, five-blade propeller and deep symmetrical radiators. The 957 of this mark were the best Spitfires of 1944, used intensively before and after D-Day in air combat, flying-bomb interception (score, 300) and ground attack. At the end of the war the refined XVIII took over, with extra fuel, bubble canopy and stronger structure. The XIX was a related PR model with even more fuel and usually a pressure cabin; in post-war service these models were restyled F.18 and PR.19.

Major Seafire versions were the XV, with single-stage low-blown Griffon, and XVII with bubble hood. Just after the war production switched to a completely redesigned family with new wings and fuselages, two-stage Griffons and a series of other changes, designated Spitfire 21 to 24 and Seafire 45 to 47.

COUNTRY OF ORIGIN Great Britain

CREW 1 (some dual conversions post-war).

TOTAL PRODUCED Spitfires: 20,334; Seafires: 2,594.

DIMENSIONS Wingspan: 11·227m (36ft 10in), **LF**: 9·931m (32ft 8in), **HF**: 12·243m (40ft 2in); length, Merlin single-stage (I,II,V,VI,Seafire I–III): 9·119m (29ft 11in), two-stage: 9·538m (31ft 3½in), Griffon: 9·96m (32ft 8in); wing area: 22·483m² (242ft²), **LF**: 21·46m² (231ft²), **HF**: 23·04m² (248ft²).

WEIGHTS Empty, **I**: 2182kg (4,810lb), **VC**: 2313kg (5,100lb), **IX**: 2545kg (5,611lb), **XIV**: 3040kg (6,700lb); max loaded, **I**: 2624kg (5,785lb), **VC**: 3078kg (6,785lb), **IX**: 4309kg (9,500lb), **XIV**: 4663kg (10,280lb).

ENGINE Rolls-Royce vee-12; **I**: Merlin III, 1,030hp; **II**: 1,150hp Merlin XII; **V,VI**: 1,440hp Merlin 45; **VII,VIII,IX,XI,XVI**: 1,520hp Merlin 61 or 1,710hp 63/70 (XVI, Packard V-1650 Mk 266); **Seafire I–III**: Merlin 45/50; **XII**: 1,735hp Griffon II, IV; **XIV, XVIII, XIX**: 2,050hp Griffon 65 or (some XVIII) 2,340hp Griffon 67.

MAXIMUM SPEED **I,II**: 574km/h (357mph), **V,VI**: 602km/h (374mph), **VII,VIII,IX,XVI**: 657km/h (408mph), **XI**: 679km/h (422mph), **XII**: 632km/h (393mph), **XIV,XVIII**: 721km/h (448mph), **Seafire III**: 566km/h (352mph), **Seafire XVII**: 623km/h (387mph).

SERVICE CEILING **I**: 10363m (34,000ft), **II**: 11340m (37,200ft), **VII, VIII, IX, XIV, XVIII, XIX**: 13410m (44,000ft), **Seafires**: 10670m (35,000ft).

RANGE 1610km (1,000 miles) except **XII**: 793km (493 miles), early **Seafires**: 1050km (650 miles), **XI**: 3220km (2,000 miles), **XIX**: 2495km (1,550 miles).

MILITARY LOAD **I**: four 7·7mm (0·303in); **IA, IIA, VA**: eight 7·7mm; **IB,IIB,VI,VII**: two 20mm and four 7·7mm; **VB,XII, Seafire III**: two 20mm, four 7·7mm 227kg (500lb) bombs; **VC**: option of four 20mm; **VIII, IX, XIV, XVI, XVIII, Seafire XV, XVII**: two 20mm, four 7·7mm (E sub-types, two 12·7mm/0·5in), 454kg (1,000lb) bombs.

Roberto Terrinoni

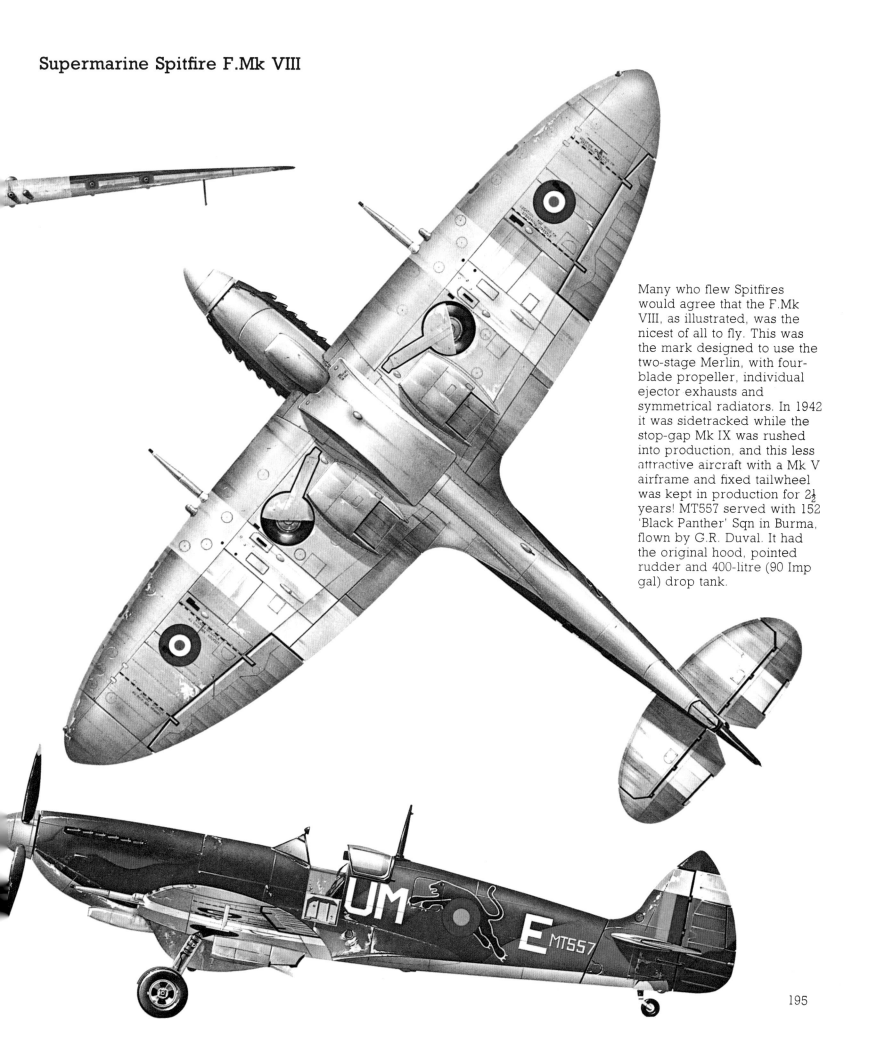

Supermarine Spitfire F.Mk VIII

Many who flew Spitfires would agree that the F.Mk VIII, as illustrated, was the nicest of all to fly. This was the mark designed to use the two-stage Merlin, with four-blade propeller, individual ejector exhausts and symmetrical radiators. In 1942 it was sidetracked while the stop-gap Mk IX was rushed into production, and this less attractive aircraft with a Mk V airframe and fixed tailwheel was kept in production for $2\frac{1}{2}$ years! MT557 served with 152 'Black Panther' Sqn in Burma, flown by G.R. Duval. It had the original hood, pointed rudder and 400-litre (90 Imp gal) drop tank.

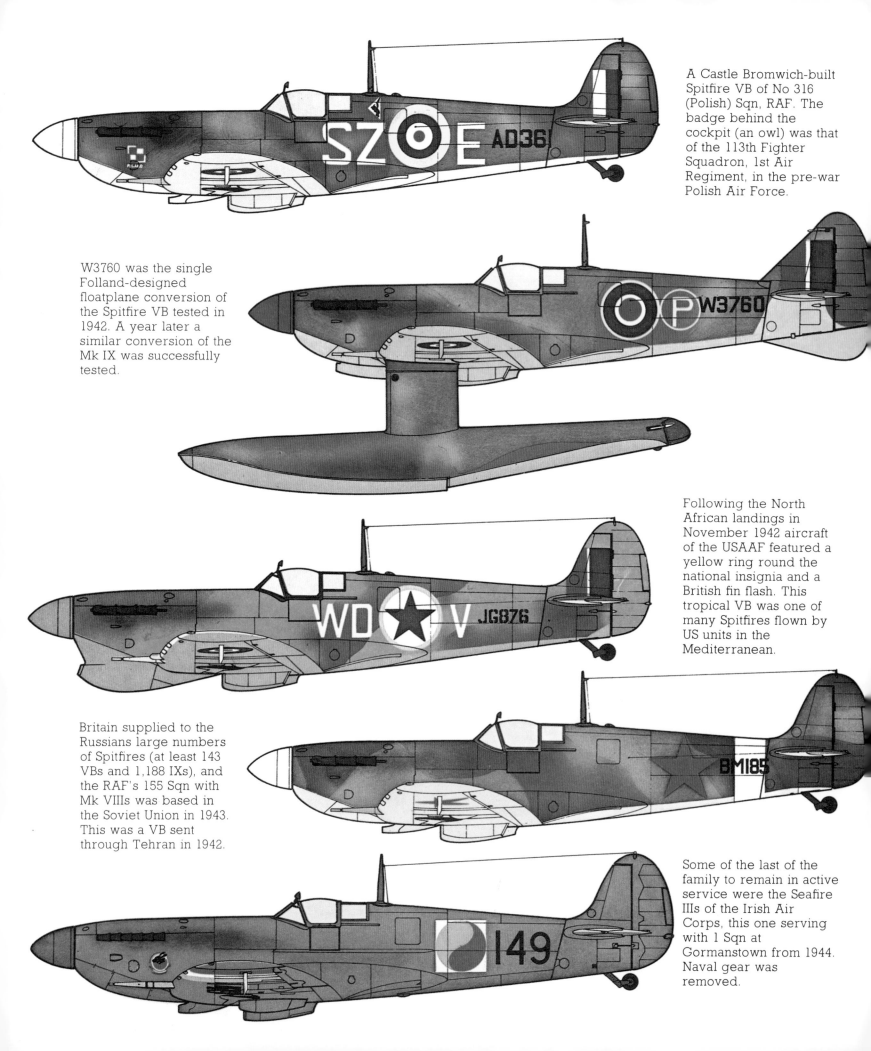

A Castle Bromwich-built Spitfire VB of No 316 (Polish) Sqn, RAF. The badge behind the cockpit (an owl) was that of the 113th Fighter Squadron, 1st Air Regiment, in the pre-war Polish Air Force.

W3760 was the single Folland-designed floatplane conversion of the Spitfire VB tested in 1942. A year later a similar conversion of the Mk IX was successfully tested.

Following the North African landings in November 1942 aircraft of the USAAF featured a yellow ring round the national insignia and a British fin flash. This tropical VB was one of many Spitfires flown by US units in the Mediterranean.

Britain supplied to the Russians large numbers of Spitfires (at least 143 VBs and 1,188 IXs), and the RAF's 155 Sqn with Mk VIIIs was based in the Soviet Union in 1943. This was a VB sent through Tehran in 1942.

Some of the last of the family to remain in active service were the Seafire IIIs of the Irish Air Corps, this one serving with 1 Sqn at Gormanstown from 1944. Naval gear was removed.

Supermarine Spitfire

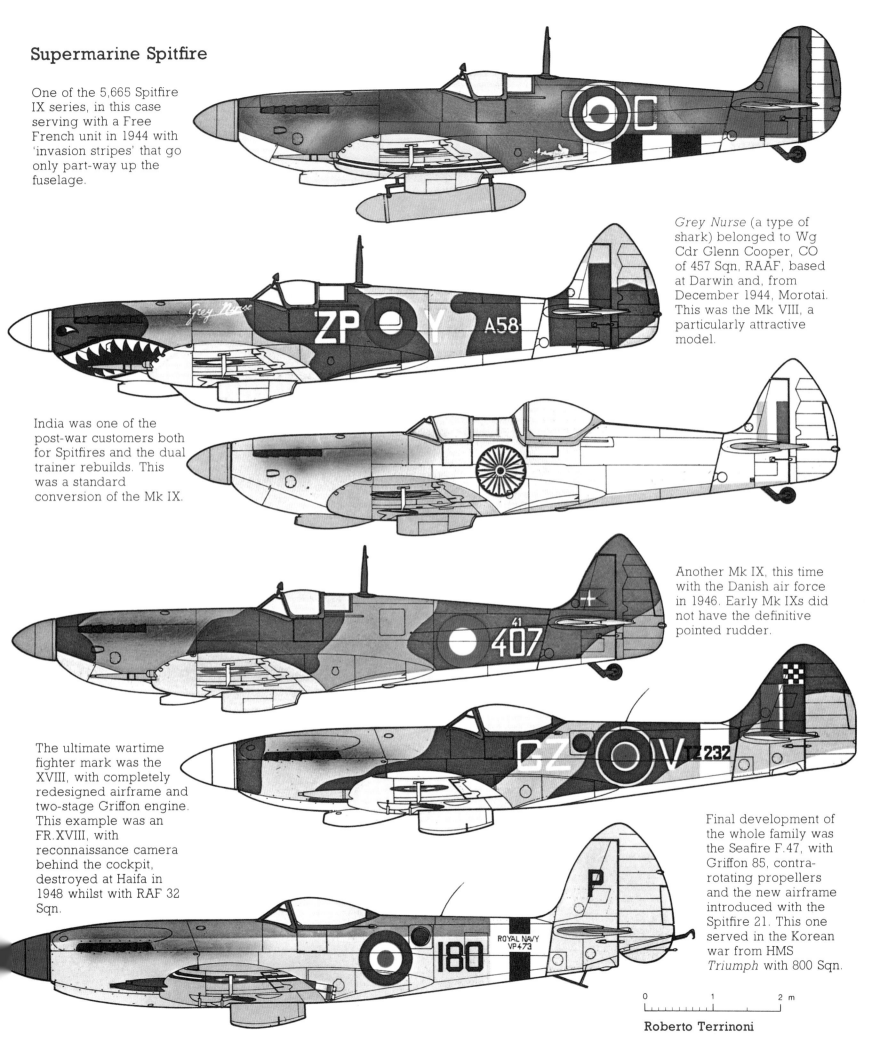

One of the 5,665 Spitfire IX series, in this case serving with a Free French unit in 1944 with 'invasion stripes' that go only part-way up the fuselage.

Grey Nurse (a type of shark) belonged to Wg Cdr Glenn Cooper, CO of 457 Sqn, RAAF, based at Darwin and, from December 1944, Morotai. This was the Mk VIII, a particularly attractive model.

India was one of the post-war customers both for Spitfires and the dual trainer rebuilds. This was a standard conversion of the Mk IX.

Another Mk IX, this time with the Danish air force in 1946. Early Mk IXs did not have the definitive pointed rudder.

The ultimate wartime fighter mark was the XVIII, with completely redesigned airframe and two-stage Griffon engine. This example was an FR.XVIII, with reconnaissance camera behind the cockpit, destroyed at Haifa in 1948 whilst with RAF 32 Sqn.

Final development of the whole family was the Seafire F.47, with Griffon 85, contra-rotating propellers and the new airframe introduced with the Spitfire 21. This one served in the Korean war from HMS *Triumph* with 800 Sqn.

Roberto Terrinoni

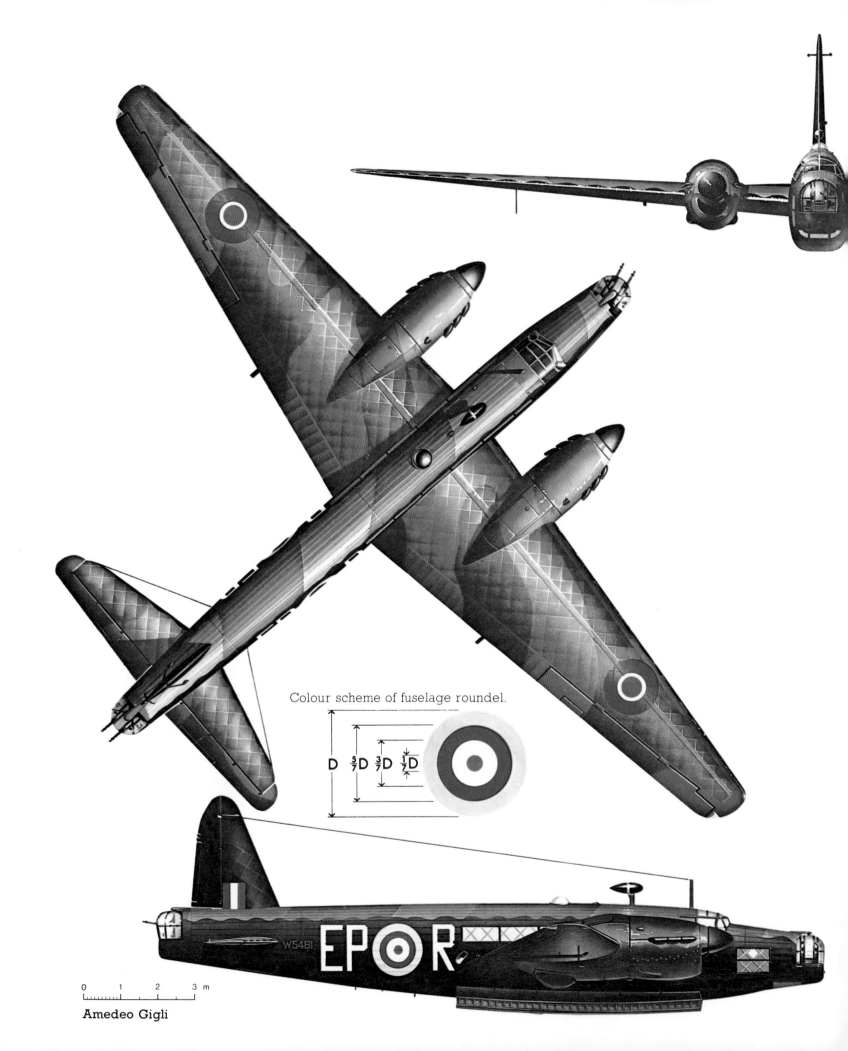

Colour scheme of fuselage roundel.

D $\frac{5}{7}D$ $\frac{3}{7}D$ $\frac{1}{7}D$

W5461 EP●R

0 1 2 3 m

Amedeo Gigli

Vickers-Armstrongs Wellington Mk II

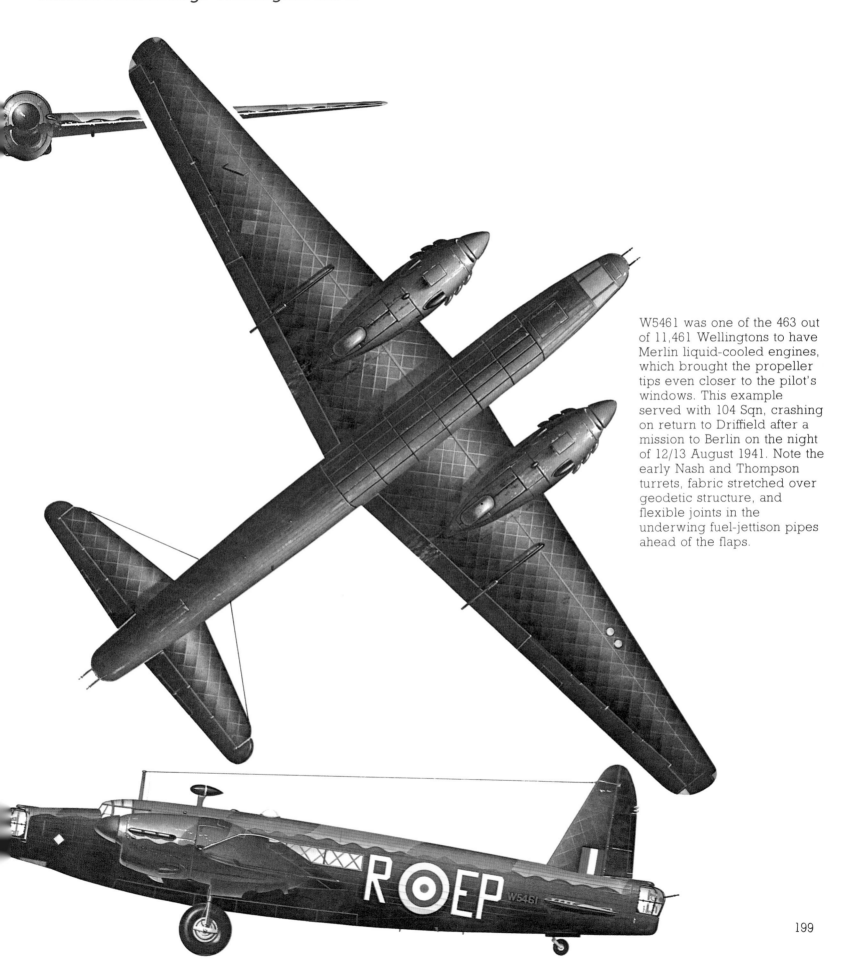

W5461 was one of the 463 out of 11,461 Wellingtons to have Merlin liquid-cooled engines, which brought the propeller tips even closer to the pilot's windows. This example served with 104 Sqn, crashing on return to Driffield after a mission to Berlin on the night of 12/13 August 1941. Note the early Nash and Thompson turrets, fabric stretched over geodetic structure, and flexible joints in the underwing fuel-jettison pipes ahead of the flaps.

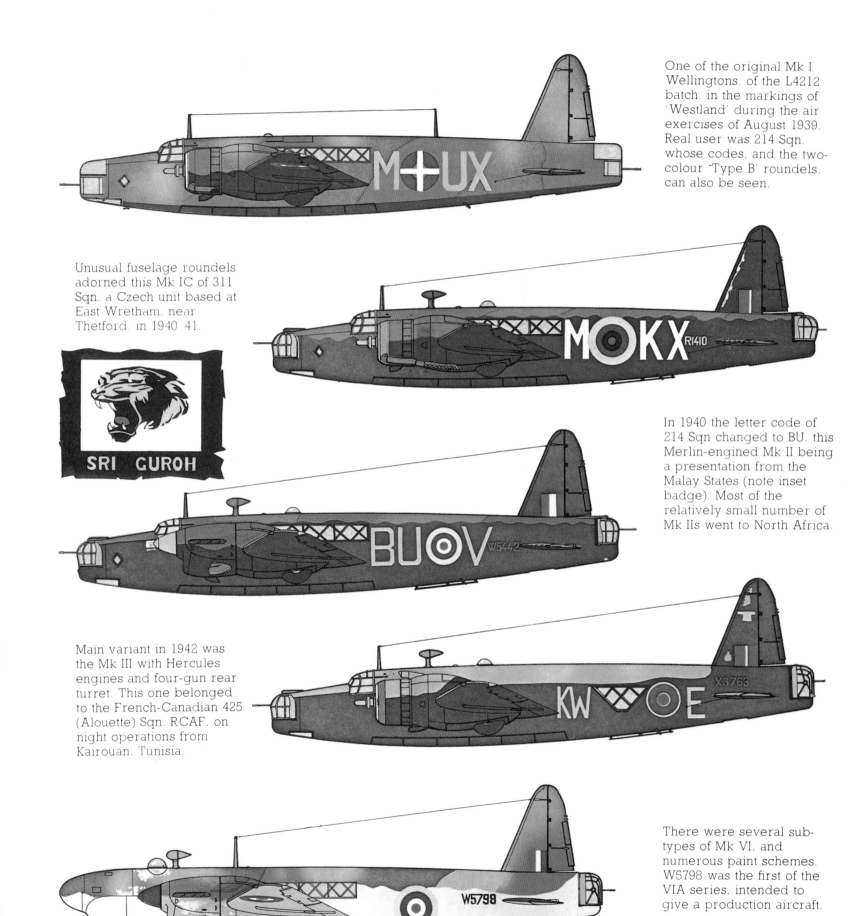

One of the original Mk I Wellingtons, of the L4212 batch, in the markings of 'Westland' during the air exercises of August 1939. Real user was 214 Sqn. whose codes, and the two-colour 'Type B' roundels, can also be seen.

Unusual fuselage roundels adorned this Mk IC of 311 Sqn. a Czech unit based at East Wretham, near Thetford, in 1940 41.

SRI GUROH

In 1940 the letter code of 214 Sqn changed to BU. this Merlin-engined Mk II being a presentation from the Malay States (note inset badge). Most of the relatively small number of Mk IIs went to North Africa.

Main variant in 1942 was the Mk III with Hercules engines and four-gun rear turret. This one belonged to the French-Canadian 425 (Alouette) Sqn. RCAF. on night operations from Kairouan. Tunisia.

There were several sub-types of Mk VI. and numerous paint schemes. W5798 was the first of the VIA series. intended to give a production aircraft.

Vickers-Armstrongs Wellington

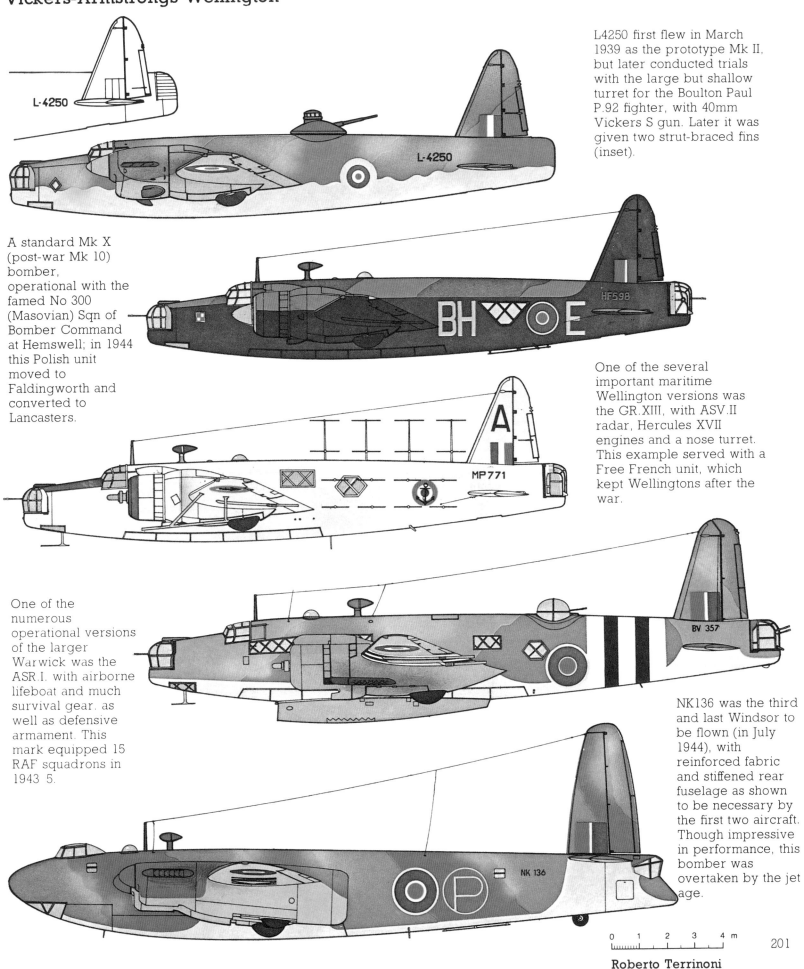

L4250 first flew in March 1939 as the prototype Mk II, but later conducted trials with the large but shallow turret for the Boulton Paul P.92 fighter, with 40mm Vickers S gun. Later it was given two strut-braced fins (inset).

A standard Mk X (post-war Mk 10) bomber, operational with the famed No 300 (Masovian) Sqn of Bomber Command at Hemswell; in 1944 this Polish unit moved to Faldingworth and converted to Lancasters.

One of the several important maritime Wellington versions was the GR.XIII, with ASV.II radar, Hercules XVII engines and a nose turret. This example served with a Free French unit, which kept Wellingtons after the war.

One of the numerous operational versions of the larger Warwick was the ASR.I. with airborne lifeboat and much survival gear. as well as defensive armament. This mark equipped 15 RAF squadrons in 1943 5.

NK136 was the third and last Windsor to be flown (in July 1944), with reinforced fabric and stiffened rear fuselage as shown to be necessary by the first two aircraft. Though impressive in performance, this bomber was overtaken by the jet age.

0 1 2 3 4 m

201

Roberto Terrinoni

Vickers-Armstrongs
Wellington

In 1932 B.N. (later Sir Barnes) Wallis, who had led structural design for the Vickers-built R.100 airship, began refining what he called 'geodetic' construction. This was a form of metal basketwork, assembled by riveting thousands of small strips and subassemblies, reminiscent of the structure of the airship. He put it into practice with the Wellesley bomber of 1935, and it reached its zenith with the larger Wellington. As a result this bomber was flexible (it was said its dimensions could never be quoted except by relating them to a particular time) but efficient and extremely tough, and in World War 2 proved able to survive extensive damage and be easily repaired. It was the only British bomber produced throughout the war, and the total number far exceeded that of any other British aircraft except the Hurricane and Spitfire.

Built to specification B.9/32, the prototype flew on 15 June 1936. After much development the Wellington I emerged in December 1937 and showed itself to be the most efficient RAF bomber. But early day sorties over the German fleet were disastrous, and shaped Bomber Command policy of attacking Germany by night. The various Mk I versions (see armament in data) were produced at an increasing rate at Weybridge, Chester and Squire's Gate (Blackpool), output by 1942 reaching four per day. By this time the batch of 400 Mk IIs had been delivered, and output henceforth concentrated on Hercules-powered versions except for one batch of 220 Mk IVs built at Chester and the experimental Mk VI. The latter, with the Mk V, used a cylindrical pressure cabin for a crew of three and had high-blown engines to fly above the level of AA fire or fighters. The 63 production Mk VIs were used for research including operational missions with Gee and other navaids, ECM and reconnaissance sensors, at heights up to 12200m (40,000ft).

By far the most important versions were the B.III, with Hercules engines and four-gun rear turret, and the similar B.X. The latter remained in production until after the war, and these marks were not displaced from front-line duty with RAF Bomber Command until 1946. From 1940 the Wellington – called the Wimpey, from Popeye's friend J. Wellington Wimpey – was by far the most important crew trainer at OTUs (operational training units), 25 of which were equipped with the Mks I and III in 1940–4. Other Mk Is were rebuilt either as transports (IX, XV, XVI) or as Coastal Command patrol aircraft with ASV.II (Mk VIII). The first such conversions carried large rings fed with powerful pulses of electric current to detonate magnetic mines from January 1940. By 1942 the VIII was fitted with radar, the Leigh searchlight and anti-submarine weapons, and it was followed by the XI, XII, XIII and XIV, all based on the Mk X but fitted with various arrangements of radar, Leigh light and weapons. The final model, the XIV, had ASV Mk III in the nose, with the aerial in a chin radome, and the Leigh light in a retractable cylinder at the rear of the weapon bay. This mark also had launchers for rockets, and served in many theatres.

By 1944, when production had passed its peak of 302 per month, about half the Wimpeys were on operations and the rest were transports, flying classrooms and engaged in numerous research programmes. The T.10, a training version of the Mk X bomber, remained in RAF service until 1953.

Back in 1936 Vickers-Armstrongs had designed a larger bomber as a replacement for the Wellington, to specification B.1/35, but this was delayed and finally flew with Vulture engines on 13 August 1939. By this time the four-engined bombers were preferred, and the Warwick finally served as the ASR.I air/sea rescue aircraft and C.III transport, in each case with R-2800 Double Wasp engines, and as the GR.II and GR.V maritime patrol aircraft with 2,520hp Bristol Centauruses. The 350 Mk I and 100 Mk III Warwicks worked extremely hard, the former carrying a lifeboat and airdropped survival packs, and the latter having up to 24 seats and a large cargo container attached under the fuselage.

COUNTRY OF ORIGIN Great Britain.

CREW Usually 6.

TOTAL PRODUCED 11,461, including 3,048 Mk I/IA/IC, 1,519 Mk III and 3,804 Mk X.

DIMENSIONS Wingspan 26·26m (86ft 2in) except long-span version of Mk V and VI: 29·92m (98ft 2in); length, normal: 19·68m (64ft 7in); wing area, except long-span V, VI: 78·04m² (840ft²).

WEIGHTS Empty, **I**: 8165kg (18,000lb), **IC**: 8417kg (18,556lb), **X**: 11940kg (26,325lb); maximum loaded, **I**: 11271kg (24,850lb), **IC**: 11703kg (25,800lb), **X**: 16556kg (36,500lb).

ENGINES **I,VIII,IX,XV,XVI**: two 1,050hp Bristol Pegasus XVIII 9-cylinder radials; **II**: 1,145hp Rolls-Royce Merlin X vee-12; **III**: 1,375hp Bristol Hercules III or XI 14-cylinder sleeve-valve radials; **IV**: 1,200hp P&W Twin Wasp R-1830-S3C4G 14-cylinder; **V**: special turbocharged Hercules VIII; **VI**: special two-stage Merlin R6SM; **X, XI, XII, XIII, XIV**: 1,675hp Hercules XVI.

MAXIMUM SPEED **I, IV, VIII, IX, XV, XVI**: 370km/h (230mph); **V,VI**: 483km/h (300mph); remainder 410km/h (255mph).

SERVICE CEILING Except for V,VI: typically 6710m (22,000ft); **V,VI, long-span**: 12192m (40,000ft).

RANGE With 680kg (1,500lb) bombs, typical: 3540km (2,200 miles).

MILITARY LOAD Normal maximum bomb load, carried internally: 2041kg (4,500lb); **X,XI,XII,XIII,XIV**: 2722kg (6,000lb), with XIV extra option of underwing rails for eight 27kg (60lb) rockets. Defensive armament: **I**: two 7·7mm (0·303in) Browning in 'roller-blind' nose turret, two in tail, one in ventral turret; **IA**: rotary nose and tail turrets, same armament; **IC**: ventral replaced by two 7·7mm (0·303in) in beam windows; **III**: new rear turret with four 7·7mm (0·303in); **V,VI**: unarmed or rear turret only; **VII**: experimental turret with 40mm Vickers S; **VIII, XIV**: usually no nose turret; **IX, XV, XVI**: usually unarmed.

Yakovlev Yak-1, 3, 7 and 9

Alexander S. Yakovlev was the chief Soviet designer of gliders and sporting aircraft in 1925–35. He then studied fighters, and when the Soviet government issued its important requirement for a new fighter in 1938 his bureau quickly designed the Ya-26 *Krasavec* (Beauty), flown in March 1939. Like its rivals it used the maximum amount of wood, though the fuselage was partly of welded steel tube. It was generally judged the best of the competing designs, and after minor changes went into production as the I-26 shortly before the German invasion in June 1941. In the new 1940 designation scheme the fighter was restyled Yak-1, and in the autumn production was transferred away from Moscow to Kamensk-Uralsk, east of the Urals, where by the end of 1941 output had increased over the pre-move peak. Thereafter more Yaks were built than any other fighter in history.

Deliberately made strong and almost unbelievably simple, the Yak-1 scored in all-round performance and manoeuvrability, gained at the expense of firepower (though the latter was equal to the Bf 109F). By late 1941 pupils were being trained on the UTI-26 or Yak-1U, a tandem trainer which often had fixed wheel or ski landing gear. At about the same time production switched to the Yak-1M, with a cut-down rear fuselage to give all-round vision. This primitive model was that selected by the French Normandie-Niemen squadron when it was formed in March 1943. By early 1942 the more powerful PF-series engine was available, and with this fitted, and several minor improvements, the fighter was redesignated Yak-7, the main versions being the 7A with original cockpit, 7B with cut-down rear fuselage and 7U (or 7V) trainer. Total production of the 1 and 7 was in the neighbourhood of 15,000.

In the spring of 1942 Yakovlev began to introduce light-alloy structure into the wing, retaining wooden skin, thus increasing the volume available for fuel. At first called Yak-7DI, this entered service late in 1942 as the Yak-9, and in fierce fighting around Stalingrad showed itself the master of German fighters in most respects except armament. In early 1943 the Yak-9T appeared, with cockpit moved to the rear to allow installation of a much larger cannon. Small numbers were built of the 9K with 45mm gun and of an anti-ship and anti-tank model with a 75mm gun. The 9D was a long-range version, and the 9DD of 1944 packed every available space with fuel for long-range interdiction and bomber escort. In 1944 a group of DDs flew to Bari in southern Italy where they operated in support of Tito in Yugoslavia. The 9B was a fighter/bomber, and the 9U a strengthened model which led to the VK-107 engine and the post-war family of later Yak-9 models based on the 9P. There were few dual-control Yak-9s, those rebuilt from fighters in Poland being dubbed *Sparka* (double-nine).

In parallel with the Yak-9 the bureau developed from the 1M a dogfighter in which range was sacrificed in return for the maximum performance and manoeuvrability. By January 1943 this entered production as the Yak-3, distinguished by a smaller wing, oil cooler moved to the wing roots and a long radiator duct. It proved so difficult to fight, even at high altitude where the 109G and 190 had previously been able to hold their own, that the Luftwaffe issued an order to 'avoid combat with Yak fighters lacking an oil cooler on the nose, and with an inclined aerial mast'. In fact most Yak-3s had no mast, the aerial wire running from fin to canopy. In 1944 the Normandie-Niemen group re-equipped with the Yak-3, scoring the last 99 of their total of 273 victories against the Luftwaffe with these agile aircraft. After the war, in May 1947, the same aircraft were given to the French unit which then flew to Le Bourget (Paris) and served for a short period as the Armée de l'Air GC III wing.

Several Communist air forces used the Yak-9P post-war, notably North Korea whose aircraft were involved in combats with UN forces in 1950–3. Many of the Yak fighters by this time had a radio direction-finding loop in the top of the rear fuselage.

COUNTRY OF ORIGIN Soviet Union.

CREW 1, except for dual-control trainer versions.

TOTAL PRODUCED About 37,000 (15,000 Yak-1s and -7s, 6,000 Yak-3s and 16,769 Yak-9s).

DIMENSIONS Wingspan, **1,7,9**: 10·0m (32ft 9¾in), **-3**: 9·2m (30ft 2¼in); length, usual: 8·65m (28ft 4½in), **9U, 9P**: 8·7m (28ft 6½in); wing area, **1,7,9**: 17·35m² (186·75ft²), **3**: 14·85m² (159·84ft²).

WEIGHTS Empty, typical **1,7,9**: 2330kg (5,137lb), **9T**: 2750kg (6,063lb), **3**: 2165kg (4,773lb); maximum loaded, **1**: 2820kg (6,217lb), **9**: typically 3200kg (7,055lb) except DD: 3300kg (7,275lb), **3**: 2660kg (5,864lb).

ENGINE Klimov vee-12 liquid-cooled developed from Hispano-Suiza design. **1**: 1,100hp VK-105PA; all subsequent wartime versions: 1,260hp VK-105PF or (-3) 1,222hp PF-2; **9U, 9P** and final version of **3**: 1,650hp VK-107A.

MAXIMUM SPEED **1,7,9**: typically 600km/h (373mph); **3**: 650km/h (403mph); **9U, 9P**: 700km/h (435mph); **3** with VK-107: 720km/h (448mph).

SERVICE CEILING Most: 10000m (32,800ft); **3**: 10800m (35,435ft).

RANGE **1,3,7**: all about 837km (520 miles); **9D**: 1400km (870 miles); **9DD**: 2200km (1,367 miles).

MILITARY LOAD **1**: 20mm ShVAK cannon, two 7·62mm (0·30in) ShKAS, wing racks for six RS-82 rockets or (usually) two bombs of 50kg or 100kg (110 or 220lb); **late 1, 7, most 9**: 20mm ShVAK and two 12·7mm (0·5in) BS; **9T**: main gun usually 37mm NS, only single BS; **9B**: internal bay for 400kg (880lb) bomb load behind pilot; **3**: guns only.

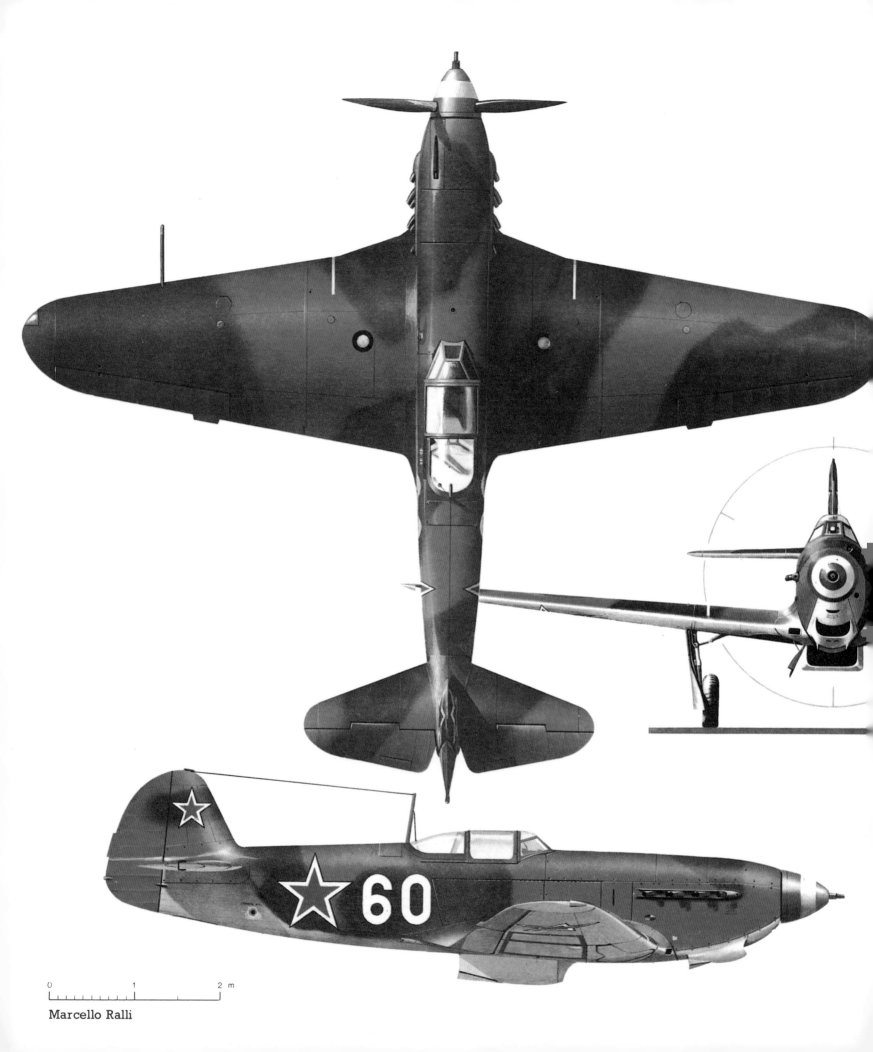

0 1 2 m

Marcello Ralli

Yakovlev Yak-9T

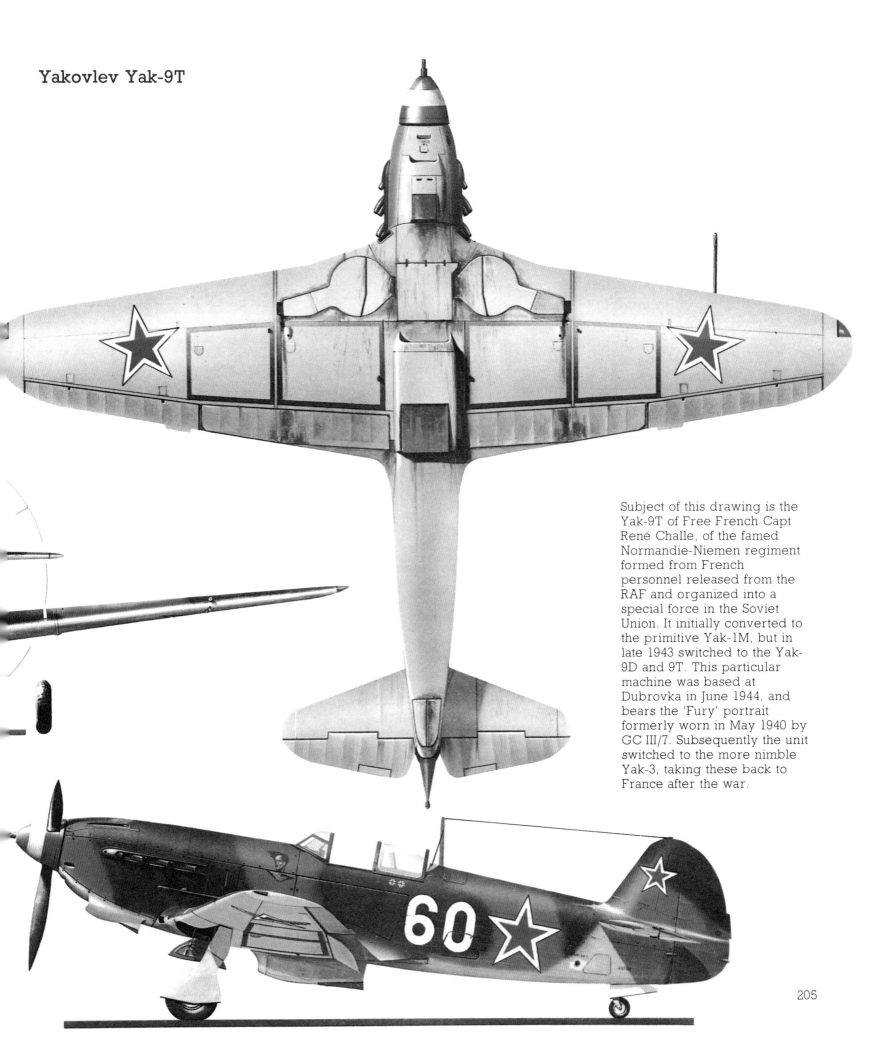

Subject of this drawing is the Yak-9T of Free French Capt René Challe, of the famed Normandie-Niemen regiment formed from French personnel released from the RAF and organized into a special force in the Soviet Union. It initially converted to the primitive Yak-1M, but in late 1943 switched to the Yak-9D and 9T. This particular machine was based at Dubrovka in June 1944, and bears the 'Fury' portrait formerly worn in May 1940 by GC III/7. Subsequently the unit switched to the more nimble Yak-3, taking these back to France after the war.

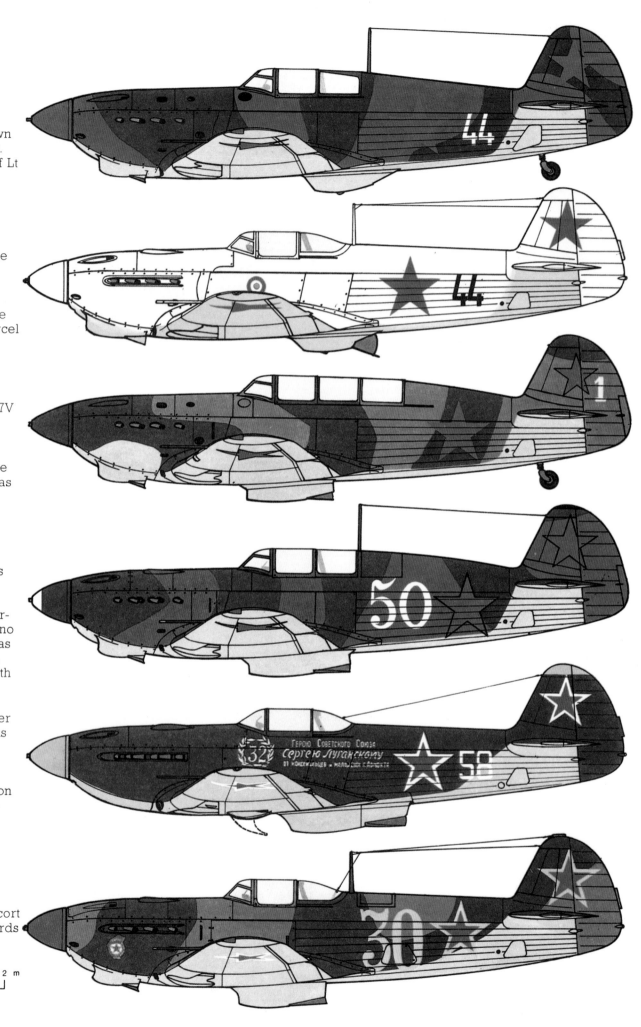

Several good photographs exist showing early production Yak-1s flown by Soviet women aces. This was the aircraft of Lt Lily Litvyak.

Yak-1M selected by the French *Normandie-Niemen* wing in 1943, shown in winter colouring. This was the machine of Sub-Lt Marcel Albert.

Still an extremely primitive aircraft, the 7V was the first two-seat conversion trainer for the Yak fighter family. Tail and tailwheel were as on Yak-1, engine was sometimes a PF.

The 7A fighter always had the PF engine plus all improvements introduced in Yak-1 production except rear-view canopy. Though no insignia appear this was the aircraft of Col A.E. Golubov, CO of the 18th Guards Fighter Regt.

The nimblest dogfighter of the whole series was the Yak-3, despite its smaller wing. This aircraft was flown by Hero of the Soviet Union Sergei Luganskii, who scored 34 confirmed victories.

A much-publicized Yak-9D long-range escort of an unidentified Guards regiment.

0   1   2 m

Marcello Ralli

Yakovlev Yak-1, 3, 7 and 9

Longest-ranged version was the Yak-9DD, which not only escorted US heavy bombers but (236th Fighter Division illustrated) flew to Bari, Italy, to help Balkan partisans.

A Yak-9T anti-armour fighter of the Polish *Vistula* regiment, probably in early 1946 when national insignia appeared.

This Yak-9T was flown to Treviso in 1946 by a Yugoslav defector. Yugoslav Russian aircraft were mostly soon grounded after the war for lack of spares.

Sparka (double nine) was the popular name of the Yak-9 trainer conversion produced in 1946 in Poland.

The ultimate wartime Yak was the 9U, with VK-107 engine and cleaned-up airframe. Entering service in October 1944, many stayed on in Germany and this example buzzed aircraft on the Berlin Airlift.

The Yak-9P was a major type with the North Koreans during the war against South Korea, and this fighter was captured by UN forces.

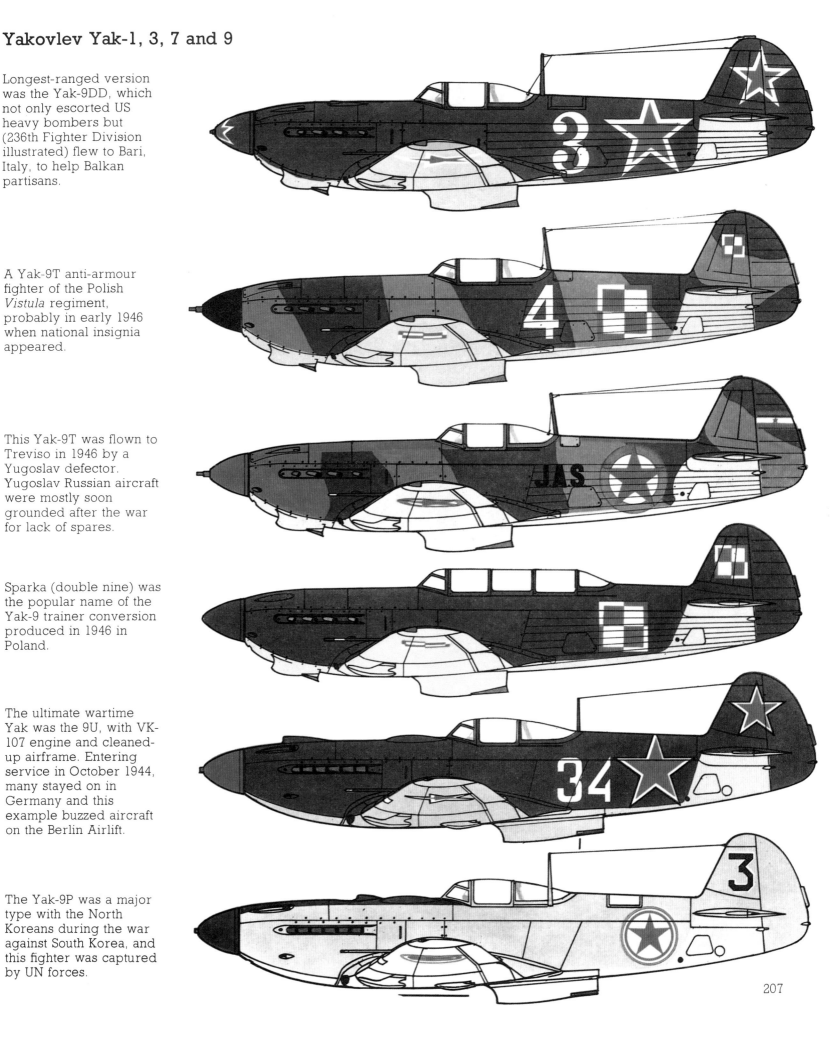

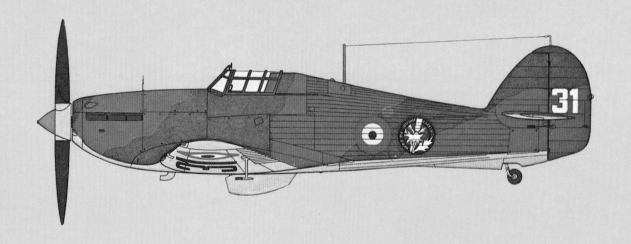